Reading the Irish Woman:
Studies in Cultural Encounter and Exchange, 1714–1960

Reappraisals in Irish History

Editors
Enda Delaney (University of Edinburgh)
Maria Luddy (University of Warwick)

Reappraisals in Irish History offers new insights into Irish history, society and culture from 1750. Recognising the many methodologies that make up historical research, the series presents innovative and interdisciplinary work that is conceptual and interpretative, and expands and challenges the common understandings of the Irish past. It showcases new and exciting scholarship on subjects such as the history of gender, power, class, the body, landscape, memory and social and cultural change. It also reflects the diversity of Irish historical writing, since it includes titles that are empirically sophisticated together with conceptually driven synoptic studies.

1. Jonathan Jeffrey Wright, *The 'Natural Leaders' and their World: Politics, Culture and Society in Belfast, c.1801–1832*

Reading the Irish Woman

Studies in Cultural Encounter
and Exchange, 1714–1960

GERARDINE MEANEY,
MARY O'DOWD
AND
BERNADETTE WHELAN

LIVERPOOL UNIVERSITY PRESS

First published 2013 by
Liverpool University Press
4 Cambridge Street
Liverpool
L69 7ZU

Copyright © 2013 Gerardine Meaney, Mary O'Dowd and Bernadette Whelan

The rights of Gerardine Meaney, Mary O'Dowd and Bernadette Whelan to be identified as the authors of this book have been asserted by them in accordance with the Copyright, Designs and Patents Act 1988.

All rights reserved. No part of this book may be reproduced, stored in a retrieval system, or transmitted, in any form or by any means, electronic, mechanical, photocopying, recording, or otherwise, without the prior written permission of the publisher.

British Library Cataloguing-in-Publication data
A British Library CIP record is available

ISBN 978-1-84631-892-4

Typeset by Carnegie Book Production, Lancaster
Printed and bound in the United States of America

Contents

Abbreviations	vii
Acknowledgements	ix
Introduction	1

The Enlightenment

1	The Enlightenment and Reading, 1714–1820	13
2	Educating Women, Patriotism and Public Life, 1770–1845	54

Emigration

3	The Emigrant Encounters the 'New World', *c*.1851–1960	87
4	Women and the 'American Way', 1900–60	130

Modernism

5	Producers and Consumers of Popular Culture, 1900–60	179
6	Sexual and Aesthetic Dissidences: Women and the Gate Theatre, 1929–60	196

Conclusion	218
Bibliography	221
Index	256

For Margaret MacCurtain,
historian, pioneering scholar of Irish women's studies
and friend

Abbreviations

AFSR	American Foreign Service Inspection Report
AIHS	American Irish Historical Society
AMP	The Arnold Marsh Papers, TCD
AOHP	American Oral History Project 2007–8
BTSP	Breaking the Silence Project, University College Cork
D/FA	Department of Foreign Affairs
D/J	Department of Justice
DIB	Dictionary of Irish Biography (Cambridge University Press, http://dib.cambridge.org)
ESP	Eason and Son Ltd Papers
ESTC	English Short Title Catalogue (http://bl.estc.uk)
GAA	Gaelic Athletic Association
IRCHSS	Irish Research Council for the Humanities and Social Science
LAI	Library Association of Ireland
MGM	Metro-Goldwyn-Meyer
NAI	National Archives of Ireland
NARA	National Archives and Records Administration, United States of America
NFC	National Folklore Collection, Ireland
NLI	National Library of Ireland
ODNB	Oxford Dictionary of National Biography (Oxford University Press, http://www.oxforddnb.com/)
PRONI	Public Record Office of Northern Ireland
QUB	Queen's University Belfast
RIA	Royal Irish Academy
S/D	General Records of the Department of State, United States of America
TCD	Trinity College Dublin
TCDMARL	Manuscripts and Research Archives Library, TCD
TLAI	The Library Association of Ireland

TLS	Tipperary Local Studies
TNA	The National Archives, UK
UCC	University College Cork
UCD	University College Dublin
UL	University of Limerick
WIDA	Women's Industrial Development Association

Acknowledgements

This book had its origins in a project funded by the Irish Research Council for the Humanities and Social Sciences (IRCHSS). The authors also gratefully acknowledge support received from the School of History and Anthropology, Queen's University of Belfast (QUB), the Department of History, University of Limerick (UL), the Department of English and the Humanities Institute, University College Dublin (UCD). We have benefitted enormously from the contributions of participants in seminars and workshops funded by the IRCHSS project in UCD, UL and QUB as well as from the feedback received at national and international conferences. We also learned a great deal from engagement with Dr Catherine O'Connor and Dr Susan Cahill, the postdoctoral fellows employed on the project.

The oral testimony for the study derives from a number of oral history projects including the UL Oral History Project, 2001 supported by the Faculty of Arts, Humanities and Social Science Research Fund and the American Oral History Project, 2007–8 funded by the IRCHSS. The projects were co-ordinated by Dr Catherine O'Connor and thanks go also to Margaret Hogan and Tony Hogan as well as the interviewees.

Leanne Calvert assisted with research and copyediting and Gráinne O'Donovan constructed the project's website.[1] Special acknowledgement should be given to Dr Noreen Giffney for her invaluable editorial assistance and advice. We would also like to thank the anonymous readers for their useful guidance and suggestions.

The archivists and librarians in the following institutions provided invaluable help: the National Library of Ireland, the National Archives of Ireland, the Public Record Office of Northern Ireland, the National Archives, UK, the National Library, Scotland, QUB library, UCD library, UL library and Special Collections, the Delargy Centre for Irish Folklore,

1 http://www2.ul.ie/web/WWW/Faculties/Arts,_Humanities_%26_Social_Sciences/Inventing.

UCD, the Department of Early Printed Books and Special Collections, Trinity College, Dublin, the Manuscripts and Archives Research Library, Trinity College, Dublin, the archive of the Presentation Sisters, George's Hill, Dublin, the Ursuline Order Archive, Blackrock, Cork, Dublin Diocesan Library and Tipperary Libraries Local Studies and Archives, Thurles. Dr Piaras MacÉinrí, University College, Cork (UCC) facilitated access to the 'Breaking the Silence: Staying at Home in an Emigration Society' online archive in the Irish Centre for Migration Studies, UCC. The authors also drew on the database produced by the Women in Modern Irish Culture Project funded by the UK Arts and Humanities Research Council.[2]

Others who assisted the authors include Dr John Bergin, Ken Bergin, Dr Enda Delaney, Tony Farmar, Siobhan Fitzpatrick, Mary Guinan-Dermody, Sister Karen Kent, Dr Rolf Loeber, Dr John Logan, Professor Maria Luddy, Valerie Norton, Dr Clare O'Halloran, Dr Rosemary Raughter, Dr Lisa Townsend and Tim Watt.

The authors are especially grateful to Sue Barnes and Rachel Clarke at Carnegie Book Production and Alison Welsby, Editorial Director at Liverpool University Press for their support and guidance.

2 http://www2.warwick.ac.uk/fac/arts/history/irishwomenwriters/.

Introduction

In 1700 few Irish women were literate. Most lived in a rural environment, rarely encountered a book or a play or ventured much beyond their own domestic space. By 1960 literacy was universal, all Irish women attended primary school, had access to a variety of books, magazines, newspapers and other forms of popular media and the wider world was now part of their everyday life. This study seeks to examine the cultural encounters and exchanges inherent in this transformation. It analyses reading and popular and consumer culture as sites of negotiation of gender roles. This is not an exhaustive treatment of the theme but focuses on three key points of cultural encounter: the Enlightenment, emigration and modernism. The writings and intellectual discourse generated by the Enlightenment made it one of the most influential forces shaping western society. It set the agenda for scientific, political and social thought for the eighteenth and nineteenth centuries. The migration of peoples to North America was another important historical marker in the development of the modern world. Emigration altered and shaped American society as well as the lives of those who remained behind. By the twentieth century, aesthetic modernism suspicious of Enlightenment rationalism and determined to produce new cultural forms developed in a complex relationship with the forces of industrialisation, urbanisation and social transformation.

This study analyses the impact of these forces in western culture on changing roles and perceptions of Irish women from 1700 to 1960. It examines the processes of cultural influence and exchange, looking at long-term alterations in behaviour and attitudes. The analysis ranges from eighteenth-century advice books to theatre in the twentieth century and will argue that international popular culture and didactic and educational material aimed at women were a locus of conflict and change.

While this study has a broad historical span, the focus is on cultural change. This facilitates tracing distinctive patterns of cultural encounter and influence at specific times rather than seeking to produce a 'one size fits all' explanation of how these forces operate for all historical periods. The organisational principle of each section is to examine the nature of the cultural encounter, how it took place and how Irish women engaged with it.

The Enlightenment

The Enlightenment has long been recognised as opening up the agenda of equality for women as well as men. If man was a rational animal so too, it was increasingly argued, was woman. The Enlightenment initiated a debate on women's intellectual ability and led to an expansion in the provision of schools for girls and a corresponding rise in female literacy. In England and colonial America, Enlightenment ideas fused with evangelical Protestantism to construct a new model of ideal womanhood which began to prevail particularly within middle-class society. The new woman was literate and actively engaged with religious reading and spiritual activities. She was often involved in philanthropic work and her local community. The new woman also believed in reading for leisure but was selective in her choice of reading. She read serious, often religious literature rather than fiction. She rarely wrote for publication herself but admired the women writers associated with the bluestocking movement in England. Her views on the role and status of women combined the intellectual equality advocated by the Enlightenment with a religious belief in the equality of all souls. At the same time, most advocates of the new model of womanhood of the late eighteenth and early nineteenth centuries rejected any notion that men and women were equal in every respect arguing instead that their different characteristics were complimentary. Women should be educated to enhance their natural instincts for motherhood and care of the home while the curriculum in boys' schools should prepare them for engagement with the public and the professional world. Young women could be given translations of classical texts to read but only young boys should be taught classical languages. By the late eighteenth century, there is also evidence of a more radical view of women's role in society. The political debate on equality infiltrated the discussion on women and a small number of writers supported the notion of societal and political equality for the sexes.[1]

The first section investigates the impact that this Enlightenment debate had on women in Ireland. The aim of chapter one is to explore the ways in which ideas about the new woman filtered into Irish society. Printed literature was the principal media through which women encountered these

---

1 For a survey of the engagement of British women with Enlightenment thought see Sarah Knott and Barbara Taylor (eds), *Women, Gender and Enlightenment* (Basingstoke: Palgrave Macmillan, 2005).

debates. Throughout the eighteenth century, Irish printers and booksellers profited from the absence of strict copyright laws and reprinted English editions of books without fear of prosecution. Large numbers of books were published in Ireland that were directed at a female readership. Many were books advising on the education and formation of young girls. The emerging Irish periodical market also relied a great deal on the reproduction of material from English journals and magazines. Thus the scores of books and periodicals that appeared on the Irish market in the eighteenth and nineteenth centuries are a key source for tracing this cultural encounter and transfer. Although often confining in their advice, the encouragement of young women's literacy skills and independent intellectual thought paradoxically incorporated what historians have identified as an early form of feminism.

The second chapter explores the impact of Enlightenment ideas on women's lives and the emergence of different versions of the new Enlightenment woman in Irish society. As elsewhere, education and philanthropy provided women with new roles as teachers, foundresses of religious congregations and published writers. While women from Protestant denominations were the first to participate in public affairs, particularly those associated with philanthropic projects, by the 1820s, Catholic women were also developing a public profile. In addition, women participated in Irish political life in a way which would not be possible in the later nineteenth century. The leisure and resources to read and engage with Enlightenment ideas were predominantly available to middle-class women. By 1850, however, rising female literacy facilitated female agency and gave more women the means by which to determine their own lives. This included the life-changing decision to leave Ireland.

Emigration

Emigration was a fulcrum of cultural exchange which influenced women's lives profoundly and defined or redefined ideas about womanhood. In the nineteenth century, knowledge of America was circulated through printed literature and letters. Information about conditions in America for women at work, in the home and at leisure was disseminated through newspapers, magazines, books and eventually film in the twentieth century. The image of the female emigrant was joined by that of the career woman, the female consumer and the American film star, among others. The values represented by these figures were not just those of modernity and progress, but also of greater personal choices for women. The transfer of these ideals was not direct but was mediated through Irish and British newspapers, magazines and books and in the twentieth century, controlled within the framework of social mores set down by successive Irish Free State governments' legislation and Roman Catholic principles. The extent to which individual Irish women accepted, rejected or adapted these external messages to suit their own lives offers an insight into how external cultural influences actually operated in women's everyday experiences. Women's accommodation of external and internal cultural influences emerges in the prevalence of American music, dance as well as film, in twentieth-century Ireland. It also challenged the prescribed church and state ideal of an Irish-speaking, rural society imbued with cultural and sexual purity.

Chapters three and four focus on the female emigrant and the female consumer of American popular culture as a conduit for cultural engagement between America and Ireland. Between 1815 and 1845 approximately one million Irish settled elsewhere. The 1845–53 Famine accelerated this movement with 2.5 million leaving between 1846 and 1855 and the departures continued despite the establishment of the Irish Free State in 1922. America was the preferred destination and at certain periods more women than men emigrated to the USA, which distinguishes the pattern of Irish departures from other European emigrant societies. Most were Roman Catholic, poor women from rural parts, single and under thirty years of age.

Chapter three examines how by 1900 America was perceived as a place where women could lead independent lives. They could find work, at good rates, could progress to better employment and have a more comfortable home, with electricity and running water, than in Ireland. They could also have a social life with other Irish and new friends, marry, delay marriage or not marry. The extent to which America offered young women independence and better living and working conditions is clear from the gendered advice and warnings emanating from the Irish Roman Catholic hierarchy. The chapter explores continuities, namely that even when work was available to young women in twentieth-century Ireland many still chose to leave, which suggests that while leaving was difficult (indeed the American 'wake' persisted into the 1950s), America offered more attractions. A final aim of the chapter is to examine the female emigrant's 'round trip' with packages, letters and temporary and permanent returnees arriving back home. She could bring money, clothes, food and news of life in America but her appearance, behaviour and presence in her home community also represented a visual image of American life that emphasised the contrast between the old and the new worlds. The confrontation of the two cultures merits investigation.

Chapter four contexualises the female emigrant alongside contrasting images of womanhood emanating from American material and popular culture. The dissemination of these images across the world remains today a matter of discussion and debate particularly in the context of American 'imperialism'.[2] Ironically the 'American way', born out of Enlightenment-inspired values of rationality, individualism and self-determination, also came full circle back to Europe in the twentieth century. The gender dimension to this cultural exchange is explored in chapter four through investigation of images of womanhood inherent in American consumerism, advertising, and popular culture in the form of film, fiction, music and dancing. From the 1930s onwards, the expanding media incorporated more sophisticated advertising strategies which targeted woman as consumers and projected certain messages about gender relations in modern America. During the period 1922 to 1960, some writers in Irish woman's magazines and in the newspapers thought that the woman worker could learn some lessons from the 'modern American career woman' or the 'career mother', who was portrayed as fashionable, clever and independent. However, the most popular reading matter in Ireland was religious magazines, which offered contrasting but equally influential messages about woman's lives in America. The strained relationship between traditional and progressive models of behaviour intensified in the middle decade of the twentieth century and is also reflected in the tension between avant garde modernism and the cultural agenda of the Irish Free State.

Modernism

Through the twentieth century, modernist aesthetics was one of the most influential frameworks adopted by literary and cultural critics. In an influential article, Miriam Hansen links modernism with modernity to include in the study of modernist aesthetics cultural practices that were manifestations of modernity. This includes 'mass-produced and mass-consumed phenomena of fashion, design, advertising, architecture and urban environment, of photography, radio and cinema'. Hansen's development of 'vernacular

---

2 For example see Lewis Galantière (ed.), *America and the Mind of Europe* (London: Hamilton, 1951); Richard Rose (ed.), *Lessons from America: An Exploration* (London: Macmillan, 1974); David Ellwood and Rob Kroes (eds), *Hollywood in Europe: Experiences of a Cultural Hegemony* (Amsterdam: VU University Press, 1994); Richard Pells, *Not Like US: How Europeans have Loved, Hated and Transformed American Culture since World War II* (New York: Basic Books, 1997), p. 9. For a comparative perspective see Franklin D. Scott, 'American Influences in Norway and Sweden', *The Journal of Modern History*, 18, 1 (March 1946), pp. 37–47.

modernism' is particularly apt for analysing cultural production and consumption by women in twentieth-century Ireland.[3]

The official discourse of the newly independent Irish state was almost equally suspicious of the foreign, the urban and the sexual and frequently associated all three in the figure of the modern young woman. However, the degree of resistance to the dominant ideology of womanhood in this period has frequently been underestimated. Irish women persistently engaged with modernity. They purchased and read foreign and mass-produced reading materials and attended American film with enthusiasm. Newspapers, books, cinema-going and shopping provided the consuming woman with further ways to engage with America.

Chapter five looks at women as cultural producers. Popular literature provided the means by which Irish women could develop public reputations as novelists and playwrights. From the nineteenth century onwards Irish women such as Katherine Cecil Thurston and L. T. Meade were highly successful purveyors of popular fiction to an international market particularly in the USA. They also promoted themselves as 'Irish women writers'.

Chapter six focuses in particular on the programme of plays produced by the Gate Theatre from its foundation in 1929 to 1960. It points to the mixture of popular and more challenging modernist productions presented in the Gate during these years. The diversity and range of work by women in this period has been overlooked until recently by Irish literary history.[4] These productions were part of the Gate's diverse programme that indicates that theatre-goers were equally willing to attend plays by Dorothy Sayers, Anton Chekhov and Eugene O'Neill and promiscuously mixed 'high' and 'low' culture. Chapter six also examines the Gate as a space of cultural and sexual dissidence in Dublin, suggesting a trace of an 'other' city, where both gender and other forms of identity were much more fluid than in official Ireland. The relationship between aesthetic and sexual freedom is a key theme in Irish writing in the post-independence period, but also an important point of intersection with both modernist and realist writing by women in the inter-war years. This chapter explores the paradox by which Christa Winsloe's *Children in Uniform* could be performed on the Dublin stage in 1934, albeit to discretely subdued acclaim, but *Gone With the Wind* could not be screened without significant cuts until 1968. Class and particularly the desire to control the cultural life of the working class are obviously key here, but analysis of Irish modernism in all its forms creates a more complex picture. The permeability of the boundaries

---

3 Miriam Hansen, 'The Mass Production of the Senses: Classical Cinema as Vernacular Modernism', *Modernism/Modernity*, 6, 2 (April 1999), p. 60.
4 Cathy Leeney, *Irish Women Playwrights, 1900–1939: Gender and Violence on Stage* (Irish Studies 9) (New York: Peter Lang, 2010).

between high and low cultural forms and the processes of cultural exchange mediate questions of the 'proper' role of women in domestic, national and international contexts.

Methodological Approaches

New electronic and printed resources have made visible the hitherto hidden diversity and scope of the cultural lives of Irish women, from subscribers to eighteenth-century journals to cinema-goers in the twentieth century.[5] Identifying and quantifying this material is insufficient for an understanding of the complex processes of cultural and social change, however. This work draws on these resources to facilitate interpretation and analysis, combining literary and historical research techniques in the multidisciplinary, collaborative mode demanded by the new range of primary material. It maps the complexity and range of the much disparaged cultural lives of these literate women, readers and writers of novels, playwrights and theatre goers, emigrants writing home and their correspondents, girls at the movies and advertising copy-writers.

This is an ambitious book which explores the relationship between historical and literary methodologies and approaches in the analysis of cultural engagements. In the course of writing this book, we have become more aware of the alternative approaches of historians and literary critics. The methods of the literary and historical scholar can lead to different insights into 'Reading the Irish Woman'. Literary analysis is primarily interpretative in its operation. It produces readings of texts, and on the basis of a detailed reading of a single key text it can propose an analysis of an entire cultural or social movement. It does not work on the basis of empirical evidence of actual social practice and it is frequently concerned with unconscious social processes and ideologies. It does offer an insight into the imaginative and philosophical lives of women readers and a trace of their desires and aspirations. It also challenges approaches which understand Irish women's cultural and social history in a predominantly national frame.

---

5   See, for example: Breaking the Silence (http://migration.ucc.ie/oralarchive/testing/breaking/narrators/); Eighteenth Century Collections Online (http://gale.cengage.co.uk/product-highlights/history/eighteenth-century-collections-online.aspx); Irish Newspapers Online (http://www.irishnewsarchive.com); Nineteenth Century UK Periodicals Online (http://mlr.com/DigitalCollections/products/ukperiodicals); Women in Modern Irish Culture Database (http://www2.warwick.ac.uk/fac/arts/history/irishwomenwriters). See also the Inventing and Reinventing the Irishwoman website. The respondents to the oral history projects were selected through personal contact. Semi-directed interviews took place.

The complexity of cultural production and consumption by Irish women indicates that 'as people move with their meanings and meanings find ways of traveling even when people stay put, territories cannot really contain cultures.'[6]

Historical analysis is grounded in empirical evidence that shapes and refines the conceptual framework. Historians require a range of sources and documents and build their arguments on the basis of a plurality of evidence. The methodology of the historian also provides a chronological context through which changes and continuities in women's lives can be discerned. These differences in approach were not easily accommodated. Understanding what we mean by terms such as 'modernisation', 'progressive', 'conservative', 'traditional', 'ideology' and 'agency' has been problematic. These words carry different meanings in the different disciplines and are contentious in both. Nevertheless, the collaborative nature of the project has led to much cross-fertilisation and interdisciplinary discussion. The overall theme of the book of cultural encounter, exchange and adaptation crosses disciplines and each discipline has brought particular insights. The engagement of women with the Enlightenment is primarily through printed texts. The role of women in this diverse intellectual movement has only become visible in recent years through collaboration between historians and literary critics.[7] Dialogue between historians and literary critics on the nature of the Irish Enlightenment has begun in recent years although there has been a more limited engagement with considerations of gender.[8] Asking how women

---

6   Ulf Hannerz, *Transnational Connections: Culture, People, Places* (London and New York: Routledge, 1996), p. 8.
7   See, for example, Sarah Knott and Barbara Taylor (eds), *Women, Gender and Enlightenment* (Basingstoke: Palgrave Macmillan, 2005); Martin Fitzpatrick, Peter Jones, Christa Knellwolf and Iain McCalman (eds), *The Enlightenment World* (London: Routledge, 2004).
8   See, for example, Graham Gargett and Geraldine Sheridan (eds), *Ireland and the French Enlightenment, 1700–1800* (Basingstoke and London: Macmillan, 1999); Máire Kennedy, *French Books in Eighteenth Century Ireland* (Studies on Voltaire and the Eighteenth Century, 2001:07) (Oxford: Voltaire Foundation, 2001); Richard Butterwick, Simon Davies and Gabriel Espinosa Sánchez (eds), *Peripheries of the Enlightenment* (Studies on Voltaire and the Eighteenth Century, 2008:01) (Oxford: Voltaire Foundation, 2008); Richard B. Sher, *The Enlightenment and the Book: Scottish Authors and Their Publishers in Eighteenth-Century Britain, Ireland, and America* (Chicago: University of Chicago Press, 2006); David Berman, 'Enlightenment and Counter-Enlightenment in Irish Philosophy', *Archiv für Geschichte der Philosophie*, 64, 2 (1982), pp. 148–65; Máire Kennedy, 'Foreign Language Books, 1700–1800' in Raymond Gillespie and Andrew Hadfield (eds), *Oxford History of the Irish Book, Volume 3: The Irish Book in English, 1550–1800* (Oxford: Oxford University Press, 2005), pp. 368–82; Michael Brown, *Francis Hutcheson in Dublin, 1719–30: The Crucible of His Thought* (Dublin: Four Courts Press, 2001). On women see especially Máire Kennedy, 'Women and Reading in Eighteenth-Century Ireland', in Bernadette Cunningham and Máire Kennedy (eds),

participated in this diverse intellectual movement compels scholars to operate in an interdisciplinary way and reveals the central significance of debates around women for Enlightenment thought. The understanding of emigration similarly benefits from interdisciplinary approaches which produce a more nuanced and gendered understanding. Early studies of emigration were predominantly concerned with male emigrants, offered the 'exile' interpretation and concentrated on one stage of the emigration process.[9] A focus on women and the 'round trip' from departure to return in some form reveals the limitations of the 'exile' interpretation and places the female emigrant at the heart of the transatlantic exchange alongside her male counterpart. The application of different methodologies, including folklore and oral history, and closer textual analysis of letters and diaries illuminates women's distinct experience. The analysis of Irish women's participation in vernacular and high modernism needs to be set in the context of broader debates about canons, cultural history and the questioning of historicism as the dominant mode of literary analysis. The mode of literary criticism brought to bear in the concluding chapters is heavily influenced by the concerns of cultural studies as a distinct discipline, but seeks to integrate them in analysis of the relationship between history and literature.

Reading the full complexity of the Irish woman requires this interdisciplinary approach. Throughout the period 1700 to 1960, women in Ireland defied official and social norms and adapted, adopted, conformed to and sometimes rejected cultural ideas and practices from home and abroad. In short, there is no one 'Irish Woman'.

The Experience of Reading: Irish Historical Perspectives (Dublin: Rare Books Group of the Library Association of Ireland and Economic and Social History Society of Ireland,1999), pp. 78–98; 'The Distribution of a Locally Produced French Periodical in Provincial Ireland: The *Magazin à la mode*, 1777–1778', *Eighteenth-Century Ireland: Iris an Dá Chultúr*, 9 (1994), pp. 83–98; Angela Bourke et al. (eds), *Field Day Anthology of Irish Writing, Volumes 4–5: Irish Women's Writing and Traditions* (Cork: Cork University Press, 2002).

9 For a recent synopsis of emigration historiography see J. J. Lee, 'Interpreting Irish-America', in J. J. Lee and Marion R. Casey (eds), *Making the Irish American: History and Heritage of the Irish in the United States* (New York: New York University Press, 2006).

The Enlightenment

1
The Enlightenment and Reading, 1714–1820

Introduction

What was the Enlightenment and how did it change society in eighteenth-century Europe? These questions have been at the core of the historiographical debate on the Enlightenment since the 1960s. For the historian of women, the questions are compounded by the imperative to identify which aspects of this complex intellectual, political and social movement impacted on women and on ideas about women. In recent years, there has been an increasing recognition among historians and literary scholars that consideration of the nature of women and their education formed an important element in enlightened discussion and debate. Philosophers, political thinkers and writers of literary fiction queried if men's and women's brains were physically similar and whether mental capacity was gender neutral. If it was, should boys and girls be educated in the same way? Irish-born John Toland argued that not only were women intellectually equal to men but that education was the means through which women could reconstruct their lives and be more active in society: 'the Parity of the intellectual Organs in both Sexes, … makes [women] equally capable of all Improvements, had they but equally the same Advantages of Education, Travel, Company, and the Management of Affairs' as men.[1] Other writers adopted a more cautious approach. While acknowledging women's intellectual ability they also maintained that women's societal role was distinct from that of men and, consequently, that they should be educated in distinct ways.[2]

---

1 John Toland, Preface to *Letters to Serena, 1704* (London: Printed for Bernard Lintot, 1704).
2 Jonathan I. Israel, *Enlightenment Contested: Philosophy, Modernity, and the Emancipation of Man 1670–1752* (Oxford: Oxford University Press, 2006), p. 573.

The significance attached to women's education led to a new public recognition of the woman reader and scholar as well as the writer. As female literacy spread in the middle decades of the eighteenth century, publishers identified women as new consumers of books and journals. Writing for women readers by men and, increasingly, by women was an important means through which new definitions of gender behaviour were disseminated. Nor was this type of writing confined to one particular genre. Conduct books, religious writings, school books, novels, poetry and, as the eighteenth century advanced, magazines were all utilised to present definitions of femininity and appropriate behaviour for girls and women. In England, some literary critics, following Nancy Armstrong's seminal study, have suggested that this literature was central to the construction of a middle-class ideal of womanhood and ultimately bourgeois ideology which came to dominate English society in the nineteenth century.[3] Others have argued that the impact of Enlightenment thinking on gender definitions was more complex and that in much of the writing 'for the ladies' there was a tension between the promotion of a passive image of the ideal woman and the advocacy of greater intellectual engagement and involvement in public activities.[4]

A small group of writers carried the equality debate to its logical conclusion and opposed the legal subordination of women, particularly in marriage and, an even smaller minority, argued for the removal of social taboos concerning women's sexual behaviour. The origins of modern-day feminism are traditionally traced to the 1790s, as radical writers such as Mary Wollstonecraft asserted the 'rights of women' alongside those of men. More recently, scholars have acknowledged that Wollstonecraft's work drew on a significant legacy of writings by men and by women which advocated greater equality between the sexes.[5] Feminist historiography has also recognised the importance of religion in the discussions on women's role and status in society and has identified religious writers as supporters of enlightened views on women, particularly in relation to their education. As Sarah Knott and Barbara Taylor note: 'In Catholic as well as in Protestant settings, religion was a key site of enlightened discussion over women's status and entitlements.'[6]

---

3 Nancy Armstrong, *Desire and Domestic Fiction: A Political History of the Novel* (Oxford: Oxford University Press, 1987).
4 See, for example, Leila Silvana May, 'The Strong-Arming of Desire: A Reconsideration of Nancy Armstrong's "Desire and Domestic Fiction"', *ELH*, 68, 1 (Spring, 2001), pp. 267–85.
5 Karen Offen, *European Feminisms, 1700–1950: A Political History* (Stanford: Stanford University Press, 2000).
6 Sarah Knott and Barbara Taylor (eds), *Women, Gender and Enlightenment* (Basingstoke: Palgrave Macmillan, 2005), p. xviii.

The aim of this section of the book is to trace the dissemination of these ideas in Ireland and to explore their impact on changing definitions of femininity and womanhood. The main medium for the exchange of ideas was print, initially through Irish reprints of London imprints.

Cultural Encounters: Print and the Debate on Women in Eighteenth Century Ireland

George Berkeley, The Ladies Library *(1714)*
One of the earliest indications of an awareness on the part of at least one well-known Irish reader of the debate on women was the publication of *The Ladies Library* in London in 1714. Although originally attributed to Richard Steele, *The Ladies Library* was compiled by a young George Berkeley, Irish philosopher and future Bishop of Cloyne.[7] The three-volume work consisted of a collection of essays on a range of topics relating to women's domestic, social and religious duties and functions. Volume one focused on education and behaviour and detailed a suitable educational curriculum for girls. The second volume included chapters on women's societal and familiar roles as daughters, wives, mothers and widows, and the final volume concentrated on women's religious duties and exercises. As a number of scholars have pointed out, *The Ladies Library* drew heavily (albeit without acknowledgment) on other contemporary printed texts on the education and formation of young girls and women.[8] Among the authors plagiarised by Berkeley were François Fénelon, *Education des filles* (1687); Richard Allestree, *The Ladies Calling* (1673); John Locke, *Some Thoughts Concerning Education* (1693); Mary Astell, *A Serious Proposal to the Ladies, for the Advancement of their True and Greatest Interest. By a Lover of her Sex* (1694); and William Fleetwood, author of *The Relative Duties of Parents and Children, Husbands and Wives, Masters and Servants...* (1705).[9] These writers differed in their attitudes to the education of women and a careful reading of the three volumes of

---

7 For the identification of Berkeley as compiler of *The Ladies Library* see Stephen Parks, 'George Berkeley, Sir Richard Steele and *The Ladies Library*', *The Scriblerian and the Kit-Cats*, 12, 1 (Autumn 1980), pp. 1–2; E. J. F. and D. B., 'George Berkeley and *The Ladies Library*', *Berkeley Newsletter*, 4 (December 1980), pp. 5–13; *ODNB* entry on Berkeley by M. A. Stewart.
8 Greg Holingshead, 'Sources for the *Ladies Library*', *Berkeley Newsletter*, 11 (1989–90), pp. 1–9; E. J. F. and D. B., 'George Berkeley and *The Ladies Library*'; Patricia Springborg, 'Introduction', in Mary Astell, *A Serious Proposal to the Ladies, Parts I and II* (London: Pickering and Chatto, 1997), pp. 23–24.
9 For a full list of the texts used by Berkeley in *The Ladies Library* see George A. Aitken, *The Life of Richard Steele* (2 vols; London: William Isbister, 1889), vol. 2, pp. 39–44; Greg Holingshead, 'Sources for the *Ladies Library*', *Berkeley Newsletter*; E. J. F and

The Ladies Library reveals contradictions and inconsistencies in the views presented. Most followed what Jonathan Israel has called the 'moderate mainstream' of enlightened thought and agreed that 'women's intellectual powers are intrinsically weaker than men's', and that the 'moral qualities desirable in women' necessitated that girls be educated differently from boys.[10]

Of all the writers whose texts were edited by Berkeley, Mary Astell held the most radical views on women's education. In *A Serious Proposal to the Ladies, for the Advancement of their True and Greatest Interest. By a Lover of her Sex*, Astell outlined her plan for the establishment of a monastery or 'religious retirement' for 'Ladies of Quality' where they could study religion and also pursue more secular learning.[11] Two years later, Astell's *An Essay in Defence of the Female Sex* was printed.[12]

Some of the other authors whose texts were transcribed by Berkeley for *The Ladies Library* were also in favour of education for young women, although they expressed their views in more moderate language than Astell. These included Anglican clergymen such as Richard Allestree and William Fleetwood. Susan Staves has argued that clergy in the Church of England supported intellectual activity by women because it helped to promote the reading of religious texts. The clergymen also recognised that the cultivation of a pious image for women writers 'could offer models of Anglican female piety and learning' that might serve as a template for other women.[13] It may have been in this spirit that George Berkeley, who had been ordained a minister in the Church of Ireland in 1710, agreed to Richard Steele's suggestion that he compile an anthology of writing addressed to women. As most of the work is extracted from other writers, it is, however, difficult to get a clear view of Berkeley's reflections on the education of women. Like many of the authors whose work he reproduced, Berkeley communicated an ambivalence about supporting women's education and its ultimate aim and purpose. In the brief passages that appear to be in his own words, Berkeley

---

D. B., 'George Berkeley and *The Ladies Library*'; Patricia Springborg, 'Introduction' to Mary Astell, *A Serious Proposal to the Ladies*, pp. 23–24.

10 Jonathan I. Israel, *Enlightenment Contested*, p. 573.

11 Mary Astell, *A Serious Proposal to the Ladies, for the Advancement of their True and Greatest Interest. By a Lover of her Sex* (London: printed for R. Wilkin at the King's Head in St. Paul's Church-Yard, 1694).

12 Mary Astell, *An Essay in Defence of the Female Sex. In which are Inserted the Characters of a Pedant, a Squire, a Beau, a Vertuoso, a Poetaster, a City-Critick, &c. In a Letter to a Lady. Written by a Lady* (London: printed for A. Roper and E. Wilkinson at the Black Boy, and R. Clavel at the Peacock, in Fleetstreet, 1686).

13 Susan Staves, 'Church of England Clergy and Women Writers', in Nicole Pohl and Betty A. Schellenberg (eds), *Reconsidering the Bluestockings* (San Marino, Calif.: The Huntington Library Press, 2003), p. 94.

seemed to share the view of John Toland and Mary Astell that women were intellectually equal to men. He opened the section on 'Ignorance' in volume one with an assertion that 'Nature has given them [i.e. women] as good Talents as Men have, and if they are still called the weaker Sex, 'tis because the other, which assumes the Name of the wiser, hinders them of improving their Minds in useful Knowledge'.[14]

Other sections of the three-volume compilation suggest, however, that Berkeley's ideas about women's education were more conservative. He did not, for example, reprint in *The Ladies Library* Astell's support for an academy for women.[15] Instead he chose a section from the second part of Astell's *Proposal* on philosophical thought.[16] Berkeley clearly believed strongly in women's social and domestic role as daughters, wives, mothers and widows and that their education and upbringing should reflect this destiny. In the chapter on modesty, he suggested that St Paul's admonition that women should remain silent was not limited to 'Ecclesiastical Assemblies'.[17]

Cultural encounters through Irish reprints

No Irish edition of *The Ladies Library* is known to have been printed. The volumes are of interest, however, because they give an insight into the views of a well-known Irish intellectual and future member of the Church of Ireland hierarchy in the early eighteenth century. Berkeley's editing of *The Ladies Library* also suggests an awareness in Ireland of contemporary English publications on the education and ideal behaviour of women. In addition, most of the key texts cited by Berkeley were reprinted in Irish editions, frequently in the same year that the first London edition appeared.

John Locke's writings were well known in eighteenth-century Ireland. According to the *English Short Title Catalogue*, there were five Irish reprints of the Locke text plagiarised by Berkeley. *Some Thoughts Concerning Education* was printed in Dublin in 1728 (two editions), 1737, 1738 and 1778. The editions that appeared in 1728 and 1737 were printed 'at the request

---

14 George Berkeley, *The Ladies Library: Written by a Lady. Published by Sir Richard Steele* (1st edition, 3 vols; London: Printed for J[acob] T[onson], 1714), vol. 1, p. 435.
15 Richard H Dammers, 'Richard Steele and "*The Ladies Library*"', *Philological Quarterly*, 62, 4 (Fall 1983), pp. 530–35.
16 Patricia Springborg (ed.), *A Serious Proposal to the Ladies, Parts I and II*, by Mary Astell (London: Pickering and Chatto, 1997), pp. xvii–xxiii.
17 George Berkeley, *The Ladies Library: Written by a Lady. Published by Sir Richard Steele*, vol. I, p. 182. Although much of this chapter is taken from Richard Allestree, *The Ladies Calling· In Two Parts. By the Author of The Whole Duty of Man: The Causes of the Decay of Christian Piety, and The Gentleman's Calling* (Oxford: Printed at the Theater, [1673]), Berkeley appears to have added the section to Allestree's text concerning Paul's message on the silence of women.

of several of the nobility of this kingdom'.[18] The text presented one of the most popular guides for parents and tutors on how to educate children in an enlightened fashion. Locke grounded his ideas in a belief in the rationality of the child. Reasoned argument and explanation were far more effective in teaching a child how to behave virtuously than strict discipline and use of the rod. Locke cautioned against corporal punishment suggesting that it only served to confirm the validity of using force and violence, adding that 'those children that have been most chastised, seldom make the best men.'[19] Parental praise and an awareness of being held in high esteem by a parent were, Locke argued, far more effective methods of instruction than strict discipline. Learning should be enjoyable with children being coaxed rather than forced. Locke advocated the use of games and toys to teach the alphabet and writing skills and argued that the use of an 'easy pleasant book' with illustrations such as Aesop's *Fables* would be more effective in teaching literacy than compelling children to read long passages from the Bible or other religious text which they would not understand.[20]

In his introductory remarks, which were copied by Berkeley for *The Ladies Library*, Locke acknowledged that his work was mainly directed at 'how a young gentleman should be brought up from his infancy, which in all things will not so perfectly suit the education of daughters; though where the difference of sex requires different treatment, 'twill be no hard matter to distinguish.'[21] In other words, Locke was not concerned to identify a gender-specific curriculum and his text could be used as a guide for the rearing and educating of girls as well as boys.

The work of Richard Allestree was also in demand in early eighteenth-century Ireland. An edition of his completed works, including his *The Ladies Calling*, was printed by subscription in Dublin in 1723. Allestree's *The Whole Duty of Man* was one of the most popular books by an English clergyman to be printed in eighteenth-century Ireland, going through a total of twelve editions from 1699 to 1800.[22] There were 253 subscribers to the 1723 volume,

---

18 Patrick Kelly, 'Perceptions of Locke in Eighteenth-Century Ireland', *Proceedings of the Royal Irish Academy*, 89C (1989), pp. 20–21. See ESTC online (http://www.estc.bl.uk) for bibliographical details of editions of Locke's work.
19 John Locke, *Some Thoughts Concerning Education* (10th edition, Dublin: R. Reilly on Cork Hill, 1737), p. 42.
20 Locke, *Some Thoughts Concerning Education*, p. 170. See also pp. 167–70.
21 Locke, *Some Thoughts Concerning Education*, p. 10.
22 Richard Allestree, *The Works of the Learned and Pious Author of The Whole Duty of Man* (Dublin: Printed for P. Dugan, 1723). There were seven Irish editions of [Richard Allestree], *The Whole Duty of Man* (Dublin: John Brocas, 1699; A. Rhames, 1714; E. Wates, 1720; S. Hyde, 1733; R. Reilly, 1737; William Watson, 1800) and five of *The New Whole Duty of Man* (Dublin: Printed for P. Wilson, 1746; Printed for P. Wilson and James Esdall, 1752; Printed for P. Wilson and T. Dylan, 1764; Printed for W. Wilson,

which included thirty-three Church of Ireland ministers, among whom was Patrick Delany, Dean of St Patrick's Cathedral, Dublin and husband of artist and literary hostess, Mary Delany. Women accounted for 9.6 per cent of the subscribers.[23] In *The Ladies Calling*, Allestree communicated the same uncertainty as Berkeley concerning the intellectual status of women. In the introduction, he noted his unwillingness to disagree with the 'received opinion' that women were 'in respect of their intellects ... below men' but he also echoed Toland and Berkeley in suggesting that if women were given the same educational opportunities as men that they would 'make as good returns of it'.[24] Despite this assertion, the main text of *The Ladies Calling* advocated a more traditional and passive role for women as chaste virgins, obedient wives and nurturing and supportive mothers and widows with little reference to intellectual activities.

There was no Irish edition of Mary Astell's *A Serious Proposal* but her *Some Reflections on Marriage* was reprinted in a Dublin edition in 1730.[25] This was an explicit indictment of the contemporary status of women in English society. It critiqued the entrapment of women in forced marriages but also seemed to suggest that women could never have parity of esteem in marriage as it was doubtful 'if a man could respect his wife when he has a contemptible opinion of her and her sex? When from his own elevation he looks down on them as void of understanding, full of ignorance and passion, so that folly and a woman are equivalent terms with him?'[26]

The existence of the Irish edition of Astell's text suggests an interest among, at least, some members of the Dublin literati in her radical views on the status of women in society. Five years later, another text which advocated a reform of the laws on marriage, entitled *The Hardships of the English Laws. In Relation to Wives. With an Explanation of the Original Curse of Subjection Passed upon the Woman. In an Humble Address to the Legislature* was published in Dublin in the same year as a London edition appeared. It has been attributed to Sarah Chapone, a friend of Mary Delany who may also have been behind the publication of the Irish edition. Delany

---

1771; Printed for William Wilson and J. Williams, 1774). See also the Dublin reprints of William Fleetwood, *The Relative Duties of Parents and Children, Husbands and Wives, Masters and Servants: Consider'd in Sixteen Practical Discourses: with Three Sermons upon the Case of Self-Murther* (3rd edition; Dublin: Samuel Fairbrother, 1726).

23 See the Inventing and Reinventing the Irish Woman website for a list of subscribers: http://www2.ul.ie/web/WWW/Faculties/Arts%2C_Humanities_%26_Social_Sciences/Inventing/Eighteenth_Century_Subscribers.

24 Richard Allestree, *The Ladies Calling in Two Parts. By the Author of the Whole Duty of Man, etc.* (8th impression; Oxford: Printed at the Theater, 1705), preface.

25 Mary Astell, *Some Reflections Upon Marriage. With Additions* (5th edition; Dublin: S. Hyde and E. Dobson, 1730).

26 Ibid., p. 31.

fostered a network of female writers and artists in Dublin and London. She and her husband were among the subscribers of a number of Irish reprints in the 1730s and 1740s.[27]

Cultural exchange: Elizabeth and Richard Griffith – A Series of Genuine Letters Between Henry and Frances *(1757)*
Another writer whose publications appeared in many Irish editions and who supported an intellectual role for women, albeit in a less radical manner than Astell and Chapone, was Elizabeth Griffith, born in Wales but brought up in Dublin.[28] In 1757 Griffith and her Kilkenny-born husband, Richard, published *A Series of Genuine Letters Between Henry and Frances*, which they claimed was an edited version of their courtship correspondence.[29] The three-volume work presented an ideal friendship between a man and a woman. Referring to themselves as Abelard and Heloise, the couple exchanged books, discussed literature and, when they met, read together. Although based in Ireland, the couple were anxious to demonstrate that they were familiar with the most fashionable literature appearing in the London market and encouraged one another to read new books and authors.

Letters Between Henry and Frances included a discussion on the intellectual ability of women with Frances (i.e. Elizabeth) presenting herself as a 'Champion, for the Honour of my injured Sex'.[30] The greater physical strength of men, she argued, has led to an erroneous belief that they also had 'greater sense and nobler Souls'. At the same time, she sardonically pointed out, 'they refused, very unfairly, the same Law of Reason, to an Horse, though they acknowledge him to be an Animal of greater Strength, than they.'[31] Women who were poorly educated were unfairly criticised for the 'Weakness of our Understandings'. More directly than Berkeley and

---

27 Sarah Chapone, *The Hardships of the English Laws. In Relation to Wives. With an Explanation of the Original Curse of Subjection Passed Upon the Woman. In an Humble Address to the Legislature* (London: W. Bowyer for J. Roberts, 1735; Dublin: George Faulkner, 1735). For Chapone's authorship of the text see the entry on Chapone in *ODNB*. For Delany's encouragement of women writers and artists see, for example, below; Patrick Kelly, 'Anne Donnellan: Irish Proto-Bluestocking', *Hermathena*, 154 (Summer 1993), pp. 39–68; Lisa Townsend, 'The Intellectual and Cultural Interests of Women in Ireland, c.1740–c.1840' (unpublished PhD thesis, Queen's University Belfast, 2007).

28 Elizabeth Eger, *Bluestockings: Women of Reason from Enlightenment to Romanticism* (Basingstoke: Palgrave Macmillan, 2010), pp. 89–90; *ODNB* entry by Elizabeth Eger; *DIB* entry by Frances Clarke.

29 See Shaun Regan, 'Locating Richard Griffith: Genre, Nation, Canon', *Irish University Review*, 41, 1 (Spring–Summer 2011), pp. 95–114.

30 Elizabeth and Richard Griffith, *A Series of Genuine Letters Between Henry and Frances* (3 vols; London: Printed for W. Johnson, 1757), vol. 1, letter 39, p. 61.

31 Ibid., letter 40, p. 62.

Allestree, Griffith gave a very spirited defence of the potential of women if they had had the benefit of a broad intellectual education:

> Henceforth therefore, I interdict you, wise Fools, from the Unjustness of any Satyr against our Sex, 'till you have, by a proper and more liberal Education, given our noble and ingenuous Natures fair Play to exert themselves. Do this, if ye dare, ye imperious Tyrants, and ye shall see, how small we will make you. Oh! Let us once be free; for know that Arts and Sciences cannot raise their Heads under despotick Sway.[32]

Letters Between Henry and Frances thus incorporated some of the more progressive ideas about women's education circulating in English printed literature. The *Letters* also testify to the circulation of such ideas in Ireland as both correspondents were resident there. Elizabeth was living in Dublin while Richard was based in his family home in Kilkenny. In the first and second editions, however, their residence was fictionalised as England in order to preserve, it was alleged, the anonymity of the couple. In the third edition, their Irish location was restored and more specific references to Ireland were included. The first edition of the courtship correspondence was published in Ireland prior to its London publication with the help of a subscription list which included the names of a significant number of Irish parliamentarians, prominent lawyers and members of the Irish administration.[33] Also among the list of subscribers were Mary Delany and other women associated with her Irish network including Letitia Bushe, the Forth sisters and members of the Hamilton family. The husband of the Irish bluestocking, Elizabeth Vesey, Agmondisham Vesey as well as Mrs Handcock, her female companion and sister of Vesey's first husband, were also among the subscribers to the Griffith volume.[34] Other well-known members of Dublin literary and

---

32 Ibid.
33 No copy of the first edition of *A Series of Genuine Letters Between Henry and Frances* (3 vols) printed in Dublin in 1757 appears to have survived. The London edition which was published in the same year included the list of subscribers. The second edition printed by S. Powell, in Crane-Lane, Dublin in 1760 also had Irish subscribers but the prominent political and literary names were less in evidence. Neither the Veseys nor members of the Delany network appear to have been subscribers to the second edition. See the online database, http://www2.ul.ie/web/WWW/Faculties/Arts,_Humanities_%26_Social_Sciences/Inventing/.
34 For the list of subscribers see the online database, http://www2.ul.ie/web/WWW/Faculties/Arts,_Humanities_%26_Social_Sciences/Inventing/. Elizabeth Vesey's first husband was William Handcock, who died in 1741. The first name of his sister is unknown. See Betty Rizzo, *Companions without Vows: Relationships among Sixteenth Century British Women* (Athens, Ga.: University of Georgia Press, 1994), pp. 218–39.

political circles on the subscription list were Dublin councillor Charles Lucas and his son Henry (then a student at Trinity College Dublin), the genealogist John Lodge, the economic reformist Samuel Madden and members of the Monck Mason family and actor and theatre manager, Thomas Sheridan. The list of names suggests not only the strong connections of the Griffiths among the social, intellectual and political elite of Dublin but also the readership for this type of publication which promoted an image of courtship and marriage as an intellectual partnership.

Cultural encounters and exchange: The bluestocking circle
In the preface to her *Novellettes, Selected for the Use of Young Ladies and Gentlemen, Written by Dr Goldsmith* (London, 1780; Dublin, 1784), Griffith identified herself with other women writers who 'have served to explode the illiberal assertion that Female genius is inferior to Male'.[35] In later writings, Griffith, however, supported a more domestic role for women than was evident in *Letters Between Henry and Frances*. In her *Essays, Addressed to Young Married Women* which first appeared in London in 1782 (an Irish edition appeared in 1790), Griffith admonished young wives to be attentive to their husbands and suggested that it was the wife's fault if the husband found other women more attractive.[36] If a husband had an affair with another woman, the wife should remember that 'to resent, or to retaliate, neither her duty nor her religion will permit'.[37] Even the leisure activity of reading was not strongly recommended by Griffith in *Essays, Addressed to Young Married Women*.

Griffith's later views may have been partly influenced by personal experience, as her husband was reported to have left her for a younger woman.[38] By that time too, Griffith was linked to the outer circle of women writers and intellectuals associated with the bluestocking movement. While the latter were strong advocates of women's education, they also shared Anglican clergymen's belief in a rather limited social role for women and would have approved of Griffith's emphasis on women's domestic and familial duties in her later writings.

Elizabeth Vesey, who was a member of a prominent Anglo-Irish family,

---

Letitia Bushe is listed as Letitia Buthe, but this is corrected to Bushe in the second edition of the letters that was published in Dublin in 1760. Griffith's first play to be published: *Theodorick, King of Denmark. A Tragedy. Never Before Published. By a Young Gentlewoman* (Dublin: James Esdall, 1752) was also printed by subscription. See the online database as above.

35 Cited in the entry on Elizabeth Griffith by Elizabeth Eger in *ODNB*.
36 Elizabeth Griffith, *Essays, Addressed to Young Married Women* (London: T. Cadell, 1782; Dublin: Sold by George Draper, 1790), p. 25
37 Ibid., p. 28.
38 Entry on Elizabeth Griffith by Elizabeth Eger in *ODNB*; entry on Elizabeth Griffith by Frances Clarke in *DIB*.

represents the most direct link between Ireland and the bluestocking network.[39] Along with Elizabeth Montagu and Frances Boscawen, Vesey hosted regular salons in her London house at which 'intelligent talk and witty repartee were more important than drink, politics, cards, or sexual encounters.'[40] The bluestocking salons were one of the most important manifestations of the impact of Enlightenment thinking on women in Britain. The meetings were visible and audible proof that women as well as men were rational beings capable of intellectual thought. There was a formal structure to the Vesey salon that distinguished it from the routine round of visiting with which middle- and upper-class women would have been familiar. The relatively large size of the salon also transformed it from a private familiar meeting to that of a semi-public one. Elizabeth Montagu's description of Vesey's salons suggests that they may also have served a quasi-political purpose, bringing together English, Scottish and Irishmen with different loyalties and beliefs who

> all gather together under the downy wing of the Sylph [i.e., Vesey], and are soothed into good humour: were she to withdraw her influence for a moment, discord would reassume her reign and we should hear the clashing of swords, the angry flirting of fans, and St Andrew and St Patrick gabbling in dire confusion the different dialects of the Erse language...[41]

The bluestocking salons, thus, expanded the intellectual and the public space in which women could function without incurring social disapproval.

Boscawen, Vesey and Montagu formed part of a wider social and literary network sustained through the salons as well as by private correspondence, the medium through which many women participated in the new 'republic of letters'.[42] Although Elizabeth Montagu published very little and Boscawen and Vesey nothing at all, the three women maintained regular correspondence with a wide range of intellectuals, men as well as women.[43] In addition, they offered patronage to women writers, often in a very practical form. Montagu, in particular, used her family wealth to assist authors to get their

---

39 Entry on Elizabeth Vesey by Barbara Brandon Schnorrenburg in *ODNB*.
40 Ibid.
41 Elizabeth Montagu to Elizabeth Carter, 4 September 1772, cited in Eger, *Bluestockings: Women of Reason from Enlightenment to Romanticism*, p.109. See also Emma Major, 'The Politics of Sociability: Public Dimensions of the Bluestocking Millennium', *Huntington Library Quarterly*, 65, 1/2 (2002), p. 180.
42 Elizabeth Eger, *Bluestockings: Women of Reason from Enlightenment to Romanticism*, pp. 87–100.
43 Entry on Frances Boscawen by Elizabeth Eger in *ODNB*.

work published. Elizabeth Vesey also provided financial help for publications aimed at women, particularly in Ireland. She was, for example, instrumental in securing the printing of an Irish edition of Montagu's *An Essay on the Writings and Genius of Shakespeare* in 1769 and, as noted already, she and her husband Aghmondisham Vesey were listed as subscribers to a number of Irish publications.[44]

The growing interest in women writers linked to the bluestocking group also contributed to the expanding market in books on the education of girls. Women associated with the network such as Anna Barbauld, Elizabeth Carter, Hester Chapone, Hannah More and Catherine Talbot all produced books that were intended to instruct young women on their education, their religious practice and their general behaviour. Barbara Taylor and other scholars have pointed to the 'feminist' charge in such texts as they encouraged girls to read and think for themselves.[45] Chapone, for example, outlined an impressive reading curriculum for her niece which, if followed, would have encouraged young women to be intellectually inquisitive and engaged.

Like other bluestocking writers, Chapone also stressed the importance of religious education. Aileen Fyffe has, however, drawn a useful distinction between writers who adhered to orthodox Anglican views and those who were members of a dissenting sect. The latter, Fyffe suggested, encouraged a more independent form of thinking among children than the former. In particular, Fyffe explored the publications of Unitarians, Anna Barbauld and her brother, John Aikin, which were also printed in Irish editions.[46] Fyffe contrasted the open approach of the Aikins to the education of children with that of the devout Anglican, Sarah Trimmer, whose books on children's education asserted the authority of the parent and an unquestioning attitude to learning.[47]

While the biography of Irish woman Elizabeth Vesey is central to the story of the bluestocking movement, there is little evidence that she attempted to form a similar group in Ireland. The most well-known literary salon of eighteenth century Ireland was organised by Mary Delany and her husband

---

44 Eger, *Bluestockings: Women of Reason from Enlightenment to Romanticism*, pp. 67–68, 81–87. For Vesey as a subscriber to Irish publications, see William H. Robinson, *The Library of Mrs. Elizabeth Vesey, 1715–1791* (Newcastle upon Tyne: W. H. Robinson, 1926) and below.

45 Barbara Taylor, 'Feminists versus Gallants: Manners and Morals in Enlightenment Britain', *Representations*, 87 (Summer 2004), pp. 125–48.

46 Aileen Fyffe, 'Reading Children's Books in Eighteenth-Century Dissenting Families', *Historical Journal*, 43 (2000), pp. 453–74. For Irish editions see note 53 below.

47 Ibid. See also Mary Hilton '"Child of Reason": Anna Barbauld and the Origins of Progressive Pedagogy', in Mary Hilton and Pam Hirsch (eds), *Practical Visionaries: Women, Education and Social Progress, 1790–1930* (Harlow: Longman, 2000), pp. 21–38.

Patrick and was attended by Jonathan Swift, Letitia Pilkington and other literary luminaries. Swift also hosted literary evenings and was noted for his patronage of women authors.[48] Mary Delany encouraged women writers and, as has already been noted, her name or that of her husband appears as a subscriber to a number of Irish printed books. Like the women who attended the bluestocking London salons, Delany also corresponded with a group of women, some of whom were also listed as subscribers to books by women authors.[49] The Swift and Delany salons thus shared some of the characteristics of the London salons. They included men and women and provided a support network for women writers. Outside of Dublin, the Edgeworth family organised socio-literary events to which they invited writers to read and discuss their work. In the 1790s and early 1800s, English-born Elizabeth Hastings, Countess of Moira, came closer to imitating the format of the London events through the gatherings of politicians, writers and intellectuals that she assembled in her Dublin house. None of these occasions, however, generated the same notoriety as the London salons of Vesey, Montagu and Boscawen.[50]

Although there was no explicit imitation of the bluestocking salons in eighteenth-century Ireland, there was a readership for books written by women associated with the bluestocking circle and, more widely, for books intended for a female readership. As the bluestocking group emerged into public prominence in England in the 1760s and 1770s, the demand for publications by women involved in the network expanded in Ireland. Nearly all of the books published by writers such as Catherine Talbot, Catharine Macaulay, Elizabeth Montagu, Elizabeth Carter, Fanny Burney, Hester Chapone and Charlotte Lennox appeared in Irish editions.[51] In the eleven-year period between 1775 and 1786, there were seven Dublin editions of Hester Chapone's *Letters on the Improvement of the Mind. Addressed to a Young Lady* which Norma Clarke has described as disseminating 'the bluestocking ideal more comprehensively than any other single production of the era'.[52] There was, also, a regional market for such books outside of Dublin. In addition to Belfast and Cork reprints, local booksellers stocked copies of the original English editions of works by

---

48 For the salons of the Delanys and Swift, see A.C. Elias Jr (ed.), *Memoirs of Laetitia Pilkington* (2 vols; Athens, Ga.: University of Georgia Press, 1997), vol. 1, pp. 283, 387.
49 Lady Llanover (ed.). *The Autobiography and Correspondence of Mary Granville, Mrs. Delany: with Interesting Reminiscences of King George the Third and Queen Charlotte*: (2 series, 6 vols; London: R. Bentley, 1861–62); Patrick Kelly, 'Anne Donnellan: Irish Proto-Bluestocking'.
50 See also chapter two, pp. 70–71.
51 See ESTC online (http://www.estc.bl.uk).
52 Norma Clarke, 'Bluestocking Fictions: Devotional Writings, Didactic Literature and the Imperative of Female Improvement', in Knott and Taylor (eds), *Women, Gender, and Enlightenment*, p. 468.

women linked to the bluestocking circle. Editions of the work of Unitarians, Anna Letitia Barbauld and her brother, John Aikin, for example, were printed in Belfast and Cork as well as in Dublin.[53] Sarah Fielding's *The Governess or Little Female Academy... For the Entertainment and Instruction of Young Ladies in their Education* was also reprinted in the three principal Irish cities.[54] In 1785, Anthony Edwards published an extensive list of the books available in his shop in Castle Street in Cork. Among the volumes for sale were publications by Elizabeth Griffith, Catharine Macaulay, Sarah Fielding, Hester Chapone, Elizabeth Carter and Catherine Talbot.[55] An interest in the debate on women was not, therefore, confined to a small elite group in Dublin.

Cultural Transfer through Translation and the Printed Word

French translations
The reprinting of English-authored books was one medium for the dispersal of the debate on women's societal role and education in Ireland. Another was the publication of English translations of writings by French authors. Despite the ambiguous attitude of eighteenth-century English society towards France, parents, governesses and teachers admired French Catholic writings on the education of girls. London publishers recognised the demand for English translations of French authors. Frequently, however, the translator thought it appropriate to edit or amend the French text to suit an Anglican readership. Through the revisions of the translators, cultural encounter thus became a form of cultural adaption as the French text was revised for an English market.

A good example of this process is the English translations of *Education des filles* authored by French Catholic cleric, François Fénelon. The text was originally published in Paris in 1687. The first English translation appeared two years later with a title which indicated that changes had been made to

---

53 John Aikin, *Evenings at Home; Or, the Juvenile Budget Opened. Consisting of a Variety of Miscellaneous Pieces* (Cork: J. Connor, 1794); John Aikin, *Lessons for Children of Three Years Old* (Dublin: R. Jackson, 1779); John and A. L. Aikin (Mrs Barbauld), *Miscellaneous Pieces in Prose* (Belfast: James Magee, 1774).

54 *The Governess; or, Little Female Academy. Being the History of Mrs. Teachum, and her Nine Girls. With their Nine Days Amusement. Calculated for the Entertainment and Iinstruction of Young Ladies in their Education. By the Author of David Simple* (Dublin: Printed for A. Bradley and R. James, 1749, 1752; Cork: printed for T. White and W. Flyn, 1769; 10th edition, Belfast, 1779; Dublin: s.n., 1791).

55 Anthony Edwards, *A Catalogue of Books, in Most Branches of Literature and Music,... Now Selling by Anthony Edwards, no 3 Castle-Street, Cork* (Cork: Printed for Anthony Edwards, 1785). See also Máire Kennedy, 'Women and Reading in Eighteenth-Century Ireland', pp. 78–98.

the original text: *The Education of Young Gentlewomen. Written Originally in the French; and From Thence Made English. And Improved For a Lady of Quality.*[56] In 1714, when George Berkeley included an extract from Fénelon's text in *The Ladies Library*, he used a more recent English translation by Anglican clergyman George Hickes which had appeared in 1707. The title agan indicated that Hickes had not only translated Fénelon's work but had also 'revised' it. Hickes's translation was popular and went through at least four London editions and was also reprinted in Glasgow and in Dublin.[57]

Fénelon presented a conservative view of girls' education. He wrote for the daughters of wealthy families who were educated at home or in elite boarding schools such as that at Saint Cyr with which Fénelon was linked.[58] There was an assumption in all of the eighteenth-century writings on female education that girls from poor families were to be trained in employable skills rather than being educated to spend their leisure time in reading suitably selected books. The school at Saint Cyr, for example, which was established by Fénelon's friend, Madame Maintenon, had an entrance qualification of '140 years of noble ancestry'.[59] For Fénelon, and for Berkeley in his selection of appropriate texts for *The Ladies Library*, the priority was the instruction of young women who were to spend their lives as wives and mothers in wealthy households. As with many other writers, Fénelon was an advocate for the education of girls, but he also believed in the 'natural weakness' of women which, he argued, was the primary reason why their education should be treated with care. Women had important social roles as household managers, teachers of young children and companions for their husbands for which they should be trained in childhood.

The attraction of Fénelon's writings for parents and guardians of children was that, like Locke, his educational theory was centred on an

---

56 Francois Fénelon, *The Education of Young Gentlewomen. Written Originally in the French; and From Thence Made English. And Improved For a Lady of Quality* (London: Printed for Nathaniel Ranew, 1699).

57 George Hickes, *Instructions for the Education of a Daughter, by the Author of Telemachus. To Which is Added, a Small Tract of Instructions for the Conduct of Young Ladies of the Highest Rank. With Suitable Devotions Annexed. Done into English, and Revised by Dr. George Hickes* (London: Printed for Jonah Bowyer, 1707, 1708, 1713, 1721; Edinburgh: Printed for James Reid, 1750; Glasgow: Printed by R. & A. Foulis, 1750, Dublin: Printed for P. Wilson, J. Exshaw, and M. Williamson, 1753). For Hickes's revisions of the original text see H. C. Barnard, *Fénelon on Education* (Cambridge: Cambridge University Press, 1966), pp. xliv–xlvi.

58 Barnard, *Fénelon on Education*, pp. xxii–xxiii. See also Madame de Maintenon, *The Ladies Monitor or Instructions for the Fair Sex, Written in French by the Celebrated Madam de Maintenon, for the Use of the Young Ladies of St. Cyr's and Now First Translated into English by Mr. Rollos* (Dublin: Printed for Richard Smith, 1758).

59 Olwen Hufton, *The Prospect Before Her: A History of Women in Western Europe, Volume 1: 1500–1800* (London: HarperCollins, 1995), p. 112.

enlightened perception of the child as a rational being. Praise and encouragement were more effective teaching tools than excessive chiding. Parents and governesses should make learning enjoyable rather than an enforced chore and they should encourage children's curiosity rather than attempt to restrict it. Children's books should be presented in an attractive fashion with short passages of text and, where possible, illustrations. Unlike in Locke's educational ideas, however, at the centre of Fénelon's ideal curriculum were stories drawn from the Bible, though in addition to religious training Fénelon believed that all 'gentlewomen' should be taught reading and writing. In a passage, later paraphrased by Berkeley, Fénelon condemned women who were unable to pronounce the words that they read or whose writing style was so deficient that they could not form or connect letters properly. Given women's future roles as household managers, they should be taught how to keep accounts and acquire knowledge of the law, particularly in relation to property and inheritance. Other subjects on Fénelon's curriculum included history, moral philosophy, music and painting. And, in a passage cited by Berkeley, Fénelon expressed his view that girls should acquire a reading facility in other modern languages to enable them to read 'good books' by some of the most acclaimed writers of eighteenth-century Europe. Classical languages were not on Fénelon's curriculum but he did not object to girls learning 'a little Latin' that would help them in their learning of other modern languages. While advocating this impressively wide-ranging curriculum, Fénelon characteristically sounded a contradictory warning note against giving young girls access to 'dangerous books' that they might read in private at home.[60] The menace posed by women reading the wrong kind of book was to be another recurring theme in the subsequent discourse on women's education.[61]

According to Máire Kennedy, Fénelon was one of the most widely known French authors in eighteenth-century Britain and Ireland.[62] Hickes's translation of *Education des filles* was printed in Dublin in 1753 while Fénelon's *Les aventures de Télémaque* was found in a significant number of eighteenth-century Irish private libraries, appearing in forty-six per cent of libraries (seventy-eight in total) for which catalogues have survived.[63] Based on the adventures of Télémaque in search of his father, Ulysses, it was

---

60 George Hickes, *Instructions for the Education of a Daughter, by the Author of Telemachus. ... Done into English, and Revised by Dr. George Hickes...* p. 243.
61 On Fénelon, see also Jean Bloch, 'Discourses of Female Education in the Writings of Eighteenth-Century French Women', in Knott and Taylor (eds), *Women, Gender and Enlightenment*, pp. 243–58.
62 Máire Kennedy, *French Books in Eighteenth-Century Ireland* (Studies on Voltaire and the Eighteenth Century, 2001:07) (Oxford: Voltaire Foundation, 2001), p. 46.
63 Ibid., pp. 19, 46, 183–90.

mainly used as a school book for French language classes. Although the focus is on the male character, Télémaque, the text also explores different representations of women including the seductress and the 'charming butterfly', a woman who is portrayed as frivolous and lacking in depth of character. Télémaque finally chooses 'un amour raisonnable' with Antipe, who is praised for 'her silence, her modest reserve, her constant employment, her industry in spinning, weaving, and embroidery, her attention to the economy of her father's house, since the death of her mother; her contempt of the ornament of dress and her forgetting, or even seeming to be ignorant of her beauty', a description which complemented the view of the ideal women that appears in the pages of *Education des filles*.[64]

The publications of French author Stéphanie-Félicité de Genlis were also widely used in the education of Irish girls. When Irish writer Sydney Owenson met the seventy-year-old de Genlis in Paris in 1816, she recalled that it was 'out of [de Genlis's] work I had been educated' and 'whose name and writings were intimately connected with all my earliest associations of books and literature'.[65] Maria Edgeworth's first attempt at publication in the 1780s was a translation of de Genlis's *Adèle et Théodore* in which the author outlined her views on children's education.[66] The book in the original French as well as in English translation was popular in Ireland as it was in England and was found listed in 29 Irish private libraries of the eighteenth century.[67]

Adèle et Théodore was in epistolary format and told the story of a father and mother who devised an experimental plan for the rearing of their two children, a boy aged six and a girl aged seven. The couple move the family home from Paris to a rural retreat, accompanied by two carefully chosen teachers including an English tutor called Bridget. The mother assumes responsibility

---

64 François De Fénelon, *Telemacus, Son of Ulysses*, edited and translated by Patrick Riley (Cambridge: Cambridge University Press, 1994), pp. 302–3; Barnard, *Fénelon on Education*, pp. xxxvii–xl.
65 Mary Campbell, *Lady Morgan: The Life and Times of Sydney Owenson* (London: Pandora Press, 1988), p. 141.
66 The work was withdrawn from publication because another translation had appeared in print. See Clíona Ó Gallchoir, *Maria Edgeworth: Women, Enlightenment, Nation* (Dublin: University College Dublin Press, 2005), pp. 12, 24–26; Maria Edgeworth, *Letters for Literary Ladies*, edited by Claire Connolly (London: Dent, 1993), pp. xviii–xix.
67 See Table 3, Top 100 French authors present in Irish private libraries, in Kennedy, *French Books in Eighteenth-Century Ireland*, pp. 183–90. For Irish reprints of the English translations see Stéphanie Félicité Genlis, *Adelaide and Theodore, or Letters on Education: Containing All the Principles Relative to Three Different Plans of Education; to That of Princes And to Those of Young Persons of Both Sexes* (Dublin: Printed for W. Jones, 1783, 1785 (2 reprints), 1794).

for the education of the daughter, Adèle, while the father teaches Théodore. De Genlis acknowledged that her pedagogical ideas were influenced by 'the wise Locke'.[68] She agreed with Locke that knowledge should be nurtured in children and was best done through play. She devised toys, games and plays for the lessons of Adèle and Théodore.[69] De Genlis also wrote her own tales and stories to read to the children which she later published and which appeared in two Irish editions in 1800.[70] As with so many other writers on girls' education, de Genlis identified woman's societal role as that of a good mother and wife. The ideal woman should 'possess solid reasoning, with all the important virtues: a general, though not a deep knowledge of the sciences; all the powers of pleasing, a knowledge of all the modern languages, without pedantry or affectation; and that, in short, she should conduct her domestic affairs like a good housewife, who pretends to no other merit'.[71] De Genlis also shared the class bias of Fénelon and other educationalists. In *Adèle et Théodore*, the mother adopted a young orphan girl, Ermine aged six-and-a-half, to whom the seven year old Adèle was to act as a mother and learn the skills of motherhood with her live doll. Ermine's education was also to be narrower than that of Adèle and to focus on practical skills.

De Genlis wrote *Adèle et Théodore* partly to refute the teachings of Jean Jacques Rousseau on the education of children. Rousseau's famous *Emile* first appeared in English translations in the early 1760s. The last section of the book dealt with the education of Sophie, the woman intended as Emile's wife. In the text, Rousseau penned a much-quoted assertion on the differences between men and women and the need, therefore, for their education to be distinct.[72] Although this passage provoked controversy,

---

68 See Stéphanie Félicité Genlis, *Adelaide and Theodore, or Letters on Education: Containing All the Principles Relative to Three Different Plans of Education; to That of Princes And to Those of Young Persons of Both Sexes* (Dublin: Printed for Luke White, 1783), p. 49.

69 This view was expanded in *Théâtre à L'usage des Jeunes Personnes. Theatre of Education. Translated from the French of the Countess de Genlis* (4 vols; Dublin: D. Graisberry, 1781, 1783, 1784).

70 See Stéphanie Félicité Genlis, *Nouvelle Méthode d'Enseignement Pour la Première Enfance. A New Method of Instruction for Children From Five to Ten Years Old, Including Moral Dialogues, the Children's Island, A Tale, Thoughts and Maxims, Models of Composition in Writing, for Children Ten or Twelve Years Old, and a New Method of Teaching Children to Draw. Translated from the French of Madame de Genlis* (Dublin: P. Wogan, 1800).

71 Stéphanie Félicité Genlis, *Adelaide and Theodore, or Letters on Education: Containing All the Principles Relative to Three Different Plans of Education; to that of Princes and to those of Young Persons of Both Sexes* (Dublin, Printed for Luke White, 1783), p. 39.

72 See R. L. Archer, *Rousseau on Education* (London, 1912), pp. 217ff.; Karen Offen, *European Feminisms 1700–1950: A Political History* (Stanford: Stanford University Press, 2000), pp. 38–41.

many women educationalists were more concerned with Rousseau's attitude towards religious education. Although de Genlis used the same device of rural isolation as Rousseau recommended for Emile, she rejected his refusal to place religious reading at the centre of the child's education.

In Ireland, as elsewhere, responses to Rousseau's views on female education were more positive than his depiction of Sophie might seem to warrant. Emily Fitzgerald, Duchess of Leinster, famously offered Rousseau a position as tutor to her large family while other women note in their correspondence that they approved of his views on education.[73] The mother of the artist and memorialist Caroline Hamilton, for example, tried to follow Rousseau's advice in the rearing and education of her children.[74] Máire Kennedy found copies of *Emile* in twenty-two Irish private libraries. There were, however, no Irish editions of *Emile* but there were four reprints of the English translation of Rousseau's *La nouvelle Héloïse* which had been published a year before *Emile* in 1761. It depicted 'a strong heroine ... in control of her family and a large estate'. As elsewhere, the popularity of *La nouvelle Héloïse* appears to have outweighed the criticisms of Rousseau's depiction of Sophie.[75]

Women linked to the Anglo-Irish Protestant class were, therefore, reading French writers on education.[76] There was also, however, a Catholic readership for such books, particularly in the small schools which were founded in rural and urban Ireland from the middle decades of the eighteenth century. These establishments were a mixture of small private schools for middle-class girls, mainly located in the towns and cities, and charity schools for the poor, often erected on rural estates or in Church of Ireland parishes. The last quarter of the eighteenth century was also the period during which the legal restrictions on the provision of Catholic education were relaxed, and this led to a corresponding expansion in the number of schools run by Catholic women. There is little information about the books read in any of these schools. Fragmentary evidence

---

73 Kennedy, *French Books in Eighteenth-Century Ireland*, pp. 49–51.
74 Jean Bloch, 'Discourses of Female Education in the Writings of Eighteenth-Century French Women' in Knott and Taylor (eds), *Women, Gender and Enlightenment*, pp. 250–51; *Eloisa: or, a Series of Original Letters Collected and Published by J. J. Rousseau. Translated From the French. In Four Volumes.* (Dublin: James Hunter, 1761, Peter Wilson, 1766, 1767, John Pasley, 1795).
75 Kennedy, *French Books in Eighteenth-Century Ireland*, pp. 49–51, 188.
76 See, for example, Máire Kennedy, 'The Distribution of a Locally Produced French Periodical in Provincial Ireland : The *Magazin à la Mode*, 1777–1778', *Eighteenth-Century Ireland: Iris an Dá Chultúr*, 9 (1994), pp. 83–98; 'Women and Reading in Eighteenth-Century Ireland', in Bernadette Cunningham and Máire Kennedy (eds), *The Experience of Reading: Irish Historical Perspectives* (Dublin: Rare Books Goup of the Library Association of Ireland and Economic and Social History Society of Ireland, 1999), pp. 78–98.

suggests, however, that texts by French authors were commonly used for the education of Irish girls.

When, for example, Teresa Mulally established a school for poor children in inner-city Dublin in 1766, she wrote that she read 'Mrs Affable' to them on a regular basis.[77] This was a reference to a very popular text entitled *Magasin des Enfans* by Jeanne Marie Le Prince de Beaumont, a French author of children's stories. The latter spent fifteen years in London where she befriended prominent members of the aristocracy including women linked to Irish landed families such as Emily Fitzgerald, Duchess of Leinster, and her daughter-in-law Pamela, who was reputed to be the adopted daughter of Stéphanie-Félicité de Genlis. Le Prince de Beaumont wrote over twenty books on the education of girls. *Magasin des Enfans* appeared first in 1756 and by the time that Teresa Mulally was using it in her Dublin school it had achieved international acclaim.[78] Written in a series of dialogues between a governess, Mrs Affable, and her pupils, the text is interspersed with fables and stories including Beaumont's famous version of the fairy tale 'Beauty and the Beast'. Although a committed Catholic, Beaumont shared many of the views on the education of girls held by Anglican ministers as well as by English women writers such as Chapone and Fielding. Clarissa Campbell Orr has noted that, like her English counterparts, Le Prince de Beaumont's views combined social conservatism with a 'clear commitment to the values of the Enlightenment. Le Prince de Beaumont's message is that women have the right to reflect on moral issues and acquire knowledge.'[79] The advertisement for the 1793 Dublin edition of *Magasin des Enfants* emphasised the didactic aim of the volume. In their conversations with Mrs Affable 'each Lady is made to speak according to her particular Genius, Temper, and Inclination ... their several Faults are pointed out, and the easy Way to mend them, as well as to think and speak, and act properly; no less Care being taken to form their Hearts to Goodness, than to enlighten their Understanding with

---

77 Roland Burke Savage, *A Valiant Dublin Woman: The Story of George's Hill (1766–1940)* (Dublin: M. H. Gill, 1940), p. 61.
78 *Magasin des enfans, ou dialogues entre une sage gouvernante et plusieurs de ses élèves de la premiére Distinction ...* was first published in London in 1756 by J. Haberkorn. An English translation appeared in Dublin in 1764: *The Young Ladies Magazine, or Dialogues Between a Discreet Governess and Several Young Ladies... By Mrs. Le Prince de Beaumont ...* (Dublin: James Hoey, Junior). There were two other Dublin editions in English (1786, 1792: John Parker) and three in French (Caleb Jenkin, 1787, H. Chamberlaine, 1788, P. Wogan, 1798).
79 Clarissa Campbell Orr, 'Aristocratic Feminism, the Learned Governess, and the Republic of Letters', in Knott and Taylor (eds), *Women, Gender and Enlightenment*, pp. 310–11.

useful Knowledge.'[80] The choice of *Magasin des Enfants* to read to poor Irish children in inner-city Dublin may have been suggested to Mulally by Irish priests or women educated in Catholic schools on the Continent. Mulally was, for example, in correspondence with Nano Nagle, the founder of the Presentation Order. Nagle had spent some time as a postulant in France and used the French *petits écoles* as a model for her establishments in Cork city.[81]

In addition to her schools for poor children, Nagle also sponsored the founding of an Ursuline convent in Cork in 1771. The members of the first community had been trained in France and brought with them French Ursuline texts as a guide for the administration of the convent and adjoining school. Among the books used by the nuns in Cork and subsequently translated into English by a member of the Irish community was a *Directory for Novices*. Mother Borgia McCarthy, who translated the *Directory*, added to the French version two chapters on 'the merit and method of instruction' of children which provide some indication of the teaching methods of the Cork-based nuns.[82] Conforming to the widely held view that the children of the poor should be taught differently from those of the middle and upper classes, McCarthy devoted one chapter to the education of the latter and a second to the instruction of the poor. Citing Fénelon, McCarthy incorporated into her text on the education of the better-off children an enlightened view on how children should be instructed. Very young children should be taught by example, and the less able should 'not be driven or forced to unreasonable exertions, neither should they be ever reproached with stupidity; on the contrary, they should be encouraged for time alone will expand the powers that lie folded up in their souls'.[83] Children should not be afraid to ask questions but rather they should be encouraged to 'speak as they think' as this was the only way that they would learn. This advice particularly applied to older girls who 'have been often known to refrain from necessary questions, lest asking them may argue ignorance'.[84] Unsurprisingly, McCarthy's advice on the education of poor children focused

---

80 *Magasin des enfans. The Young Ladies Magazine: or, Polite Tutoress. Containing Dialogues Between a Governess and Several Young Ladies of Quality* (Dublin: John Parker, 1793). See also the advertisement for printer James Hoey's Dublin edition: *Books Printed by and for James Hoey, Junior* (Dublin: s.n., 1763).
81 Roland Burke Savage, *A Valiant Dublin Woman: The Story of George's Hill (1766–1940)*, pp. 67–109.
82 Sister Ursula Clarke, *The Ursulines in Cork since 1771* (Cork: Ursuline Convent, Blackrock, Cork, 2007), pp. 58–59.
83 Mother Borgia McCarthy, *A Directory, for Novices of Every Religious Order; Particularly Those Devoted to the Instruction of Youth. Translated from the French* (Cork: W. Ferguson, 1817), p. 107.
84 Ibid., p. 118. See also chapter two.

on skills-training and the preparation of the children for work in service or other low grades of employment.

With regard to the teachers of children, McCarthy expressed approval of the novices studying in order to prepare for teaching. She also, however, gave the conventional warning on the dangers of the literary lady: 'Do not aim at instructing in an original and learned manner. There is no temptation more dangerous for those who are destined to instruct than a desire to appear learned.'[85] In short, McCarthy's views on education incorporated enlightened thinking but did not offer support for the more radical ideas concerning the equality of men and women.

Although the nuns in the Cork convent provided the finance to have the *Directory* privately printed for circulation within the Ursuline community, the Cork printers recognised the commercial potential of the volume for a lay readership and advertised it in their shop window as a 'Directory to the Heads of Families'.[86] Later in 1834 when Mother Borgia McCarthy asked the London publisher George Keating to produce a small print-run for the new Ursuline convent in Charleston, USA, he too commented on its suitability for use by 'mothers, governesses or any others having to perform the duty of monitoring the minds of youth and their manners and sentiments'. Keating urged McCarthy to consider editing a new book based on the *Directory* to be entitled 'Practical Little Book for Mothers'.[87] Keating, who specialised in publishing Catholic literature, was interested in producing a text aimed specifically at Catholic mothers based on the ideas and values of French educationalists. The volume never appeared although McCarthy and Keating collaborated again on the publication of *The Ursuline Manual*.[88]

Irish-language translations and cultural influences
From the early Christian period, Irish scribes translated and circulated manuscripts from Continental Europe. This tradition continued to flourish in the late seventeenth and eighteenth centuries. Although most Irish-language texts were circulated in manuscript form in the eighteenth century, Lesa Ní Mhunghaile and other scholars have explored the ways in which Irish language intellectuals engaged with the expanding English-language print culture.[89] One popular text in circulation throughout the eighteenth century

---

85 Ibid., p. 117.
86 Clarke, *The Ursulines in Cork since 1771*, p.59.
87 George Keating to Mrs McCarthy, 21 June 1834 (Ursuline Convent, Blackrock, UCB/03400).
88 See chapter two, pp. 63–64.
89 Les Ní Mhunghaile, 'Bilingualism, Print Culture in Irish and the Public Sphere, 1700–*c*.1830', in James Kelly and Ciarán Mac Murchaidh (eds), *Irish and English Essays in the Irish Linguistic and Cultural Frontier, 1600–1900* (Dublin: Four Courts Press,

was a translation by Domhnall Ó Colmáin of Erasmus's 'Assembly or Parliament of Women'. The first manuscript versions of 'Párliament na mBan' date to between 1696 and 1703. Like George Hickes and other translators of continental publications, Ó Colmáin edited and revised the original manuscript. The first section of the manuscript is a translation of Erasmus's 'Assembly or Parliament of Women' but the author added on to Erasmus's text a discussion on the education of women. Using the format of a parliament of women, the text presents a series of speeches or sermons by the female members of the parliament on sins such as lust, envy, laziness, backbiting and drunkenness. The women parliamentarians decreed that girls be sent to school until the age of twelve and the most intellectually able given access to more advanced study in the liberal arts including grammar, rhetoric, philosophy, arithmetic, astrology, geometry and poetry. Women should also be permitted to study theology, law and medicine. In other words, women should have access to the same educational curriculum as men. The parliament also agreed that the women should be given the public authority ('ughdarrás puiblighe') to enforce their decrees.[90] The text was written by Ó Colmáin for his young pupil, James Cotter, and in many ways fits into the category of an Irish version of a conduct book.

Although unpublished, 'Párliament na mBan' was a popular text and there are extant over forty manuscript copies dating from 1696 to the second half of the nineteenth century.[91] In the debate on education, the author seems to have adopted a radical approach to women's education. Máirín Ní Dhonnchadha has, however, pointed out that there are three versions of the text dating to the period 1697 to 1703. The first version was mocking in its tone towards the female parliamentarians, assigning them nicknames that meant the opposite to the moral message that they were conveying, a tactic that also undermined the sincerity of their statements.[92] In his third and final version, however, Ó Colmáin revised the text to make it less satirical and more respectful of the women in the assembly. The author changed the women's surnames to those of well-known Munster families and added a section on a local Munster woman who had taken a vow of chastity and

---

2012), pp. 218–42; Eoghan Ó Néill, *Gleann an Óir. Ar Thóir an Staire agus na Litríochta in Oirthear Mumhan agus i nDeisceart Laighean* (Dublin: An Clóchomhar Tta, n.d.), pp. 79–85.

90 Brian Ó Cuív (ed.), *Párliament na mBan* (Dublin: Dublin Institute for Advanced Studies, 1952), p. 2; N. Bailey (ed.), *The Colloquies of Erasmus* (3 vols; London: Gibbings & Co., 1900), vol. 3, pp. 114–22.

91 Ó Cuív, 'Introduction', in *Párliament na mBan*; N. Bailey (ed.), *The Colloquies of Erasmus*, pp. ix–xxix.

92 See also Máirín Nic Eoin, *B'ait Leo Bean. Gnéithe den Idé-Eolaíocht Inscne i dTraidisiún Literatha na Gaeilge* (Dublin: An Clóchomhar Tta, 1998), pp. 132–39.

lived the life of a nun even though female religious communities were banned in Ireland at the time. Ní Dhonnchadha suggests that this version of 'Párliament na mBan' could have been used as a 'devotional text for Catholic Ladies' and, consequently, the decrees on women's education might also be taken more seriously.[93] Ó Colmáin's manuscript could, therefore, be included in a catalogue of Irish-authored writings that engaged with, revised and adapted Enlightenment views on women's education.

Cultural Encounters and Adaptation: Irish Writers Influenced by English Publications

Wetenhall Wilkes

In the first half of the eighteenth century there was clearly, therefore, interest among an Irish reading public in writings on the education and upbringing of girls. Although many parents and teachers relied on translations or revisions of English, French or other continental writers for advice, a small number of Irish authors identified the commercial potential of this market. Among the most successful was Trinity graduate Wetenhall Wilkes. Born in Kilmore in County Cavan, Wilkes published *A Letter of Genteel and Moral Advice to a Young Lady. To Which is Digested into a New and Familiar Method, a System of Rules and Information, to Qualify the Fair Sex to be Useful and Happy in Every Stance*, by subscription in Dublin in 1740. Although not in holy orders when he wrote the book, Wilkes subsequently became an Anglican minister.[94]

Addressed to Wilkes' young teenage niece, *A Letter of Genteel and Moral Advice to a Young Lady* opened with a long section on the merits of a religious education which included fairly traditional guidance on Christian behaviour. Wilkes advised his niece to follow the Christian virtues of charity, compassion and humility, avoid the sins of vanity and pride, dress modestly and choose her friends with care. Husbands should be obeyed and humoured rather than criticised for their faults by their wives. Wilkes was, however, a little more relaxed than other clerical writers in his views on how his niece should spend her leisure time. He counselled her to engage in gaming and playing of cards 'sparingly' but did not prohibit them altogether.[95] In the last section, Wilkes discussed the merits of a good education for a young woman as well as giving some advice on choosing a husband. He not only advised

---

93 Máirín Ní Dhonnchadha (ed.), 'Medieval to Modern, 600–1900', in Angela Bourke et al. (eds), *Field Day Anthology of Irish Writing, Volume IV: Irish Women's Writing and Traditions* (Cork: Cork University Press, 2002), p. 160.
94 See *ODNB* entry by Katherine O'Donnell.
95 Wetenhall Wilkes, *A Letter of Genteel and Moral Advice to a Young Lady* ... (Dublin: Printed for the Author, 1740), pp. 121–22.

that she learn to read and write well but also how to order her thoughts into a structured argument: 'The Perfection of our Nature is to know; that is to be able to frame clear and distinct ideas; to form true judgments and to deduce proper Consequences ... Reading is useful but thinking is necessary.'[96] Although Wilkes instructed his niece to 'cultivate and adorn your understanding with the Improvements of Learning' that were 'suitable to your Sex', his recommended reading was as appropriate for a boy as for a girl. He suggested that she read Socrates and Plutarch's *Lives* in translation as well as the writings of other Greek and Roman writers including Plato, Seneca, Pythagoras and Cicero for examples of exemplary lives as well for their morals and reasoning. While Wilkes had no objection to women learning French, Italian or Latin, he stressed the importance of an expertise in English reading and writing 'since it is English that one educated in England and Ireland must have constant use of'.[97]

Wilkes also included in his ideal syllabus for a young girl authors identified with Enlightenment thought in France. On his reading list, for example, was a popular science book by French scientist, Bernard le Bovier de Fontenelle, 'Conversations on the Plurality of Worlds' (1686) which had been printed in an English translation in Dublin in 1687.[98] In the preface to the original version of this book, Fontenelle indicated that he was writing mainly 'pour les femmes' and that he aimed 'not just to educate women about science but also to "enlighten" them and by so doing activate them in society'.[99] Fontenelle was a favoured guest at the salons organised by women in late seventeenth-century Paris and the English title of his most famous book reflected his awareness of his female readership.[100] Other French writers recommended by Wilkes were Fénelon, Pascal, Boileau and Voiture. Dublin reprints of translations of the work of all these authors had also appeared in the 1730s.[101]

---

96 Wilkes, *A Letter of Genteel and Moral Advice to a Young Lady*, pp. 106–7.
97 Wilkes, *A Letter of Genteel and Moral Advice to a Young Lady*, p. 103
98 *A Discourse of the Plurality of Worlds. Written in French, by the Most Ingenious Author of the Dialogues of the Dead. And Translated into English by Sir W. D. Knight* (Dublin: Andrew Crook and Samuel Helsham, 1687); Another translation appeared in Dublin in 1728: *Conversations With a Lady, on the Plurality of Worlds. Written in French, by Mons. Fontenelle, ... Translated by Mr. Glanvill...* (Dublin: William Forrest, 1728).
99 Jonathan Israel, *Radical Enlightenment. Philosophy and the Making of Modernity 1650–1750* (Oxford, Oxford University Press, 2001), p. 82.
100 Nina Rattner Gelbart, 'Introduction' to *Conversations of the Plurality of Worlds*, translated by H. A. Hargreaves (Berkeley: University of California Press, 1990), p. xv. For the English title of Fontenelle's work see note 98 above.
101 Blaise Pascal, *Thoughts on Religion, and Other Curious Subjects. Written Originally in French by Monsieur Pascal. Translated into English by Basil Kennet, D.D. ...* (Dublin: George Faulkner, 1739); Monsieur Voiture, *The Works of the Celebrated Monsieur Voiture* (2 vols; Dublin: Samuel Fairbrother, 1731); Nicolas Boileau-Despréaux, *The Lutrin: an Heroic-Comical Poem. In Six Cantos. By Monsieur Boileau. To Which is*

There were 427 subscribers listed for *A Letter of Genteel and Moral Advice to a Young Lady*, although Wilkes subsequently complained that he had not received all the money that had been promised.[102] The volume clearly found a readership in Ireland because a second edition was printed in 1741 without the support of a subscription list. Almost a quarter of the subscribers (106) to the first edition were women and included Mary Delany as well as a scattering of titled ladies. Church of Ireland ministers also featured strongly in the subscription list, constituting about nine per cent of the total. Among them were Jonathan Swift, who ordered twenty copies, Hugh Boulter, the archbishop of Armagh who subscribed for ten copies, Mary Delany's husband, Patrick, dean of Down who signed up for six copies and the bishop of Elphin who subscribed for four books. Other subscribers included Daniel Falkiner, the lord mayor of Dublin and John Elwood, vice-provost of Trinity College Dublin. Wilkes had appealed to Swift and others for financial assistance and some of the subscriptions may have been a form of charity. Wilkes' text, however, proved popular, particularly in London, where by 1766 eight editions had been printed.[103]

In addition to his letter of advice to his niece, Wetenhall Wilkes was also the author of a strong defence of women's education in *A Letter to a Lady in Praise of Female Learning*, which was printed in Dublin in 1739.[104] This short text recounted the story of a debate that had taken place in a coffee house in Dublin on the merits of female education. In the debate, Wilkes articulated why he was in favour of the education of women while his opponents argued that their domestic roles meant that there was no necessity for them to acquire literacy.[105] Wilkes cited the example of Queen Elizabeth to suggest that learned women existed in the past who could serve as role models for women in early eighteenth-century Ireland. And he asserted women's right to education, in enlightened and modern language, which he linked to a Christian message on the virtues of a knowledge of God and of one's duty in life:

> Since Women as well as Men have intelligent Souls, why should they be debarr'd from the Improvements of them? If it were intended by

---

Prefix'd, Some Account of the Author's Writings, and this Translation: by N. Rowe, Esq (Dublin: S. Powell, 1730).

102 See the advertisement at end of the first edition of *A Letter of Genteel and Moral Advice to a Young Lady*. For the list of subscribers see the online database, http://www2.ul.ie/web/WWW/Faculties/Arts,_Humanities_%26_Social_Sciences/Inventing/.

103 See ESTC online (http://estc.bl.uk).

104 Although anonymous, the introduction to *A Letter to a Lady in Praise of Female Learning* (Dublin: J. Jones, 1739) is signed 'W.W.'. A second edition was published in London as *An Essay on the Pleasures and Advantages of Female Literature* (London: Printed for the Author, 1741). See also *ODNB* entry on Wilkes by Katherine O'Donnell.

105 *An Essay on the Pleasures and Advantages of Female Literature* ..., pp. 5–11.

Nature that Man should monopolize all learning to himself, why were the Muses female? Who ... were the Mistresses of all the Sciences and the Presidents of Musick and Poetry? Since Heaven has not deny'd the Faculty of thinking to the fair Sex; why should they be confin'd to low and home bred Studies? ... Nothing can be more reasonable than that Women, as well as men, should have light enough to lead them to the Knowledge of their Maker and the Sight of their own Duties. They have an equal right to furnish themselves with sold and useful Knowledge ...[106]

Wilkes' account of a debate on the merits of women's education in a Dublin coffee house along with the prominent names that appeared on the subscription list for the first edition of *A Letter of Genteel and Moral Advice to a Young Lady* is further evidence of the interest in the subject in Dublin in the early decades of the eighteenth century.

Enlightened teachers
Another way in which we can assess the influence of Enlightenment writers on Irish educationalists is to look at the publications of teachers and their views on education. The writings of two Irish-based school teachers indicate their engagement with progressive views on pedagogy. Samuel Whyte opened an 'English Grammar School' in Dublin in 1758 which was attended by boys and girls, while David Manson established a co-educational school in Belfast. The educational ideas of both men had much in common and were clearly influenced by Enlightenment thought. They believed, like Locke, that learning should be engaging and enjoyable. Clearly inspired by Locke, Manson devised a card game to teach the alphabet and basic numeracy and penned 'A plan for the improvement of children in virtue and learning, without the use of the rod'.[107] In a similar fashion, Whyte encouraged his students to write poetry and present private performances of their literary work. Whyte also published a collection of poetry which included many written by his female as well as his male pupils.[108]

106 *An Essay on the Pleasures and Advantages of Female Literature* ..., p. 17.
107 David Manson, *Directions to Play the Literary Cards Invented for the Improvement of Children in Learning and Morals From Their Beginning to Learn Their Letters, Till They Become Proficients in Spelling, Reading, Parsing and Arithmetick* (Belfast: Printed for the Author, 1764); *A New Pocket Dictionary; Or, English Expositor* (Belfast: Daniel Blow, 1762). See also Paul J. Kane, 'The Life and Works of David Manson, a Belfast School-Teacher 1726–1792' (unpublished MA thesis, Queen's University Belfast, 1984); entry in *ODNB* by Thomas Hamilton, revised by Linde Lunny.
108 Samuel Whyte, *The Shamrock: or Hibernian Cresses. A Collection of Poems, Songs, Epigrams, etc. Latin as Well as English, the Original Production of Ireland. To Which are Subjoined, Thoughts on the Prevailing System of School Education, Respecting Young*

Both Manson and Whyte actively supported the education of girls. Among those who attended Manson's school were members of the McCracken and Joy families including Mary Ann McCracken and her sister, Margaret.[109] One of the games devised by Manson for his pupils divided the class into a replica of the social hierarchy of real life. The boy and girl who excelled at their morning lessons were appointed the king and queen while others were nominated as members of the 'royal society' according to their academic performance and ability to repeat lines of grammar. Further down the academic ranking were the pupils who could only remember a small number of lines and were designated as tenants and under-tenants. Manson not only taught his pupils English grammar through such games but also instructed them on how the constitution worked. The king and queen had the privilege of calling a parliament on Saturdays when there was no formal class. Other games designated pupils as chancellors and vice-chancellors to explain the meanings of words. In his description of the rules for the games, Manson implicitly assumed that the pupils were male and female. In the 'royal society', surrounding the king and queen, there were princes and princesses, dukes and duchesses and lords and ladies. Girls as well as boys sat in parliament and took on the role of chancellor and vice-chancellor.[110]

In 1772 Samuel Whyte published his 'Thoughts on the Prevailing System of Education, Respecting Young Ladies as Well as Gentlemen: with Practical Proposals for a Reformation' as an addendum to his collection of poetry, *The Shamrock*, and three years later he published an extended version as a separate pamphlet.[111] Whyte's text was essentially a critique of the quality of teachers that he had encountered in Ireland and what he perceived as the haphazard and unstructured education that they dispensed. He was, not surprisingly, an advocate of the formal structure of the English grammar school over private tutoring. As the title of his pamphlet implied, Whyte included girls' education in the 'revolution in education' that he proposed and rejected the argument that girls should not attend public schools. Asserting that 'women are endowed with a rational soul and improvable faculties' Whyte denounced

---

Ladies as Well as Gentlemen: With Practical Proposals for a Reformation (Dublin: R. Marchbank, 1772). See also J. T. Gilbert, *The Streets of Dublin* (Dublin: James Gilbert, 1851), pp. 27–34; entry on Whyte in *DIB* by Patrick Geoghegan.

109 Mary McNeill, *The Life and Times of Mary Ann McCracken, 1770–1866: A Belfast Panorama* (Dublin: Allen Figgis, 1960), pp. 43–48.

110 David Manson, 'The Present State and Practices of the Play-School in Belfast', included as an appendix to *A New Pocket Dictionary; Or, English Expositor* (Belfast: Daniel Blow, 1762).

111 Samuel Whyte, *Modern Education, Respecting Young Ladies as Well as Gentlemen* (Dublin: R. Marchbank, 1775).

the fact that 'there are no Colleges, or Academies, no established System of Instruction for Ladies.' He expressed his admiration for educated French women who could engage in intellectual conversation and recommended a similar model for Irish women: 'In the Name of all that is good and sensible! Let us throw off this Tyranny of Custom, and give the Minds of our Females a more liberal and proper cast.'[112] While adhering to the common belief that women should be educated to make them better companions for men, Whyte's pamphlet is remarkable for its radical language and his belief that women had a 'right to literature'.[113]

The teaching and publications of Manson and Whyte were, therefore, an important means through which new Enlightenment ideas on women's education were disseminated in Ireland. Both men utilised the expanding Irish print market to promote their views on pedagogy. The emergence of a magazine and periodical-reading culture in eighteenth-century Ireland also enhanced the access Irish readers had to the latest intellectual fashions.

Cultural Encounters through Reading: Periodicals as Disseminators of New Images and Definitions of Womanhood

As Ballaster et al. have suggested, the production of the magazine brought reading from the coffee shop to the drawing room. The miscellaneous format of the magazine also allowed for tensions and contradictions in the public discourse to be presented alongside one another. The same magazine might include a short piece advocating that women learn to read classical languages alongside another warning against the dangers of the over-education of young girls.[114]

The Ladies Journal

The first Irish periodical dedicated to women readers appeared in 1727. The anonymous male editor announced in the first issue of *The Ladies Journal* that he intended to be a 'Champion' for women, and in the second issue he declared that there was 'an absolute necessity, for the ladies being as learned as the *Gentlemen*'.[115] In the next issue of *The Ladies Journal*, the editor, like Wetenhall Wilkes, cited examples of literary women whose scholarly work testified to women's intellectual ability. They included the poet, Sappho, the

---

112 *Modern Education, Respecting Young Ladies as Well as Gentlemen*, pp. 48–49.
113 Ibid., p. 49.
114 Ros Ballaster, Margaret Beetham, Elizabeth Frazer and Sandra Hebron, *Women's Worlds: Ideology, Femininity and Women's Magazines* (London: Macmillan, 1991), pp. 7, 14.
115 *The Ladies Journal*, 24 January 1726/7, p. 11.

Pythagorean philosopher, Theano, and in more recent history, Margaret, the daughter of Thomas More who had translated her father's Latin works, Queen Elizabeth and the poet Katherine Phillips. From his own time, the editor noted two writers with Irish connections, Susan Centlivre and Eliza Haywood and added that he could have 'mentioned several ladies of our own nation were it not for offending their modesty by publishing their names'.[116] The editor expressed an enlightened view of education and women's right to it as he proclaimed that 'learning is of an Universal Extension; like the Sun, it denies not it's Rays and benign Influence to any that will but open their Eyes; other Treasures may be Monopoliz'd or engross'd but this is increased by Communication and Difusion.'[117]

The Ladies Journal appeared in twenty-two weekly issues and consisted of eight pages per issue.[118] The content was a mixture of short stories usually with a moral about love and friendship and poetry. The intended readership appears to have been the social elite of mainly Protestant Dublin. The editor refers to musical concerts and other social engagements that he attended in the city. The journal was written to provide 'instruction and amusement' for women who participated in such events. Although its intended readership was socially limited, *The Ladies Journal* was, nonetheless, the first Irish periodical to encourage and publish correspondence and poetry from women, albeit anonymously. In one of the last issues the editor printed 'An hymn to learning' by a 'young lady' who wanted to 'give ... an idea of what might be expected from them if their education was agreeable to their capacity and merit'.[119]

The Female Spectator
The Ladies Journal is of interest, therefore, because it suggests the existence in early eighteenth-century Dublin of a readership for a periodical which was not only directed at women but supported women writing for publication and learning. More particular evidence of a readership in Ireland for periodicals dedicated to women readers is provided by the publication of Irish editions of work by Eliza Haywood. A precursor of the bluestocking movement, Eliza Haywood was the first English woman to establish a reputation as a novel writer. She was also a drama critic, editor of two periodicals and writer of political commentary.[120]

Haywood spent some time in Ireland in 1714–16 as an actor in the Smock Alley Theatre and there was, therefore, not surprisingly, an Irish interest in

116 *The Ladies Journal*, 2 February 1726/7, pp. 19–20.
117 *The Ladies Journal*, 2 February 1726/7, p. 20.
118 Alison Adburgham, *Women in Print. Writing Women and Women's Magazines from the Restoration to the Accession of Victoria* (London: Allen & Unwin, 1972), p. 77.
119 *The Ladies Journal*, 29 June 1727.
120 Entry for Eliza Haywood by Paula R Backscheider in *ODNB*.

her published work. A number of her novels appeared in Dublin editions from 1724 through to 1755.[121] Haywood also edited the *Female Spectator* which appeared in twenty-four issues over a two-year period, from 1744 to 1746. The appearance of the *Female Spectator* was a significant event in women's relationship with a public press as it was 'the first magazine by and for women'.[122] The content of the *Female Spectator* was far more diverse than that of *The Ladies Journal*. Haywood's editorial aim was to combine entertainment with guidance to women on how to lead virtuous lives. Although writing in a popular genre, Haywood shared the common view that a woman's destiny was to be a good wife and mother but that girls should be educated and take an interest in improving their minds through reading. In her opening statement in volume one of the *Female Spectator*, Haywood announced that 'reading is universally allowed to be one of the most improving as well as agreeable amusements.'[123]

Haywood communicated advice to her female readership through the telling of illustrative short stories. As in her novels, Haywood advocated that young, unmarried women be given a certain amount of freedom. In the first volume she reprimanded parents who forced marriages on their children. In Haywood's view, the key to a successful marriage was mutual companionship and shared interests. The couple should take time to get to know one another before they married.[124]

The *Female Spectator* was written in a lively and accessible style and appealed to Irish as well as to English readers. Irish interest in Haywood's periodical was evident in 1746 when Dublin publishers George and Alexander Ewing published a four-volume composite collection of the *Female Spectator*. The volumes were clearly popular as two more editions were published by the Ewings by the following year.[125] The first Dublin edition was printed with the aid of subscribers whose names were listed in the preliminary pages to the first volume. There was a total of 357 subscribers of whom 138 (38.7 per cent) were women.[126] It is worth noting that just over half of the

---

121 See *ESTC* online (http://www.estc.bl.uk).
122 Helen Koon, 'Eliza Haywood and the "Female Spectator"', *Huntington Library Quarterly*, 42, 1 (Winter 1978), p. 44. See also Adburgham, *Women in Print: Writing Women and Women's Magazines from the Restoration to the Accession of Victoria*, pp. 95–103; Shawn Lisa Maurer, 'The Periodical', in Ros Ballaster (ed.), *The History of British Women's Writing, 1690–1750* (Basingstoke: Palgrave Macmillan, 2010), pp. 163–66.
123 *The Female Spectator*, 1 (Dublin: George and Alexander Ewing, 1746), p. 1. See also *ODNB* entry on Haywood by Paula R. Backscheider.
124 *Female Spectator*, vol. 1, pp. 23, 77–80.
125 The National Library of Ireland has copies of the first and third editions.
126 See the online database, http://www2.ul.ie/web/WWW/Faculties/Arts,_Humanities_%26_Social_Sciences/Inventing/.

women subscribers were designated as single, using the prefix of 'Miss'. This suggests that the periodical had a particular appeal for young women. The subscribers also, however, included a scattering of the social elite of Irish society, with two bishops, two viscounts and two viscountesses, five army captains and six Church of Ireland ministers listed. Máire Kennedy has identified twenty-two booksellers among the Irish subscribers to the *Female Spectator* which also indicates a more general interest in Haywood's publications.[127] The addresses of most of the subscribers is not included but, where it is noted, 42.3 per cent had addresses in Ulster (see table 1).

Table 1 Geographical Location of Subscribers to the *Female Spectator* (Dublin, 1746)

Place	Number	Percentage
Ulster	22	42.3
England	9	17.3
Munster	9	17.3
Dublin	4	7.7
Unknown	4	7.7
Leinster	2	3.8
Connacht	1	1.9
Scotland	1	1.9
Total	52	

Nine subscribers came from Belfast while others were based in Downpatrick, Coleraine and Monaghan. Merchants from southern towns in Limerick and Waterford were also listed among subscribers to the *Female Spectator*. The geographical range suggests that Haywood was well known in Ireland and that there was a readership, particularly among young literate women for her work.[128]

Walker's Hibernian Magazine
When Irish-produced periodicals and magazines began to appear in increasing numbers in the middle decades of the eighteenth century, printers and editors (often the same person) recognised the commercial value of

127 Kennedy, 'Women and Reading in Eighteenth-Century Ireland', p. 91.
128 Kennedy, 'Women and Reading in Eighteenth-Century Ireland', pp. 89–92.

appealing to women readers. For example, when *The Magazine of Magazines* was first published in Limerick in 1751, its editor noted that

> We promise ourselves that those of our own class will not fail of being our friends; ... But above all, we should sue for the protection and patronage of the fair sex; ever desiring them to be our encouragers. Nor indeed do we at all doubt they will be so, as they may be assured their cause will never be forgotten here; for, alas! they know not how strenuous advocates they have in our club.[129]

The *Hibernian Magazine* (subsequently, Walker's *Hibernian Magazine*) first appeared as a bi-monthly publication in 1772. It proved to be among the most popular and long lasting of Irish magazines. Politically radical, successive editors supported the Volunteers, the United Irishmen and Catholic Emancipation. The editors were also very aware of political developments outside Ireland and printed extensive reports on events in France as well as in the new American republic.

The commercial success of *Walker's Hibernian Magazine* was partly due to the attention it paid to women readers. The editors cleverly tapped into the growing female literate market. The contents of the magazine presented a complex picture of women in modern society. They included items that were directed at a female readership and were to become familiar features in women's magazines of the nineteenth and twentieth centuries. Among the regular features were articles on the latest fashion as worn, particularly, in the highest social circles in London, embroidery insets that could be used to trace the latest designs on cloth, copies of music scores and serialised fiction. The front cover of the magazine often included an engraving of a well-known actress who had appeared on the London stage (and might also have visited Dublin) or the wife of the lord lieutenant, dressed in a fashionable gown.[130]

Alongside the items that were directed explicitly at a female readership, *Walker's Hibernian Magazine* also included articles that discussed issues relating to women. Prominent among the themes highlighted was the debate on women's education. Most of these articles were anonymous and many were extracts from recently printed books.[131] Others may have been written

---

129 *The Magazine of Magazines* (Limerick: Andrew Walsh, 1751), vol. 1, p. iii.
130 See, for example, the engravings of the countess of Buckingham in *Walker's Hibernian Magazine*, May 1774; February 1778; and actress, Mrs Barry in May 1774. See also December 1772; April 1774.
131 See for example, 'A Comparative View of Both Sexes', June 1781; 'On the Intrinsic Merits of Women', July 1781; 'Moral and Intellectual Excellence of the Fair Sex', June 1786; 'On Female Authorship', August 1789; 'Letter on Female Education', October 1799.

by Samuel Whyte, as the views expressed were very close to his opinions on the instruction of girls. The editor of the periodical was clearly sympathetic to Whyte's educational ideas and printed long extracts on 'Female education' from *The Shamrock* before its publication in 1772.[132]

Walker's Hibernian Magazine also printed short pieces from books by English writers associated with radical views on women's status in society. In 1791, extracts from Mary Wollstonecraft's critique of Edmund Burke appeared in the magazine; and in March of the following year, a short piece from *A Vindication of the Rights of Women* on 'modesty' was printed not long after the first edition had appeared in London.[133] In 1798, following the publication of William Godwin's *Memoir*, the editor reprinted the extract in the March issue of that year and in April he reproduced on the front page of the periodical an engraving of Wollstonecraft along with a critique of Godwin's work and its revelations about Wollstonecraft's private life.[134] Periodicals like *Walker's Hibernian Magazine*, thus served as a medium through which the more radical views on women's role and status in society were communicated to an Irish readership.

However, despite the editor's admiration for Mary Wollstonecraft and efforts to appeal to women readers, *Walker's Hibernian Magazine* did not actively encourage women to contribute items for publication. He printed a small number of poems attributed to women but no prose. The pioneering work of *The Ladies Journal* was not, therefore, advanced by successive editors of *Walker's Hibernian Magazine*.

The Parlour Window
By contrast, in late eighteenth-century England, a number of periodicals appeared that not only identified the commercial potential of women readers but also published writings by women and, in some cases, were edited by women. These included the *Lady's Magazine or Entertaining Companion for the Fair Sex* which was first published in 1770 and the *Lady's Monthly Magazine* which began in 1798 and was edited by a 'company of

---

132 See Mary O'Dowd, *A History of Women in Ireland, 1500–1800* (Harlow: Pearson, 2005), pp. 214–15. See also *Letters Lately Printed in the Freeman's and Hibernian Journals, under the Signature of P. Leyal: Addressed to His Grace the Duke of Leinster. And now Republished at the Desire of the Apollo Society, and of Several Respectable Citizens* (Dublin: James Porter, 1780).

133 *Walker's Hibernian Magazine*, March 1791; March 1792. For an extract from Macaulay, see November 1793.

134 *Walker's Hibernian Magazine*, March 1798. Extracts from Wollstonecraft's work were also published in the first issue of *Sentimental and Masonic Magazine* in 1792. All of Wollstonecraft's books were printed in Irish editions between 1788 and 1798. See ESTC online (www://estc.bl.uk).

ladies'.[135] Copies of these English magazines were advertised in Irish newspapers and were read by women in Ireland but it was not until the mid-1790s that similar Irish-produced periodicals began to appear.[136]

In 1795, the first issue of *The Parlour Window* appeared in Dublin. The editors identified themselves as two women but did not give their names. The opening statement of the new periodical noted that 'I am persuaded that the timidity natural to our Sex, has prevented many things worth reading, from being Printed; and that many Female writers have (thro' delicacy) Published their Works under A Masculine Signature.'[137]

Despite the proto-feminist tone of the first editorial statement, the literary content of *The Parlour Window* was rather mundane and its purpose was not always clear. The stated aim was to provide moral lessons in a more palliative form than 'dry moral essays or even the instructive tale, be the latter ever so instructive'. The core of the eight issues of the periodical was, nonetheless, an 'instructive tale' that told the story of a young woman, Caroline, deprived of her family's wealth because her father married for love rather than money. Caroline is presented as a model to be emulated. She is well versed in English literature and prone to quoting Pope, Shakespeare, Spencer or other literary luminaries at opportune moments. Caroline admires and finds solace in the beauty of nature rather than material wealth. In the course of the serialised story, the value of reading and education for women is praised although the author repeats the standard mantra on the danger of reading novels. A young woman who was educated in the 'too great freedom of a public school' is depicted reading Rousseau's *Héloïse* and warned by an older woman of the danger of doing so. The latter is, however, careful to point out that Rousseau had correctly warned that 'inflammatory novels, (and we have too many of them,) and some kind of poetry, actually affect the mind, as strong liquors do the head and the blood, both create a sort of feverish feel, that a modest well regulated mind, should blush to FEEL.'[138]

The editors of *The Parlour Window* remained anonymous for the eight issues of their publication but the Bodleian Library copy suggests that the authors of the 'instructive tale' were 'Mrs Eustace and her sister'. Mrs Eustace along with Mr and Mrs Peter La Touche were also listed among what were called the 'annual subscribers', of whom there were a total of five. It is likely that it was this group which provided most of the finance for the

---

135 Adburgham, *Women in Print: Writing Women and Women's Magazines from the Restoration to the Accession of Victoria*, pp. 129–41, 212–16.
136 Kennedy, 'Women and Reading in Eighteenth-Century Ireland'.
137 *The Parlour Window*, p. 1.
138 *The Parlour Window*, pp. 133–36, 155–56.

enterprise. *The Parlour Window* also generated interest and support among a wider group of upper-class women in late eighteenth-century Dublin. Almost sixty per cent of the 245 subscribers were women. They included members of the leading aristocratic and peerage families as well as four countesses and five viscountesses. Among the men who subscribed were the attorney general, two members of parliament and two bishops. The final issues were dedicated to Lady Cavendish, the wife of the Lord Lieutenant who was also listed among the subscribers.[139] The support of Lady Elizabeth La Touche and her husband Peter for *The Parlour Window* might suggest a Protestant evangelical origin for the periodical. Another woman associated with evangelicalism in eighteenth-century Ireland was Lady Arbella Denny, who was the subject of a panegyric in the third issue of *The Parlour Window*.

Despite support from the Irish political and ecclesiastical elite, *The Parlour Window* failed to make an impression on the literary public and ceased publication after eight issues. The editors expressed a sense of frustration that sales of the periodical were limited to the subscribers and that they had also incurred considerable personal expense to maintain the publication. *The Parlour Window* manifested the tensions that English historians have identified in periodical literature of the eighteenth century. While the appeals to the woman reader, the support for women's education and the provision of printed space for women's writings endorsed the 'loosely pro-woman position' of Enlightenment thinkers, *The Parlour Window* also conveyed a more restrictive message that identified the separate qualities of women. As Kathryn Shevelow has noted, the entrance of women into the public world of periodical literature was a 'process of simultaneous enfranchisement and restriction'.[140]

The New Magazine

In his introductory statement to the first issue of *The New Magazine: a Moral and Entertaining Miscellany* in January 1799, the editor wrote of his intention 'to make this compilation agreeable to men of sense, yet to my fair countrywomen, it will be found peculiarly adapted; and I make no doubt but my list of subscribers will shew as many female names, as any other catalogue of the kind in Ireland'. The editor used the nom de plume of 'Philanthropus' but he has been identified as James Delap by Anne Markey.[141] As editor of *The New Magazine,* Delap encouraged the 'literary youth of both sexes' to contribute

---

139 For a list of subscribers, see the online database, http://www2.ul.ie/web/WWW/Faculties/Arts,_Humanities_%26_Social_Sciences/Inventing/.
140 Kathryn Shevelow, *Women and Print Culture: The Construction of Femininity in the Early Periodical* (London: Routledge, 1989), pp. 1–2.
141 Anne Markey, 'Irish Children's Fiction, 1727–1820', *Irish University Review*, 41, 1 (Spring–Summer 2011), Special Issue on 'Irish Fiction, 1660–1830', p. 121.

to the periodical but acknowledged that he was particularly relying on contributions from the 'fair part of our species'.[142] The editor was thus expecting his publication to appeal not just to women as readers but also as writers.

Delap was partly justified in his expectation of female subscribers. Of the 110 individuals listed as subscribers to *The New Magazine*, forty-one (37.2 per cent) were women. The number of individual subscriptions was relatively low by comparison with other eighteenth-century Irish publications but among these were orders for a significant number of copies. Belfast printer and bookseller, William Magee ordered fifty-six copies while the Cork printer, James Haly subscribed for twenty-four copies and another printer, E. Webb from Waterford, ordered fourteen copies.[143] The attraction of *The New Magazine* for booksellers was probably that it was directed at a youth readership and could be purchased in bulk for use in schools. Although the editor shunned political contributions or articles that were identified with a particular religious sect, there may, like *The Parlour Window*, have been a connection between *The New Magazine* and evangelical Protestantism as well as with the Quaker community. The addresses of most of the subscribers are not noted but of those that are, there is a preponderance of towns where a co-educational Quaker school had been established, and the surnames of some individual subscribers also suggest they were members of the Society of Friends.[144] A significant number of the books reviewed in *The New Magazine* were listed as imported into Ireland or printed by John Gough, a schoolteacher who taught in the Quaker schools in Cork, Dublin and Lisburn.

The fact that the Quaker schools were co-educational may have made the content of *The New Magazine* particularly appealing for use by teachers. It was the first periodical directed at young people which included strongly Irish content. A regular feature was a topographical article on an Irish town starting with Kilkenny and including Limerick, Youghal, Clonmel, Belfast, Lisburn, Killarney, Armagh and Hillsborough. There was also a strong moral undercurrent to many of the articles in *The New Magazine*. While the editor noted that his publication was not explicitly religious, he expressed his intention of including 'entertaining stories, from which good morals can be extracted'.[145]

---

142 *The New Magazine*, January 1799.
143 See the online database, http://www2.ul.ie/web/WWW/Faculties/Arts,_Humanities_%26_Social_Sciences/Inventing/.
144 There was a total of twenty-four orders of copies of *The New Magazine* from Cork; an order of nine books from Lisburn; nine from Mountmellick and fourteen from Waterford. The Dublin subscribers are not identified by address. The subscribers were listed at the end of each volume. See the online database, http://www2.ul.ie/web/WWW/Faculties/Arts,_Humanities_%26_Social_Sciences/Inventing/.
145 See, for example, *The New Magazine*, January 1799.

Such views concurred with much of the literature authored by the English writers admired by *The New Magazine*. Delap wrote approvingly of English women writers such as Anna Laetitia Barbauld, Sarah Trimmer and Hannah More. The lives of these women were presented as exemplary and as models that could be followed by his women readers in Ireland. Delap expressed his preference for authors of educational and religious tracts and empathised with the religious priorities of More and Barbauld and probably also with their espousal of evangelical Protestantism.[146]

In addition to Delap's biographical studies of women writers, *The New Magazine* included a regular feature reviewing books written for children and youth as well as publications concerned with the education of children, most of which were written by women. The reviews, which appear to have been written by Delap, ranged from short summaries of new books to more extensive critical reviews accompanied by lengthy extracts. They also usually included details of the Irish editions of the books and their respective cost. In many instances, it was noted that the book had not yet appeared in an Irish edition. Thus, *The New Magazine*, like *Walker's Hibernian Magazine*, was a medium through which women could learn of the latest publications and ideas on the education of children. For example, three books by the English philanthropist Priscilla Wakefield were reviewed in brief paragraphs with a note that they were all imported into Ireland by the printer John Gough.[147]

The New Magazine lasted for only two years. The editor announced that he was ceasing publication with a bitter and disillusioned statement on the preference of readers for novels:

> But to what purpose is it to write, to select, to publish, with ever so much care, judgment and ability, when a preference, a decided preference is given to those writings which only tend to amuse, without any one good or useful end or aim; but the conversation of such people, and the reading of such books as simply amuse, are much more eagerly sought than those which tend to instruct. Witness the avidity with which Novels are sought; ….
>
> While there is so little relish for works of a serious and moral tendency, it appears to be of little use to continue any longer a miscellany, whose aim has been to carry instruction along with amusement.[148]

---

146 *The New Magazine*, March 1799.
147 *The New Magazine*, January, 1799.
148 *The New Magazine*, March 1799.

Conclusion

Irish publishers' lists of books confirm Delap's conclusion that the most popular publications among young women readers in eighteenth-century Ireland were novels rather than advice books or 'instructive tales' that they may have been compelled to read by teachers, parents or guardians. Nevertheless, the publishers' lists and those of subscribers to Irish publications indicate that there was an interest in books that engaged with the contemporary debate in England and elsewhere on female education and the societal role of women. Most of the texts available in Ireland could be categorised as part of what Jonathan Israel described as, the 'moderate mainstream' of Enlightenment thought on women.[149] While their authors were not opposed to the expansion of women's intellectual horizons, they also asserted the distinctive gender characteristics of men and women and the necessity of educating girls separately from boys and for a different function in society. It is also possible, however, to trace a thinner but nevertheless continuous thread of publications that advocated a more radical view based on the equality of the sexes. From Mary Astell's and Sarah Chapone's condemnation of the laws on marriage through to Mary Wollstonecraft's *A Vindication of the Rights of Women*, eighteenth-century Irish readers had access to texts that critiqued the contemporary status and subordinate role of women.

There are two chronological peaks in the publications in Ireland on women's education. The first dates to the early decades of the eighteenth century from the 1710s through to 1740. The books that appeared at this time had links with the Dublin Protestant elite associated with George Berkeley, Mary and Patrick Delany and Jonathan Swift. The Delanys and their circle of friends are prominent among the lists of subscribers to books by and about women. The second peak occurs in the 1790s and forms part of the wider radicalisation of Irish society among, in particular, Irish dissenters. Extracts from publications on the debate on the education of women including those by Mary Wollestonecraft appeared in *Walker's Hibernian Magazine* alongside reports on the proceedings of the Volunteers and the United Irishmen. The publications of David Manson and James Delap also date to this period. In addition, Irish readers had access to Irish reprints of the works of English women authors, many of whom were connected to the bluestocking network which flourished in the middle decades of the century.

The main readers of these publications were from English-speaking Protestant and dissenter Ireland: women like Belfast-based Martha McTier or Mary Ann McCracken, both of whom expressed approval of Mary

---

149 Israel, *Enlightenment Contested: Philosophy, Modernity, and the Emancipation of Man 1670–1752*, p. 573.

Wollstonecraft's publications. It is clear, however, that new ideas on women's education were also trickling through to Catholic Ireland. Irish-language writers, such as Domhnall Ó Colmáin, were familiar with the European debate on women. Catholic teacher Teresa Mulally and Mother Borgia McCarthy from the Cork Ursuline convent could also be categorised as sympathetic to the 'moderate mainstream' of Enlightenment thought on the education of girls. By the early decades of the nineteenth century, literature linked with English bluestocking women and writers who promoted the education of girls was also being read in private schools attended by mainly Catholic pupils.[150]

Mary Peckham Magray has argued that, by the 1830s, Irish nuns drawn from middle-class families 'were well on their way to establishing themselves as the leading molders and reproducers of the developing modern Irish Catholic culture'.[151] Magray defined this culture in two ways: the advancement of the Romanisation of Irish Catholicism and the embourgeoisement of Irish society through the training of Irish girls in appropriate and inappropriate behaviour. The conclusions of Magray and the literary scholar, Nancy Armstrong, have much in common. While Armstrong identifies eighteenth-century women writers as having a powerful influence on the embourgeoisement of English Victorian society, Magray attributes the same task in Irish society to female religious. Both writers fail, however, to consider the complexity of the process of cultural construction and transfer and, in the Irish context, Magray overlooks the impact of the Enlightenment on the development of women's education in Ireland. There was often a tension in the writings of women writers, such as those linked to the bluestocking circle, between identifying a narrow social role for women and the encouragement to women to expand their intellectual horizons. Nonetheless, the 'feminist charge' to be found in the seemingly pious writings of Hester Chapone and others had the potential to provoke women into breaking through some of the behavioural restrictions of bourgeois society. Similarly, the behavioural advice of Mother McCarthy to the pupils of the Ursuline Convent wavered between encouraging them to read and think for themselves and curtailing the sort of books that were considered appropriate reading for young ladies.

The relationship between a reader and a book is problematic for the historian. It is difficult to make a direct connection between a publication and its impact on individual readers or on society in general. A book or

---

150 See chapter two and Antonia McManus, *The Irish Hedge School and Its Books, 1695–1831* (Dublin: Four Courts Press, 2004), pp. 182–217, 245–56.
151 Mary Peckham Magray, *The Transforming Power of the Nuns: Women, Religion, and Cultural Change in Ireland, 1760–1900* (New York: Oxford University Press, 1998), p. 106.

periodical may have been purchased but not necessarily read and absorbed by Irish women readers. We can document recommendations and gifts of conduct literature by older relatives to daughters or nieces but it is more difficult to find any reference to them in the correspondence of women. Good examples of this complexity are Mary Ann McCraken and Martha McTier, both of whom lived in late eighteenth-century Belfast and were sympathetic to the radical politics advocated by their respective brothers. Both women admired Mary Wollstonecraft's writings on the status of women but neither engaged publicly in politics. Yet, as the next chapter makes clear, both McCracken and McTier were born into a generation of women who did begin to construct new public images and widen out the sphere within which women could function without encountering social disapproval.

2

Educating Women, Patriotism and Public Life, 1770–1845

Introduction

Chapter one traced the amassing in eighteenth century Ireland of printed literature on the education of women and, more widely, on the role and contribution of women in society. Interest in this type of literature declined in the early nineteenth century. By 1800, there is a noticeable absence in the pages of *Walker's Hibernian Magazine* of articles that focused on the merits of female education or that discussed the role of women. They were replaced with items that were to become the standard fare of women's magazines: advice on marriage and married life, serialised romantic tales and fashion.[1] The unsuccessful attempts in the 1790s to produce periodicals for women readers were not repeated in subsequent decades. Instead, the new weekly or monthly publications of the early nineteenth century were aimed at a Catholic and nationalist readership and did not have an explicit gender dimension to their marketing

---

1 See, for example, 'The Land of Matrimony: On Precepts for Promoting Conjugal Happiness' by 'A Lady', in *Walker's Hibernian Magazine*, July 1810. Other periodicals searched for this study include *The Monthly Pantheon or General Repository or Politics, Arts, Science, Literature and Miscellaneous Information* (1809), which included articles entitled 'Hints to the Fashionable World for the Year 1809' (March 1809); 'The Mirror of Fashion. To Shew the Very Age and Body of the Times, its Form, and Pressure' (April 1809); and 'Irish Varieties. Fashion for May' (May 1809). *The Belfast Monthly Magazine* published a series of articles on education in the 1810s but they mainly related to the education of poor children. See for example, 'For the Education of Female Children' (31 October 1812); 'On the Lancastrian System of Education' (31 January 1812); 'Observations on Female Charity-Schools' (31 August 1812); 'Remarks on Apprenticing Female Children on their Leaving a Charity School' (30 September 1812); 'Plan of a Female Benefit Club' (30 April 1814); 'Biographical Sketch of Elizabeth Carter' (31 January 1814). Women were listed among the prize winners for mathematical puzzles in *The Literary and Mathematical Asylum* (1823).

strategies.[2] A small number of magazines such as the *Dublin Family Magazine or Literary and Religious Miscellany* (Dublin, 1829) were produced for a school market but, unlike in the 1790s, they did not focus specifically on female readers.

For most of the nineteenth century there were no Irish-produced magazines directed at a female readership. The first, *Lady of the House* appeared in 1890.[3] Prior to that date, Irish women were among the readers of the expanding number of women's magazines that were published in London. The most successful in the early nineteenth century was *La Belle Assemblée*, which was one of the first to feature full-page engravings of women's fashions from London and Paris. Other items advertised in *La Belle Assemblée* included luxury consumer items like furniture, silverware and paintings.[4] The commercial potential of the middle-class woman consumer was increasingly recognised by English publishers.

The most successful nineteenth-century women's magazine was the *Englishwoman's Domestic Magazine*, edited by Samuel and Isabella Beeton, from the early 1850s. It set the model for future women's magazines. By contrast with their eighteenth-century predecessors, the editors of the *Englishwoman's Domestic Magazine* produced their magazine for the middle-class woman in charge of a household. Their emphasis was on 'homemaking' and, as Samuel Beeton wrote in the first issue, the magazine was for women who wanted 'to make home happy'. The articles in the *Englishwoman's Domestic Magazine* were a successful mixture of practical household advice, serialised fiction and accounts of the latest fashions, which were often accompanied by patterns and dressmaking guidance on how to recreate them. The *Englishwoman's Domestic Magazine* had an Irish readership. The correspondence and query page of the magazine regularly included Irish

---

2 See, for example, *The Dublin Saturday Magazine. A Journal of Instruction and Amusement Comprising Irish Biography and Antiquities* (Dublin: J. Mullany, 1847); *Duffy's Irish Catholic Magazine: A Monthly Review, Devoted to National Literature, the Fine Arts, Antiquities, Ecclesiastical History, Biography of Illustrious Irishmen, and Military Memoirs. ...* (Dublin: James Duffy, 1847–[1848]); *The Catholic Penny Magazine: Published Weekly, Under the Inspection of Catholic Divines* (Dublin: T. & J. Coldwell, 1834–35).
3 See p. 33 below.
4 Irene Dancyger, *A World of Women: An Illustrated History of Women's Magazines* (Dublin: Gill and Macmillan, 1978), pp. 33, 47–50; Alison Adburgham, *Women in Print: Writing Women and Women's Magazines from the Restoration to the Accession of Victoria* (London: Allen and Unwin, 1972), pp. 218–28; Margaret Beetham, *A Magazine of Her Own? Domesticity and Desire in the Woman's Magazine, 1800–1914* (London: Routledge, 1996). There are copies of *La Belle Assemblée* available in the National Library of Ireland, a deposit which suggests Irish interest in the periodical.

correspondents. Irish readers also inserted notices in the classified lists of family births, deaths and marriages.[5]

Paradoxically, while the public debate on women's education faded in the early decades of the nineteenth century, there were more women being educated. The early nineteenth century witnessed an increase in the number of schools available for the education of girls and a corresponding rise in female literacy. Similarly, while the periodical literature seemed to assume that most women spent their time in the home and on domestic duties, the 1820s and 1830s were marked by an expansion in the public space in which women could move without social disapproval. The widening of women's access to the public sphere has long been recognised by historians as one of the most significant ways in which Enlightenment ideas made an impact on women's lives. The aim of this chapter is to explore how the public profile of many Irish women changed in the early nineteenth century as they gained access to education and, as a result, could participate more fully in public life. As in the eighteenth century, there continued to be a tension in the perception of women's role in society. As the public discourse increasingly emphasised the domestic and the private, educational, political and economic developments in the early decades of the nineteenth century constructed new images for Irish women and womanhood in the public sphere.

The Educated and Educating Woman

> My grandmother, though an earl's daughter, could write only a short letter, containing a few kind sentences, in a very large hand, spelling very ignorantly, and yet she was considered a sensible woman, and had energy enough to establish a little school, at Inistiogue, where girls were taught to make lace, at a time when there were scarcely any schools for the poor in Ireland. ... Lady Betty must have had ... some taste for literature if we may judge from her having left her name on many of the best authors of that day. She read, I have heard, well and committed to memory many passages from Young[6] and Milton while sitting at her work.[7]

---

5 Ros Ballaster, Margaret Beetham, Elizabeth Frazer and Sandra Hebron, *Women's Worlds. Ideology, Femininity and the Woman's Magazine* (London: Macmillan, 1991), pp. 89–93; online search of the *Englishwoman's Domestic Magazine* (Nineteenth Century UK Periodicals, Gale Cengage Learning).

6 Probably Edward Young, *The Complaint, or, Night-Thoughts on Life, Death, and Immortality* (1742–46), which was reprinted five times in eighteenth-century Dublin.

7 Caroline Hamilton, 'Reminiscences' in NLI, MS 4811.

Thus, in her memoirs, written in the mid-1820s, Caroline Hamilton wrote of the educational achievement of her grandmother, Lady Elizabeth Fownes, and drew attention to the irony of a semi-literate wealthy woman establishing schools for the poor. Unlike her ancestor, Hamilton could read and write lucidly, leaving behind several volumes of reminiscences of her family which she composed 'for my children'.[8] In her memoirs, Hamilton detailed the care which her mother, Sarah Tighe (née Fownes), took with the education of her children. Having read Jean Jacques Rousseau's *Emile*, Tighe sent her sons to public school in England while she employed 'every kind of master, at first an English and afterwards an Irish governess' for her daughters.[9] In addition, Caroline, who became an accomplished artist, had a drawing master, 'my mother caring little what expense she incurred for our improvement'.[10]

Hamilton also wrote of the considerable effort and attention that her aunt, Theodosia Blachford, gave to the education of her daughter, Mary Tighe. Blachford, who had been virtually self-taught, was dismissive of governesses and agreed with the fashionable view, inspired by Enlightenment thinking and texts such as de Genlis's *Adèle et Théodore*, that mothers should be involved in the teaching of their daughters as much as possible. Although she sent her daughter to school and employed drawing and music masters for her, Blachford also devoted a considerable amount of time to Mary's education. She encouraged Mary to improve her writing skills through the transcribing of literary texts and to learn French and Italian by reading and translating books in both languages.[11] With her mother's encouragement, Tighe kept a journal in which she 'noted down every book she read and her observations upon them'.[12]

Caroline Hamilton's writings thus chart the changing pattern of the education of middle- and upper middle-class women. She was born in 1777 and her cousin and sister-in-law Mary Tighe was born five years earlier, in 1772. They were members of the first generation of middle- and upper-class Irish women for whom a formal education in their childhood was the norm rather than the exception. As Hamilton noted of her grandmother's generation,

> Half a century ago, a governess was not considered as at present an indispensable member of every gentleman's family. An old nurse

8 Ibid. and NLI, MS 4810.
9 NLI, MS 4811.
10 Ibid.
11 NLI, MS 4810, pp. 13–16; Harriet Kramer Linkin (ed.), *The Collected Poems and Journals of Mary Tighe* (Lexington: University of Kentucky Press, 2005), pp. xx, 240–53; See also the *DIB* entry for Mary Tighe by Harriet Kramer Linkin.
12 NLI, MS 4910, p. 34. The journal has not survived.

generally taught to read and the parish clerk, to write and if a young lady professed any taste for literature, she was permitted to read what she pleased in her father's library which generally consisted of old romances, books of divinity, and tedious histories.[13]

In this way, her grandmother learnt to read but not to write with fluency. A similar transition can be traced in the family of Belfast merchant and landowner, William Tennent. Tennent's mother, Anne was clearly an enthusiastic reader who sent numerous requests for books to her son. All of the book orders were, however, communicated through her husband's correspondence. The Tennent family archive in the Public Record Office of Northern Ireland is a rich one with extensive correspondence between members of the family in the last quarter of the eighteenth and early nineteenth centuries but it contains only one letter by Anne Tennent, which suggests that although she was an enthusiastic reader she found writing more difficult. Her son, William, however, took care to educate all his daughters (legitimate and illegitimate). Each was sent to school for a number of years and wrote articulate and clear letters to their father.[14]

The generation of Irish women born in the last quarter of the eighteenth century were, therefore, better educated, on the whole, than their antecedents. Nor was this phenomenon limited by class or by religion. Niall Ó Ciosáin has explored the available historical data on literacy skills of women in the early nineteenth century. Relying mainly on the statistical information provided in the printed reports of the 1841 census, Ó Cíosain's analysis suggests that the growth in the number of schools had made a significant impact on female literacy by that time. The census data indicates that 47 per cent of the Irish population over five years of age could read in 1841 and of those 44 per cent were women. There were regional differences in the literacy rates. The number of women able to read was noticeably higher in Ulster although more women in Leinster and Munster had both reading and writing skills.[15] Thus, in the decades before the Famine in Ireland (1845–53), the transition in female literacy was well under way. The reading ability figure for Ulster reflects the Protestant emphasis on literacy, but the expansion in Catholic education in the course of the early nineteenth century helped to reduce the denominational imbalance. As

13 Caroline Hamilton, 'Anecdotes of Our Family, Written for My Children' (NLI, MS 4810, pp. 1–2); Linkin (ed.), *The Collected Poems and Journals of Mary Tighe*, p. 247.
14 See the Tennent papers in PRONI, D1748. There is a digitised catalogue which can be consulted in PRONI but many of the family letters remain uncatalogued. The authors are grateful to Leanne Calvert for her work on this source.
15 Niall Ó Ciosáin, *Print and Popular Culture in Ireland, 1750–1850* (London: Macmillan Press, 1997), pp. 31–32.

noted in chapter one, the foundation of private and church-run schools for girls as well as boys burgeoned in the last quarter of the eighteenth century. The rise in literacy rates was also assisted by the establishment of the government-funded primary school system in 1831, which created a national network of free schools.[16]

Although the principal focus was on teaching basic literacy skills to young children, more advanced schools for older girls also began to be advertised in Irish newspapers at this time. They catered for girls over the age of nine or ten and were essentially secondary schools that built on the literacy skills which the children had learnt elsewhere, either in a school or at home. The academic curriculum in some of these establishments was surprisingly rigorous and was often modelled on a French or English prototype.

In the 1790s, Sydney Owenson and her sister, Olivia spent three years as borders in a French Huguenot school in Clontarf outside Dublin.[17] The school was under the management of Madame Terson who, according to Owenson, modelled the discipline in the school on that of Saint Cyr with which Fénelon was associated.[18] Saint Cyr had a strong academic reputation and its principle aim, according to one contemporary, was 'to give the state well-educated women'.[19] Like Saint Cyr, the school day in the Clontarf school followed an impressive schedule and, as recommended by John Locke, was divided between healthy outdoor exercise and academic study. School activity began at six in the morning in the summer months and seven in the winter. Upon rising, weather permitting, the girls bathed in the sea. Following this, prayers were said and the pupils received instruction in English grammar and geography before they had their breakfast. After breakfast, there was time for exercise and recreation in the school grounds. Classes resumed again at twelve and continued until three. Dinner was served about four and then time was allocated for walking either along the seashore or in the grounds of Clontarf Castle. A two-hour study period started at seven o'clock after which the girls had supper and then retired to bed. On average, therefore, the pupils in Madame Terson's school spent about seven hours

16 D. H. Akenson, *The Irish Education Experiment: the National System of Education in the Nineteenth Century* (London: Routledge and Kegan Paul, 1970); Deirdre Raftery and Susan Parkes, *Female Education in Ireland 1700–1900: Minerva or Madonna* (Dublin: Irish Academic Press, 2007).

17 Lady Sydney Morgan, *Lady Morgan's Memoirs: Autobiography, Diaries, and Correspondence*, edited by W. H. Dixon (2 vols; London: W. H. Allen, 1862), vol. 1, pp. 98–108. Following Terson's retirement, the Owenson girls attended a school in Dublin city centre for a number of years. Ibid., pp. 110–11.

18 Ibid., p. 103. Madame Terson had taught at the Huguenot school in Portarlington but had moved to Clontarf on Dublin bay for health reasons.

19 See the entry on Françoise, Marquise de Maintenon in The Catholic Encyclopedia, http://www.newadvent.org/cathen/09548b.htm (accessed 25 October 2012).

a day on academic study. The subjects taught included English grammar and writing, the French language, geography and history, arithmetic and drawing. Prayers and all conversation were conducted in French.[20]

Owenson described the education that she and her sister received in Clontarf as 'the best instruction that the best masters could bestow and we were subjected to a discipline which ... was the very best ever introduced into a female seminary in any country'.[21] Madame Terson's establishment clearly had a reputation as a good school for girls. There were thirty to forty pupils at the school when the Owensons joined it and among them were the daughters of parliamentarian Henry Grattan and of Church of Ireland ecclesiastical, Richard Marlay.[22] Owenson's description suggests that French Enlightenment ideas on education directly impacted on the lives of the daughters of the leading members of the Irish Protestant elite. It was probably also at the Clontarf school that Owenson became familiar with the publications of Madame de Genlis.[23]

Schools for middle-class girls, particularly in the main cities, could also be based on English or Scottish models. This seems to have been particularly the case in Belfast where schools provided a solid academic education as well as training for employment for girls and boys. In January 1828, for example, the *Belfast Newsletter* published the names of the boys and girls who had excelled in the recent examinations held in the Belfast School in North Street. The subjects examined were spelling, reading, grammar, parsing, sacred history, writing, arithmetic, algebra and geography. Both sexes were taught similar academic subjects but the advertisement for the school noted that it prepared the boys for college while the girls were instructed in 'plain and fancy work'.[24] Similarly, in July 1828, the English and Mercantile School in Belfast published the names of the boys and girls who had been rewarded with premiums. The names of the girls in the 'Ladies School' were listed separately but again the subjects examined indicate a solid academic curriculum. They included spelling, reading, history, grammar, parsing, geography, writing and arithmetic. Letter-writing and 'bills of parcels'[25] were also listed among the subjects studied, which

20 Lady Sydney Morgan, *Lady Morgan's Memoirs: Autobiography, Diaries, and Correspondence*, pp. 103–5.
21 Ibid., p. 98.
22 Marlay was bishop of Clonfert (1787–95) and later bishop of Waterford and Lismore (1795–1802). See Lady Sydney Morgan, *Lady Morgan's Memoirs: Autobiography, Diaries, and Correspondence*, pp. 101, 105.
23 See chapter one.
24 *Belfast Newsletter*, 1 January 1828.
25 A bill of parcels was the invoice of goods drawn up by a shopkeeper or manufacturer for a customer. It would include such details as the date, the name of the shopkeeper and customer, an itemised list of the goods sold and the cost and details of payment.

suggests that the girls were also being trained for employment or assisting in a family business.[26]

Whilst such schools were primarily aimed at girls from Protestant and Presbyterian families, the impact of the new emphasis on an academic curriculum can also be documented in schools frequented predominantly by Catholic children. The daughter of Daniel O'Connell, Ellen, recalled in her memoir of her father that while in the first decade of the nineteenth century 'almost all the Catholic ladies of Ireland' attended a boarding school managed by 'two old maids the Misses O'Rourke who had been educated in France', she implied that Catholic girls also attended Huguenot day schools in Dublin in the 1820s and 1830s.[27] Antonia McManus also pointed to the advanced nature of the literature being taught in some of the hedge schools for poorer children in the early 1820s. Among the books listed as being used in such schools in 1825 were Eliza Haywood's *Female Spectator*, Charlotte Lennox's *Female Quixote*, Lady Mary Wortley Montague's letters, Madame de Sevigné's letters and the novels of Samuel Richardson.[28]

The early decades of the nineteenth century was also the period during which convent schools began to flourish. While many concentrated on the teaching of literacy and practical skills to poor children, the Catholic hierarchy were also anxious to support more elite schools for the daughters of the Catholic middle and upper classes. Their model was the French or Belgian convent school which had been favoured by many wealthy Catholic families in the eighteenth century. The Bar convent school in York was also popular as a school for middle-class Irish girls, particularly in Dublin. By the 1800s, however, the Bar was used as a training location for Irish women intending to return to Ireland to establish religious communities and schools. The founder of the Loreto Order, Mary Teresa Ball, for example, spent three years at the York convent as a teenager and later returned to enter the novitiate there in 1816.[29] Mary Aikenhead was also a professed nun in the York convent although she used the French order of the Daughters of Charity as the prototype for her new Irish order of the Sisters of Charity.[30]

The first successful Irish-based Catholic school that provided an advanced education for girls was run by a branch of another French order,

---

26 *Belfast Newsletter*, 1 July 1828. For a similar type of school in Dublin, see the reference to the annual examinations at Russell Place Boarding and Day School in *Freeman's Journal*, 9 August 1820.
27 'Recollections of Daniel O'Connell by His Daughter, Ellen Fitzsimon', 1876 (NLI, MS 1504).
28 Antonia McManus, *The Irish Hedge School and Its Books, 1695–1831* (Dublin: Four Courts Press, 2004), pp. 182–217, 245–56.
29 *DIB* entry by Frances Clarke.
30 *DIB* entry by Marie O'Leary.

the Ursulines. The nuns in Cork were, by the 1810s, endeavouring to establish a strong academic ethos in imitation of the schools established by the order in France. In 1813, the school introduced a biannual system of examinations for which pupils were rewarded with premiums and certificates at a formal prize-giving ceremony.[31] By 1840, Ursuline boarding schools were also established in Thurles, Limerick, Sligo, Waterford, Lifford and Galway, catering mainly for daughters of the mercantile and commercial classes of those towns. These schools also had a strong French ethos.[32]

As noted in chapter one, the nuns teaching in Ursuline schools spent time thinking and writing about pedagogy.[33] They also wrote their own school textbooks. This was particularly the case in Cork. Mother Ursula Young, for example, published two books on Irish history in 1815. Young's general history of the United Kingdom of England and Ireland was accompanied by a teacher's aid, which listed questions that could be asked through a study of the volume.[34] Although the introduction to the history included a denunciation of the 'insinuating accents of a Voltaire or a Rousseau' and warned against an 'incautious selection' of books that denigrated religion, the main text consisted of a patriotic interpretation of Irish history.[35] The book was, however, considered politically biased by educational inspectors who denounced its use in a Christian Brothers' school in Dublin. The inspector's report assumed that the book was written by the nationalist-minded Christian Brothers rather than by a member of the Ursuline Order.[36] The curriculum devised by the Ursulines for the school

---

31 Sister Ursula Clarke, *The Ursulines in Cork since 1771* (Cork: Ursuline Convent, Blackrock, Cork, 2007), p. 56. By 1831 there were monthly examinations in Catechism; spelling; geography; vocabulary; globes; the solar system; English grammar; chronology; rivers; English; French; English, French and Roman history; mythology; phrases; verbs; French reigns; translation and repetition; English reading; 'attention to rule'; speaking French; carriage and work; politeness; neatness in person; arithmetic; order; tables (Ursuline Convent Archive, Blackrock, UCB/01505).

32 On the foundation of Ursuline convents, see Sister M. St. Dominic Kelly, *The Sligo Ursulines: The First Fifty Years 1826–1876* (Sligo: privately published, 1987).

33 See chapter one, p. 33.

34 Ursula Young, *A History of the United Kingdom of Great Britain and Ireland ... Compiled from Various Authors and Intended Chiefly for the Young Ladies Educated at the Ursuline Convents* (2 vols; Cork: W. Fergusson, 1815); *A Sketch of Irish History Compiled by Way of Question and Answer, for the Use of Schools* (Cork: J. Geary, 1815); *Questions on the History of the United Kingdom of Great Britain and Ireland. Intended Chiefly for the Young Ladies Educated at the Ursuline Convent, Cork* (Cork: J. Geary, 1815). See also *A System of Chronology Facilitated by the Mnemonics for the Use of the Young Ladies Educated at the Ursuline Convent* (Cork: 1841).

35 Alfred O'Rahilly, 'An Ursuline Writer on Irish History', *Journal of Cork Historical and Archaeological Society*, 47 (1942), pp. 77–86.

36 Ibid.

in Cork, therefore, had a French base but was clearly adapted to meet Irish circumstances.

Another model that the Ursulines adopted for Irish Catholic use was that of the conduct book. In the 1820s, Mother Borgia McCarthy penned the *Ursuline Manual* 'for the spiritual good and formation to piety of the Young Ladies' educated in the Cork convent.[37] The volume provided a daily guide for prayer and religious practice. In addition, the introduction advised girls on their wider conduct in life. Cautioning girls to take care when choosing their companions and avoid reading novels, romances and attending the theatre, the *Manual* presented a message that would have been familiar to the readers of advice books written by Protestant women writers. Yet, like the latter, there was a tension between McCarthy's encouragement of intellectual activity and the passivity of her advice on the girls' behaviour. She presented St Catherine of Alexandra as a model for young girls to emulate 'in the use to be made of mental acquirements'. The patron saint of girls' education would never, according to McCarthy, have made 'an ostentatious show' of her learning. The ideal young woman might be educated but she did not boast in public about it.[38]

The French ethos of the Ursuline convent and school in Cork is evident from the significant number of French books still to be found in the convent archive. In addition to the *Ursuline Manual*, McCarthy and her colleagues also translated a number of French religious texts into English. It is possible to identify at least fifteen books produced by nuns attached to the Cork convent from 1812 through to 1860. Some related to the rule and regulations of the Ursuline Order and were addressed to young novices as they entered the convent. Other texts were, however, written for the laity and provided spiritual guidance as well as advice on conduct and behaviour.

The commercial possibilities of some of these texts, in the booming market of conduct and devotional books for girls, were recognised by Irish and English publishers. By the end of the nineteenth century, ten editions of the *Ursuline Manual* had been printed in Dublin, fourteen in North America and two in London. *The Month of Mary: A Series of Meditations on the Life and Virtues of the Holy Mother of God, Particularly Adapted for the Month of May. By a Member of the Ursuline Community, Blackrock, Cork* had appeared in six editions by 1853.[39] The Dublin publisher was Richard Coyne,

---

37 *The Ursuline Manual, or, a Collection of Prayers, Spiritual Exercises, etc. Interspersed With the Various Instructions Necessary for Forming Youth to the Practice of Solid Piety: Originally Arranged for the Young Ladies Educated at the Ursuline Convent, Cork* (Cork: 1825; London: Keating and Brown, 1825, 1827, 1830; Dublin: R. Coyne, 1835, 1846).
38 *The Ursuline Manual*, pp. xiv–xv.
39 The original title, *Meditations for the Month of Mary, On the Life and Virtues of*

described as the 'printer and bookseller to the College of Maynooth'.[40] The Ursuline publications clearly formed part of the burgeoning number of Irish printed books sponsored or approved by the Catholic hierarchy in the early decades of the nineteenth century.[41]

The pedagogical example set by the Ursuline community in Cork was followed by others. Nuns who taught in the Ursuline convent in Waterford penned books on botany and architecture for use in their school in the early nineteenth century.[42] When the newly established Loreto Order opened its boarding school for girls in Rathfarnham on the outskirts of Dublin in 1822, it too placed great emphasis on the academic strength of its curriculum. The students were taught English, arithmetic, the 'natural sciences', geography, history, French, Italian, Spanish, painting and needlework. There were also masters instructing in the usual female 'accomplishments' including music, dancing, riding and drawing. As in Cork, the pupils took regular exams which were assessed by external examiners.[43] The teachers also looked to French convent schools for their curriculum and pedagogical direction. Among the books authored by teachers in the school were a history of France and religious texts, some of which were translations from French originals.[44]

---

    the Holy Mother of God: Adapted for the Use Both of Religious Persons and Seculars, indicates that it was intended for use by the laity. The sixth edition was printed in Cork by J. O'Brien in 1853. See also *Spiritual Consolation, or A Treatise on Interior Peace. Translated from the French of Père Lomber. Interspersed with Various Instructions Necessary for the Promoting the Practice of Solid Piety. Translated By the Authoress of the "Ursuline Manual"* (Dublin: Richard Coyne, 1835); *The Spirit of Prayer. A New Manual of Catholic Devotion with the Epistles and Gospels for the Sundays and Principal Festivals Throughout the Year. By a Member of the Ursuline Community, Cork* (Cork: J. O'Brien, 1850); *The Catholic Offering: Counsels to the Young on Their Leaving School and Entering into the World. By a Member of the Ursuline Community, Blackrock, Cork* (Dublin: James Duffy, 1859).

40 On Coyne see entry in *DIB* by C. J. Woods. See also the correspondence between Mother Borgia McCarthy and the London publisher George Keating in the Ursuline Archive, Blackrock, Cork.

41 See Hugh Fenning, 'The Catholic Press in Munster in the Eighteenth Century', in Gerard Long (ed.), *Books Beyond the Pale: Aspects of the Provincial Book Trade in Ireland before 1850* (Dublin: Rare Books Group of the Library Association of Ireland, 1996); Sister Ursula Clarke, *The Ursulines in Cork since 1771*, pp. 65, 84–86.

42 See Rolf Loeber and Magda Stouthamer-Loeber, '18th–19th Century Irish Fiction Newsletter' (1999), no 9. Unpublished. Copy in QUB Library. See also *A Compendious and Impartial History of England from the Invasion of the Romans to the Close of the Reign of William the Fourth for the Use of Catholic Youth. By a Member of the Ursuline community, St Mary's Waterford* (Dublin: James Duffy, 1844).

43 William Hutch, *Mrs. Ball: A Biography* (Dublin: James Duffy, 1879), pp. 92–93, 144.

44 Ibid., pp. 154–55.

New Public Images for Women:
The Educated Lady

If it is possible to discern the influence of the Enlightenment on educational developments in Ireland, can we also identify how these developments impacted on the changing public image or construction of the Irish woman? Most obviously, the expansion in girls' education opened up the profession of teaching for women. While private tutoring or employment as a governess had been available for much of the eighteenth century to women of a certain class but with little or no family income, the role of a teacher/manager of a commercial school brought women more into the public world. They were compelled to advertise their premises in newspapers and were among the small number of women listed in urban trade directories in Belfast and Dublin. Some ran their premises in conjunction with a spouse who looked after a complementary school for boys while single or widowed women often had sisters or daughters as assistants.[45]

The nun as a public figure is also more in evidence during this period. In 1777, despite the resistance of their patron, Nano Nagle, the nuns in the Ursuline convent in Cork donned the full habit of their French order – a visual sign of the new image.[46] And by the 1820s, the habited nun must have been a familiar figure in Irish society as the number of female religious working outside the strict rules of cloister increased. It is worth noting in this context that Mary Aikenhead and Mary Teresa Ball both had portraits of themselves dressed in their full habit, a very public display of the new Irish nun.[47]

As the graduates of the new education began to emerge in the early nineteenth century, the educated lay woman and the woman reader gained a new recognition, particularly in the urban communities of Belfast and Dublin. The 'literary lady' no longer required quite such vigorous defending as was the case in the eighteenth century. When in 1828, Isabella McCracken, niece of Mary Ann, finished her secondary education in Coleraine with laudatory comments from her teacher, she continued her reading and her studies by herself. She attended a lecture course on moral philosophy in the newly opened Belfast Institution and made extensive lecture notes. McCracken also kept a list of the books that she read which amounted to over 250 volumes in the years 1829–46. McCracken's reading was wide-ranging

---

45 Mary O'Dowd, *A History of Women in Ireland, 1500–1800* (Harlow: Pearson, 2005), pp. 210–12.
46 Entry in annals for 1777 in Ursuline Archive, Blackrock, Cork.
47 The portrait of Mary Aikenhead (1845) is by N. J. Crowley and is in St Vincent's Hospital, Dublin. Mary Frances Ball had her portrait painted by J. P. Haverty in 1834. The original is in Rathfarnham Abbey, Dublin.

and included works on Greek and Roman history as well as the latest novels by contemporary writers. In August and September 1831, for example, McCracken noted that she had read translations of work by Diogenes Laertius, Demosthenes, Isaeus, Xenophon, Plato and Aristotle. Later in the decade her reading included more fiction. In the three years from 1837 to 1839, McCracken recorded that she had read among other works Jane Austen's *Mansfield Park* and *Pride and Prejudice*, Charles Dickens' *Oliver Twist*, Maria Edgeworth's *Belinda* and Walter Scott's *Ivanhoe*.[48]

McCracken was also a member of the Linenhall Library, which from its foundation in 1788 admitted a small number of women, including McCracken's aunt, Mary Ann. Other public libraries were increasingly available, at least to some women. Sydney Owenson recalled in her memoirs that when she lived as a young woman with her father in Kilkenny, she was given access to the diocesan library in the town where she 'took the opportunity of fluttering over a quantity of genuine old Irish books; which study engendered a state for Irish antiquity, which never afterwards slumbered'.[49] Later, the antiquarian and founding member of the Royal Irish Academy, Joseph Cooper Walker, took a scholarly interest in Owenson's use of Irish history in her novels. He advised Owenson to consult the Academy's library assuring her that any 'of the members could get you access ..., where you might pass two or three hours with pleasure and advantage'.[50]

The advanced study undertaken by Isabella McCracken after she left school was not unique. Antiquarian studies attracted a number of women in the late eighteenth and early nineteenth century. Charlotte Brooke was the first to publish the results of her research and translation work on Irish poetry. Other women, such as the Countess of Moira, pursued their antiquarian studies in a more private fashion, but she, like the bluestocking women of the mid-eighteenth century, maintained a correspondence with a number of writers and scholars, including Walter Scott. Sydney Owenson also made use of letters to connect with scholars for advice about her historical novels although, like the Countess of Moira, she read and researched widely herself. In 1811 she began research for her novel *O'Donnell* and wrote of having being lent by a 'good old Irishman ... 20,000 volumes of old Irish books to make extracts from ... I am just going to work pell mell, looking like a little conjurer, with all my blacklettered books about me.'[51]

---

48 Eliza McCracken's papers in the Tennent papers (PRONI, D1748/G/378); Lisa Townsend, 'The Intellectual and Cultural Interests of Women in Ireland, c.1740–c.1840' (unpublished Ph.D. thesis, Queen's University Belfast, 2007), pp. 49–50, 61–66.
49 Lady Sydney Morgan, *Lady Morgan's Memoirs: Autobiography, Diaries and Correspondence*, vol. 1, p. 119.
50 Ibid., p. 315.
51 Ibid., p. 515. For the Countess of Moira, see Granard Papers in PRONI, T3765.

The antiquarian interests of Brooke, Owenson, Lady Moira and Maria Edgeworth were, of course, part of a wider revival of antiquarianism in late eighteenth-century Ireland.[52] The Royal Irish Academy was established in 1782 and its founding members included the most well-known historians and antiquarians of the time. Women were not admitted as members of the Academy, although it is worth noting that among the founding members were strong supporters of women's education. They included R. L. Edgeworth, who wrote texts on education with his daughter Maria, Daniel Beaufort whose daughters, Lucia and Harriet, were not only well educated but also later became authors of antiquarian and botanical texts and Joseph Cooper Walker, who offered practical support to Sydney Owenson and Charlotte Brooke in their antiquarian and historical research.

Charlotte Brooke famously applied for the post of housekeeper of the Academy in 1787. She withdrew her application when she realised that she did not have sufficient support among the members, one of whom advised her to seek employment as a governess. Lesa Ní Mhunghaile has, however, recently pointed out that Brooke's application had divided the members of the Academy, many of whom were sympathetic to her and were impressed by her scholarship and knowledge of Gaelic poetry. It was members of the Academy who first suggested to Brooke that she publish a book based on her transcriptions and translations of Irish poetry and, according to Ní Mhunghaile, founding members including Walker, Charles Vallancey, Charles O'Conor and Sylvester O'Halloran all offered support and advice to Brooke when she was compiling *Reliques of Irish Poetry*.[53] Walker and others also successfully solicited subscriptions for the publication of the volume while another member of the Academy, Daniel Beaufort, negotiated on Brooke's behalf with booksellers. Among the 278 subscribers to *Reliques of Irish Poetry* were thirty members of the Academy.[54] In her preface to the volume, Brooke acknowledged, in particular, the support that she received from Walker.[55]

---

52 Clare O'Halloran, *Golden Ages and Barbarous Nations: Antiquarian Debate and Cultural Politics in Ireland, c.1750–1800* (Cork: Cork University Press, 2004); Ann de Valera, 'Antiquarian and Historical Investigations in Ireland in the Eighteenth Century' (unpublished MA thesis, University College, Dublin, 1978).
53 Lesa Ní Mhunghaile, 'Anglo-Irish Antiquarianism in County Longford in the 1780s: The Case of Charlotte Brooke', in Martin Morris and Fergus O'Ferrall (eds), *Longford: History and Society* (Dublin: Geography Publications, 2010), p. 237.
54 *Reliques of Irish Poetry: Consisting of Heroic Poems, Odes, Elegies, and Songs, Translated into English Verse: With Notes Explanatory and …* (Dublin: George Bonham, 1789), pp. ix–x; Lesa Ní Mhunghaile (ed.), *Charlotte Brooke's 'Reliques of Irish Poetry'* (Dublin: Irish Manuscripts Commission, 2011).
55 Ní Mhunghaile, 'Anglo-Irish Antiquarianism in County Longford in the 1780s', pp. 245–47.

The Royal Irish Academy initiated a series of essay competitions in the early nineteenth century in which women were permitted to participate. The first woman to have her prize essay published in the *Transactions of the Royal Irish Academy* in 1815 was Harriet Kiernan. Her contribution was entitled 'Essay on the Influence of Fictitious History on Modern Manners'.[56] The essay developed the familiar argument that novel-reading introduced readers to low moral standards. It concluded with a sentiment that would have received support from men like Daniel Beaufort and Joseph Cooper Walker, that the 'youth, of both sexes' should be given a 'virtuous and religious education' which would 'enlarge and elevate the mind'.[57] In 1828, Beaufort's daughter, Lucia, was the second woman to have her essay published in the *Transactions*. Entitled 'An Essay upon the State of Architecture and Antiquities, Previous to the Landing of the Anglo-Normans in Ireland', the text was a wide-ranging survey of Irish antiquities and was accompanied by fifteen drawings penned by Beaufort.[58]

Women were not elected as full members until the twentieth century, but the Academy admitted four women as honorary members before 1845. Three were women who had achieved international recognition for their research or contributions to the advancement of knowledge: Princess Ekaterina Daskova (1791), who had visited Ireland in 1779 and had been appointed Director of the Imperial Academy of Arts and Sciences and president of the Russian Academy by Empress Catherine the Great; the Scottish scientist, Mary Somerville (1834); and the British astronomer, Caroline Herschel (1838). The fourth female honorary member was Maria Edgeworth who was elected in 1842.[59] Although this might not appear as a very impressive record, the Royal Society in London did not elect its first honorary female member until 1945.[60] Daskova was nominated as a member of the American Philosophical

---

56 *Transactions of the Royal Irish Academy*, 12 (1815), pp. 61–97. Kiernan may have been related to George Kiernan who published an article on a water pump in the *Transactions of the Royal Irish Academy*, 13 (1818). See also R. B. McDowell, 'The Main Narrative', in T. Ó Raifeartaigh (ed.), *The Royal Irish Academy: A Bicentennial History 1785–1985* (Dublin: Royal Irish Academy, 1985), pp. 16–17.
57 Kiernan, 'Essay on the Influence of Fictitious History on Modern Manners', p. 97.
58 *Transactions of the Royal Irish Academy*, 15 (1828), pp. 101–241.
59 The authors are grateful to Siobhan Fitzpatrick, the librarian in the RIA for this information.
60 In 1781, Daskova was elected as a member of the American Philosophical Society. In 1835, Herschel and Somerville were elected honorary members of the Royal Astronomical Society. Herschel was also awarded the gold medal of the Prussian Academy of Sciences in 1846. See also Georgina Ferry, 'The Exception and the Rule: Women and the Royal Society 1945–2010', consulted online at http://rsnr.royalsocietypublishing.org/content/early/2010/06/30/rsnr.2010.0043.full (accessed 8 March 2011); Richard Holmes, 'The Royal Society's Lost Women Scientists', *The Observer*, 21 November 2010, consulted online at http://www.guardian.co.uk/science/2010/nov/21/royal-society-lost-

Society in 1789 but the next female members were not appointed to that organisation until 1869.[61]

There was, therefore, some recognition of the woman scholar, scientist, writer and antiquarian by the Irish intellectual elite through the Royal Irish Academy in the early nineteenth century. When Sir William Rowan Hamilton became president in 1838, he asked Maria Edgeworth for advice on how to promote the literary activities of the Academy and invited her to contribute an article on the topic for the *Transactions*. Edgeworth declined the invitation but she did make some suggestions to Rowan Hamilton on ways in which the Academy could take the lead in literary matters in Ireland. Among Edgeworth's proposals was the admission of women to the evening discussions in the Academy. Her intention appears to have been to endeavour to widen out the social circle of the Academy and make its discussions available to a larger audience. As Clare O'Halloran notes, Edgeworth wrote to Rowan Hamiltion that she had in mind the social events that accompanied meetings of the Royal Society in London and which helped to make science a fashionable topic of conversation in the city. Rowan Hamilton's response to Edgeworth's proposal revealed some of the limits of the Irish male intellectual's attitude to the female intellectual. While admitting that the Academy 'ungallantly' omitted women from its activities, he listed a number of practical objections to the idea that they be admitted as visitors. There was not enough space in the Academy's rooms to accommodate women and, as there was a waiting list for men to be admitted as members, it would not be possible to add to the numbers by permitting women to attend. Rowan Hamilton also reminded Edgeworth that the Academy was disimilar to other societies as it was also a corporation run by the members. When the Academy's business was being discussed, the male visitors were asked to leave but Rowan Hamilton thought it would not be possible to ask the ladies to leave in the same manner.[62]

While Rowan Hamilton was clearly struggling to find reasons why women should not be admitted as visitors to the Academy, he did note that other learned societies in Dublin were more open to women members. Edgeworth's suggestion was probably also prompted by the increased access that women had to public lectures and more widely to public spaces in the early nineteenth century. Women had attended public lectures in Dublin in

---

women-scientists (accessed 8 March 2011). In 1869, Mary Somerville was elected to the American Philosophical Society.

61 Mary Somerville was among the three women elected in 1869. The authors are grateful to Charles B. Greifenstein, Manuscripts Librarian at the American Philosophical Society for this information.

62 Clare O'Halloran, '"Better Without the Ladies"': The Royal Irish Academy and the Admission of Women Members', *History Ireland*, 19, 6 (November/December 2011), p. 43; correspondence between Edgeworth and Rowan Hamilton, RIA MS 24 F 23.

the eighteenth century but the choice of public lectures available widened in the early decades of the nineteenth century. In Dublin, in January 1820, for example, there were public lectures on steam engines, metallurgy and the geology of Ireland. In June, ladies and gentlemen could attend lectures on the natural history of Greenland and in August Mr Donovan advertised a series of lectures on pharmacy in Apothecaries Hall while Edward Whyte, son of the schoolteacher Samuel, announced his annual course of lectures at the English and Classical Academy in Grafton Street.[63] Women in Dublin could register for conversational classes in French as well as benefitting from a choice of dancing and riding classes. In addition, Mrs Richards offered 'to teach an elegant and perspicious running hand' in four to six lessons.[64] Also in January 1820, ladies and gentlemen were invited to view a number of exhibitions in Dublin including a 'panorama of the magnificent scenery of the frozen regions' in 'Marshall's Splendid New Pavillon' in Lower Abbey Street.[65] In Belfast, at the same time, women could attend lectures on a range of subjects including natural history, zoology and chemistry. From the 1830s, the meetings of the Belfast Natural History Society were open to women.[66]

At a less public level, Maria Edgeworth seems to have regretted the absence of a literary salon in the Dublin of the 1830s. Rowan Hamilton was clearly horrified at her suggestion that the Academy take on this role, not least because 'the giving or attending such soirées would ... draw me off too much from science ... and private study.' The death of the Countess of Moira in 1807 had brought to an end the only signficant salon in the city.[67] Sydney Owenson, like Maria Edgeworth, critically compared the socio-intellectual life of Dublin with that of London. She too attempted to fill the gap with her own salon when she and her husband moved into their house in Kildare Street in the 1820s. Rowan Hamilton also revealed to Maria Edgeworth in 1838 that Lady Morgan had proposed a plan 'for Dublin, by which the late provost and I were to have had the honour of being associated with her, in giving, all three weekly parties; but the hint was thrown away'.[68] The provost in question was Bartholomew Lloyd who was also president of the Academy and had died suddenly in 1837. Morgan's proposal suggests that she shared

---

63 *Freeman's Journal*, 13, 21, 28 January 1820; 9 June 1820; 2, 26 August 1820.
64 *Freeman's Journal*, 12, 13, 18, 19, 20 January 1820.
65 *Freeman's Journal*, 2 August 1820. See also Kevin Rockett and Emer Rockett, *Magic Lantern, Panorama and Moving Picture Shows in Ireland, 1786–1909* (Dublin: Four Courts Press, 2011), pp. 117–49.
66 Townsend, 'The Intellectual and Cultural Interests of Women in Ireland, *c.*1740–*c.*1840', pp. 169–71.
67 *DIB* entry on Elizabeth Hastings, Countess of Moira, by Rosemary Richey.
68 RIA MS F 23 3, Sir William Rowan Hamilton to Maria Edgeworth, 12 January 1838.

Edgeworth's vision of a meeting of intellectual men with like-minded women in a social setting.

The Public Image of the Woman Writer

Edgeworth and Owenson were, of course two of the most well-known women of their generation. The editors of *A Guide to Irish Fiction, 1650–1900* noted the increase in the number of published female authors in the forty years from 1780 to 1820 and the corresponding decrease in the use of pseudonyms by women writers.[69] The woman writer had become an acceptable social figure. Maria Edgeworth and Sydney Owenson each constructed a public image as an Irish woman writer although they differed in their emphasis and presentation.

Maria Edgeworth's first novel, *Castle Rackrent*, appeared in 1800 and was followed by a series of novels over the next twelve years which established Edgeworth's reputation as one of the outstanding novelists of her time.[70] Apart from her novels, Edgeworth wrote didactic texts on education and the rearing of children and her first published work, *Letters for Literary Ladies* (1798), supported the notion of the educated woman. Her last novel, *Helen*, also presented a strong argument in favour of women's education.

Following her father's death in 1817, Edgeworth developed a 'literary social presence' in London. She had a wide circle of literary acquaintances including Sir Walter Scott and William Wordsworth who visited her in her home in Edgeworthstown, Co. Longford. Edgeworth also engaged with the public world of literary discourse as her work was reviewed, mostly favourably, in the most prominent periodicals of early nineteenth-century Britain. As she gained a public reputation as a writer, she created a role as a literary patron, offering advice and support to other writers, particularly women. Although Edgeworth was from a landed Anglo-Irish background, she dealt with her publishers in a professional manner and astutely negotiated the terms of her contracts. According to W. J. MCormack, she was 'the most commercially successful novelist of her age'.[71]

---

69 Rolf Loeber et al., *A Guide to Irish Fiction, 1650–1900* (Dublin: Four Courts Press, 2006), p. lxxxiv. A similar trend is noted for women poets by Anne Coleman, *A Dictionary of Nineteenth Century Irish Women Poets* (Galway: Kenny's Bookshop, 1996). The majority of the published Irish women poets of the nineteenth century were born after 1830 and did not begin their publishing careers until the late 1840s or later. Only a small number established a public reputation in the early decades of the century.
70 See *ODNB* entry by W. J. McCormack and the *DIB* entry by Edwina Keown.
71 *ODNB* entry by W. J. McCormack. For Edgeworth's negotiations with her publishers see also Townsend, 'The Intellectual and Cultural Interests of Women in Ireland, c.1740–c.1840', p. 106.

Edgeworth cultivated an image of a 'literary lady' who engaged with the literary worlds of London and to a lesser extent of Dublin and Ireland. Her public image was similar to that of the English bluestocking women and her correspondence with Rowan Hamilton suggests that she would have liked to have emulated the London salons of the group in Dublin. Many of Edgeworth's publications fitted into the socially conservative agenda of the bluestocking women. Edgeworth baulked at the idea of being described as a writer of novels, preferring to refer to her novel *Belinda* as a 'moral tale' rather than a novel because 'so much folly, error and vice are disseminated in books classed under this denomination.'[72] Edgeworth's *Letters for Literary Ladies* also rehearsed much of the discussion on women's education that would have been familiar to women writers linked to the bluestocking movement.[73] Like More's *Strictures on Modern Education*, the two-volume *Practical Education* that Edgeworth wrote with her father, Richard Love Edgeworth, critiqued Rousseau's theories on the education of children.[74]

Sydney Owenson's public image as an Irish woman writer was in sharp contrast to that of Edgeworth. Unlike the latter, Owenson embraced the idea of being designated as an Irish novelist and she hoped to emulate the commercial success of English women novelists such as Fanny Burney.[75] Owenson, however, also looked to French women writers for suitable models. She was particularly taken by Germaine De Staël, whose public image as a writer of French national stories Owenson tried to adapt to an Irish setting.[76]

Owenson's third novel, *The Wild Irish Girl*, was a commercial success. Seven editions appeared within a two-year period from 1805 to 1807. The novel confirmed Owenson's public image as the Irish woman novelist. As

---

72 Cited in *ODNB* entry by W. J. McCormack.
73 *Letters for Literary Ladies: To Which is Added, an Essay on the Noble Science of Self-Justification* (London: printed for J. Johnson, 1795).
74 Catherine Toal, 'Control Experiment: Edgeworth's Critique of Rousseau's Educational Theory', in Heidi Kaufman and Chris Fauske (eds), *An Uncomfortable Authority: Maria Edgeworth and Her Contexts* (Newark, Del.: University of Delaware Press, 2004), pp. 212–31; Jessica Richard, '"Games of Chance": Belinda, Education, and Empire', ibid., pp. 192–211.
75 Mary Campbell, *Lady Morgan: The Life and Times of Sydney Owenson* (London: Pandora Press, 1988), p. 39.
76 Julie Donovan, *Sydney Owenson, Lady Morgan and the Politics of Style* (Bethesda: Maunsel & Co., 2009), pp. 9, 96; Clíona Ó Gallchoir, 'Germaine de Staël and the Response of Sydney Owenson and Maria Edgeworth', in Eamon Maher and Grace Neville (eds), *France–Ireland: Anatomy of a Friendship – Studies in History, Literature and Politics* (Frankfurt am Main: Peter Lang, 2004); Lionel Stevenson, *The Wild Irish Girl: The Life of Sydney Owenson, Lady Morgan (1776–1859)* (New York: Chapman and Hall, 1936), pp. 111–12.

Julia Donovan has detailed, Owenson fostered her public identification with the main female character in the novel, Glorvina, a well-read young Irish woman who was also an accomplished harpist, singer and dancer. Owenson 'acted out the role of Glorvina in her own life signing off on her letters as "Glorvina" and attending parties where she donned ancient Celtic costume'.[77] The wild Irish girl, and the image that it created, was so popular that shopkeepers in Dublin advertised 'Glorvina' mantles and scarlet cloaks while fashionable women wore Glorvina bodkins.[78]

Owenson and Edgeworth also in different ways espoused the right of women to literature and engaged with the emerging feminist writings. In the writings of both authors, women were usually the central characters. Owenson more consciously than Edgeworth related her writing to early European feminism. Her novel, *Woman, or Ida of Athens* which was published in 1809 was inspired by de Staël's *Corine ou l'Italie* (1807).[79] Owenson's stated aim in the novel was 'to delineate the character of woman in the perfection of its natural state'.[80] This theme was developed further in Owenson's last book, *Woman and her Master* which argued that men and women had complementary characteristics but that of superior intelligence was allotted to women.[81]

Edgeworth and Owenson both cultivated public profiles as writers in different ways. Other women authors were more hesitant about emerging into the public world of print. The Quaker Mary Leadbeater was fifty years of age before she published a book of poetry in her own name in 1808,[82] although she had been writing since she was a teenager. As Nini Rodgers suggests, it is likely that Leadbeater circulated her poems and extracts from her journal among family and friends long before she became a published author.[83] Between 1811 and 1823, Leadbeater published a series of books in dialogue format that provide advice on household management and virtuous behaviour to Irish peasants. The first, *Cottage Dialogues* was a commercial success with four editions appearing between 1811 and 1813. Leadbeater's fame as a woman writer was, however, posthumous and

---

77 Julie Donovan, *Sydney Owenson, Lady Morgan and the Politics of Style*, p. 3.
78 Ibid., p. 72.
79 It was published in London by Longman, Hurst, Rees and Orme
80 Stevenson, *The Wild Irish Girl: The Life of Sydney Owenson, Lady Morgan (1776–1859)*, pp. 111–12.
81 Sydney Owenson, *Woman and her Master* (2 vols; London: Henry Colburn, 1840).
82 Leadbeater's first volume of poetry: *Extracts and Original Anecdotes for the Improvement of Youth* had been published anonymously in 1794 (Dublin: R. M. Jackson).
83 Nini Rodgers, 'Two Quakers and a Utilitarian: The Reaction of Three Irish Women Writers to the Problem of Slavery, 1789–1807', *Proceedings of the Royal Irish Academy*, 100C, 4 (2000), pp. 140–41; entry on Leadbeater by Maria Luddy in *ODNB*.

developed following the publication of her 'Annals of Ballitore' by her niece, Elizabeth Shackleton.[84]

Another woman who, like Leadbeater, slowly emerged as a public writer was Anna Doyle Wheeler. Born in County Tipperary in 1785, Wheeler was privately educated and by her teenage years was reading widely in French philosophy and political thought. According to her daughter, Rosina, Doyle Wheeler 'tainted by the ... poison of Mrs Wollstonecraft's book supported the French Revolution'.[85] Following her separation from her husband, Doyle Wheeler lived in France for some time and befriended social reformers there. She also became a close friend to Irishman William Thompson and collaborated with him when he authored *An Appeal of One Half the Human Race, Women, Against the Pretensions of the Other Half, Men, to Retain Them in Political, and thence in Civil and Domestic Slavery* which appeared in 1825. Thompson acknowledged in an introductory letter to the text that he had been strongly influenced by his discussions with Doyle Wheeler on the status of women. The *Appeal* fused together the demands of eighteenth-century writers for the better education for women with the call of British and French radical writers for institutional reform of church and state. It was not, however, until the late 1820s that Wheeler developed an independent public profile through public lectures in London on women's rights.[86]

The Philanthropic Woman and Protestant Evangelicalism

Despite the women writers' championing of women as heroines and intellectuals, a far more acceptable public role for women remained that of the philanthropist and carer of the poor, particularly indigent women and children. As David Garrioch has argued, 'philanthropy was central to the Enlightenment's definition of itself. Those two key elements of behaviour that were such central characteristics of the enlightened individual, sensibility and sociability, were both inextricably linked with philanthropy.'[87] English historians have documented the extent to which evangelical Protestantism created a new public role for wealthy women in the middle decades of the

---

84 *The Leadbeater Papers. The Annals of Ballitore With a Memoir of the Author* (2 vols; London: Bell and Daldy, 1862). See also entry in *DIB* by Maureen E Mulvihill.
85 Dolores Dooley, *Equality in Community: Sexuality Equality in the Writings of William Thompson and Anna Doyle Wheeler* (Cork: Cork University Press, 1996), p. 59.
86 Mary O'Dowd (ed.), 'The Political Writings and Public Voices of Women, *c.*1500–1850', in Angela Bourke et al. (eds), *The Field Day Anthology of Irish Writing, Volume 5: Irish Women's Writing and Traditions* (Cork: Cork University Press, 2002), pp. 63–64.
87 David Garrioch, 'Making a Better World. Enlightenment and Philanthropy', in Martin Fitzpatrick et al. (eds), *The Enlightenment World* (London: Routledge, 2004), p. 496.

eighteenth century. Some, like Selina Hastings, Countess of Huntingdon, had links with women in Ireland and were the means through which a small network of Irish women became enthusiastic supporters of evangelical religion.[88] As with their English counterparts, women from landed families established small charitable projects on their family estates while others developed a more public profile through their involvement in projects that had the support of the Irish parliament.[89] In the 1790s, *Walker's Hibernian Magazine* presented the wealthy woman philanthropist as an ideal public role model for other women as it published as its frontispiece engravings of Irish women associated with charity work. In March 1794, for example, the magazine printed an engraving of Lady Fitzgibbon, the wife of the Lord Chancellor, seated at a spinning wheel alongside a text that praised her public and private work for the indigent.[90] In February 1796, the cover engraving was of Elizabeth Latouche who had a public profile as a supporter of charity projects, particularly on her family estate at Delgany.[91]

The expansion of Protestant missionary work in the first half of the nineteenth century also extended the public work of women as they joined a myriad of voluntary organisations contributing to Sunday school teaching, the temperance movement and evangelical societies distributing bibles and other religious tracts. As David Hempton and Myrtle Hill note, 'women gave their time, commitment and local knowledge to the furtherance of these causes, and the result was a growing professionalism and a considerable broadening of physical and spiritual horizons.'[92]

The opening of public space to the woman philanthropist led indirectly to a widening of women's participation in Irish political life. The consumer market and, more particularly, the country of origin of manufactured goods were inextricably linked to the demand for parliamentary reform and projects to improve the Irish economy. In public discourse, commentators linked the wealthy woman consumer of Parisian fashions and other imported luxury goods with Irish poverty. From the middle decades of the eighteenth century, aristocratic women associated with the court at Dublin Castle constructed a more positive image of the woman consumer

---

88 On the 'new role' for women created by the expansion of Protestant evangelicalism see Jane Rendall, *The Origins of Modern Feminism: Women in Britain, France and the United States* (Basingstoke: Macmillan, 1985), pp. 93–96. On women in Ireland see David Hempton and Myrtle Hill, *Evangelical Protestantism in Ulster Society, 1740–1890* (London: Routledge, 1992), pp. 129–42. See also Nancy Cott, 'Passionlessness: An Interpretation of Anglo-American Sexual Ideology, 1790–1840'. *Signs*, 4 (1978), pp. 219–36.
89 O'Dowd, *A History of Women in Ireland, 1500–1800*, pp. 43–70.
90 *Walker's Hibernian Magazine*, March 1794.
91 *Walker's Hibernian Magazine*, February 1796.
92 Hempton and Hill, *Evangelical Protestantism in Ulster Society, 1740–1890*, p. 199.

who rejected foreign manufactured goods in favour of buying Irish. The prototype of the virtuous woman consumer was enhanced in the 1770s when Irish women were urged to imitate the 'American ladies' who had led the boycott against the purchase of imported British goods. The woman consumer who shunned the latest imported fashions in favour of often less flattering home-manufactured clothes was a politically important construct that prevailed into the twentieth century.[93]

The Catholic Lay Woman and Irish Patriotism

The Protestant evangelical woman pioneered the role of the publicly active woman in Ireland. Gradually, however, in the last quarter of the eighteenth century, Catholic lay women also began to emerge into the public sphere as sponsors of schools, orphanages and other institutions for the poor. The trend began in urban centres where women, such as Nano Nagle and Teresa Mulally, became involved in teaching poor children.[94]

Like her Protestant counterpart, the Catholic lay woman frequently entered the public sphere as a fund-raiser. In the 1760s, Teresa Mulally, for example, pioneered a fund-raising scheme in the parish where her school was based. The format of the account established by Mulally allowed for subscriptions to be paid on a weekly, monthly, quarterly or annual basis. This enabled Mulally to look for contributions from parishioners from varied economic backgrounds: from wealthy Catholic families as well as from women traders in inner-city Dublin.[95]

The role of the Catholic lay woman as fund-raiser was enhanced in the early decades of the nineteenth century as more Catholic charitable institutions were established. Newspapers such as the *Freeman's Journal* also began to list the donors, male and female, who had contributed to particular funds.[96] The egalitarian parish-based funding scheme that

---

93 Mary O'Dowd, 'Politics, Patriotism, and Women in Ireland, Britain and Colonial America, *c*.1700–1780', *Journal of Women's History*, 22, 4 (Winter 2010), pp. 15–38; Padraig Higgins, *A Nation of Politicians: Gender, Patriotism, and Political Culture in Late Eighteenth-Century Ireland* (Madison: University of Wisconsin Press, 2010); Martyn J. Powell, *The Politics of Consumption in Eighteenth-Century Ireland* (Basingstoke: Palgrave Macmillan, 2005).

94 See entry by Noreen Giffney on Nagle in *DIB*. See also *ODNB* entry by Rosemary Raughter, and T. J. Walsh, *Nano Nagle and the Presentation Sisters* (Dublin: M. H. Gill, 1959).

95 See account for subscribers in Presentation Order Archive, George's Hill, Dublin; R. Raughter, 'A Discreet Benevolence: Female Philanthropy and the Catholic Resurgence in 18th-Century Ireland', *Women's History Review*, 6 (1997), pp. 465–84.

96 *Freeman's Journal* regularly printed notices of Catholic charities in which women were

Mulally used was also adapted by the Catholic Association founded by Daniel O'Connell in 1824.[97] Although women were not admitted as members of the Association, there were no gender restrictions on the collection of the Association's Catholic Rent and contributions from women were welcome from the start. The Association also encouraged women to form separate female committees locally to contribute to a 'Ladies' Catholic Rent'. A clever method of encouraging donations was to follow the model of the charity organisations and print the names of those who made the largest donations in the newspapers.[98] Newspapers that were supportive of O'Connell, such as the *Freeman's Journal* and *The Pilot*, published long lists of individual donations including those made by women. Although most contributions came from well-off business and merchant families, the published lists also included donations made by household servants.[99] The Catholic Association thus, perhaps unintentionally, drew more Irish women of all economic classes into the public sphere. Among the papers of the Catholic Association in the Dublin Diocesan Library is an undated printed address to the ladies of the County Dublin parishes of Rathfarnham, Bohernabreena and Swords, urging them to contribute to this fund. Nineteen women are listed as donors, including two female servants. It is the earliest known Irish political circular specifically addressed to women and is striking evidence of the way in which fund-raising for the Catholic Association widened women's political involvement.[100] It is impossible to assess the exact contribution of women to the Catholic Rent but a statistical analysis of the printed names suggests that women represented between ten and fifteen per cent of the total.

In addition to fund-raising, large numbers of women attended the public meetings of the Catholic Association. The gallery in meeting places (which was often the local Catholic church) was reserved for women attendees.[101]

---

involved. See, for example, *Freeman's Journal*, 26 January 1825; 19 September 1836. See also *Drogheda Journal*, 1 January 1825, which noted the women involved in the town's Catholic Female Charity School; *The Pilot*, 29 December 1828, listed the female and male subscribers to a fund for the establishment of a Catholic free school in Dublin by the Education Society under the auspices of the Catholic archbishop of Dublin.

97 For a more detailed study of women and O'Connellite politics see Mary O'Dowd, 'O'Connell and the Lady Patriots: Women and O'Connellite politics, 1824–1845', in Allan Blackstock and Eoin Magennis (eds), *Politics and Political Culture in Britain and Ireland, 1750–1850: Essays in Tribute to Peter Jupp* (Belfast: Blackstaff Press, 2007), pp. 283–303.

98 Initially, donations of ten shillings or over were listed but over time the names of those who made smaller subscriptions were also printed.

99 See, for example, *Freeman's Journal*, August 1828; *The Pilot*, 5 December 1828.

100 Papers of the Catholic Association, Dublin Diocesan Library.

101 See, for example, *The Times*, 25 October 1828; Thomas Wyse, *Historical Sketch of the*

As one report of the Leinster provincial meeting in a Kilkenny chapel in 1828 noted, 'there were women without end in the gallery.'[102] A separate female space was also regularly provided at the dinners organised by the Association following the major town rallies.[103]

The leadership of the Catholic Association sanctioned the public participation of women in its campaign for a number of reasons. Firstly, and perhaps, most importantly, it recognised the value of women as fund-raisers. Secondly, in his speeches, O'Connell presented the movement that he led as more than a political organisation. It represented the moral force of the Irish people, which included men, women and children. The visible presence of women at the meetings of the Catholic Association endorsed that view. There was also a significant charitable dimension to the Catholic Association which facilitated the involvement of women.[104] The funds accumulated through the rent were managed like a charity and used for a variety of philanthropic causes. The Association, for example, sponsored schools for the poor as well as a 'seminary for young Catholic girls' and made regular donations to the Catholic Book Society formed to disseminate Catholic texts among the poor.[105] Thus the work that the women did on behalf of the Association could be presented as philanthropic rather than as involvement in a political organisation that might be perceived as men's business.

A third reason why women were welcome as supporters of the Catholic Association relates to the influence of British radicalism on the political ideas of Daniel O'Connell. Like other radicals, O'Connell had voiced his support in theory for the equality of men and women. As a young law student in London in 1796, he had read Mary Wollestonecraft's *A Vindication of the Rights of Women* (1792). He noted in his journal his concurrence with Wollstonecraft's views on the status of women but that he had not yet decided 'what portion of power in the government of the world ought to be entrusted to the female

---

Late Catholic Association of Ireland (2 vols; London: Henry Colburn, 1829), vol. 2, p. lvi; *Drogheda Journal*, 5 February 1825; 29 June 1825; 7 January 1826; 27 September 1826; 3 January 1827; 16 January 1828.

102 Account by Thomas Creevey cited in James A. Reynolds, *The Catholic Emancipation Crisis in Ireland, 1823–1829* (New Haven, Conn.: Yale University Press, 1954), p. 30.

103 Mary O'Dowd, 'O'Connell and the Lady Patriots: Women and O'Connellite politics, 1824–1845', pp. 283–303.

104 See the 'Report on the Practicability of Forming the New Catholic Association – Agreed to at the Aggregate Meeting held 13th July 1825', printed in Thomas Wyse, *Historical Sketch of the Late Catholic Association of Ireland*, vol. 1, appendix, pp. xxxix–xlvii.

105 See Minute Book of the Proceedings of the Catholic Association, September–October 1828 (NLI, MS 3290); Charles Chenevix Trench, *The Great Dan: A Biography of Daniel O'Connell* (London: Jonathan Cape, 1984), p. 144; *Freeman's Journal*, 19 April 1824. See also the minutes of the Financial Committee of the Association, 1826–35 (Dublin Diocesan Archives, Catholic Association papers, 55/2).

sex'.[106] Like many of his contemporaries, O'Connell's views on women were rooted in his belief in the special characteristics of what he referred to as the 'better and softer sex'.[107] In one of his longest speeches on female qualities, O'Connell spoke of his own relatives: his granddaughters, daughters, mother and his late wife in affectionate terms that stressed their familiar rather than their public role. Women, he claimed, had 'a purity which stripped them of vice, and made celestial all the tender affections which so peculiarly belong to them. Oh, they watched over our childhood – soothed the cares of youth and the sorrows of manhood – cheered and supported old age, and even smoothed the dreary path which leads to the grave.'[108]

The particular characteristics that O'Connell associated with women did not preclude their participation in public life. In fact, O'Connell's utilisation of moral force as a political instrument could be said to have enhanced women's political role. A good example of this is O'Connell's defence of women's right to petition parliament for the abolition of slavery in terms which stressed their moral authority: 'if ever the female had the right to interfere, it was upon that occasion.' O'Connell also argued that the strength of the anti-slavery movement lay in the fact that it was a 'complete expression of public opinion.... [The petitions] were signed by persons in every grade, and of every age, and of every class; and both sexes united in demanding, that slavery should be put to an end.'[109] O'Connell used very similar rhetoric in Ireland. Like the anti-slavery movement, he argued that Catholic Emancipation was a morally just demand and that the campaign to

---

106 Arthur Houston (ed.), *Daniel O'Connell: His Early Life, and Journal, 1795–1802* (London: Pitman Press, 1906), p. 102. See also Oliver MacDonagh, *The Hereditary Bondsman: Daniel O'Connell 1775–1829* (London: Weidenfeld and Nicolson, 1988), p. 42.
107 *The Times*, 25 November 1841. See also his acknowledgement of the address from women in Kilkenny in October 1840 (*Freeman's Journal*, 16 October 1840).
108 *Freeman's Journal*, 16 October 1840. Neither O'Connell's wife nor any of his daughters took a prominent role in his political campaign although they did on occasion appear at meetings with him. William Fagan suggested that one of O'Connell's daughters may have contributed to the Catholic journal *The Dublin Review* sponsored by her father. See William Fagan, *The Life and Times of Daniel O'Connell* (2 vols; Cork: J. O'Brien, 1847–48), vol. 2, p. 594.
109 House of Commons debate on the abolition of slavery, 3 June 1833, p. 315, col. 1: http://hansard.millbanksystems.com/commons/1833/jun/03/ (accessed 3 March 2012). See also Clare Midgley, *Women Against Slavery: The British Campaigns, 1780–1870* (London: Routledge, 1992), p. 64. For O'Connell and the anti-slavery campaign see Douglas Riaich, 'Ireland and the Campaign against American Slavery, 1830–1860' (unpublished Ph.D. thesis, University of Edinburgh, 1975), chapter 3; Maurice J. Bric, 'Daniel O'Connell and the Debate on Anti-Slavery, 1820–50', in Tom Dunne and Laurence J. Geary (eds), *History and the Public Sphere: Essays in Honour of John A. Murphy* (Cork: Cork University Press, 2005), pp. 69–82. The authors are grateful to Dr Nini Rodgers for these references.

achieve it transcended quotidian politics, which made it an appropriate cause for women to support. Nonetheless, O'Connell did not endorse women's participation in more routine political affairs.

The ambiguity of O'Connell's attitude to women in the public sphere was evident during the 1840s campaign to repeal the Act of Union. In some ways, women's role in the Loyal National Repeal Association (LNRA), founded by O'Connell in April 1840, represented an advance on their work for the Catholic Association.[110] Women were once again valued as fund-raisers and, as before, the names of subscribers and collectors of large sums of money were published in the newspapers.[111] Unlike in the earlier campaign, however, women were admitted as members of the LNRA and were permitted to sit in the main hall as well as in the gallery.[112]

Two months after the establishment of the LNRA, the World Anti-Slavery Convention in London met in London in June 1840. The British organisers of the convention objected to the presence of women among the American delegates but O'Connell famously defended the right of the women to attend. He repeated his belief that the 'mind has no sex' and after some initial hesitation, wrote in favour of the women delegates being admitted to an 'equal share and right of discussion'.[113] O'Connell was, however, careful to guard against establishing any more general rights for women that might be applied in England or in his own organisations in Ireland. He pointed out that the customs concerning the status of women at public meetings in England and North America were different. While in England women did not sit on the platform, they did do so in the United States and, therefore, the London convention should respect this practice.[114]

O'Connell was uncharacteristically silent on Ireland in his letter to the American women, perhaps because he was aware that women in Ireland had

---

110 Mary Ray, the daughter of the secretary of the Association, was the first woman to recruit twenty Repealers and she was enrolled as the first female member of the Association (see *Freeman's Journal*, 5 January 1841). The authors are grateful to Dr Jackie Hill for this reference.
111 Based on a selective analysis of names listed in *Freeman's Journal*.
112 *Freeman's Journal*, 2 October 1840.
113 Jacqueline Van Voris, 'Daniel O'Connell and Women's Rights, One Letter', *Éire–Ireland*, 17, 3 (1982), pp. 37–38. See also F. B. Tolles (ed.), *Slavery and 'The Woman Question': Lucretia Mott's Diary of Her Visit to Great Britain to Attend the World's Anti-Slavery Convention of 1840* (*Journal of the Friends Historical Society*, Supplement 23) (Haverford, Pa. and London: Friends' Historical Association and Friends' Historical Society, 1952); Kathryn Kish Sklar, '"Women Who Speak For an Entire Nation": American and British Women at the World Anti-Slavery Convention, London, 1840', in Jean Fagan Yellin and John C. Van Horne (eds), *The Abolitionist Sisterhood: Women's Political Culture in Antebellum America* (Ithaca, NY and London: Cornell University Press, 1994), pp. 301–33.
114 Jacqueline Van Voris, 'Daniel O'Connell and Women's Rights, One Letter', p. 38.

taken a more prominent role in political agitation than they had in England. The debate on the American delegation at the anti-slavery convention had, however, revealed the level of opposition to women's engagement with public agitation in England. It may have been for this reason that O'Connell thought it necessary to set limits to the involvement of women in the Repeal campaign. In December 1840, he asserted that while women were welcome to attend meetings of the LNRA, it was a breach of rules to address them directly from the platform: 'although we are most happy in being cheered and honoured by their presence amongst us, still they are not considered to be present.'[115]

The involvement of women in the public world of politics was not a new development in the 1820s. Women from all social backgrounds had participated in a variety of ways in Irish political life since the 1770s.[116] What was new in the 1820s, however, was the incremental rise in the number of women who participated in public and often overtly political events. It is not possible to estimate precisely the numbers of women who were engaged in various ways in O'Connell's campaigns, but given the widespread popularity of the campaigns led by O'Connell it must have involved hundreds of thousands of women. Even those who could not read could participate in the political debate, as measures were taken in the 1820s and again in the 1840s for public readings of the proceedings of the Dublin meetings.[117]

If a more intense politicisation of women can be detected in Ireland during the O'Connellite era, to what extent is this manifest in the views expressed by women? Although it is possible to explain the participation of women in the Catholic Association as an extension of their involvement in charity organisations, it is clear from the statements of the women that they were politically aware and knowledgeable about the specific demands of the Catholic Emancipation and Repeal campaigns. The letters that accompanied the group subscriptions sent in by women usually included an explicit identification of the women with the political causes of Emancipation and Repeal and the absence of any apology for their participation, as women, in public affairs. In one of the earliest printed letters in 1824, Emily McNevin, on behalf of a group of women in Loughrea, wrote of her 'enthusiastic zeal for civil and religious liberty' and explained that O'Connell had convinced her and the other women that 'our cause is the cause of justice'.[118] In 1840, other women defended their support for repeal of the union through reference

115 *Freeman's Journal*, 22 December 1840.
116 See O'Dowd, *A History of Women in Ireland, 1500–1800*, pp. 43–70.
117 See the painting by George Mulvany entitled *Reading the Nation*. Prominent in the picture of a group of people listening to the reading of the newspaper are two young women.
118 *The Times*, 31 December 1824.

to Irish history and the role of women in it. The women in Limerick, for example, recalled 'the noble example shown by the women of Limerick in 1691' while in Kilkenny it was noted that in 'the struggle for national independence the women were not inactive'. The latter group also justified their involvement in political affairs by recalling that 'it was one of our sex who brought the tyrant upon Erin's green valleys; it is, therefore, the more specially our duty to tender our humble aid to burst the tyrant chain'.[119]

In October 1840, O'Connell visited the Ursuline Convent in Waterford city where an address was read to him by one of the girls. It asserted unequivocally the identification of the convent girls with the cause of Repeal: 'We are all Repealers here. Are we not? Yes; a thousand times yes. We are devoted to you, and unworthy of the high name of Irish girls would we be could any power on earth make us flinch from your standard…'[120] Like the Irish history taught at the Cork convent, the French model of an Ursuline education was being adopted to suit the circumstances in Ireland in the 1840s.

Conclusion

The historiography on the history of women in Ireland traditionally identifies the last decades of the nineteenth century as a time of advancement for women in intellectual and political life.[121] Yet, in the fifty years before the Great Famine, the figures for female literacy grew rapidly, more women received a structured education and it became respectable for women to hold strong political views and express those views in public venues. In some respects, it could be argued that women were freer to participate in mainstream political movements in the pre-Famine period than they were later in the century. O'Connell may have set limits to women's participation in the Repeal movement in later years, but he never banned women from attending public meetings as the Irish Parliamentary Party was to do in the early twentieth century. Political rhetoric in the early nineteenth century encouraged women to become involved in political campaigning, but at the end of the century it was concerned to set limits to female engagement

---

119 *Freeman's Journal*, 16 October 1840. This was a reference to Derbfhorgaill (*c.*1108–93), queen-consort of Bréifne who allegedly eloped with Diarmait Mac Murchada, the Leinster lord who was believed to be responsible for bringing the first Norman soldiers to Ireland. See the entry by Máire Ní Mhaonaigh in *DIB*.
120 *Freeman's Journal*, 31 October 1840.
121 See, for example, Rosemary Cullen Owens, *A Social History of Women in Ireland* (Dublin: Gill and Macmillan, 2005); Alvin Jackson, *Ireland 1798–1998: Politics and War* (Oxford: Blackwell, 1999).

with public life. The advancements made by women in the first half of the nineteenth century are documented in the *Dictionary of Irish Biography*, which charts a two-fold increase in entries between 1800 and 1850 as women philanthropists, foundresses of religious community, educators, writers, artists, antiquarians and scholars gained public recognition and respectability.

There was a class dimension to the public advancement of women at this time. The women who appeared in publicly visible roles were nearly all from middle- or upper-class backgrounds, although their religious affiliation was clearly more diverse. Women in rural Ireland, particularly among the small tenant and labouring classes had neither the leisure nor the means to read books and newspapers. The O'Connellite campaigns were strongest, particularly among female supporters, in the towns and cities. Yet, it would be misleading to suggest that education only made an impact on the lives of middle- and upper-class women. The acquisition of literacy skills through private and state-funded schools widened the employment opportunities of young rural as well as urban women and gave them a means through which to exercise some control over their lives. Kerby Miller et al have pointed to the 'strong positive correlation between literacy and emigration' and the rise in female emigration as more women learnt to read and write.[122] Young women in the early decades of the nineteenth century could read for themselves the literate culture associated with emigration in the form of letters, shipping advertisements as well as newspaper reports on the new world. As, the next section makes clear, the single Irish female emigrant represented a significant proportion of the Irish-American community in the 1820s and 1830s. Literacy, female agency and emigration are thus inextricably linked.

There is little tangible evidence that Irish women believed that women were treated more equitably in North America than they were in Ireland. The second section in this volume indicates, however, that many had absorbed the popular view of America as a land of liberty and freedom and, by osmosis, the rhetoric associated with the proto-feminism of Enlightenment thought. When women wrote of their desire to travel to the land of 'happiness' and of 'liberty' and 'freedom', they were, although they may not have known it, revealing the influence of the Enlightenment on their use of language and, by extension, their mode of thought.[123]

---

122 Patrick O'Sullivan (ed.), *Irish Women and Irish Migration* (London: Leicester University Press, 1995), p. 46.
123 See chapter three, pp. 90, 121. Kerby Miller, David N. Doyle and Patricia Kelleher '"For Love and Liberty": Irish Women, Migration and Domesticity in Ireland and America, 1815–1920', in Patrick O'Sullivan (ed.), *The Irish World Wide: History, Heritage, Identity, Volume 4* (London and Washington: Leicester University Press, 1995), p. 48.

Emigration

3
The Emigrant Encounters the 'New World', c.1851–1960

Introduction

Irish women's encounters with Enlightenment ideas about female education and societal roles were complex and defining for some women. The first section argued that there was a radical and a moderate view on women's role and status emanating from contrasting concepts of equality between the sexes. Roman Catholicism, embourgeoisement and Enlightenment influences combined to shape the values of Catholic society as well as to define female behaviour in the pre-Famine period. The two chapters in the first case study in the volume, suggest that most women were influenced one way or another by at least a moderate view of equality. By the eve of the 1845–53 Famine, the woman reader, the school-going girl, the female religious and the woman patriot had expanded definitions of womanhood at least for upper- and increasingly middle-class women. This would continue with the female emigrant who is the focus of the next case study. She also exercised an element of choice and control over her life albeit within the wider context of the family.

Emigration became an integral part of Irish society. Irish arrivals in the USA peaked at 1.8 million in 1890, and ten years later the second generation Irish in America exceeded 3.3 million. By 1931 mass migration to the USA almost ceased.[1] When emigration to the USA resumed after 1945, it was still small relative to Britain, but significant in terms of the 'continuity of

---

1 Tracey Connolly, 'Emigration from Independent Ireland: 1922–1970' (unpublished Ph.D. thesis, University College Cork, 1999), p. viii; Patrick J. Blessing, 'The Irish in America', in Michael Glazier (ed.), *The Encyclopedia of the Irish in America* (Notre Dame, Ind.: University of Notre Dame, 1999), p. 454.

Irish migration ... and the perpetuation of Irish and ethnic community life'.[2] In other words, despite the decline in departures for the USA after 1931, a depth of contact was set and the encounter became two-way in the form of the 'return tide' of emigrants, money, letters and packages.[3] On the eve of the Famine, the concept and reality that was 'America' had already changed many Irish women's lives, both those leaving and those staying behind. The latter's lives were continuously effected by the subsequent indirect contact with American society and in time the 'return tide'. This chapter examines how knowledge of America entered Irish women's lives through the emigrant experience; the nature of that two-way encounter; and finally how the emigrant experience extended Irish women's horizons so that an expanded concept of 'America' evolved over time.

All that can be known for definite about nineteenth-century emigrants is that they 'took those steps up the gangway and onto the ship'.[4] The 'push–pull' explanatory model for emigration defines the push factors as religious and political oppression, lack of employment, population pressure and the pull factors as a tolerant society, greater economic and social opportunities, better working conditions and higher standards of living. Towards the end of the nineteenth century, additional push factors such as personal improvement and pull factors such as the appeal of urban centres became significant. Obviously the timing was occasionally influenced by specific personal, national and international events. But there is also 'uncertainty' about the relative influence of any one factor on the emigrant and if the decision to leave was even a 'rational' one.[5] Nonetheless, the very step onto the gangway represented a break with family, home and place and some change in the lives of the individual and community was inevitable. This applied to men

---

2 Kerby Miller, *Emigrants and Exile* (New York: Oxford University Press, 1985), p. 199; Linda Dowling Almeida, 'A Great Time to Be in America: The Irish in Post-Second World War New York City', in Dermot Keogh, Finbarr O'Shea and Carmel Quinlan (eds), *Ireland: The Lost Decade in the 1950s* (Cork: Mercier Press, 2004), p. 206; Mary E. Daly, *The Slow Failure: Population Decline and Independent Ireland, 1920–1973* (Madison: University of Wisconsin Press, 2006), p. 260.
3 Arnold Schrier, *Ireland and the American Emigration* (Chester Springs, Pa.: Dufours Editions, 1997), p. 151.
4 Caitriona Clear, *Social Change and Everyday Life in Ireland, 1850–1922* (Manchester: Manchester University Press, 2007), p. 63.
5 Enda Delaney, 'Irish Migration to Britain, 1921–71: Patterns, Trends and Contingent Factors' (unpublished Ph.D. thesis, Queen's University Belfast, 1997), pp. 33–36; Enda Delaney, 'Gender and Twentieth-Century Irish Migration, 1921–1971', in Pamela Sharpe (ed.), *Women, Gender and Labour Migration: Historical and Global Perspectives* (London: Routledge, 2001), pp. 209–24; Padraic Travers, 'Emigration and Gender', in Mary O'Dowd and Sabine Wichert (eds), *Chattel, Servant or Citizen: Women's Status in Church, State and Society* (Belfast: Institute of Irish Studies, 1995), pp. 187–99.

and women alike.[6] Recent research suggests that the traditional view of seeing women as 'secondary emigrants' is less relevant for any stage of the process. Women were actively involved in the decision, whether it was their own or that of family or friends.[7] The implication of female agency in the decision to leave for the USA suggests that by 1850 the female emigrant was an integral figure in the transatlantic relationship.[8] Moreover, as outlined in chapter two, the continuing expansion in female education, with the acquisition of reading and writing skills as well as the gradual abandoning of the Irish language, enabled more emigrants to be better informed about emigration while also preparing them for the challenge that lay ahead in the public rather than the private world. The availability of letters, advertisements for shipping lines in posters, newspapers and guidebooks, as well as the extension of the National School system of education from 1832 onwards strengthened the link between education, literacy and emigration, as noted in chapter two.[9] Towards the end of the century, F. L. Dingley, a State Department official, who conducted a survey of the emigrant countries in western Europe, commented that the majority of the emigrants out of Queenstown, the busiest emigration port in Ireland, could read and write.[10]

Cultural Engagement:
Knowledge of American life, 1600–1914

From the seventeenth century onwards America, shaped in part by the Enlightenment influences of liberalism and republicanism, was seen as a place of religious toleration, political freedom, a place where land could be obtained and a country of urban and industrial growth rather than a place of oppression, poverty and failure. Chapter one revealed how the concept of republican America was present in radical periodical literature read by

---

6 William E. Van Vugt, *Britain to America: Mid-Nineteenth Century Immigrants to the United States* (Urbana and Chicago: University of Illinois Press, 1999), p. 122; See also Chantelle Erickson, *Leaving England: Essays on British Emigration in the Nineteenth Century* (Ithaca, NY and London: Cornell University Press, 1994).
7 Travers, 'Emigration and Gender', p. 189; Van Vugt, *Britain to America*, p. 122; See also Erickson, *Leaving England*.
8 See also Daly, *The Slow Failure*, p. 14.
9 Sarah Roddy, '"The Emigrants' Friend"? Guides for Irish Emigrants by Clergymen c.1830–1882', in Ciara Breathnach and Catherine Lawless (eds), *Visual, Material and Print Culture in Nineteenth-Century Ireland* (Dublin: Four Courts Press, 2010), pp. 244–57.
10 F. L. Dingley, *European Emigration: Studies in Europe of Emigration Moving Out of Europe, Especially that Flowing to the United States* (Washington: Bureau of Statistics, Dept of State, 1890), p. 286.

women. For the Irish, many of the early-stage emigrants were from Ulster, and were Presbyterian, Protestant, Society of Friends (Quaker) and, to a lesser extent, Roman Catholic, who were escaping government oppression, continuous political upheaval and rising rents, while those who went as indentured servants were escaping poverty. Writing in 1808 when America had provided a home for her co-religionists and allowed them to progress within Thomas Jefferson's Democratic–Republican party, Margaret Wright, a County Tyrone-born Presbyterian woman, described America as the 'land of freedom and of liberty ... the land of promise flowing with milk and honey to those labouring under Egyptian bondage'.[11] Between one-half and two-thirds of those who left before 1845 were family groups. Moran suggests that because a family of five could find £60 to pay the fares and maintain themselves for fifteen months upon arrival, they were comfortable in Ireland.[12] These pre-Famine emigrants were equally desirous to take advantage of the new economic, as well as religious and political opportunities to improve their lives. While these women may not have read Thomas Paine or Thomas Jefferson, they had a concept of America, albeit a vague one based on letters, newspapers and periodicals such as *Walkers' Hibernian Magazine* and the *Freeman's Journal*. When Quaker Margaret Boyle Harvey returned to Cork from Philadelphia in 1809, she commented that 'the lower class of people here think it [America] is a wonderfully fine place.'[13]

From the 1820s onwards more poorer Catholics began to emigrate and came to see America in similar transforming terms.[14] During the nineteenth century between 250,000 and 400,000, 'overwhelmingly Catholics', received 'full or partial' assistance to travel to north America from government, landlords and philanthropists.[15] These groups were close to the bottom of the economic scale and, unlike the middle-class and wealthy women in chapters one and two, left behind few personal diaries, though letter-writing continued to be one of the main mediums for women's writing as in the

---

11 Dennis Clark, 'Irish Women Workers and American Labor Patterns: The Philadelphia Story', in Patrick O'Sullivan (ed.), *The Irish World Wide: History, Heritage, Identity. Volume 4: Irish Women and Irish Migration* (London: Leicester University Press, 1995), pp. 112–30; Kerby Miller et al. (eds), *Irish Immigrants in the Land of Canaan: Letters and Memoirs from Colonial and Revolutionary America, 1675–1815* (Oxford: Oxford University Press, 2003), p. 48.
12 Gerard Moran, *Sending Out Ireland's Poor: Assisted Emigration to North America in the Nineteenth Century* (Dublin: Four Courts Press, 2004), p. 18.
13 Friends Historical Library, Dublin, Ireland, 'Journal of Margaret Boyle Harvey 1786–1832', p. 19.
14 Miller, *Emigrants and Exile*, p. 195.
15 Kerby A. Miller, 'Review – Sending Out Ireland's Poor: Assisted Emigration to North America in the Nineteenth Century', *Journal of Social History*, 38, 3 (Spring 2005), pp. 784–86; Moran, *Sending Out Ireland's Poor*, pp. 17–29.

eighteenth century. Most wanted to escape the poverty and destitution although 'others were indecisive'. It could be argued that these early Catholic groups would have gone anywhere and that America meant little to them. Yet, once settled, the role of the letter might have been life-changing for family and friends at home.[16] This type of private writing, as noted in chapter one, was a way that women communicated with one another and maintained bonds. It was, therefore, an important a medium of exchange. Letters could include money, contribute to chain migration and sustained contact with the home community into the twentieth century.[17] By 1827, Alexander Carlisle Buchanan informed the Select British Parliamentary Committee on Emigration: 'they send home flattering letters, and they send home money to assist in bringing out their friends.'[18]

In these early decades, observers also saw an increasing number of young Irish women arriving into New York harbour alone. Chapter two suggests that women by 1820 had more freedom to shape their own lives and these departures offer further evidence of this continuity albeit for different reasons. Although fewer in number than young men, together the single women comprised 60 per cent of the Irish classified as labourers or servants arriving into New York in 1836. On the eve of the 1845–53 Famine, as table 3.1 reveals, a significantly high proportion of women already featured among Irish emigrants to the USA.

Table 3.1 Females per 1,000 Males among Emigrants from Britain and Ireland to the USA, 1841

	Among all immigrants	Among adults aged 15 years or older
Scots to the USA	521	551
English to the USA	615	529
Welsh to the USA	702	700
Irish to the USA	805	758

Source: Erickson, *Leaving England*, p. 192.

---

16 Moran, *Sending Out Ireland's Poor*, pp. 23, 26.
17 David Steven Cohen (ed.), *America: The Dream of My Life* (New Brunswick, NJ: Rutgers University Press, 1990), p. 3.
18 *British Parliamentary Papers 1826–7 (237), 1826–7, v2, Second Report from the Select Committee on Emigration from the United Kingdom* (reprint Shannon: Irish University Press, 1968), p. 74, qs 870, 891.

In other words, along with married women, young single Irish women left for the USA before 1845.[19] For these single women, America meant getting work most likely as domestic servants, maintaining contact with home and bringing out siblings and friends. Their subsequent actions and motivations would remain unknown for the most part and undoubtedly those who arrived destitute fared least well of all. Yet, the pattern was set. By 1840 the prevalence of Irish women in domestic service was a feature of urban life in the north-east at least. Five years later, US port officials described young Irish women immigrants as 'servants' or 'spinsters' who were influenced by claims in letters that 'young women who can wash and sew well can find plenty of employment' in US cities.[20] Some prospered, as approximately nineteen per cent of the depositors in the New York City Emigrant Industrial Savings Bank were Irish-born females working in private domestic service and had arrived in the USA between 1816 and May 1845.[21]

The extent to which this positive image of America as a place of paid work, wealth and prosperity was transforming Irish society by influencing people to leave, was already creating anxiety in some circles. From the 1790s, emigrants' guidebooks on sale in Ireland warned the Irish against emigrating and outlined the dangers and hardships. In 1818, Thomas Addis Emmet, the Irish-American lawyer, politician and United Irishman, believed that most Irish emigrants 'set out with false notions', and William Murphy, a Cork doctor, stated in 1827 that there was 'a great want of correct knowledge ... with respect to ... America' within the local farming community. Ten years later, the Irish Charitable Society in Boston accused the Irish emigrants of viewing America as 'sort of a half-way stage to Heaven, a paradise ... the very El Dorado of Spanish romance' and in the mid-1840s the Irish Emigrant Society in New York warned Irish emigrants 'against entertaining any fantastic idea, such as that magnificence, ease and health, are universally enjoyed' in America.[22] Despite this, the powerful myth of America as a place of progress for women and men was reinforced by the arrival of money for the passage and remittances to alleviate hardship in Ireland, particularly in western parts.

By mid-century, dependence on American relatives had become another

---

19 See Erickson, *Leaving England*, pp. 192–93.
20 Margaret Lynch-Brennan, *The Irish Bridget: Irish Immigrant Women in Domestic Service in America, 1840–1930* (Syracuse, NY: Syracuse University Press, 2009), p. 41; Miller, *Emigrants and Exile*, p. 200.
21 Lynch-Brennan, *The Irish Bridget*, p. xix.
22 Kerby Miller and Bruce D. Bolling, 'Golden Streets, Bitter Tears: The Irish Image of America during the Era of Mass Migration', *Journal of American Ethnic History*, 10, 1/2 (Fall 1990–Winter 1991), pp. 18, 17.

fundamental part of life for many.[23] Asenath Nicholson, the Quaker philanthropist who toured Ireland in 1844 and 1845, visited a house located two miles outside Johnstown, County Kilkenny. It was the home of the family of a domestic servant, Mary H., who worked for her in New York, and she commented that the £40 sent home 'not only kept her mother in tea and bread but had given them all the "blessed tobacco" besides'. Mary H. had visited home also by then and her mother recalled that she had insisted on 'overturnin'' the cabin and cleaning beds and floors. Later Nicholson visited Cahirciveen, County Kerry, where she met a 'tidy well-dressed young woman whose dialect and manner was so much like the Americans' that she asked if she had been there. The woman replied that she had worked in New York for ten years and had returned to look after her sick mother. On the eve of the Famine, therefore, Nicholson noticed that other 'servant girls' had returned from America because a 'great change' was evident in their 'dress, manner and language'. She continued

> She ceases to be a beast of burden and the basket on her back, which she throws off, she will never lift again. She confines her services more to the inside of the cabin and this undergoes a manifest change for the better.[24]

Against the background of famine, death, disease, destitution and evictions in mid-century, more married couples and unmarried women emigrated than ever before. Miller suggests that the image of America as a 'free country' still held sway but that most just wanted to escape. In this battle for survival, there could have been little gender difference in the perception that anywhere was better than where they lived.[25] In the 1860s the availability of 'free land' for men and single and widowed women through the Homestead Acts refined this view.[26] However, Hoerder's transnational scholarship on European emigrant societies suggests that women emigrants may not have considered this opportunity to own land in the same way as men. He argues that married women were more cautious because while it would mean a 'better future' for their families, it might also mean geographical

---

23 Miller, *Emigrants and Exile*, p. 271; Lynch-Brennan, *The Irish Bridget*, pp. 57–58.
24 Asenath Nicholson, *Ireland's Welcome to the Stranger: On An Excursion Through Ireland in 1884 & 1845, for the Purpose of Personally Investigating the Condition of the Poor* (New York: Bakker and Scrivner, 1847), pp. 88, 246.
25 Kerby A. Miller, '"Revenge for Skibbereen": Irish Emigration and the Meaning of the Great Famine', in Arthur Gribben (ed.), *The Great Famine and the Irish Diaspora in America* (Boston: University of Massachusetts Press, 1999), pp. 183–87.
26 'The Homestead Act, 1862', http://www.nps.gov/jeff/historyculture/upload/homestead.pdf (accessed 16 July 2010).

and social isolation.[27] While 'an unusually large proportion' of Famine emigrants travelled in family groups and some succeeded in establishing themselves on American farms, most Catholics settled in America's cities and towns. By 1855, almost 176,000 Irish-born residents were living in New York city and comprised approximately twenty-eight per cent of the total population. Subsequent emigration followed this pattern.[28] In other words, women and men from rural backgrounds sought and found work in urban areas and in the 'lowest paid, least skilled and most dangerous and insecure employment'.[29] America, as a place of free land, held less sway with those who came from Irish rural backgrounds. Not only did they change their lives by leaving for America, but they adjusted them further by working in urban areas and this was particularly true for young women.

In the post-American Civil War years, America assumed further transformative powers with 'industrialisation, the growth of cities, the expansion of factories and mechanization.' It came to be perceived as a 'country of speed, great size and huge factories' but also one where women were perceived to be 'treated better … [and] … could get jobs'.[30] This contrasted with the other options available to Irish women. Firstly, there was industrialised and urbanised Britain where women could also find work but which was a less popular destination. Irish subservience in Britain manifested through continued poverty, prejudice and discrimination persisted until well into the twentieth century. In 1853, Reverend Alexander Peyton, Catholic parish priest of Blarney and Whitechurch in Cork, who was sent by Archbishop Cullen to the USA to collect funds for the Irish Catholic University, later published a series of letters in the *Cork Examiner* and an advice pamphlet. He commented that 'when contrasting the encomiums passed upon Irish servant maids in America, for their virtue, piety and honesty, with the advertisement for servants in England, "No Irish need apply", I was forced to admit that the English have no respect for these enobling qualifications.'[31] Indeed it

---

27 Dirk Hoerder, 'From Dreams to Possibilities: The Secularization of Hope and the Quest for Independence', in Dirk Hoerder and Horst Rössler (eds), *Distant Magnets: Expectations and Realities in the Immigrant Experience, 1840–1930* (New York/London: Holmes and Meier Publishers, 1993), p. 8.

28 Kerby A. Miller and Bruce D. Bolling, 'The Pauper and the Politician: A Tale of Two Immigrants and the Construction of Irish-American Society', in Arthur Gribben (ed.), *The Great Famine and the Irish Diaspora in America* (Boston: University of Massachusetts Press, 1999), pp. 197, 203; Miller, '"Revenge for Skibbereen"', pp. 182, 189.

29 David Fitzpatrick, *Irish Emigration 1801–1921* (Studies in Irish Economic and Social History 1) (Dundalk: Dundalgan Press, 1990), p. 15; Miller, '"Revenge for Skibbereen"', p. 189.

30 Hoerder, 'From Dreams to Possibilities', p. 8.

31 Rev. Alex. J. Peyton, *The Emigrant's Friend; or Hints on Emigration to the United States of America Addressed to the People of Ireland* (Cork: J. O'Brien, 1853), p. 46.

was not until the inter-war period in the twentieth century that Irish female emigration to Britain overtook male emigrant rates.[32]

Life in America also offered young, Irish, Catholic women, mainly from the western parts, more than was on offer in Ireland. Clear's recent re-evaluation of evidence relating to marriage states that historians can be sure of just three conclusions in the period 1850–1922: 'Irish people in general married at a lower rate than the European norm ... they married comparatively late ... the average age of brides in 1911 was 29 [years], that of bridegrooms 33 [years].'[33] A link can be made between emigration and marriage, namely that as soon as young Irish women realised that there was 'no husband and no job at home', they departed in greater numbers than men, particularly in the 1890s.[34] This raises the question as to whether America, the predominant location, might have been seen as offering them a better chance to find a husband. Diner's earlier work on the Irish in New York, Boston, Milwaukee, Buffalo, Pittsburgh, Detroit and other centres of Irish population suggest that the rate of marriage among the Irish in America 'did outpace' that in Ireland although it was less frequent than any other immigrant group. This she interprets as an Irish-American hesitation to marry.[35] In other words, Irish women knew that going to America might not necessarily mean breaking with familial and religious traditions. Yet for others, America might have equated with delaying marriage or not marrying at all. Perhaps some took heed of 'the ... prominent Irish women – labour leaders, school teachers, religious leaders, and actresses – [who] never married' and led independent lives.[36] There is no evidence to suggest that delaying or not marrying was influenced by the emerging American suffrage movement or feminist ideology. Yet, in 1920, more Irish women were single than in other immigrant groups with one-quarter unmarried, suggesting a desire to shape their own lives.[37]

---

32 Donald M. MacRaild, *The Irish Diaspora in Britain, 1750–1939* (Basingstoke: Palgrave, 2011), pp. 190, 30.

33 Clear, *Social Change and Everyday Life in Ireland*, p. 74.

34 Donald Harman Akenson, *The Irish Diaspora: A Primer* (Toronto and Belfast: Institute of Irish Studies, 1996), pp. 38, 166; David Fitzpatrick, '"A Share of the Honeycomb": Education, Emigration and Irishwomen', in Mary Daly and David Dickson (eds), *The Origins of Popular Literacy in Ireland: Language Change and Educational Development, 1700–1920* (Dublin: TCD and UCD, 1990), p. 175; Kerby A. Miller, *Ireland and Irish America: Culture, Class and Transatlantic Migration* (Dublin: Field Day, 2008); Lynch-Brennan, *The Irish Bridget*, pp. 25–26.

35 Hasia Diner, *Erin's Daughters in America: Irish Immigrant Women in the Nineteenth Century* (Baltimore: Johns Hopkins University Press, 1983), pp. 46–47.

36 Diner, *Erin's Daughters*, p. 49.

37 Doris Weatherford, *Foreign and Female: Immigrant Women in America 1840–1930* (New York: Schocken Books, 1986), p. 221.

Irish women who had entered the religious life also developed a concept of America which could be life-changing. As noted in chapter two, nuns exercised important cultural influence over society, but the religious life was also a form of independent life. Convent life became popular in the early nineteenth century and this popularity continued into the twentieth century. There was an 'eight-fold' increase in the number of women who 'refused marriage' and entered a convent with a dowry.[38] This path provided not just another powerful alternative to marriage as well as fulfilment of spiritual needs, but also offered an attractive 'emotional and material experience'.[39] Once fully professed into a religious order, most nuns had little or no control in their futures. Previous generations of persecuted post-Reformation believers saw America as a religious refuge but in the nineteenth and twentieth centuries, Roman Catholic authorities in Ireland, Rome and the USA viewed it as a site for missionary work, particularly among the recently arrived Irish communities.[40] Irish nuns were at the centre of that mission, which was driven mostly by the invitation of bishops, priests and religious orders in the USA. Along with nuns and postulants travelling out, aspirants were encouraged to join orders in either Ireland or the USA and then depart for the American mission. Several thousand young women responded to these campaigns. They had a different American dream from that of their sisters and friends because the economic motivation was not their primary concern. In the USA, educated middle-class young women who entered with dowries went on primarily to become teachers and principals, nurses and matrons working in teaching, health care and social services just as in Ireland. Moreover, by the end of the nineteenth century, the dowry was replaced by education as a requirement for entry in the USA. These women were not 'submissive servants of the male clergy' due to their 'pioneering' work. Hoy describes Irish nuns in the USA who came to dominate the provision of Catholic education as 'heroes'. This description could be applied to all missionaries irrespective of destination. However, the developmental state of the American Catholic Church in a rapidly progressing society and economy, did allow for a certain unity of vision about their American mission and also

---

38 Clear, *Social Change and Everyday Life in Ireland*, p. 37.
39 Mary Peckham Magray, *The Transforming Power of the Nuns: Women, Religion & Cultural Change in Ireland, 1750–1900* (New York: Oxford University Press, 1998).
40 The following is based on the work of Suellen Hoy, *Good Hearts: Catholic Sisters in Chicago's Past* (Urbana and Chicago: University of Illinois Press, 2006); Suellen Hoy and Margaret MacCurtain, *From Dublin to New Orleans: The Journey of Nora and Alice* (Dublin: Attic Press, 1994); Suellen Hoy, 'The Journey Out: The Recruitment and Emigration of Irish Religious Women to the United States, 1912–1914', *Journal of Women's History*, 6/7 (Winter–Spring 1995), pp. 64–98.

fulfilled individual women's occupational and professional hopes within the religious life.[41]

But it was the association of America with paid work in the post-Famine period which changed the lives of so many young, single, Catholic women. Despite the expansion in the variety of paid work opportunities in Ireland, the occupational choices for an increasingly literate and numerate, young, English-speaking female who sought paid employment in Ireland were decreasing. In 1861, 26 per cent of women were in employment, falling to 19.5 per cent in 1911. An expanding area of female employment was as workers in shops and stores particularly in urban centres, although the *Freeman's Journal* in December 1881 compared their circumstances to a 'system of slavery'. A constant source of employment for women in Ireland throughout the nineteenth century was domestic service. By 1911 one working women in three was in service.[42] For women employed as domestic servants in Ireland and those who were unemployed, not only was work available in the USA but they also had regulated hours and wages.[43] As noted earlier, soon after the Famine, Irish female servants virtually monopolised domestic service in America's cities and became an integral part of the 'new middle-class culture' whereby households had to have '"live-in" servants'. Reverend Alexander J. Peyton commented after his trip in the early 1850s:

> Irish servant-maids in America have contributed much to the honour and dignity of our country; their virtuous conduct, their strict attention to religion, the faithful honest and conscientious performance of their respective duties, have elicited the marked approbation of their employers…[44]

While the Catholic Church became less supportive of emigration, as will be seen, the number of women who declared themselves to be domestic servants in the US census increased from 559,908 in 1860 to 1,012,133 in 1920. The 1900 US census indicated that fifty-four per cent of the women in servant employment were Irish-born. The Irish 'Bridget' was an 'integral part' of the

---

41 Hoy, *Good Hearts: Catholic Sisters in Chicago's Past*, pp. 4–10.
42 Clear, *Social Change and Everyday Life in Ireland*, pp. 24–37; Stephanie Rains, *Commodity Culture and Social Class in Dublin 1850–1916* (Dublin: Irish Academic Press, 2010), p. 100; Tony Farmar, *Privileged Lives: A Social History of Middle-Class Ireland 1882–1989* (Dublin: A. & A. Farmar, 2010), pp. 63–64; Mona Hearn, *Below the Stairs: Domestic Service Remembered in Dublin and Beyond, 1880–1922* (Dublin: Lilliput Press, 1993), p. 111.
43 Hoerder, 'From Dreams to Possibilities', p. 8.
44 Peyton, *The Emigrant's Friend*, p. 46.

middle-class American home.[45] The reality of domestic life was often marked by a difficult settling-in period as the women got used to the modern or American ways of cleaning, cooking and laundry and experienced prejudice, discrimination, exploitation, a loss of personal freedom and loneliness.[46] Some domestics found work in hotels and boarding houses while other women worked in mills and factories usually manufacturing textiles and clothes.[47] Cohen's study of female-headed households in Greenwich, New York between 1880 and 1910 indicates the presence of 'asymmetrical wage scales' among male and female linen workers as was the case in Gilford, County Down, but Irish female emigrants considered pay rates in domestic service at least 'better than anything available at home' and Irish female domestic servants who lived-in also received bed and board.[48] It is difficult to ascertain if these women attained independence and power in their American lives, and if Irish-born women had less opportunity for upward mobility. But Kenny concludes that despite obstacles and difficulties, 'they generally prospered ... carving out new lives for themselves, financing the passage of siblings to America, and supporting their families back in Ireland.'[49]

45 Diane M. Hotten-Somers, 'Relinquishing and Reclaiming Independence: Irish Domestic Servants, American Middle-Class Mistresses, and Assimilation, 1850–1920', in Kevin Kenny (ed.), *New Directions in Irish-American History* (Madison: University of Wisconsin Press, 2003), pp. 227–43; Diner, *Erin's Daughters*, pp. 80–94; Clark, 'Irish Women Workers', p. 120; Lynch-Brennan, *The Irish Bridget*, p. xvii; Janet Nolan, *Ourselves Alone: Women's Emigration from Ireland 1885–1920* (Lexington: University Press of Kentucky, 1989), pp. 73–90.
46 Hotten-Somers, 'Relinquishing and Reclaiming Independence', pp. 227–43; Diner, *Erin's Daughters*, pp. 80–94; Nolan, *Ourselves Alone*, pp. 73–90; Kenny, 'Part 3. The World of Work. Editor's Introduction', in Kenny (ed.), *New Directions*, p. 161; D. A. Katzman, *Seven Days a Week: Women and Domestic Service in Industrializing America* (New York: Oxford University Press, 1978), pp. 7–14, 267–69; Fay Dudden, *Serving Women: Household Service in Nineteenth-Century America* (Middletown, Conn.: Wesleyan University Press, 1983), pp. 193–235.
47 Blessing, 'The Irish in America', p. 531; Lynch-Brennan, *The Irish Bridget*, p. xvii; Clark, 'Irish Women Workers', p. 118.
48 Marilyn Cohen, 'The Migration Experience of Female-Headed Households: Gilford, Co. Down, to Greenwich, New York, 1880–1910', in O'Sullivan (ed.), *Irish Women*, pp. 130–45; Timothy J. Hatton and Jeffrey G. Williamson, 'After the Famine: Emigration from Ireland, 1850–1913', *Journal of Economic History*, 53, 3 (September 1993), p. 577; Kenny, 'Introduction', in Kenny (ed.), *New Directions*, p. 161. Foley and Guinnane stated that US wages were higher than in Ireland during the second half of the nineteenth century. Marc C. Foley and Timothy G. Guinnane, 'Did Irish Marriage Patterns Survive the Emigrant Voyage? Irish-American Nuptuality, 1880–1920', *Irish Economic and Social History*, 26 (1991), p. 18.
49 Cohen's study of Gilford and Greenwich in 1880–1910 indicates that many women emigrated hoping for a better life but that this was not realised at least for female-headed households. See Cohen, 'The Migration Experience of Female-Headed Households', p. 143; Kenny, 'Introduction', in Kenny (ed.), *New Directions*, pp. 160–61.

The pattern set in the pre-Famine period remains identifiable; Reverend Peyton noted in 1853 that Irish domestic servants 'remit their hard earned wages' and in 1868 the member of parliament John Francis Maguire who toured the USA in 1866, believed that Irish girls living in American cities sent home more money than their male counterparts.[50] Later on in the 1880s and 1890s, one of the reasons why philanthropist Vere Foster favoured assisting young, single women to emigrate to the USA in his second scheme was because 'they are the least able to get themselves out, and because … they are generally the most liberal in sending home help to bring out their brothers and sisters and parents, if they wish to go.'[51] Reports from his correspondents were peppered with references to money and tickets being sent home. In February 1880, Maria Corrigan in Ballaghadreen, County Mayo, had received £3 from an aunt in America, while Catherine Flanagan and Mary McCann had their passages paid by friends who had emigrated earlier.[52] Margaret McCarthy threatened to send no more money unless her family joined her in America. In this case a 'mutual obligation' existed between a daughter who had left, saved and sent the ticket price home and her family, who were expected to join her.[53] Remittances in the form of bank drafts, cash and pre-paid passage tickets came through banks, mercantile houses, shipping firms, exchange agencies, private letters and returning emigrants. Between 1848 and 1900, Irish-Americans sent $260 million back to Ireland, and forty per cent or $104 million was in the form of prepaid tickets.[54] In the mid-1860s, John Francis Maguire cited evidence that Irish women in New York, San Francisco and Lowell also sent money to Ireland.[55] One of the many exchange agencies was founded by Patrick Donohoe, editor of the *Boston Pilot*, which remitted more than $180,000 annually from female Irish domestic servants in Boston by the 1880s.[56]

50 Peyton, *The Emigrant's Friend*, p. 46; John Francis Maguire, *The Irish in America* (New York: D. & J. Sadlier, 1868), pp. 321–22; entry on John Francis Maguire by Stefanie P. Jones in *DIB*.
51 Quoted in Anne O'Connell, 'Assisted Female Emigration: Vere Foster's Scheme, 1880–1896' (unpublished Ph.D. thesis, University of Limerick, 1998), p. 6.
52 O'Connell, 'Assisted Female Emigration', pp. 73, 148.
53 Ruth-Ann Harris, '"Come You All Courageously": Irish Women in America Write Home', *Éire-Ireland*, 36, 1/2 (Spring–Summer 2001), p. 175.
54 Timothy J. Meagher, 'The Fireman on the Stairs: Communal Loyalties in the Making of Irish America', in J. J. Lee and Marion R. Casey (eds), *Making the Irish American: History and Heritage of the Irish in the United States* (New York: New York University Press, 2006), p. 617.
55 Maguire, *The Irish in America*, pp. 277, 319.
56 Schrier, *Ireland and the American Emigration*, p. 106; Harris, '"Come You All Courageously"', p. 175; Margaret Lynch-Brennan, 'Ubiquitous Bridget: Irish Immigrant Women in Domestic Service in America, 1840–1930', in Lee and Casey (eds), *Making the Irish American*, p. 341.

By the turn of the century seventy-five per cent of young female emigrants had their passage paid by a sister and all were going to join a sister in the USA. Murphy suggests that sibling bonds were strengthened but so was the idea that women could prosper in the USA.[57] The hopeful emigrant Péig Sayers in Dingle, County Kerry, was disappointed when 'ná raibh fheidir lei [Cháit Jim] an costas a chur chugam' [she was unable to send me the cost]. She did not receive the price of the ticket because her friend hurt her arm and was unable to work.[58] Money also went towards buying land, building houses, improving houses, paying bills, the price of dowries and buying animals. In the early 1880s two young nuns sent back money to families in the west of Ireland to buy a horse to do the work of gathering seaweed which they had both done for their families.[59] Indeed John Millington Synge's experiences in Wicklow, west Kerry and Connemara between 1898 and 1905 revealed that female emigrants' money from America maintained many families in those areas.[60] Food, knitted gifts, photographs, rings, watches and clothes were also sent, representing the continuous presence of American material goods in Irish life and reinforcing the positive American encounter but also sharply contrasting it with life in Ireland.[61]

Relatives received money to leave but learned from letters that conditions in America could be transforming. Lynch-Brennan's work on domestic service indicates that while living spaces and food were not always adequate, Irish girls still flocked into domestic service.[62] By early 1900, even the lowliest paid domestic servant living in Brooklyn who might have lived in a 'tiny space in a stuffy attic', had a room of her own. It was 'dry' and she had 'creature comforts' such as 'running water, gas light and work indoors made easier by modern conveniences'. In New York, many lived in

---

57 Maureen Murphy, 'The Fionnuala Factor: Irish Sibling Emigration at the Turn of the Century', in Anthony Bradley and Maryann Gialanella Valiulis (eds), *Gender and Sexuality in Modern Ireland* (Amherst: University of Massachusetts Press, 1997), pp. 85–101.
58 Peig Sayers, *Peig* (Dublin: Comhleacht Oideachas na hÉireannn, undated), p. 123.
59 Grace Neville, '"She Never Then After That Forgot Him": Irishwomen and Emigration to the United States in Irish Folklore', *Mid-America: An Historical Review*, 74, 3 (October 1992), p. 279; Grace Neville, 'Land of the Fair, Land of the Free? The Myth of America in Irish Folklore', in Anthony Coulson (ed.), *Exiles and Migrants: Crossing Thresholds in European Culture and Society* (Brighton: Sussex University Press, 1997), p. 65; Hoy, 'The Journey Out', p. 91, fn. 41.
60 John Millington Synge, 'The Inner Land of Mayo', in Alan Price (ed.), *Collected Works, Volume 2: Prose* (London: Oxford University Press, 1966), pp. 305–6.
61 Neville, '"She Never Then After That Forgot Him"', p. 279; Neville, 'Land of the Fair, Land of the Free?', p. 63; Grace Neville, 'Dark Lady of the Archives: Towards an Analysis of Women and Emigration to North America in Irish Folklore', in O'Dowd and Wichert (eds), *Chattel, Servant or Citizen*, p. 212.
62 Lynch-Brennan, *The Irish Bridget*, pp. 93, 113.

the neighbourhoods of Brooklyn Heights, Carroll Gardens or Park Slope, which meant access to 'gardens and tree-lined streets and the expanse of Prospect Park'. A domestic servant could participate in parish activities in the expanding neighbourhoods or in one of the Irish community-organised picnics and dances and meet friends from home. During her leisure time she could shop in nearby New York or take the streetcar to Coney Island. In other words, despite loneliness and unhappiness at times, she enjoyed a 'measure of privacy, independence and autonomy' which contrasted vividly with her previous life of little or no financial or material resources.[63] While she may not have contrasted her new autonomous life with the patriarchal, restricted life predominant in rural Ireland, as some scholars argue, she did not reject what she encountered in America and instead transferred information about these hallmark activities of a modern society back home to family and friends.[64]

Scholars who have worked on letters acknowledge their problematic nature, particularly in terms of veracity. Miller's study based on over 5,000 letters and folklore testimonies notes that letters were often responsible for disseminating the view that America was a 'veritable paradise'. Yet, letter-writers provided negative as well as positive information about their lives in America, in particular that working lives were harsh.[65] Another aspect of the negative experience was the physical and moral danger some young girls encountered not just in America but during the journey and sometimes family in America were less than welcoming of the new arrival.[66] Moreover, letters did not always contain money. The disappointment could be acute. Some parents blamed themselves for forcing emigration upon their children and others held a long-lasting resentment which reinforced the idea that America was a materialistic place where family ties mattered little.[67] The

---

63 Murphy, 'The Fionnuala Factor', p. 85; Lynch-Brennan, *The Irish Bridget*, pp. 121–49.
64 Hotten-Somers, 'Relinquishing and Reclaiming Independence', pp. 227–43; Diner, *Erin's Daughters*, pp. 80–94; Nolan, *Ourselves Alone*, pp. 73–90; Kenny, 'Introduction' in Kenny (ed.) *New Directions*, p. 161; Katzman, *Seven Days a Week*, pp. 7–14, 267–69; Dudden, *Serving Women: Household Service in Nineteenth-Century America*, pp. 193–235.
65 Miller, '"Revenge for Skibbereen"', p. 190; Kerby Miller, "Paddy's Paradox: Emigration to America in Irish Imagination and Rhetoric', in Hoerder and Rössler (eds), *Distant Magnets*, p. 267; Anna Kelly, 'I Went to America', *The Bell*, 3, 5 (February 1942), pp. 353–56.
66 See Clark, 'Irish Women Workers' for evidence of Irish women who were 'jobless and homeless' in Philadelphia in the 1870s. See O'Connell, 'Assisted Female Emigration', pp. 33–45 on Charlotte Grace O'Brien's work; John Nolan, 'Mission of Our Lady of the Rosary', in *Irish Ecclesiastical Record* (September 1891), pp. 776–85.
67 Miller, 'Paddy's Paradox', p. 283; Hoerder, 'From Dreams to Possibilities', pp. 10–11; Murphy, 'The Fionnuala Factor', pp. 85–101.

empty letter and negative information should have had a dissuasive effect on young women thinking of emigrating but it did not. Instead, Miller maintained that the receiver of the letter in Ireland selected what they wanted from it.[68] It was the descriptions of enjoyment gained from a train journey across America, from work as a maid, from leisure time and earning and spending money that were more influential. Harris takes this further to suggest that young Irish women may have interpreted positive information from their female relatives and friends as evidence of independence and autonomy in America.[69]

The returner in the pre-1914 period
Such impressions may have been reinforced by the returned female emigrant. Following Nicholson's observation about the pre-Famine period, while just 2.1 per cent of all Irish emigrants to the USA returned between 1899 and 1910, more women than men returned in this turn-of-the-century period.[70] Return could last for any length from three, six, or twelve months to permanent stays.[71] Murphy's work on 1898 and 1906 suggests that many single women returned from the USA for short visits. American-born Margaret Dineen, a single woman travelled to Ireland alone in 1898 to attend the 'great celebration in honour of "Wolfe Tone"' and returned again in 1907 for the Dublin International Exhibition.[72] Others came back with enough money to marry and set up businesses with their husbands.[73]

This reality had also infiltrated English- and Irish-language literature, memoirs and songs. Schrier has outlined many emigrant ballads and among the best known are Percy French's 'Donegan's Daughter' (1897) and 'The Emigrants' Letter' (1910).[74] Female emigration was a regular concern of the popular writer Rosa Mulholland and following from her 1888 novel, *A Fair Emigrant*, in which second-generation Irish-American heiress 'Bawn

68 Miller, 'Paddy's Paradox', p. 267.
69 Harris, '"Come You All Courageously"', pp. 170–75.
70 Neville, '"She Never Then After That Forgot Him"', p. 285; Neville, 'Dark Lady of the Archives', p. 210. Wyman suggests that because so many women worked in domestic service where they were in close contact with American life, they were more easily assimilated and less likely to return. Mark Wyman, *Round-Trip to America: The Immigrants Return to Europe, 1880–1930* (Ithaca, NY and London: Cornell University Press, 1993), p. 78; Lynch-Brennan, *The Irish*, p. 57.
71 Diane Dunnigan, 'Coming Home: Return Migration to Ireland, 1890–1920', paper presented to the Migrations in Irish History Symposium, National University of Ireland, Maynooth, 8 June 2011.
72 Murphy, 'The Fionnuala Factor', pp. 85–101.
73 Neville, 'Land of the Fair, Land of the Free?', pp. 66, 68; Neville, '"She Never Then After That Forgot Him"', p. 286.
74 Schrier, *Ireland and the American Emigration*, pp. 97–102.

Desmond' returns, she commented that 'America is a very levelling place'. Her 1908 novel, *The Return of Mary O'Murrough*, dealt specifically with the female returner and can be read as favouring or rejecting emigration.[75] The poet Martin Ó Direáin recalled returners in *Feamainn Bhealtaine*. One of John Millington Synge's informants in Mayo told him that so many women returned that 'there is hardly a marriage made in the place that the woman hadn't been in America.' Irish domestic servant Margaret Hegarty returned from New York to County Kerry, married and stayed permanently, albeit in unhappy circumstances. Synge also described the 'perfectly clean' cabins of returned female 'yanks', the presence of photographs of the 'Sistine Madonna' on the walls of their homes unlike the 'hideous German oleographs on religious subjects' in most Irish cabins, and the wearing of 'new American blouses' in some places.[76]

This evidence does not fully support the contention of an 'americaniz[ing of] the mentality of the Irish female whether or not she emigrated'. However, it does suggest that by the beginning of the twentieth century, the returned female 'yank', whether she stayed for long or short periods, represented cultural difference.[77] Contemporaries agreed. F. L. Dingley, a US State Department official charged with visiting the main emigrant countries in western Europe, accounted for the 'phenomenon' of the 'increase in the swarm of young [Irish] women' to the USA because it 'is singularly adapted by its sense of fair play to woman to give her an independent career'.[78] By then a similar view was embedded in the folklore; America was 'favouring girls more than boys', girls could do 'much better in America than at home' and it transformed women from 'docility to financial independence'. Unsurprisingly the latter was unwelcomed by the largely male respondents in the National Folklore Commission project because it made women 'arrogant, critical and difficult to please'.[79] Nonetheless, young, single Irish women and their families regarded America as a place of opportunity more than exile, a place where personal ambition and hopes could be met as well as decent living conditions secured for themselves and their families left behind.[80] Thus, the traditional explanation that women did not desire to

75 Rosa Mulholland, *A Fair Emigrant* (London: Keegan, Paul Trench, 1888), p. 194; Rosa Mulholland, *The Return of Mary O'Murrough* (Edinburgh and London: Sands, 1908).
76 Murphy, 'The Fionnuala Factor', pp. 86–92; Lynch-Brennan, *The Irish Bridget*, p. 57.
77 Lynch-Brennan, *The Irish Bridget*, p. 58; David Fitzpatrick, 'The Modernisation of the Irish Female in Rural Ireland', in P. O'Flanagan (ed.), *Rural Ireland: Modernisation and Change 1600–1900* (Cork: Cork University Press, 1987), p. 163.
78 Dingley, *European Emigration*, p. 308.
79 Neville, 'Land of the Fair, Land of the Free?', pp. 66, 68; Neville, '"She Never Then After That Forgot Him"', p. 286.
80 See Hoerder, 'From Dreams to Possibilities', pp. 1–27.

emigrate and did so only to accompany their 'menfolk' or to rejoin them can be questioned.[81] Irish women, like German women, held an image of life in America characterised by higher status, greater freedoms, employment opportunities and economic independence.[82]

The entrenchment of this idea of America and its consequences for Irish rural life was such that some Irish Roman Catholic clerics promulgated the view that leaving for any reason other than political pressure was unacceptable, and women were a particular focus for such views. In 1903, Fr. Joseph Guinan, then a curate in Athlone, County Westmeath, published the first of his eight novels, *Scenes and Sketches in an Irish Parish Or Priests and People of Doon by a Country Curate* which accepted that the eldest girl, 'Rosie', 'now about twenty years of age, seeing no chance of employment at home, resolved to emigrate' to America. Fr. Guinan preferred to see 'Rosie' stay in the 'mud wall cabin' than become 'victim of hellish agencies of vice'.[83] The Catholic Truth Society, founded in 1899 to promote an interest in Irish and Catholic themes, published millions of cheap penny booklets in the following years. Among the concerns of its writers who included the Irish–Ireland advocate Mary Butler and Mulholland, was the continuous flow of emigrants. The former lamented the dilution of a Gaelic Ireland culture.[84] When the character 'Moya' in Mulholland's 'The Hungry Death' was forced to emigrate with 'Coll', it was 'for better times' than were available in Inis Meáin in the west of Ireland.[85] Against the background of papal condemnation of every form of liberalism including individualism and 'unrestricted competition', beginning with the 1864 *Syllabus of Errors* through to the tenure of Pope Pius X (1903–14), Catholics were urged, in Lee's words, 'to save their souls in Holy Ireland rather than to hazard them for the world's goods among American heretics'.

Ironically, although lamenting emigrants' departure, it was the Catholic, conservative, patriarchal values embedded in rural economy and society which condemned them to leave.[86] Moreover, these young Catholic women were

---

81 Travers, 'Emigration and Gender', p. 187 also deals with the issue.
82 Hoerder, 'From Dreams to Possibilities', pp. 23, 15.
83 Rev. J. Guinan, *Scenes and Sketches in an Irish Parish Or Priest and People of Doon By a Country Curate* (3rd edition; Dublin: M. H. Gill, 1903), pp. 34–47.
84 Mary Butler, 'A Medieval Modern', *The Catholic Bulletin and Book Review*, 4 (November 1914), p. 684; see also Mary Butler, *Modern Fashions in Ladies' Dress* (Dublin: Irish Messenger Office, 1927), p. 4.
85 Stephen James Meredith Brown (ed.), *Ireland in Fiction, 1910: A Guide to Irish Novels, Tales, Romances, and Folk-Lore* (New York: reprinted Burt Franklin, 1970), p. 322; Rosa Mulholland, 'The Hungry Death', reprinted in *Irish Monthly*, 42 (June–July 1914), pp. 297–310, 366–73.
86 Maurice Curtis, *A Challenge to Democracy: Militant Catholicism in Modern Ireland* (Dublin: The History Press Ireland), pp. 11–12; J. J. Lee, *Ireland, 1912–1985: Politics and Society* (Cambridge: Cambridge University Press, 1989), p. 383; see also Kerby

blamed by the Catholic hierarchy for being more susceptible than young men to 'some bright vision beyond the Atlantic'. Similar paternalistic views also influenced the Catholic clergy in New York to establish the Missionary of Our Lady of the Rosary for female, but not male, Irish emigrants.[87] Between 1884 and 1890 the Mission priests gave valuable help to 25,000 Irish women, but noticed in 1891 that the arrivals now wanted to 'improve their social position' as well as secure a livelihood. In turn, this personal aim led fewer women to turn to the Mission, which was heavily criticised by Catholic clergy.[88] An assistance programme in Boston run by the Charitable Irish Society of Boston and the Saint Vincent de Paul Society, which also aimed to prevent young Irish women from engaging in immoral behaviour, had the additional aim of preventing proselytizing. By 1913, it also had experienced a decline in the demand for its services.[89] Both programmes could also be seen as part of the Catholic Church's efforts in America and Ireland, to ensure that the behaviour of Irish emigrant women accorded with a moral code. Notwithstanding this position, it was the comment from Denis Lee from Goresbridge, County Kilkenny, who followed his sister to America in 1903 that America was 'a good country, especially for girls', providing work and an opportunity for self-improvement that echoed the views of Irish women and their families.[90] Lee was identifying a pattern present since the early nineteenth century. Indeed, there was some recognition of this in Boston at least, where the Irish Charitable Society moved to establish an employment bureau in 1918.[91]

The Appeal of America, 1922–60

National independence was widely expected to signal the end of emigration through the provision of employment.[92] Instead unemployment increased

---

Miller, 'Emigration, Ideology and Identity in Post-Famine Ireland', *Studies: An Irish Quarterly Review*, 75, 300 (Winter 1986), p. 515–27; Miller, 'Paddy's Paradox', p. 279.

87 See Diarmaid Ferriter, *The Transformation of Ireland 1900–2000* (London: Profile Books, 2004), pp. 44–45; Nolan, 'Mission of Our Lady of the Rosary', pp. 776–85.

88 Nolan, 'Mission of Our Lady of the Rosary', p. 784.

89 Deirdre M. Moloney, 'A Transatlantic Reform: Boston's Port Protection Program and Irish Women Emigrants', *Journal of American Ethnic History*, 19, 1 (Fall 1999), pp. 50–66.

90 National Folklore Collection (hereafter NFC), Delargy Centre for Irish Folklore, University College Dublin, MS 1409, Denis Lee, Patrick and Michael Silke.

91 Moloney, 'A Transatlantic Reform', p. 61.

92 J. J. Lee, 'Emigration 1922–1998' in Glazier, *The Encyclopedia of the Irish in America*, p. 263. Delaney suggests that there was a gross underestimation of the numbers of people emigrating to Britain. Delaney, 'Irish Emigration', pp. 70–76, 135–36; Ferriter, *The Transformation of Ireland 1900–2000*, p. 330.

rapidly after 1920 and was accompanied by widespread distress and hardship. Women's employment stagnated or declined from the 1920s to the 1980s. In the inter-war period, government policy in Ireland sent out certain messages to women who regarded paid employment as a way of fulfilling personal aims.[93] Between 1926 and 1935, the marriage bar was extended to all civil service posts. In 1936, the Conditions of Employment Act permitted the Minister for Industry and Commerce to prevent women from working in certain industries. These restrictions could be justified in the short term on the grounds of poor economic circumstances, but the marriage bar remained in place until 1974. Throughout the period, the state made it clear in the respective reports on technical education in 1926, seasonal migration in 1937–38 and youth unemployment in 1951 that female ambition, particularly among poorer classes, should be confined to the domestic environment.[94] Clear has shown that many women, particularly those who were married, were too busy surviving to be overly concerned about these restrictions on their earning ability and other limitations on their personal life and citizenship roles.[95] But the economic climate and legislative framework affected their daughters, who continued to leave.

Throughout the first three decades of the twentieth century, for every eight males leaving, ten females departed.[96] Evidence presented to the inquiry into the decline of the Irish language was littered with references to the personal and familial assumption of emigration to the USA for young women and men. Dr Bartley O'Beirne, the Tuberculosis Officer for County Galway, indicated in 1925 that girls in his area 'were waiting for their time to go to America'.[97] America remained the favoured destination and even after the depression hit the US economy, in 1929 when M. K. McGurl, a teacher in Spiddal, County Galway, asked his pupils what would they like to do when

93 Mary E. Daly, *Women and Work in Ireland* (Studies in Irish Economic and Social History 7) (Dundalk: Dundalgan Press, 1997), pp. 43–44; Mary E. Daly, 'Women in the Irish Free State, 1922–39: The Interaction between Economics and Ideology', *Journal of Women's History*, 6, 4/5 (Winter–Spring 1995), p. 102. Women workers left Woolworths upon marriage. Barbara Walsh, *When the Shopping Was Good: Woolworths and the Irish Main Street* (Dublin: Irish Academic Press, 2011), p. 122.
94 *Commission on Technical Education* (Dublin: Stationery Office, 1927), recc. 76; *Report of the Inter-Departmental Committee on Seasonal migration to Great Britain, 1937–8* (Dublin: Stationery Office, 1938); see Louie Bennett's minority comment in *Report on Youth Unemployment, 1951* (Dublin: Stationery Office, 1951), p. 74.
95 See Caitriona Clear, *Woman of the House: Women's Household Work in Ireland 1922–61* (Dublin: Irish Academic Press, 2000).
96 Robert E. Kennedy, Jr., *The Irish: Emigration, Marriage and Fertility* (Berkeley and London: University of California Press, 1973), p. 80.
97 *Coimisiún na Gaeltachta, Reports and Minutes of Evidence* (Dublin: Stationery Office, 1926), Minutes of evidence, Dr Bartley O'Beirne, MD, DPH, TB Officer, Co. Galway, 3 June 1925, p. 4.

they grew up, one after another the whole class said one word 'America'.[98] As economic conditions worsened in the USA and emigration to Britain escalated and rumours circulated in Ireland that visa restrictions to the USA would be reduced, US Consul General Henry H. Balch in Dublin reported an increase in callers and letters. He stated that 'in the main the demand for immigration visas is from impecunious relatively young, country-women who desire to seek employment in the United States as domestics.' But he was also convinced that 'for a long time to come it must attract the younger generation of this country' because so many Irish had settled there.[99] From 1946 to 1952, 16.2 per cent of total departures, equivalent to 19,400 people, emigrated to 'overseas' destinations and largely to the United States.[100] Once again most of those leaving were from the western counties, aged under thirty years, and in the 15–19 years age-range, more women than men departed.[101] Between 1951 and 1961, ten per cent of total departures went to the USA and over half of them were women.[102] America was embedded in popular mentality and was still part of the life-cycle in some parts of Ireland.

Continuing from the nineteenth century, Irish women departed for America because it was still equated with employment, better working and living conditions and, increasingly, personal fulfilment. Female participation in the US labour force increased from 18.3 per cent in 1900 to 22 per cent in 1930, unlike in Ireland where the number of women 'gainfully employed' fell from 30 per cent in 1926 to 24.1 per cent in 1951.[103] Mairead's two aunts and cousins who left Crusheen, County Clare, for America in the 1920s because 'there was nothing [in terms of work] for them' locally except in domestic service. Over 80,000 women were 'maids' in the USA in 1926, one-quarter of all working women. Many left for the USA and immediately after arriving

---

98 M.K. McGurl, 'Stray Thoughts on Library Matters', *Irish Library Bulletin* 8, 10 (October 1947), pp. 180–81.
99 National Archives and Records Administration (hereafter NARA), General Records of the Department of State (hereafter S/D), American Foreign Service Inspection Report (hereafter AFSR), Dublin, Ireland, July 1938, pp. 6, 7, 12; NARA, S/D, RG 49, roll 1231.9, Sidney A. Belovsky and Henry Balch, 9 November 1934.
100 *Report of the Commission on Emigration and Other Population Problems 1948–54* (Dublin: Government Publication Office, 1955), table 27, p. 317.
101 Delaney, 'Irish Migration to Britain', pp. 270–71.
102 Connolly, 'Emigration from Independent Ireland: 1922–1970', p. 149; Daly, *The Slow Failure*, p. 188, table 3. See also Manuscripts and Archives Research Library, Trinity College Dublin (hereafter MARLTCD), The Arnold Marsh Papers (hereafter AMP), MS 8301, S.S. 1 (a) for further on emigrant women to the USA in the 1920s and later Britain.
103 Evan Roberts, 'Labour Force Participation by Married Women in the United States: Results from the 1917/19 Cost-of-Living Survey and the 1920 PUMS', http://users.pop.umn.edu/~eroberts/evanrobertssshapaper.pdf. There are many caveats about the methodology employed in this paper; http://www.cso.ie/census.pdf.

in New York found house-cleaning work.[104] These young women could have worked as servants in Ireland or Britain either in private houses, hospitals or increasingly in hotels, but similar work in America offered a path to better paid work, a future, and for many, joining family and friends.[105] Nora Joyce did housework in Dundrum, County Dublin, for two years but emigrated to join her sister. In 1920s America, she secured domestic work but quickly moved to 'better' paid work; 'I got more dollars. From seven dollars a week to twelve dollars.'[106] An emigrant from the Gaeltacht area in Ring, County Waterford, Mary Terry Kelly who worked in the Irish College departed in 1923 because 'Ní raibh morán airgead ann ag an am sin. Dúirt mé go dtiocfainn anseo.' [There was not a lot of money around at the time. I said I would come here.] Soon she was earning twelve dollars a week.[107] Although conditions for domestic servants in the USA deteriorated during the 1919–21 recession, there was 'discord' between the 'maids and mistresses' during the 1920s and reform did not come until the late 1930s. Some live-in servants enjoyed a set day off each week, limits on the nature of their work and minimal standards of accommodation. Moreover, some emigrants believed it was now the 'land of hope and glory for the housemaid, where the electrical appliances turned kitchen drudgery into play'.[108]

In Ireland, the 'maid problem' rumbled on into the 1940s and the 'shortage of female domestic servants' was raised in Dáil Eireann in 1946. Long hours, unsuitable time off and wearing a uniform instead of an overall characterised domestic servants' working conditions in middle-class homes. In 1950, Irish women were criticised for treating their employees as 'something labelled servant' and the Irish Housewives' Association unsuccessfully called for a code of employment and wage rates to be established by the government.[109] The young women who worked in service preferred to do so in Britain rather than Ireland, but America still held its attraction. In the late 1950s, the

---

104 University of Limerick Oral History Project 2001 (hereafter ULOHP), Mairead, born 1937, retired nurse, Clarecastle, County Clare, interviewed 27 May 2001 (hereafter Tape 3); Farmar, *Privileged Lives: A Social History of Middle-Class Ireland 1882–1989*, p. 131.
105 *Commission on Emigration*, p. 127; Connolly, 'Emigration from Independent Ireland: 1922–1970', p. 20.
106 'Nora Joyce', in Ide O'Carroll, *Models for Movers: Irish Women's Emigration to America* (Dublin: Attic Press, 1990), p. 38.
107 'Mary Terry Kelly', in O'Carroll, *Models for Movers*, p. 48.
108 Alana Erickson-Coble, *Cleaning Up: The Transformation of Domestic Service in Twentieth Century New York* (London: Routledge, 2006), pp. 45, 83, 46.
109 Clear, *Woman of the House*, pp. 66–67; *Woman's Life*, 15 August 1936; *Parliamentary Debates Dáil Eireann* (hereafter *PDDE*), 101, 27 June 1946; *The Irish Housewife*, 1 (1946), pp. 31–33, 9 (1956), pp. 58–59, 2 (1948–49), p. 45, 4 (1950), p. 103; *Irish Times*, 15 July 1949.

Kerryman carried advertisements for 'general domestics for first class homes' in America; the fare would be advanced to girls aged between eighteen and forty years, no experience was required, the wage was stated and full board offered.[110] At her first job in America in 1955, Frances Newall Coen earned thirty dollars a week working as a cook for the Brickley family living on Reservoir Avenue in Chestnut Hill in Boston. She left to 'make more money' and earned fifty dollars a week working for the Kruegers.[111] Mary Walsh earned forty dollars a week childminding a Catholic family in Brookline where there was also a cook from Gort, County Galway. Later she moved to a cooking job where 'you're not as tied down' and earned fifty dollars each week.[112]

The range of paid occupations for women in Ireland evident in the 1926 census was described as a 'story of infinite romance and adventure'.[113] In addition to domestic service, work was now available in the growing commercial sphere and in the professions. The arrival of Woolworths in 1914 with better rates of pay and conditions, contrasted sharply with those available in drapery houses, particularly in rural places, where junior apprentices received accommodation, food and lodgings but no wages as late as 1965.[114] The same range of occupations and many more were available in Britain and in the USA. An unnamed Roman Catholic priest explained to 500 Irish emigrants just arrived into New York harbour in July 1922 that American girls became secretaries, book keepers, stenographers and clerks with 'good salaries, short hours and a day off each week'.[115] The *Women of 1923* yearbook found that 'overalls, grease and heavy manual labour no longer had any terrors' for women. They could work as stevedores, dock labourers, sailors and deckhands, blacksmiths, machinists, carpenters, brick makers, tin smiths, wood choppers and freight agents.[116] American women drove trucks, cleaned streets and were plumbers and there was always clerical and factory work. Even though immigrant labour was still exploited, second-generation Irish women were educated to higher levels and infiltrated nursing, teaching, clerical work and other professions. In other words, while

110 TCDMD, AMP, MS 8301, Summary of Memoranda, S.S.115, p. 145; *The Kerryman*, 2 March 1957, 5 September 1959.
111 'Frances Newall Coen – 1950s', in O'Carroll, *Models for Movers*, pp. 75–76.
112 'Mary Walsh – 1950s', in O'Carroll, *Models for Movers*, p. 72.
113 Caitriona Clear, 'Women in de Valera's Ireland, 1932–48: A Reappraisal' in Gabriel Doherty and Dermot Keogh, *De Valera's Ireland* (Cork: Mercier Press, 2003), p. 105; Caitriona Clear, '"The Women Can Not Be Blamed": The Commission On Vocational Organisation, Feminism and "Home–makers" in Independent Ireland in the 1930s and '40s' in O'Dowd and Wichert (eds), *Chattel, Servant or Citizen*, p. 180.
114 Walsh, *When the Shopping Was Good*, p. 121.
115 *Irish Independent*, 11 July 1922.
116 *Irish Times*, 28 December 1922.

most first-generation immigrant Irish Catholic women in the USA lived in ghettoes and later on in suburban neighbourhoods, socialised in Irish organisations and were attended to by Roman Catholic clergy, soon they or at least their daughters made compromises and adopted the prevailing standards of the majority, particularly in a swiftly industrialising and changing society. The *New York Times* reported on 4 May 1927 that young Irish women arriving wanted to be stenographers, not servants. When Bridget Dirrane felt 'the strains of over-working' as a nurse, she became a catering supervisor in the Duncan Park Hotel in Boston.[117]

Against the background of post-World War Two economic depression in Ireland and boom conditions in Europe and America, the 'Feminine Angle' column in the *Kerryman* drew attention to the presence of American women workers in traditional industries but also in new areas such as transportation as pilots and mechanics. Such work gave them financial independence because American women controlled seventy-six per cent of the money in savings banks in the USA.[118] Eimear, who left for Boston from Connemara in the 1950s, commented that 'America seemed to be offering the golden opportunities ... [to] become a whole person – jobs and work and development, just growing.' She found work immediately in a factory in Lynn, Massachusetts, but moved to another factory where the 'money was much better'. Around twenty of her friends from home joined her.[119] By the 1950s, forty per cent of all American women aged over sixteen years held a job, despite the rise of the cult of domesticity.[120] Even in the improved economic climate of 1960s Ireland, emigration persisted, albeit at a slower pace, because to use Mary Walsh's words about returning to America after a journey home in 1961, 'it was easy to find work.'[121]

A further feature of the American world of paid work was noticed by Irish women. Most American married women continued to work in the home but from the 1920s to 1960s more worked in the paid public sphere. Of course it was a necessity for poorer families. The educated Dirrane commented that 'there was no marriage embargo on workers in the USA. A young girl could have two or three jobs and be married as well.'[122] This latter information

---

117 Erickson-Coble, *Cleaning Up*, p. 182, fn. 40; see Bridge Dirrane, *A Woman of Aran* (Dublin: Blackwater Press, 1997).
118 *Kerryman*, 22 April 1950; 29 April 1950; 14 October 1950; 4 November 1950; 16 December 1950; 25 December 1954.
119 O'Carroll, *Models for Movers*, pp. 65, 66.
120 Connolly, 'Emigration from Independent Ireland: 1922–1970', pp. 158, 171; Vivyan C. Adair and Sharon Gormley, 'Women and Work', in Carl E. Van Horn and Herbert A. Schaffner (eds), *Work in America: An Encyclopedia of History, Policy and Society* (Oxford: ABC–Clio, 2003), p. 603.
121 'Mary Walsh – 1950s', p. 72.
122 Dirrane, *A Woman of Aran*, p. 51. Dirrane is not fully informed here, see chapter one.

made an impression on Noreen in Moycullen, County Galway, whose brother emigrated. She knew that married women in America could work after marriage, could go to clubs and 'had more freedom' than their Irish counterparts.[123] Similarly, Patricia from Kilkenny who had step-sisters in America, knew that some married women in America could choose to work outside the home or 'to stay at home' with their children.[124] Irish women with children became 'fixtures' as waitresses in the major restaurant chains, Schraffts, Lintons and Horn and Hardart, from the 1920s to 1970s.[125] The implication was that American women's working lives equally meant hard work often in the low-paid, unregulated, twenty-four-hour world of unskilled work, but that their income-earning abilities were not ended once married.

America and Other Life Choices

The link between family structure, land-inheritance practices and migration patterns has been demonstrated for the post-Famine period.[126] In the twentieth century, insufficient and inadequate urban and rural employment and housing did not encourage marriage to take place at the average life stage, between 18 and 30 years of age.[127] Bridget McLaughlin Creggagh from Carrenmullen, Malin Head, County Donegal, knew her future husband 'pretty well' when he emigrated to the USA for work in March 1925 and soon she followed. Aged twenty years she arrived in Boston in August and soon her friend 'came to call on her', and after he secured a licence as a brewery engineer they married five years later. In the interim she worked as head waitress at Groton School and was in domestic service in Brookline.[128] Sarah Anne and her two friends, Mai and Mary Bann, emigrated from Leenane, County Mayo, to New York, in 1928 and all three worked exceptionally hard. Sarah Anne admitted later that until she met her husband 'I never thought

---

123 American Oral History Project 2007–8 (hereafter AOHP), Noreen, born 7 March 1928, housewife, Moycullen, Co. Galway, interviewed 30 January 2008 (hereafter Tape 1).
124 AOHP, Patricia, born 1948, housewife, Kilkenny, interviewed 15 November 2007 (hereafter Tape 4).
125 Clark, 'Irish Women Workers', p. 125.
126 See Delaney, 'Irish Migration to Britain', pp. 98–100; Travers, 'Emigration and Gender', p. 187.
127 *Commission on Emigration*, p. 69; Lindsay Earner-Byrne, 'Reinforcing the Family: The Role of Gender, Morality and Sexuality in Irish Welfare Policy, 1922–44', *History of the Family*, 13, 4 (2008), pp. 360–69; James Meenan, 'Some Causes and Consequences of the Low Irish Marriage Rate', *Statistical and Social Inquiry Society of Ireland*, 15, 3 (1932–33), pp. 19–27, http://www.tara.tcd.ie/bitstream/2262/4681/1/jssisiVolXV19_27.pdf.
128 'Bridget McLaughlin – Donegal woman', in O'Carroll, *Models for Movers*, pp. 40–41.

I'd get a man.'[129] Once in America, Almeida indicates that the 'typical' immigrant in the post-World War Two years found work, then 'tended to marry, settled down in the communities to which they migrated and sent their children to Catholic schools.'[130] Gaining a job in America made marrying, as well as delaying it, possible.

Nora Joyce expected to get married but not in her home in the Aran Islands in the 1920s, because she saw arranged marriages, women bearing 'ten, eleven, twelve' children and living with in-laws. She emigrated in 1928 and met her husband in the following two or three years. But she 'didn't want to get married and be poor. I didn't want to get married and not have heat in the house. There was no rush in getting married.' She worked as a domestic servant until she married and progressed from living in apartments to having her 'own place' because she knew 'how to save' and bought 'bargains'. She had three children, bought a second house which was rented out but eventually returned to work because 'what would I be doing around the house? It's good for you.'[131] Another who delayed marriage was the nurse Bridget Dirrane who had met her future husband, Ned, in Dublin before she went to America: 'it was the first time I fancied him.' But it did not stop her emigrating to Boston in 1927 and once there she met him again and started going out with him 'for a few years prior to our marriage' in 1932. Even though they were both in their thirties when they married, which was an age as late as at home, they were both working and had sufficient money to rent an apartment, and a few days after their wedding Bridget started a new job nursing in Forest Hill Hospital in Jamaica Plains where she 'worked long and hard, doing much overtime and being paid a good rate per hour' while her husband's pay as a manual labourer increased over time also.[132] Mary Terry Kelly 'wasn't anxious to get married' at all. She worked as a cook in homes, schools and hotels and was well paid, had a circle of friends, went to dances every Saturday night and sometimes on Thursdays, and 'had lots of fun'. Eventually she married and had two sons.[133]

Some women who married were able to exercise an element of independence also through limiting the size of their families. One study concluded that Irish-born women in the USA in 1910 were 'more likely to

---

129 AOHP, Brigid, born 1928, housewife, Moycullen, Co. Galway, interviewed 25 February 2008 (hereafter Tape 7) and Theresa, born 1927, housewife, Moycullen, Co. Galway, interviewed 25 February 2008 (hereafter Tape 6).
130 Linda Dowling Almeida, 'Irish America, 1940–2000', in J. J. Lee and Marion R. Casey (eds), *Making the Irish American: History and Heritage of the Irish in the United States* (New York: New York University Press, 2006), p. 553.
131 'Nora Joyce', pp. 38–39.
132 Dirrane, *A Woman of Aran*, pp. 50–53.
133 'Mary Terry Kelly', p. 50.

control their fertility' than other immigrant groups and more likely to use contraception than the native-born white population.[134] The birth control movement was well established in the USA by the inter-war period, with Margaret Sanger a prominent advocate. Although it was frowned upon by Catholic conservative forces, as was the case in Ireland, the relatively smaller size of Irish-American families compared to their Irish counterparts could not have gone unnoticed by women in Ireland.[135] Mary did not emigrate with the aim of marrying either and like so many other young Irish women she was a practising Roman Catholic. When she did marry during the 1960s, she believed in 'birth control, in family planning and I also believe you should have a free will'. She had two sons. She associated return to Ireland with 'happiness' but America meant a 'broadening of horizons' due to educational and business opportunities for the married woman.[136] At eighteen years of age, Eimear emigrated from Connemara in the early 1960s but planned it during the previous years. She did not go to America to marry but her 'idea of America at that time was to go and make some money, save it and come back and live in Ireland'. She saw America offering 'golden opportunities ... I was going to be transformed overnight by coming to America. Become a whole person – jobs and work and development, just growing.'[137] Eimear was acutely aware that she was embarking on a new life in America.

This sense of freedom for young women was reaffirmed in accounts of socialising in America. By the 1920s dancing, shopping, cinema-going and eating out were all part of women's social lives. Their revelling in a new-found independence, even if tinged by sadness, also emerges in early 1960s testimony from Eimear and her friends who were members of an alcohol abstinence association and enjoyed its social gatherings. They also went to dance halls in Boston and supported Gaelic Athletic Association football teams. Mary Walsh and her friends, who worked in a wealthy neighbourhood outside Boston, found 'plenty of opportunity' to attend dances, ball games, the Mission Church and meet up three or four times each week. Eileen and Bridie O'Donnell had Thursday as their day off work in their childminding jobs in Brookline in Boston between 1959 and 1963, and they 'went into town, spent money and went dancing ... hopefully we'd get a date'.[138]

Another trend that continued from the early nineteenth into the twentieth centuries was that America offered some young women an opportunity

---

134 Thomas Guinane, *The Vanishing Irish: Households, Migration and the Rural Economy in Ireland, 1850–1914* (Princeton: Princeton University Press, 1997), p. 264.
135 Cohen, *America: The Dream of My Life*, p. 38.
136 'Mary Walsh – 1950s', pp. 69–71.
137 'Eimear (alias) – 1950s', in O'Carroll, *Models for Movers*, pp. 64–65.
138 'Nora Joyce', pp. 35, 37; 'Mary Terry Kelly', p. 49; 'Eimear (alias), pp. 66–67; 'Mary Walsh – 1950s', p. 72; 'Eileen Newell – 1950s', in O'Carroll, *Models for Movers*, p. 84

to proceed with a religious vocation and embark on missionary work as teachers and nurses. In 1922, the Sisters of the Incarnate Word and Blessed Sacrament of Corpus Christi (Texas), Franciscan nuns (Illinois), Sisters of St Joseph (Indiana) and Sisters of Mercy (Texas and Georgia) visited Ireland offering young women the opportunity to join as postulants.[139] In July 1932 the Mother House of the Sisters of Charity Congregation in San Antonia, Texas, requested Irish visas for postulants to enter the USA.[140] With less importance afforded to the need for a dowry and greater emphasis placed on being educated, these young women chose to serve God in America, not Ireland. There was a further reason that might have been influential. US Consul General in Dublin Henry Balch believed in 1938 that 'not all Irish girls who enter American orders to train to become nuns remain at the end'.[141] Perhaps some used it as a way to bypass the usual visa restrictions to get into America but subsequently left the order. The missionary work to the USA continued into the 1950s. Six members of the Irish Sisters of Charity left Shannon Airport on 22 September 1953 to establish the first house of the community in the USA.[142] It is likely that they had no say in their departures but missionary work in the USA might have entailed fewer hardships than in African or Asian countries. Indeed Clark suggests that for many the religious life in America represented 'high religious idealism' yet also brought with it 'the prospect of higher ethnic social status and education'.[143]

Undoubtedly as the twentieth century unfolded, the changes wrought in Irish women's lives by emigration to America were softened somewhat for themselves and their families, particularly in western and southern counties, by the reality that America was regarded as an extension of home. Most women went to relatives and friends in America, which contained the largest Irish-born community living outside Ireland between 1871 and 1951.[144] In 1938, US Consul Balch commented that practically all of the 'young country-women' who contacted the Dublin legation had 'quite close relatives or friends in the United States ... [who] indicate their willingness to ensure their support'.[145] These familial bonds still made departures less traumatic for all. One witness to the Coimisiún na Gaeltachta (Commission of Inquiry into

---

139 *Irish Independent*, 21 July 1922; 11 August 1922; 26 July 1922; 2 August 1922; 24 August 1922; 29 August 1922.
140 National Archives of Ireland (hereafter NAI), Department of Foreign Affairs (hereafter D/FA), Letter Books, President, 1932, Walshe to Permanent Secretary to the President, 24 September 1932.
141 NARA, RG 59, IRFS, Dublin 1938.
142 *Irish Times*, 23 September 1953.
143 Clark, 'Irish Women Workers', p. 123.
144 *Commission on Emigration*, table 95, p. 126.
145 Neville, 'Dark Lady of the Archives', p. 204; NARA, S/D, AFSR, Dublin, Ireland, July 1938, p. 12.

Irish-speaking areas) in 1925 commented that for Connemara people when they got to America 'they are amongst their own people, their own relatives ... if they came to Dublin they would know nobody.'[146] Almost thirty years later, many people along the western seaboard from Donegal to Kerry had more relations in America than in Ireland.[147] Bridget Dirrane from Inishmore emigrated in 1927 to 'Boston to be specific. Boston is the place where so many Inishmore people before me had gone.'[148] Similarly, in the 1950s a Donegal woman, Katie, recalled 'you would feel more at home in Boston than you would in Malin.'[149] This suggests that eighteenth- and nineteenth-century chain migration created extended family- and friend-based networks with strong geographical links that persisted into the twentieth century, thereby further reducing the trauma of departure and offering some security upon arrival. America was still new and different for these women motivated by economic factors, but it was no longer the alien and hostile place predicted by the Roman Catholic Church at the turn of the century.

Cultural Exchanges:
The 'Return Tide' in the Twentieth Century

Money

The impact of emigrants' gains in America through the medium of the return tide of money, letters and packages continued to alter life in Ireland. In the 1920s, ninety-five per cent of those leaving had passages paid by relatives in America, which emphasised the strength of family ties.[150] Prior to the practical cessation of emigration to the USA, emigrant remittances, mainly from America, comprised 3.4 per cent of gross domestic product and about 10 per cent of the merchandise imports.[151] In 1933, US Consul Balch

---

146 *Coimisíun na Gaeltachta*, 'Evidence furnished but not examined', 16 June 1925, 17 June 1925, 1 October 1925, p. 22.
147 TCDMD, AMP, MS 8301 summaries of evidence 153 fols., S.S. 1 (a) Congested Districts; NFC, MS 1407, Seán Tom Ceárnaí.
148 Dirrane, *A Woman of Aran*, pp. 45–47.
149 NFC, MS 1411, Conall C. O Beirn.
150 Hilary O'Kelly, 'Parcels from America: American Clothes in Ireland, *c*.1930–1980', in Alexandra Palmer and Hazel Clark (eds), *Old Clothes, New Looks: Second Hand Fashion* (Oxford: Berg, 2005), pp. 83–99; R. C. Geary, 'The Future Population of Saorstat Éireann and Some Observations On Population Statistics', *Journal of Statistical and Social Inquiry Society of Ireland*, 15, 6 (89th session, 1935–36), p. 32, http://www.tara.tcd.ie/bitstream/2262/4900/1/jssisiVolXV15_35.pdf.
151 Cormac O'Grada and Brendan M. Walsh, 'The Economic Effects of Emigration: Ireland' in Beth J. Asch (ed.), *Emigration and Its Effects On the Sending Country* (Santa Monica, Calif.: Rand, 1994), p. 137.

estimated that American remittances amounted to approximately $15 million, and five years later he calculated that Ireland received annually from the USA approximately $11,150,000 in emigrants remittances, $2,250,000 expenditure by American tourists and more than $30 million paid to the Irish Hospital Sweepstakes Trust.[152] As the US economic depression gathered pace there was a drop in remittances, but by 1947 American remittances and legacies comprised $13.2 million, equalling almost half of Ireland's dollar earnings. It is likely that remittances from Britain exceeded those from North America in the 1940s.[153] The impact of such monies on western communities was noted. In the 1920s, Reverend S. J. Walsh, parish priest for Aran Island off the coast of County Donegal, believed that the 'government would have had to be supporting the Aran Islands for the past three years were it not for America'.[154] Ten years later, the *Irish Monthly* noted the 'dearth of remittances' in western Ireland and described it as 'a prop on which it has relied for a very long time'. Informants to the emigration commission in 1948 from the western seaboard counties agreed.[155] Folklore informants looking back from the mid-1950s admitted that if 'you needed money you had no place else to turn your face' and accepted that 'the people have gained through the prosperity of America.'[156]

Although the Folklore Commission material is replete with references to sons, brothers and uncles sending money home, an exception was Micheál Ó Conaire from County Galway, who recalled an old man saying 'O Lord, poor was the house I had until my first daughter went over.'[157] However, emigrant women confirmed that they sent assistance home. In the 1920s, Nora Joyce sent money home to Inis Meán off County Galway, three or four times a year, including in August to buy turf for the winter.[158] In the same decade Mary Terry Kelly emigrated from a small farm in County

---

152 NARA, S/D, RG 59, roll 1231.7, Balch to US Secretary of State, 9 November 1934; NARA, S/D, AFSR, Dublin, Ireland, July 1938, p. 2.
153 *Coimisiún na Gaeltachta*, Minutes of evidence, 20 August 1925, p. 4; L. O'Cathasaigh, 'The Gaeltacht and Its Problems', *Irish Monthly*, 60, 704 (February 1932), p. 102; Connolly, 'Emigration from Independent Ireland: 1922–1970', p. 44; Geary, 'The Future Population', pp. 25, 26; Bernadette Whelan, *Ireland and the Marshall Plan 1947–1957* (Dublin: Four Courts Press, 2000), p. 328; see also J. P. McHale, 'Ireland and the US Dollar', *Irish Monthly*, 78, 930 (December 1950), p. 566; NAI, D/FA, 305/57I, External Affairs Memorandum, May 1948; Daly, *The Slow Failure*, p. 258.
154 *Coimisiún na Gaeltachta*, Minutes of evidence, 20 August 1925.
155 O'Cathasaigh, 'The Gaeltacht and Its Problems', p. 102; MARLTCD, AMP, MS 8301, S.S. 1 (a), Congested Districts, M. 23, S. 22, p. 42.
156 NFC, MS 1411, Conall C. Ó Beirn; MS 1409, Proinnsias De Búrca; MS 1408, Matthew O'Reilly.
157 NFC, MS 1409, Micheál Ó Conaire: 'Ó a Thighearna, ba glas a' teach a bhí agam no go ndeacha an chéad inghean liom anon!'
158 'Nora Joyce', p. 38.

Waterford and sent money home even though her parents 'never pressured her' to do so.[159] Even after marriage, some women continued the practice. Mairead's married aunts always sent money to their siblings and father in Crusheen, County Clare, and to their married sister in nearby Clarecastle. Mai was remembered for sending money every few weeks, Lily sent money for her sister's birthday and to mark St Patrick's Day, Easter and Christmas events.[160] Throughout the period, Eilis' sisters who settled in Connecticut sent dollars home to County Clare even though she recognised that it 'wasn't easy for them to help us a lot'. Throughout the 1930s, the money was used to buy a turkey and extra coal for the fire. Sometimes Eilis' father could not afford to pay the grocery bill in the local shop and on one occasion her 'father was so desperate ... he told the shopkeeper to send the bill to one of my sisters in the States whose address he gave. My sister paid the bill and from then onwards, she paid our monthly grocery bill so that we could eat. That went on for some time.'[161] By 1955 after three or four generations of departures from the Blasket Islands, 'a good lot of money or remittances' had come from America and it was used to buy food, clothes, pay debts or rent, improve houses or lands, buy land, pay costs to the USA and buy drink.[162] Similarly in Donegal it paid for animals, houses, funeral costs and debts incurred particularly in the local shop.[163] Katherine John (neé McLaughlin), was known to have sent home money to build 'big slate houses' in Goorey, County Donegal, but there were few signs of improvement to a house in Castle Plunkett in County Roscommon, paid for by a daughter who emigrated in 1922.[164] Sean Murray's sister, Annie, regularly sent home money which helped to fund his post-primary education in 1930s County Cavan.[165] Pattern days, sibling's birthdays, communions and confirmations, Christmas and Easter could be marked also by the arrival of dollars, along with donations to the Roman Catholic Church in Tullyroan, County Leitrim.[166]

159 'Mary Terry Kelly', p. 49.
160 ULOHP, Tape 3.
161 ULOHP, Eilis, born 1920, Ennis, Co. Clare, interviewed 16 August 2001 (hereafter Tape 5).
162 NFC, MS 1407, Seán Tom Ceárnaí.
163 NFC, MS 1411, Conall C. Ó Beirn.
164 NFC, MS 1411, Conall C. Ó Beirn; MS 1409, James J. O'Donnell.
165 University College Cork (hereafter UCC), Irish Centre for Migration Studies, Breaking the Silence Project (hereafter BTSP), Sean Murray, http://migration.ucc.ie/oralarchive/testing/breaking/narrators/.
166 ULOHP, Tape 3; NFC, MS 1407, Tadhg Ó Murchadha; MS 1411, Conall C. Ó Beirn; MS 1409, Thomas Duggan; MS 1409, Liam Ó Briain. Pattern days were parish religious celebrations held on the feast day of the local patron saint. American money paid for gravestones. 'American Material Culture in Ireland: Headstones and Monuments' (ongoing project directed by B. Whelan).

An empty letter was noted also.[167] Nonetheless, in 1960, emigrants' remittances and foreign pensions comprised 3.2 per cent of personal income in Ireland and a figure as high as 10.5 per cent in County Mayo, 7.0 per cent in County Donegal, 6.3 per cent in County Longford and 6.2 per cent in County Leitrim. The percentage would decrease during the 1960s but the importance of it to families in western parts was noticeable.[168] Irrespective of whether money came from female or male relatives, it confirmed certain notions about emigration, for example, it could ease financial burdens, while also giving siblings the means to emigrate and thus bring sadness into a household again.

Parcels

Similarly, the arrival of a parcel caused mixed reactions. In Ennis in County Clare in the 1950s, it was greeted with great 'excitement' by all residents living on the street; 'it was like ... a social outing.'[169] Eilis was 'always so afraid' her father could not pay the customs duty.[170] Peggy's friends were sent secondhand 'very fussy, frilly and sequined' dresses belonging to American cousins who were of 'a bigger frame'. Their father thought they were 'wonderful' and insisted they be worn to the local dance but the girls 'hated them'. They used to bring their own clothing to change into and 'dreaded these American things'.[171] Brigid in the 1950s would 'wear them sometimes' but they could be 'very loud and you wouldn't wear them, you wouldn't want to wear them'.[172] Matt's sisters in 1940s and 1950s Offaly 'were reared on American parcels' although again 'wearing something new' might provoke jibes from class mates; 'oh ye got an American parcel didn't ye.'[173] However, Carmel born in the Liberties in Dublin city in 1938 could still remember 'one particular dress' among the many clothes that her aunt sent home from America and 'it was gorgeous.'[174] Maura from Ennis in County Clare, related that in 1950s Ennis, 'men had a good suit on a Sunday and a white shirt and a tie and ordinary clothes for the week' while women's clothes were 'dull, they were usually navy ... a navy jacket and skirt and sensible shoes'. The

---

167 NFC, MS 1411, Conall C. Ó Beirn; MS 1409, Thomas Duggan.
168 Connolly, 'Emigration from Independent Ireland: 1922–1970', pp. 173–74; NESC, *The Economic and Social Implications of Emigration* (Dublin: NESC, 1991), p. 242.
169 AOHP, Maura, born 1947, teacher, Ennis, Co. Clare, interviewed, 7 January 2008 (hereafter Tape 8).
170 ULOHP, Tape 5.
171 ULOHP, Peggy, housewife, Johnstown, Co. Kilkenny, interviewed 4 April 2001 (hereafter Tape 8).
172 AOHP, Tape 7.
173 ULOHP, Matt, born 1920s, auctioneer, Birr, Co. Offaly, interviewed 24 October 2001 (hereafter Tape 9).
174 AOHP, Carmel, born 27 April 1938, housewife, Dublin, interviewed 30 January 2008 (hereafter Tape 3).

American 'tartan style … multi-coloured … short sleeve' shirts for men were recalled and the 'shoes … lovely heavy coats with fur around the collars … the absolute colour' and the 'beautiful jewellery' and 'hair bands' for women. Even the clothes of a 'fashion conscious' aunt of Maura's did not match the American clothes for 'colour or a lovely frilly blouse' and 'different styles'.[175] Eilís' sisters sent 'parcels with … nice, warm, winter clothes … lovely, warm pyjamas and slippers … At Christmas we got … books, games and many other toys. One year I got a beautiful doll which I cherished very much.'[176] Brigid's uncles did not send 'that many parcels home' but her sister-in-law, Mary, sent her a 'big parcel of baby clothes' that were 'nicer' than anything at home.[177] Noreen, a mother of six children, welcomed the children's clothes and 'blouses' with 'big frills' and a suit for herself. Indeed a local woman in Moycullen used to copy some of the American frocks and embroider them.[178]

O'Kelly suggests that parcels 'more often than not' were sent by a female.[179] But the response to such clothes depended on the economic circumstances of the household and the kind of clothes sent. O'Kelly concludes that the American parcel was about 'economy and utility but it was also about memories and dreams'.[180] The permanence of memories of the effect of such clothes on individuals and a household in both rural and urban areas is noticeable. Their ability to transform by introducing new styles and colours was signalled in Maura Laverty's work. In *Never No More*, published in 1942, 'Lizzie Doyle' sent to her sister 'Maggie' a 'plentiful supply of clothes' including fur coats, leather handbags, silk stockings, clinging, vivid, wonderful frocks and a silken chemise, which changed her from a good-looking girl into a 'raving beauty', drew 'Denis Carroll's' attention to her and consoled her at other times.[181] Two years later in *No More than Human*, Laverty related how 'Delia Scully' from Ballyderrig used the reference point of a 'cape Molly McDermott sent home from America' for her mother, to illustrate the differences between Ireland and America.[182]

In addition to receiving clothes and shoes, Mairead's family in Clarecastle, County Clare received bed linen from her aunts in Connecticut.[183] Food

---

175 AOHP, Tape 8.
176 ULOHP, Tape 5.
177 AOHP, Tape 7.
178 AOHP, Tape 1.
179 O'Kelly, 'Parcels from America', p. 87.
180 O'Kelly, 'Parcels from America', p. 95.
181 Maura Laverty, *Never No More: The Story of a Lost Village* (London: Longmans, 1942), p. 70.
182 Maura Laverty, *No More than Human* (London: Longmans, 1944), p. 19.
183 ULOHP, Tape 3.

parcels of tea, sugar, flour, prunes and rice were much appreciated particularly between 1941 and 1946 when rationing was in place.[184] Immediately after the war, when Aine's aunt came home to Moycullen in County Galway, and brought half a pound of tea, 'it was better than a thousand pounds now' because 'everything was rationed'.[185] For some families, the arrival of money, clothes and packages could, and did, make the difference between a comfortable and uncomfortable existence at particular times. Moreover, the packages confirmed an image of America as the 'greatest place', according to Theresa. Her sister-in-law, Sarah Anne, who emigrated in 1928 with her friends Mai and Mary from Leenane, County Mayo, sent parcels home with gifts for Theresa's children. But Theresa knew the parcels also meant they had 'worked hard … scrubbed floors … they did everything and anything that girls do'. She emphasised that 'it would be the girls now I'm talking about. They worked terribly hard.'[186] Even Carmel from the Liberties in Dublin, whose aunt and brother 'went over' to America before and after the World War Two 'always got the impression that it was a great place there … they must have loads of money'.[187]

Letters

Along with the parcels came the letters, most of which were now written in English. Significantly, Nora from Passage West, County Cork, who knew emigrants in America and England in the 1950s, believed that people who went to America 'kept in touch with families' because 'they were further away' whereas 'some people who went to England lost touch more easily'.[188] Outlining 'how they were getting on themselves in America', letters also helped to create an impression of America as a prosperous place and shaped some young people's ambitions.[189] Letters could provide information on work and educational opportunities, wage levels, the standard of living, as well as family news and photographs. Deirdre, whose three uncles, godfather and aunt emigrated to America, believed that women corresponded with home because 'men weren't … great communicators' and men were even less inclined to write if there was only a male relative in the home place as was

---

184 UCC, BTSP, Mary McGrath. ULOHP, Tape 3; Anna Lexmond, American Irish Historical Society (hereafter AIHS) Oral History Project, New York, volunteer, interviewed 21 August 1997.
185 AOHP, Tape 1; Aine, born 12 December 1930, housewife, Moycullen, Co. Galway, interviewed 30 January 2008 (hereafter Tape 2); Tape 3.
186 AOHP, Tape 7; Tape 3.
187 AOHP, Tape 3.
188 ULOHP, Nora, born 1939, Clarecastle, Co. Clare, interviewed 25 May 2001 (hereafter Tape 4).
189 ULOHP, Tape 5.

the case with her widowed father.[190] When a letter arrived into Mairead's house in the morning, her mother would read it and then read it again to the children after their return from school. The letter was 'so important' and she thought 'once I read the letters, wouldn't I love to go there. That it was a great country.'[191]

However, Mrs George Sweeney from County Donegal, who emigrated for nine years and returned, explained in 1955 that while many people accepted the clichéd expression often repeated in letters, 'I am well and working and making money', she knew that the 'real truth of the matter was that there were far more poor and hungry people in one of its big cities than there is in Inishowen altogether'.[192] Others at home were also aware of the 'hardships', as one respondent put it, and that the recurrent message of 'all well and doing well' in the letters was often a 'false picture'. Life in America was known by some at home to be 'so different and so unfriendly' and it was impossible to go to mass on Sundays in some parts. Workplaces such as factories were often dangerous, domestic service was 'hard work ... down on their hands and knees to scrub floors' and older people could struggle to survive.[193] It was still the case that emigrants who were unsuccessful were more likely to lose contact with their home communities. Indeed a 'great number of girls' who emigrated from north-west Mayo at the end of the nineteenth century were never 'seen or heard about anymore'.[194] Seán Ó Dúbhda in Báile na Gall, Dingle, County Kerry, believed in 1955 that 'bad or shameful news' was rarely written, instead it was brought home 'by word of mouth'. According to him, three themes permeated letters and songs about America; it was '(a) A beautiful country, no matter what's said, for those who are able to earn their bread, (b) The land of liberty, (c) The land of the free.'[195]

Irish political and religious leaders were in no doubt about the changes which such information and the remittances were having on Irish society. By the late 1920s and after decades of continuous departures from the west of Ireland to America, one witness commented to the Coimisiún na Gaeltachta that 'The eyes of the youth of the Gaeltacht are on America ...

---

190 AOHP, Deirdre, born 1928, nurse, Hospital, Co. Limerick, interviewed 9 January 2008 (hereafter Tape 5).
191 ULOHP, Tape 3.
192 NFC, MS 1411, Mrs George Sweeney.
193 NFC, MS 1411, Conall C. Ó Beirn; for reference to Irish domestic servants see Dirrane, *A Woman of Aran*, pp. 50–51. Brendan Malin in 'The American Scene: Not For Me This Life of Rush, Noise and Bustle', *The Kerryman*, 4 April 1953, criticised the 'exaggerated impression of wealth conveyed' by American letters and visitors.
194 Hoerder, 'From Dreams to Possibilities', p. 6; NFC, MS 1410, Charles Doherty.
195 NFC, MS 1407, Seán Ó Dúbhda.

they are encouraged to emigrate to the States by those who have gone there ahead of them, and who, in many cases, send prepaid passages.' Another witness commented that young people looked to America because of the lack of employment but others saw that it offered a 'better education' and 'better spirit' than in Ireland and 'even if they have to work hard, they will be independent anyway.'[196] Thirty years later, the Commission on Emigration and Other Population Problems report accepted that the positive information made a 'more favourable' impression 'than the facts warrant'.[197] This position may underestimate the more nuanced understanding that many had gained of America from letters and photographs. Deirdre, whose aunt, three uncles and godfather emigrated before she was born in 1927, agreed that the letters and accompanying photographs gave the impression that 'everything was wonderful' but 'it had no reality to our everyday life you know.'[198] Yet, other women noticed the differences in living standards between the two countries particularly when relatives returned to visit.

The returner

The Irish return rate continued to be low into the twentieth century, as noted above. The returnees, whether for short or long stays, were seen particularly by women to expect certain standards in domestic facilities. Johanna, who witnessed three generations of emigration in County Tipperary, recalled a sense of embarrassment 'when they came home first' because there 'was no such thing as the toilet or bath or anything like that'.[199] Brigid, living in Moycullen, County Galway, whose sister-in-law and her two sisters began to return for holidays in the 1950s and 1960s, recalled that when the 'yanks came home' they stayed in her house 'before we got the running water' and it was 'very hard'.[200] Similarly, in 1970s Clarecastle an American relative had to go to 'neighbours down the road, who had a bathroom, for his bath'.[201] It was not until the late 1950s that over half of rural households had electricity, and even in 1971 forty-two per cent of rural homes lacked a supply of running water and less than one-third of rural households contained a fixed bath.[202] It was not surprising, therefore, that accommodation and amenities

---

196 *Coimisiún na Gaeltachta*, Minutes of evidence, 16 June 1925, p. 11, 17 June 1925, p. 22, 1 October 1925, p. 22.
197 *Commission on Emigration*, pp. 135, 174.
198 AOHP, Tape 5.
199 ULOHP, Johanna O'Dwyer, born 1907, Thurles, Co. Tipperary, interviewed 28 March 2001 (hereafter Tape 1).
200 AOHP, Tape 7.
201 ULOHP, Tape 3.
202 Mary E. Daly, '"Turn On the Tap": The State, Irish Women and Running Water', in

in houses sometimes underwent a transformation with the imminent arrival of American visitors. Mairead remembered the occasion when a first cousin visited Clarecastle, County Clare, from New York in the early 1960s: 'we painted, we papered ... a new bathroom went in ... you name it, it was in the house.'[203] The returnee noticed change also. Mary McGrath, who began to come back from New York to east Clare in the 1960s, identified the addition of bathrooms within the house as 'change' in Ireland.[204] The improvement in facilities, specifically bathrooms, for the American visitor suggests an awareness that Irish standards of domestic amenities were lacking particularly in rural areas, and made a deep impression on Irish women. At the very least, visiting Americans drew attention, to use Nora's description, to the 'very backward' nature of rural Ireland particularly felt by women in the home,[205] while Mairead felt that her visiting American relatives, starting in the 1950s, 'seemed to have had so much more than we had, far more than we had'.[206] The difference was more of a reality for Tom Kennedy's mother, who worked as a domestic servant in New York, returned from America in the late 1940s and married a farmer while her sister in New York remained single, owning a town house, a house and land in the Catskills, had a chauffeur-driven car and later owned apartment buildings.[207]

The phenomenon of the permanent returnee emerges in the folklore memories from the turn of the century and Murphy's research has identified that some women returned for a short stay while the 'self-dowered' woman settled permanently.[208] Each census between 1926 and 1961 indicates that every county had American-born residents.[209] Already in 1925, the presence of returned single women with money was noticed in County Galway, the wider Gaeltacht area along the western seaboard and in west Kerry.[210] In 1955, Seán Tom Ceárnaí provided an overview of the incidence of returned

---

Maryann Gianella Valiulis and Mary O'Dowd (eds), *Women and Irish History* (Dublin: Wolfhound Press, 1997), pp. 206–7, 218; Central Statistics Office. *That Was Then, This Is Now: Changes in Ireland, 1949–99* (Dublin: Government Publications Office, 2000), p. 22.

203 ULOHP, Tape 3.
204 UCC, BTSP, Mary McGrath.
205 ULOHP, Tape 4.
206 ULOHP, Tape 4.
207 AIHS Oral History Project, Tom Kennedy, 23 July 1997.
208 O'Grada and Walsh, 'The Economic Effects of Emigration', p. 110; Miller, *Emigrants and Exile*, p. 353.
209 *Census of Population of Ireland, 1926*, III (Dublin: Stationery Office, 1965), table 6a, p. 152; *Census of Population of Ireland, 1961*, III (Dublin: Stationery Office, 1965), table 3, p. 84.
210 *Coimisiún na Gaeltachta, Reports and Minutes of Evidence*, Minutes of evidence, Dr Bartley O' Beirne, MD, DPH, TB Officer, Co. Galway, 3 June 1925, p. 4 and Dr Seaghan P. MacEinri, Coiste Gnotha, Conradh na Gaedhilge, 16 June 1925, pp. 7, 12.

emigrants in the Blasket Islands, off the north-west Kerry coastline: 'if the returned yanks with their families were taken [out] of the population there would not be many left.'[211] But it was not just a west coast phenomenon. In Kilrane, County Wexford, in 1955, Tess Hayes and Mrs Keating (formerly Moore) were identified among the 'returned yanks'.[212] This trend emerged also in recent testimony obtained for counties Clare, Cork, Galway, Offaly and Limerick city.[213] Male informants believed there were 'hundreds' of returned women in the Inishowen peninsula in north Donegal, and at least five alive in 1955 in Ballyhillion. Their presence led to a view that 'there is no one as easy pleased ... as a woman who has spent a while in America.' They were seen as so desperate to marry that even a 'bottle washer', an 'old "scriosán" of a man', a 'beggar', 'the worst looking "fixture" in the place' or a small farmer sufficed their needs just to stay at home.[214] The females who returned to Claregalway with savings which served as a dowry had 'no difficulty in finding husbands'. Many 'such brides' were known of in County Roscommon in 1954. Women 'often came home with plenty of money and married farmers' in County Cavan.

Mícheál MacÉnrí of Bangor Erris in County Mayo, was hostile towards all returned Americans; 'they were the great swanks ... with all their money and jewellery.' He reserved his greatest invective for the 'girls' who came home as 'great swanks and finding all the faults ... with everything and everybody ... I'm telling you they took men here after spending their time in America, that they would not get lookin at before they went to America.' According to him, other returned women without money deceived other suitors into marriage. Another informant seemed equally derogatory of the women who returned to County Galway, with dowries or 'fortunes' because 'some of them would not be too young either. People would say when such a one got married – "she was only an old yank, but she had the money."'[215] A less harsh view was present in Kerry. Jeremiah Murphy recalled in his memoir about Kilquane, north Kerry, between 1902 and 1925, that

> many of them [emigrants] saved some money and returned for a trip or desired to settle down on a farm ... The girls especially were prime targets of the young farmers contemplating matrimony and they provided almost unfair competition for the other girls left at home.

211 NFC, MS 1407, Seán Tom Ceárnaí.
212 NFC, MS 1407, John Murphy, Richard Joyce.
213 ULOHP, Tapes 3, 4, 1, 9 and Tomás, born 1919, Limerick city, interviewed 27 June 2001.
214 NFC, MS 1411, Conall C. Ó Beirn. 'Scriosán' translates as an eraser or rubber.
215 NFC, MS 1409, Thomas Duggan; MS 1409, James J. O'Donnell; MS 1410, James Argue, Micheál MacÉnrí; MS 1409, Michael Galvin.

They were smart looking, well dressed and their manners and speech were a distinct asset ... when asked if they were going to marry a farmer, some retorted, "I guess, I'm too wise for that."[216]

In south Kerry, when returnees 'went as sons-in-laws, or daughters-in-law into other farms – they were always readily accepted, as they had "the name of money"'. Another informant put it that 'girls' gave their 'savings as dowry, felt quite happy and reared families at home'.[217] Undoubtedly some did and it fulfilled their wants. Nora Murphy from County Galway, who returned before 1955 to improve her health, ended up staying for a few years and got married. Her experience illustrated that marriage was a natural expectation for many women and male suitors got a good deal also: 'most of the girls who came home got married – if they had some money, it was easy for them to get a husband and a place unless they were too old.'[218] Other reasons accounted for women returning also. Eimear returned in the early 1960s: 'Once I had my money saved, my goal was reached, I headed home. I stayed home for almost a year. I was returning to the nest. It was a much freer life. You weren't as restricted. That's the difference between this country and Ireland ... People don't enjoy life. It's all clock and time.'[219] Breda Walsh identified the fast pace in her daily office work in New York as a notable feature of her life which changed upon return.[220] Similarly Mary McGrath, who emigrated in 1953, worked in health insurance companies in New York, married and returned later, said it was 'easier to be oneself in Ireland'.[221] In other words, Eimear and Mary wanted a less restricted working and home life for themselves.[222]

Women returned to retire also. Nellie Owens who emigrated from Edenderry, County Offaly, to America in 1900, worked in a department store and then in the Hotel Commodore in New York, married there but returned with her husband in 1927 and 'lived on their savings'. Similarly, George McGuire's aunt returned to County Wexford 'after making an awful lot of money in America' which he inherited after her death.[223] The ability of

---

216 Jeremiah Murphy, *When Youth Was Mine: A Memoir of Kerry* (Dublin: Mentor Press, 1998), p. 20.
217 NFC, MS 1407, Tadgh Ó Murchadha, J. O' Keefe.
218 NFC, MS 1409, Nora Murphy.
219 'Eimear (alias)-1950s', p. 67.
220 UCC, BTSP, Breda Walsh.
221 UCC, BTSP, Mary McGrath.
222 NFC, MS 1408, Richard Joyce. See also testimony about women returning with money by Dr Bartley Ó Beirne, TB Officer, Co. Galway to Coimisiún na Gaeltachta on 13 June 1925 and by Dr Seaghan P. MacEinri, Conradh na Gaeghilge on 16 June 1925, *Coimisiún na Gaeltachta, Reports and Minutes of Evidence*.
223 NFC, MS 1408, John Quigley.

these female returnees to use their labour and create wealth for themselves in America made their presence in a rural society, where women had fewer opportunities, noteworthy. Many of the single women settled into traditional roles but did so on their own terms while married women had chosen their partners and possessed savings. Indeed it might be suggested that much of the begrudgery centred on their income-earning ability.

Those who stayed permanently, settled down to retirement or to make a living on a farm, pub or shop. In Edenderry, County Offaly, the returnees were 'level-headed people who did not "show off" their wealth'.[224] In south Kerry, returnees were 'never idle, having acquired the habit of hard work and constant "driving" during their time in America.' Continuing from the late nineteenth century, returned women in the area were known 'to cultivate tidiness and cleanliness', not only in the home but also in the dress and personal appearance of themselves and other members of the family,[225] while female returnees to Castlerea, County Roscommon, were 'mostly good hard-working' women who had a reputation for 'being economical'.[226] The impact of female returnees around Killala, County Mayo, merited a full-page article in the newly established *Irish Farmers Journal* in 1959. Journalist Joan Curran reported on the number of people who had returned to farm. Three of the four women, Mrs Sheila McDonnnell, Mrs Massey and Mrs Nancy Jordan, had returned from the USA and came to Curran's attention because of their work with county agricultural instructor, Terry Gallagher, who gave advice on vegetable-growing and poultry-rearing.[227] Eimear believed that even having worked hard in the USA and coming back with money in the 1950s 'you had to prove yourself.'[228] The qualities noticeable in the returned emigrant to Edenderry, County Offaly, were 'love of work and industry, personal cleanliness, thrift, early to rise in the morning, efficiency in their work. The women were good housekeepers and good cooks. The men folk improved their homes and farms. They showed no class distinctions.'[229] While these informants identified and praised the work ethic of the returned Americans, many of the 1955 informants agreed that their ways were not copied and indeed some soon fell out of their American ways. In other words, their transformation was at surface-level only and was deliberately set aside perhaps due to the need to integrate into the local community.[230]

224 NFC, MS 1408 Matthew Mangan.
225 NFC, MS 1407, Tadgh Ó Murchadha.
226 NFC, MS 1409, Thomas Duggan.
227 *Irish Farmers Journal*, 29 August 1959.
228 'Eimear (alias)', p. 67.
229 NFC, MS 1408, William Byrne.
230 UCC, BTSP, Breda Walsh, interview, listen/log summary.

The returnee also elucidated the differences between American and Irish 'ways'. Breda Walsh who worked in the AT&T telephone company, a popular occupation for English-speaking Irish women, and who returned with her husband, John, in 1961 defined the 'American ways' as 'businesslike' and involved doing everything 'pretty fast' and the 'Irish ways' as 'easy going' at a 'nice and easy pace', to which she soon adapted.[231] Oonagh O'Malley, a young architect who graduated from University College Dublin in 1958, returned to urban Dublin in the early 1960s, because a 'good quality of life' in America required 'wealth' whereas in Ireland as a single, working woman she was able 'to support a better lifestyle' in the capital city. Although she experienced discrimination in the workplace in Ireland, earning just sixty per cent of the male salary, in America professional women were equally underpaid but she found they were expected to be 'sexy' not 'blue stocking'. Thus, after her return while the marriage ban remained in the Irish Civil Service, pay inequality persisted and there were 'small cars and cold houses', she was 'happy' in Ireland. As a young, middle-class, returned 'yank' who was used to higher standards of living in America, she could accept Irish standards because it was home, where her parents resided. Despite the persistence of defined roles for Irish women in relation to work, she was happy to escape the 'modern American woman' stereotype.[232] Nancy Jordan, who worked as a nurse in the USA where she earned a good salary, came home to west Mayo, married a farmer, Michael, and had three children by 1959. A sense of relief was noticeable in her comment that 'we have a milking machine, electricity and a car. And we will soon be sinking a well to lay on water to the house too.' But she and Sheila McDonnell and Mrs Massey also paid tribute to the assistance received from the National Farmers' Association, the farmers' co-operative movement and the help of Gallagher the county Agricultural Instructor.[233] They had returned used to higher standards of living, but could see that modernising forces were slowly permeating Irish rural life.

The clothing and behaviour of returned emigrants also transmitted certain messages about the individual's transformation to prosperity or, as Philip Tobin from County Wexford and the Silke brothers in County Galway put it, they had become 'gentry'.[234] Men and women noted that male returnees often had more than one suit and tie in colours other than blue, and check shirts were associated with returnees.[235] The male returnee's watch, chain,

231 UCC, BTSP, Breda Walsh.
232 UCC, BTSP, Oonagh O'Malley.
233 *Irish Farmers Journal*, 29 August 1959.
234 NFC, MS 1408, Phlip Tobin; MS 1409, Patrick and Michael Silke.
235 NFC, MS 1411, Conall C. Ó Beirn; MS 1409, Seán Glennon, Thomas Moran.

cufflinks and diamond-studded ring came to define him also.[236] By 1910 some Irish women had adopted the 'yankie style' and wore capes which hung from the shoulders and fastened at the neck with one button.[237] Theresa and Brigid agreed that returned women, like men, had 'more than one rig-out'. They had 'winter clothes', 'spring clothes', 'different styles'.[238] Johanna in Thurles, County Tipperary, took it further and said 'they were more stylish.' The impact on children may have been intense. Eimear lived in Connemara in the 1950s and she remembered the 'great excitement' when a 'yank' would arrive. They would arrive 'in all their finery and it was very impressive to a fourteen or fifteen year old who was running around in her bare feet'.[239] Some times the clothes were considered 'too loud' but the general opinion held in Tadhg Ó Murchadha's Kerry locality was that the individual 'must be possessed of great wealth', or as Mairead in Clarecastle, County Clare, put it, the 'Americans when they came home ... had full and plenty.'[240] The 'chief effect of their dress' in Claregalway was 'to reinforce the idea th[at] America was a wonderful country'.[241] Such impressions were perhaps more noticeable in rural than urban parts.

The male returnee also permeated literature intended for a female audience. 'RMH' writing in *Woman's Mirror* in April 1948 penned a fictional story about meeting the returned 'Jay Sullivan'. Titled 'I Met an American', the writer noted 'really the way the girls gazed at him was too bad! anyone would think he was Adonis. Just because he was an American. I refused to admit that he was good looking.'[242] 'RMH' implies that a certain American look in a man was attractive to women and their association with wealth brought them attention also. Maura Laverty penned 'Courtship by Proxy' in *Woman's Life* magazine, recounting the 'timidity of a returned American (man)' who was 'responsible for 'Nora's' unhappiness' because she mistakenly believed 'portly, prosperous ... kindly middle-aged' 'J. J. Blake' was interested in her. Eventually the returnee 'J.J.' brought happiness to 'Nora' and her mother 'Nuala' by marrying the latter and buying the former and her future husband 'Tom' a house.[243] 'J.J.'s American experience had improved life for all.[244]

236 NFC, MS 1407, Tadgh Ó Murchadha, Seán Ó Dúbhda; MS 1408, Joseph Wade, ULOHP, Tape 8.
237 NFC, MS 1408, Matthew Mangan; MS 1411, Conall C. Ó Beirn; Mairead Dunleavy, *Dress in Ireland* (London: B. T. Batsford, 1989), p. 168.
238 AOHP, Tape 7, Tape 6.
239 'Eimear (alias) – 1950s', p. 64.
240 NFC, MS 1407, Tadgh Ó Murchadha; ULOHP, Tape 3.
241 NFC, MS 1409, Seán Glennon.
242 *Woman's Mirror*, April 1948.
243 *Woman's Life*, 18 July 1936.
244 NFC, MS 1407, Tadgh Ó Murchadha. Recollections of emigrants who had not

Conclusion

Enlightenment ideas influenced views about women's roles and also informed perceptions of America as a place of personal and political freedom. From the beginning of the nineteenth century when young, mainly Catholic women, largely from rural Ireland, encountered America they exercised independence. The circumstances surrounding departure were usually tinged by sadness, the settling-in marked by the harsh realities of life in an urban environment and traditional familial roles replicated. Nonetheless, America equated with the public world of greater life choices, higher standards of living and ambition. Although America was no longer the primary destination after 1931, contact with later generations remained strong and seemed to be sustained through female agency. America became an extension of the private domestic world of home for many Irish, Catholic families.

Even though some failed to prosper, America transformed the lives of many Irish emigrant women and in time the cultural encounter became two-way and the 'return tide' brought welcomed and unwelcomed change to their families in Ireland. It fuelled 'imaginings' about America and offered evidence of personal success along with reducing material difficulties for families and highlighting differences in living standards between the two countries, which were particularly manifest in the home environment.[245] The female emigrant, just like her male counterpart, was at the centre of the transfer of American ideas, behaviour and money to Ireland. But the female departees, their letters, parcels and some returnees increasingly personified the idea of America as a place of opportunity and prosperity for men and women alike which contrasted with life in Ireland in the century after the 1845–53 Famine. Additionally, it might also be suggested that this Irish female emigrant experience in the USA contributed in the long term to the expansion of the horizons and expectations of those women who stayed behind. The latter also encountered America in the twentieth century through other avenues.

---

prospered in America are not extensive. For further on this see Bernadette Whelan, 'The Idea of America in the New Irish State, 1922–60', in David T. Gleeson (ed.), *The Irish in the Atlantic World* (Charleston: University of South Carolina Press, 2010).
245 O'Kelly, 'Parcels from America', p. 80.

4

Women and the 'American Way', 1900–60

Introduction

This chapter demonstrates that Ireland's encounter with America was neither one-way nor static. Emigration illustrated the outward and inward nature of the contact. Another dimension to the twentieth-century American–Irish connection is the engagement that occurred through various cultural influences arising from reading, consuming, cinema-going and dancing. Each of the latter activities was complex and the encounter was negotiated and mediated by internal constraints relating to income, location and interest, and external constraints relating to societal and religious mores and the predominance of the British and Continental economic, political and cultural hinterland. Neither should it be forgotten that as with emigration, Irish cultural influences were exported to America.[1] Nonetheless, unlike Ireland, America's national wealth and natural resources underpinned its great power status and its cultural hegemony, which was pervasive. Throughout the twentieth century, print, audio and visual media carried messages and information about American society into rural and urban homes.

America was perceived to offer women a better life and autonomy. In the twentieth century the lived experiences of American women underwent important changes. American women did not get the vote until 1920 and faced official and unofficial marriage bars in some occupations such as clerical work and public school teaching until the passage of the 1964 Civil Rights Act. The nuclear family, which centred on woman as homemaker and man as breadwinner, was the ideal and this mirrored the situation in Ireland. However, the expansion in the American economy meant that the

---

1 See J. J. Lee and Marion R. Casey (eds), *Making the Irish American: History and Heritage of the Irish in the United States* (New York: New York University Press, 2006).

'American way' also brought equal access to education, increased female participation in the labour force, expanded economic opportunities, earnings and advancement.[2] Furthermore, as the companionate marriage became the ideal, parents exerted less influence over the choice of partners. The availability of divorce and birth control offered married and single women greater independence in their lives and in the 1960s would begin to undermine traditional gender relations.[3] This reading of American cultural history identifies the housewife and mother, the career woman and the female citizen during war time, as prominent models of American womanhood but not as defining figures. The single or married female shopper and the film star were other archetypes. Moreover, not all women experienced the 'American way', as it was white, middle-class women who benefitted most from educational and employment opportunities until the late twentieth century.[4]

This chapter analyses material and popular culture which has been interpreted in various ways by cultural theorists who have perceived it in terms of dichotomies such as popular/low versus elite/high culture, masculine versus feminine, public versus private or production versus consumption. There is also the 1960s view that popular culture in the form of film, radio, recorded music and television was not simply a 'top-down' phenomenon but also a 'bottom-up' one and that the owners of the new media propagated 'hegemonic' beliefs and values including ideas about gender construction and female behaviour.[5] Undoubtedly, Irish women learned about America and American women's lives through the emigration process but there were other channels. Following from the eighteenth- and nineteenth-century representation of women in the media, this chapter unravels how the American woman was constructed in books, magazines, newspapers, music and film available to Irish women and how Irish women negotiated these often complex and contradictory messages.[6] While American cinema became

---

2   Eric Olin Wright, 'American Society: how it actualy works', www.ssc.wisc.edu~wright/contemporaryAmericanSociety.htm (accessed 2 January 2012).
3   Sally G. McMillen, 'Marriage and Divorce', in Paul S. Boyer (ed.), *The Oxford Companion to United States History* (Oxford: Oxford University Press, 2001), p. 473; Donald T. Critchlow, 'Birth Control and Family Planning', in Boyer (ed.), *The Oxford Companion to United States History*, p. 77.
4   Jeanne Boydston, 'Women in the Labor Force', in Boyer (ed.), *The Oxford Companion to United States History*, pp. 834–35.
5   Martha Bayles, 'Popular Culture' in Boyer (ed.), *The Oxford Companion to United States History*, pp. 608–10.
6   Quoted in Janet Fink and Katherine Holden, 'Pictures From the Margins of Marriage: Representation of Spinsters and Single Mothers in the Mid-Victorian Novel, Inter-War Hollywood Melodrama and British Film of the 1950s and 1960s', *Gender and History*, 11, 2 (July, 1999), pp. 233–55.

a dominant cultural and social activity in Ireland from the 1920s onwards, Irish, British and American newspapers, magazines and books were more accessible.

Cultural Encounters: Newspapers, Magazines and Books

Availability of and access to reading materials
By 1900, just twelve per cent of the Irish population were illiterate and while few were educated to secondary level, most women were educated to primary level at least.[7] Previous chapters have established links between literacy and emigration and with the demand for printed material in the English (but not the Irish language) and with the dissemination of new ideas about women. But literacy was not the sole requisite of a mass reading public; location was important, along with having leisure time, spare money and, for some, a passion for reading.[8] Reading materials such as newspapers, magazines, comics and books could be bought from newsagents, stationers, railway bookstalls, chain-stores, independent newsagents, shops and post offices in towns and villages and, as was the case in earlier times, could be ordered directly from the publisher. For those with few resources material could be borrowed from the circulating libraries, the expanding free public library service and from friends and family.[9] In other words, women and men of all classes and creeds could access some form of reading material. After 1918, sales of newspapers, periodicals and cheap novels from both urban and rural areas showed modest expansion. By 1955, Eason and Son Ltd carried 22 daily newspapers and 356 weekly newspapers and magazines including 321 British, 57 Irish and 12 American titles.[10]

The magazine market, particularly for women, was another growth

---

7 Diarmaid Ferriter, *The Transformation of Ireland 1900–2000* (London: Profile Books, 2004), p. 88.
8 Niall Ó Ciosáin, 'Oral Culture, Literacy and Reading, 1800–1850', in James H. Murphy (ed), *The Oxford History of the Irish Book, Volume 4: The Irish Book in English 1800–1891* (Oxford: Oxford University Press, 2011), pp. 175, 191; Bernadette Lally, *Print Culture in Loughrea, 1850–1900: Reading, Writing and Printing in an Irish Provincial Town* (Dublin: Four Courts Press, 2008), pp. 25–26.
9 L. M. Cullen, *Eason and Son: A History* (Dublin: Eason and Son, 1989), pp. 168–72; Public Record Office Northern Ireland (hereafter PRONI), Eason and Son Ltd Papers (hereafter ESP), D3981/2/1. Woolworths opened in 1914 and sold 'novels (by the best authority)'. Barbara Walsh, *When the Shopping Was Good: Woolworths and the Irish Main Street* (Dublin: Irish Academic Press, 2011), p. 77.
10 Cullen, *Eason and Son: A History*, pp. 172, 178; Elizabeth Russell, 'Holy Crosses, Guns and Roses: Themes in Popular Reading Material', in Joost Augusteijn (ed.), *Ireland*

market. Chapter one chronicled how eighteenth-century editors identified the commercial potential of the female reader. In the nineteenth century, wealthy middle-class women in Ireland subscribed to English women's magazines, such as the *Englishwoman's Domestic Magazine*.[11] In 1890 *Lady of the House*, a monthly publication of 'feminine and general interest' directed at urban middle-class women was launched by publisher Henry Crawford Hartnell in Dublin.[12] By 1920, the British *Woman's Weekly*, established in 1911 as a template for middle- and working-class women's magazines, ranked fourth in sales of ten British weekly titles sold throughout Ireland.[13] Irish-produced titles directed at women from a wide variety of social backgrounds included *Model Housekeeping: The Magazine of Practical Ideas* (1927) (formerly *Everyday Housekeeping*), the weekly *Mother and Maid* (1932), *Irish Women's Mirror* (1932), the *Modern Girl and Ladies Irish Home Journal* (1935) and *Woman's Life: The Irish Home Weekly* (1936). Among the monthlies were the *Modern Girl and Ladies' Home Journal* (1935), *Dublin Ladies' Journal* (1937) and *Woman's Digest* (1947).[14] Publishers and retailers offered magazines at a range of prices to suit most women's pockets but borrowing also facilitated circulation.[15] Eason's sales of women's weeklies more than any other category halted the post-World War Two decline in the firm's profits.[16] Other magazines available were the *Messenger* produced by the Society of Jesus Order, or the niche publications: *The Irish Housewife* published by the Irish Housewives' Association and *The Irish Countrywoman*, organ of the Irish Countrywomen's Association.[17]

American magazines
By the late nineteenth century, American subscription magazines had gained a foothold in British markets; more copies of the genteel, 'quality' literary monthlies such as *Harper's Monthly*, *Century Magazine* and *Scribner's*

---

in the 1930s: New Perspectives (Dublin: Four Courts Press, 1999), pp. 11–29; PRONI, Eason and Son Ltd Papers, D398/1/2/1, Order Sheet, 2 April 1955.

11 See chapter two; John Tebbel and Mary Ellen Zuckerman, *The Magazine in America, 1741–1990* (New York: Oxford University Press, 1991), p. 27. Magazines directed at American women began to appear in the 1790s.

12 Hugh Oram, *The Advertising Book: The History of Advertising in Ireland* (Dublin: MO Books, 1986), p. 12.

13 PRONI, ESP, D398/19/1, 'Eason and Son, Ltd Order Sheet, 1904'; Cullen, *Eason and Son: A History*, pp. 82, 179, 336.

14 Caitriona Clear, *Woman of the House: Women's Household Work in Ireland 1922–1961* (Dublin: Irish Academic Press, 2000), pp. 93–94; Catherine Conway, 'Recipe for Success in Women's Word: Irish Women's Magazines in the 1930s', http://www.ucd.ie/pages/97/conway.html (accessed 4 April 2012); Oram, *The Advertising Book: The History of Advertising in Ireland*, p. 423

15 See PRONI, ESP, D398/19/1, 'Eason and Son, Ltd Order Sheets' for various periods.

16 Cullen, *Eason and Son: A History*, pp. 172, 178, 374.

17 Clear, *Woman of the House*, p. 36.

Magazine were sold in Britain than similar-priced British monthlies. The *Ladies' Home Journal* and others had English editions.[18] Similar developments took place in Ireland. By 1882, American periodical literature for a general audience included the *Detroit Free Press* and 'high class' *Atlantic Monthly*, *The Century* (later *Scribner's Monthly*), *St Nicholas* (a 'young people's magazine') and *Harper's Monthly* were available in Ireland.[19] Also circulating was the slightly cheaper but similarly 'snobbish' and literary *The Smart Set*. These few titles had a small circulation within educated, literary circles.[20] American publishers were associated with much of the 'new' magazine journalism'. *Harper's* was already known for its size, over 400 pages in length, and the number, quality and variety of illustrations, layout and content. The fiction consisted of 'very readable novels running from month to month', most of which were 'characteristically American' and, therefore 'more interesting'. *Harper's* was 'distinctively American'.[21] Hartnell imported American publishing practices such as targeting the mass female audience, interactive content and having complex covers.[22] American publishers and editors had also found ways to accommodate the dichotomy in femininity, between the mother and wife role and that of the 'new' remunerated working woman, which would be exported to Europe also.[23]

In the inter-war period, the explosion in American publishing was experienced in Ireland. The 'ideal' Catholic journal was considered by Fr McInerney writing in the *Irish Monthly* in 1924 to be *America*, a weekly.[24] But it was popular and 'pulp' fiction magazines such as *Broadway and Hollywood Movies*, *Breezy Stories* and *Crime Busters*, targeted at the mass audience and reliant on advertisements and cheaply priced, which were in demand. In addition to the Eason's network, the Woolworth company sold 'cheap' American magazines in its shops.[25] A market also existed for

18 Frank Luther Mott, *A History of American Magazines: 1741–1850* (Harvard: Harvard University Press, 1938), p. 229.
19 'An American Magazine', *Hibernia*, 1, 1 (April 1882), pp. 54–55.
20 Katharine Tynan, *Twenty-Five Years: Reminiscences (1913)* (London: Smith, Elder and Company, 1913), pp. 280–81.
21 'An American Magazine', pp. 54–55.
22 Oram, *The Advertising Book: The History of Advertising in Ireland*, p. 12.
23 Ros Ballaster, Margaret Beetham, Elizabeth Frazer and Sandra Hebron, *Women's Worlds: Ideology, Femininity and the Woman's Magazine* (London: Macmillan, 1991), pp. 84–86.
24 M. H. McInerney, 'Constructive Work for Catholic Irishwomen', *The Irish Monthly*, 52, 610 (April 1924), p. 193.
25 *Our Girls*, 1, 1 (October 1930); National Archives Ireland (hereafter NAI), Department of Justice (hereafter D/J), H305/18/1483, C. Watt, F. W. Woolworth and company, Liverpool, 5 April 1933 to the Chief Superintendent, Civic Guards, Dundalk, Irish Free State.

out-of-date issues, cheaply priced at between two and three pence with multiple copies of single issues available.[26]

Following the supply disruptions during World War Two and the imposition of currency restrictions in Ireland and Britain in the late 1940s, it took some time for deliveries of American magazines to be restored.[27] In 1945, Eason's had a 'considerable waiting list' for extra supplies of American titles. In the same year, Eason's notified its newsagents that 'we are now in a position to supply extra copies of imported popular comics, picture papers and women's periodicals' for all classes of women.[28] American titles were available, such as *Vogue, Harper's Bazaar, Ladies Home Journal, Time, Look, Redbook, Saturday Evening Post, Life, Collier's Weekly* ('America's liveliest weekly'), *Better Homes and Garden* (a 'high class' American monthly), and the *New Yorker*. The American monthly romance magazine, *Modern Romances*, the *Modern Woman* and *Home Companion* were carried by Eason's.[29] America's 'most popular romance and screen magazines' *Movie Spotlight, Western Movie* and *Intimate Romances* offered the 'best value ... in American magazines for a long time'.[30] By the late 1950s other American titles, *Life, Golf Illustrated, Tarzan, Modern Romances* and *Woman and Beauty* also featured in the Eason's' order list and bulletin which were distributed to booksellers and newsagents and were sold in its Limerick, Waterford, Galway, Dun Laoghaire and Dublin outlets.[31] *Reader's Digest*, the *New Haven Journal, Time, Life* and *National Geographic* were obtained through informal networks and libraries.[32] These American titles, directed at all categories of buyer, were few in number compared to Irish and British titles until the post-war years.

How did the woman buyer of books obtain them? Most people had

26 NAI, D/J, H305/18/1483, Frank O'Reilly, Catholic Truth Society of Ireland to Secretary, D/J, 31 March 1930.
27 *Eason's Bulletin*, 1, 8 (December 1945), p. 24; *Eason's Bulletin*, 2, 4 (July 1946), p. 1; *Irish Library Bulletin* (October 1947), pp. 177–80; *Irish Independent*, 1 May 1952; *Eason's Bulletin*, 7, 2 (Autumn 1956), p. 5; *Eason's Bulletin*, 6, 2 (June 1950), pp. 5–6.
28 *Eason's Bulletin*, 3, 1 (May 1947), p. 1.
29 *Eason's Bulletin*, 3, 5 (September 1947), p. 3; *Eason's Bulletin*, 6, 1 (May 1950), p. 3.
30 NLI, *Irish Retail Newsagents Gazette, Booksellers' and Stationers' Review*, 12 (December 1950), p. 3.
31 See for example PRONI, ESP, D398/19/1, 'Eason and Son, Ltd Order Sheet, Week Ending 26 February 1955; *Eason's Bulletin*, 7, 2 (Autumn, 1956); *Eason's Bulletin*, 7, 3 (Christmas 1956); PRONI, ESP, D398/19/1, 'Eason and Son, Ltd Order Sheet, Week Ending 26 February 1955'.
32 ULOHP, Tape 5; ULOHP, Tape 6; Cullen, *Eason and Son: A History*, pp. 82, 275; AOHP, Tape 8; NAI, D/FA, 219/3, Brennan to Secretary, 8 January 1940. Tipperary Local Studies (hereafter TLS), The Library Association of Ireland (hereafter TLAI), 'Laoighis Co. Library Service, February 1933–January 1934', Eibhlin Ni Ruaidh, Runai.

access to books through school and people purchased books through the expanding retail network of newsagents, booksellers and shopkeepers or acquired them directly from publishers. Thousands of cheap, paperback books were sold weekly by Woolworths and Eason's and the circulating libraries and the local library met other peoples' needs.[33] Building on the Public Libraries Act (Ireland) 1855 and the Carnegie Library network (1903), the public library service developed countrywide during the twentieth century.[34] By 1944, twenty-four of the twenty-six counties had a public library and a total stock of over one million volumes.[35] Yet, library borrowing figures suggest that just seven to fifteen per cent of the population were active borrowers in the early 1950s, although this does not take into account that library books once read were also lent within and between families and friends before being returned to the library.[36] Neither should the public's enthusiastic response and welcome of the new service be under-estimated particularly when borrowers overcame great physical challenges to attend the library branch.[37]

What types of books were available to the buyer or borrower? The attraction of fiction continued from the nineteenth century into the inter-war period. Crime, murder mystery, thriller and romance books were best-sellers for Eason's and the 'best-selling lines' in Woolworths' stores were cheap paperback novels and thrillers.[38] Professor John F. W. Howley commented in 1931 that 'the fiction department is the storm centre of the Irish public library' because the books were easy to read and entertained.[39] Regarding urban book buyers, in November and December 1934 a survey of seven

33 In the early 1920s, a circulating library run by the Dominican order in North Adelaide Street in Dublin allowed girls to borrow one book and one magazine. Switzers store operated a circulating library in the 1930s. McInerney, 'Constructive Work for Catholic Irishwomen', p. 265; *Irish Times*, 24 November 1934.
34 In 1952, fifty-two per cent of the population served by the county libraries lived in rural areas.
35 'Editorial note', *An Leabharlann*, 14, 1 (January 1956), p. 3; Mary Guinan-Dermody, 'The Establishment of a "Workers' University": A History of Tipperary Joint Libraries Committee, 1927–66' (unpublished MA dissertation, University of Limerick, 2004), pp. 23, 61.
36 Guinan-Dermody, 'The Establishment of a "Workers' University"', pp. 23, 61; Desmond J. Clarke, 'Presidential Address', *An Leabharlann*, 13, 4 (December 1955), pp. 169–76.
37 S. O'Conchubhair, 'A Day with Monaghan's Mobile Library', *An Leabharlann*, 15, 2 (December 1957), pp. 68–71.
38 Cullen, *Eason and Son: A History*, pp. 172, 178; Caroline Kanerick, '"A Jazzed and Patchwork Modern": "Future" Girls and Modern Masculinities in the Early Popular Romances of Berta Ruck', *Women's History Review*, 19, 5 (November 2010), pp. 685–702; Walsh, *When the Shopping Was Good*, p. 86.
39 John F. W. Howley, 'Fiction and Culture', *An Leabharlann*, 1, 4 (May 1931), p. 6; 'Editorial', 1, 4 (May, 1931), p. 1.

book shops and two circulating libraries in Dublin city recorded that fiction was most popular followed by books on travel, Shakespeare's plays, politics, science, botany, history, poetry and religion.[40]

During the war years, despite supply difficulties, one librarian claimed it was possible to get any book that you wanted, in a city or town at least.[41] The County Dublin Libraries Committee in 1941 reported that more non-fiction was being borrowed.[42] Outside Dublin a survey of six towns reported that the best-selling books were still in the fiction category.[43] By 1945, people borrowed whatever they could get and fiction was more popular than non-fiction.[44] Although library book stocks continued to decline, the murder story, the western and the ordinary romance were still widely borrowed in urban and rural libraries followed by 'better class' fiction, then books on the war, biography and travel.[45]

Within the fiction category, as was the case with magazines and newspapers, British authors dominated in the inter-war period. For example, over 50 per cent of the titles purchased by the County Tipperary library service in 1928 were Irish and by 1931 this had declined to approximately 11 per cent, while British and Commonwealth writers increased from 40 to 67 per cent, US writers from 5 to 13 per cent and Continental writers comprised 8 per cent of the books bought.[46] Two years later, all libraries received the Library Association of Ireland (LAI)'s 'book list no. 1' which could be obtained 'without risk of rejection'. It contained 96 titles all of which were fiction of the crime, thriller, detective and romance variety and were written by 5 Irish authors, 16 US authors and 75 British/Commonwealth authors.[47] Book shops in Dublin in winter 1934, sold 30 British-penned works, 18 Irish, 3 Continental and 2 American.[48] Twenty

---

40 *Irish Times*, 24 November 1934.
41 Foley, 'A Minstrel Boy with a Satchel of Books', p. 211; 'Public Libraries and the War', *Irish Library Bulletin*, 1, 3 (March 1940), p. 22.
42 'Librarian's Symposium', *Irish Library Bulletin*, 2, 10 (October 1941), pp. 141, 143–44, 146.
43 *Irish Times*, 19 February 1944.
44 David Barry, 'What the Public Read', *Irish Library Bulletin*, 6, 6 (November–December 1945), pp. 114–16.
45 Mary Casteleyn, *A History of Literacy and Libraries in Ireland :the long traced pedigree* (Aldershot Gower: Grafton Book, 1984), p. 222; J. Sullivan, 'Librarian's Year', *Irish Library Bulletin*, 6, 6 (November–December, 1945), pp. 115–16; 'Librarian's Symposium', *Irish Library Bulletin*, 7, 1 (January, 1946), pp. 16–18.
46 TLS, Tipperary Joint Library Selection Committee (hereafter TJLSC), Minutes 28 November 1928, 15 April 1931.
47 TLS, LAI, Advisory Committee on Book Selection, 'Book list no. 1 to obtain without risk of rejection', 1933.
48 These figures are based on 'What Dublin Is Reading' in the *Irish Times*, 10 November to 29 December 1934.

years later, a breakdown of a sample of 56 titles reviewed in *Model Housekeeping* includes 37 written by British authors, 4 by Americans, 4 by Irish authors and 2 by European authors.[49] As with newspapers and magazines, much of the book stock available to book buyers and borrowers in the inter-war period was fiction and British and Irish authors dominated. However, American authors attained popularity and many came to define 'fiction'.

American authors
At the end of the nineteenth century, the work of Henry Longfellow, John Whittier, Bret Hart, Mark Twain, Nathaniel Hawthorne, Frances Hodgson Burnett and Henry James was 'fully appreciated' by *Hibernia*'s readers.[50] Hawthorne and Harriet Beecher Stowe's *Uncle Tom's Cabin* was 'famous' and one of the 'greatest lights of American fiction'. Louisa May Alcott's *Little Women* was on many Irish women's 'must read' list.[51] In 1921, Catholic writers Katherine Bregy, Agnes Repplier, Louise Guiney and Susan Emergy were known about.[52] Isabel Ostrander was the 'cleverest writer of detective stories'.[53] It is worth noting that references to American authors did not feature prominently in the debates on the passage of the Censorship of Ireland Act (1929) which was directed at banning indecent and obscene literature.[54] The American fiction writers most borrowed in the 1930s were Lucille Papin Borden, Isabel C. Clarke and Mary Theresa Waggaman, Elizabeth Garver Jordan, Mary Johnson, Elizabeth Madox, May Stanley, Steward Edward White, Ruth Comfort Mitchell and Sophie Kerr. Other popular American writers were the prolific murder/thriller writers William Blair Morton Ferguson, Valentine Williams and Dorothy Rice.[55] Librarians credited the 1939 film version of Margaret Mitchell's *Gone With the Wind*, published in 1936, with creating new readers.[56]

During the war years, librarians in urban and rural Dublin and Counties

---

49 *Model Housekeeping*, 28 (December 1955), pp. 117–18; 28 (January 1956), p. 165; 28 (February 1956), p. 213; 32 (March 1960), p. 255; 32 (May 1960), p. 447.
50 'An American Magazine', *Hibernia*, 1, 1 (April 1882), pp. 54–55.
51 *Freeman's Journal*, 3 January 1879; *Times Pictorial*, 22 August 1942; *Connacht Tribune*, 13 December 1913.
52 McInerney, 'Constructive Work for Catholic Irishwomen', p. 193.
53 *Irish Independent*, 29 May 1922; *Irish Times*, 14 June 2011.
54 Martin, *Censorship in Two Irelands*, pp. 61, 85; *PDDE*, 21 February 1929, vol. 28, col. 268; *PDDE*, 27 February 1929, vol. 28, col. 482. http://historical-debates.oireachtas.ie.
55 Maureen Honey (ed.), *Breaking the Ties that Bind: Popular Stories of the New Woman 1915–30* (Norman: University of Oklahoma Press, 1992), pp. 28, 336; TLS, LAI, Advisory Committee on Book Selection, 'Book list no. 1 to obtain without risk of rejection', 1933.
56 *Irish Times*, 20 July 1940.

Wicklow and Waterford respectively reported that Mitchell's book headed the list as borrowers' and readers' favourite along with *All This and Heaven Too* by American Rachel Field, which had been turned into a film in 1940.[57] The 1943 survey of six provincial bookshops in smaller towns revealed that among the best-selling books in the fiction category was *The Robe* by the popular American religious writer Lloyd Douglas. It sold over two million copies worldwide.[58] Among the American authors featured in the 'American Scene' column in the *Irish Library Bulletin* in late 1946 were Wendell L. Willkie, Eve Curie, Harry W. Flannery, James Thurlow and Francis Parkinson Keyes along with old favourites Kathleen Norris, E. S. Gardner, Booth Tarkington, Marguerite F. Bayliss and Rose Franken.[59] Among 'Andrée's' recommendations in *Model Housekeeping* were Kay Boyle's *Generation without Farewell*, Reed de Rouen's *Split Image*, Robert Banning's *All Is Not Butter* and Jonathan Latimer's *The Mink Lined Coffin*.[60] By the 1950s, the County Tipperary librarian insisted on dealing with a range of bookshops which stocked 'American publications'.[61] The prominence of women and ethnic writers in American fiction, and increasingly regional writers, did not go unnoticed in Ireland in the post-war period.[62] American titles became more prominent in retail outlets, booksellers' windows, booksellers' recommended lists and on library shelves and, if banned, behind counters, and therefore increasingly available to urban and rural borrowers and buyers.

Cultural Exchange:
Negotiation between the Reader and the Message

Ballaster et al. have identified that not all buyers were readers and, that, all readers negotiate with the text and bring different 'interpretative and

---

57 'Librarian's Symposium', *Irish Library Bulletin*, 2, 10 (October 1941), pp. 141, 143–44, 146, 'Librarian's Symposium', *Irish Library Bulletin*, 3, 1 (January–February 1942), pp. 13–14.
58 *The Bell*, 6, 4 (July 1943), p. 298; http://movies.nytimes.com (accessed 1 December 2009); Gary Scott Smith, 'Lloyd Cassel Douglas', in John A. Garraty and Mark C. Carnes (eds), *American National Biography*, vol. 6 (New York and London: Oxford University Press, 1999), pp. 799–800; http://www.catholicauthors.com; Clive Bloom, *Bestsellers: Popular Fiction Since 1900* (Basingstoke: Palgrave Macmillan, 2002), p. 146.
59 'Librarian's Symposium', *Irish Library Bulletin*, 7, 1 (January 1946), pp. 16–18; 'American Scene', *Irish Library Bulletin*, 7, 10 (October 1946), p. 94; 'Autobiographies from America', *Irish Library Bulletin*, 8, 6 (June 1947), p. 112; 'American Short Stories', *Irish Library Bulletin*, 8, 6 (June 1947), p. 119.
60 *Model Housekeeping*, 22 (September 1950), p. 543.
61 TLS, TJLSC, minutes, 25 April 1952.
62 *Irish Times*, 19 October 1946.

critical practices' to reading and indeed individuals may extract different meanings depending on time and place.[63] In the Irish context, after 1922 Catholic figures believed that reading was popular among all classes and needed to be controlled through censorship.[64] Almost thirty years later, Desmond Clarke, incoming president of the Library Association of Ireland, wanted the working-class female child to be weaned from the comic-strip, the 'diet of *Peg's Paper* ... the *News of the World* and ... the tabloids'.[65] Similarly librarians confirmed that the working class and middle class were avid readers of newspapers.[66] They could also see that female borrowers read books just as much as male borrowers. Men, women and children often overcame great physical challenges to attend the library branch.[67] Increasingly librarians categorised female readers as 'the factory girl', 'the lady of leisure', the 'housewife' and the 'juvenile'.[68] This classification of female readers had evolved from the US publishing industry, which segregated the market.[69] Bookshop owners in Dublin adopted a similar strategy and used attractive window displays and good bookbinding to catch the eye of the 'housewife, the businessman or child' reader.[70] In late 1950s urban Cork, housewives, juveniles and clerical workers were the 'best' readers and merchants the 'worst'.[71]

Publishers and editors of newspapers also identified women as readers, with columns dedicated to their interests. Extending back to the eighteenth century, syndicated columns from English newspapers appeared in Irish

63 Ballaster et al, *Women's Worlds*, p. 6.
64 M. H. McInerney, 'Constructive Work for Catholic Women (continued)', *The Irish Monthly*, 52, 611 (May 1924), pp. 262–68; http://www.tipperarylibraries.ie/.pdf; TLS, LAI, 'Recommendation for improvement of public county library services 1952/53'; *Irish Times*, 23 December 1924.
65 Ballaster et al., *Women's Worlds*, p. 110; Desmond J. Clarke, 'The Appreciation, Care and Use of Books', *An Leabharlann*, 12, 1 (March 1954), pp. 5–13.
66 *Irish Library Bulletin*, 7, 1 (January 1946), pp. 16–18.
67 'Report from P. J. Madden, Cork County librarian', *An Leabharlann*, 17, 3 (September 1959), pp. 89–96; O'Conchubhair 'A Day with Monaghan's Mobile Library', pp. 68–71; Sean Bohan, 'The Donegal County Library Service', *An Leabharlann*, 13, 2 (June 1955), pp. 81–85.
68 'Kilkenny County Libraries Committee, 7th Annual Report for 12 months to 1937', *An Leabharlann*, 6, 3 (December 1938), p. 88; Clarke, 'Presidential Address, Desmond J. Clarke'; Desmond J. Clarke, 'Books and the Countryman', *An Leabharlann*, 10, 2 (September 1950), pp. 49–58; F. MacMurchadha, 'The Countrywoman: Rural Culture and the County Library', *An Leabharlann*, 10, 5 (September 1952), pp. 144–50; Foley, 'A Minstrel Boy with a Satchel of Books'; A. R. Eager, 'Some Thoughts on the Classification of Fiction', *An Leabharlann*, 11, 3 (September 1953), pp. 67–69.
69 Bloom, *Bestsellers: Popular Fiction since 1900*, p. 10.
70 'Editorial Note', *An Leabharlann*, 13, 2 (June 1955), p. 63.
71 Senator Anthony Barry, 'Library Achievement', *An Leabharlann*, 17, 3 (September 1959), pp. 89–96.

newspapers. Between 1923 and 1925, 'Our Ladies Column' was carried often on the front page of the weekly *Leitrim Observer*.[72] The daily *Cork Examiner*, ran a 'Woman's World' column in the 1920s.[73] 'Of Interest to Lady Readers' and 'Woman's World' appeared in the 'Ladies Page' in the daily *Irish Independent* at this time.[74] These imported columns from English newspapers were directed at the urban-based woman reader with money. By 1929, a series in the *Irish Independent* was re-titled to 'Ladies Page' from 'Woman's World'.[75] On the other side of the political and religious divide was the *Irish Times*, which printed syndicated English columns directed at women readers.[76] In the 1940s and 1950s 'Especially for Women' ran in the *Irish Independent* and Nuala Costello and 'Marese' offered health and beauty advice to the younger girl, the older woman, the convalescent, the outdoor woman, the career woman and the dieter.[77] Barbara Dickson (Candida)'s column entitled 'An Irishwoman's Diary' in the *Irish Times* featured encounters and conversations with women of all nationalities.[78] The *Irish Press* did not carry a woman's page on the basis that its news was of interest to 'all readers' but Máire Comerford was woman's editor and wrote regular columns directed at women.[79] An established provincial newspaper, the *Kerryman*, offered 'The Feminine Angle' in the 1950s which provided the usual mix of advice on clothes, shoes, cosmetics, cooking, diet and advertisements for food, medical and household goods.[80] 'It's a Woman's World' written by an Irish journalist in the *Tipperary Star* in 1959 included information relating to personal appearance, home and family but also news about shop sales, fashion shows and the activities of the Irish

72 *Leitrim Observer*, 23 June 1923; 18 August 1923; 2 August 1924; 31 January 1925.
73 *Cork Examiner*, 29 January 1925; 21 May 1925.
74 *Irish Independent*, 14 October 1924; 16 December 1924; 9 December 1924; 24 November 1925; 20 November 1925; 27 April 1926; 28 September 1926; 7 June 1927; 10 October 1922.
75 *Irish Independent*, 22 October 1929; 15 April 1930; 22 April 1930; 29 April 1930; 30 May 1930; 4 July 1930; 2 August 1932; 17 April 1934; 4 February 1935; 12 March 1935; 2 April 1935; 28 May 1935; 2 July 1935.
76 *Irish Times*, 21 May 1923; 26 May 1930; 30 August 1930; 31 January 1931; 27 October 1933; 22 April 1932; 25 January 1937; 26 June 1937.
77 *Irish Independent*, 28 December 1945; 18 December 1945; 31 January 1946; 6 September 1947; 14 November 1949; 27 October 1951; 16 May 1951; 25 February 1954; 25 October 1954; 19 September 1957; 11 October 1950; 11 June 1951; 7 April 1952; 19 May 1952; 25 October 1954; 22 August 1955; 23 May 1955; 13 June 1955; 26 September 1955; 13 October 1959; 26 January 1960.
78 See 'Candida' columns in the *Irish Times* from 18 March 1949 to 17 July 1953; *Irish Times*, 27 August 1958.
79 Clear, *Woman of the House*, p. 82.
80 *Kerryman*, 22 April 1950; 29 April 1950; 14 October 1950; 4 November 1950; 16 December 1950; 25 December 1954.

Countrywomen's Association.[81] Increasingly Irish newspaper publishers, owners and editors, like their British and American counterparts, produced women's magazines for 'women readers *as* women' and for women as 'consumers'.[82]

Messages about America

Different views of American society were conveyed to women depending on the context. Readers in the late nineteenth century encountered Longfellow and Cooper's literature about westward expansion and frontier adventure, and Hawthorne's romantic Gothic fiction with New England at its cultural centre. America's radical strain relating to slavery and women's rights emerged in Stowe's *Uncle Tom's Cabin* anti-slavery novel and contrasted with Twain's classic *The Adventures of Huckleberry Finn*. Alcott championed similar radical ideas in her popular romantic literature. In the pre-World War One period, Henry James gave readers a contrasting view of American naïveté and European sophistication. There were many other subtexts to their work and that of other writers who presented images of American society. It was in the twentieth century that American literature came of age.[83]

In the 1920s, there was the traditional, conservative Catholic part of American society represented in Bregy, Repplier, Guiney and Emergy and praised by Catholic reviewers for their 'high spiritual tone'.[84] During the 1930s, Irish library borrowers still read Catholic writers, such as Lucille Papin Borden, Isabel C. Clarke and Mary Theresa Waggaman, and learned about morals and faith among other Catholic themes. Lloyd Douglas' *The Robe*, a strongly religious and moralistic book, was a best-seller in provincial bookshops in the 1940s.[85] Frances Parkinson Keyes's work, particularly *The River Road*, was popular in the 1940s and 1950s with librarians because of its portrayal of Catholic themes, conventional morality, intergenerational families and in the southern setting. For some Keyes presented 'the American way of life'.[86]

A second trend was the mass-produced American fiction set in urban,

---

81 *Tipperary Star*, 3 January 1959; 10 January 1959; 17 January 1959; 24 January 1959; 14 March 1959; 9 May 1959; 11 June 1959.

82 Ballaster et al., *Women's Worlds*, p. 6.

83 Devane was convinced that American women wrote most about birth control and in turn, Irish women read it, imported, circulated and used birth-control devices. Richard Devane, SJ, 'Indecent Literature: Some Legal Remedies', *Irish Ecclesiastical Record*, 25 (February 1925), p. 194.

84 McInerney, 'Constructive Work for Catholic Irishwomen', p. 193.

85 *The Bell*, 6, 4 (July 1943), p. 298; http://movies.nytimes.com/movie/41635/The-Robe/details; Smith, 'Lloyd Cassel Douglas'; http://www.catholicauthors.com; Bloom, *Bestsellers: Popular Fiction since 1900*, p. 119.

86 'American Short Stories', *Irish Library Bulletin*, 8, 6 (June 1947), p. 119.

industrial contexts. The murder/thriller, unconventional crime tales of William Blair Morton Ferguson, Valentine Williams and Dorothy Rice opposed the 'cosy' British tradition of the amateur detective such as Agatha Christie, Dorothy L. Sayers and Arthur Conan Doyle. The 'hard-boiled' work of Isabel Ostrander, the 'cleverest writer of detective stories', reflected the 1930s economic hardship and depression with bankruptcy featuring in some stories.[87] This mass-produced popular fiction was directed at all classes of people. The romance category offered little that was distinctively American, save that the urban setting became more prominent and there were more women and ethnic writers. Sophie Kerr, who became managing editor of the *Woman's Home Companion*, published twenty-six books from 1916 to 1953, many of which reflected changing attitudes towards working women. Similarly, fiction writer Kathleen Norris, who wrote best-sellers about wealthy elites in California, published up to the 1940s. Mystery writer E. S. Gardner, who wrote for pulp magazines, published into the 1970s. Rose Franken wrote sentimental dramas on middle-class sensibilities. The stereotyping of American society in *Nobody's Fool* by Philadelphia-born Charles Vale presented 'the disillusioned and sentimentally cynical executives, the capable sluts ... [and the] common man' who was 'too virtuous to be credible'.[88] In the mid-1950s this representation was more refined in the assortment of characters in Merle Miller's *Reunion*: 'a successful New York lawyer, a professional horse-backer, a Connecticut newspaper editor, a lieutenant in the regular army, a farmer from Iowa, a mechanic, a New York warehouse worker, and an escaped lunatic ... [and] their womenfolk ... though (and this seems to be typical of American fiction) two of the wives are planning to run away with someone.' These characters represented a 'microcosm' of American life.[89] Jonathan Latimer's 1960 thriller *The Mink Lined Coffin* combined 'Hollywood ... a hated film star, script writers, directors, technicians, lots of drink, scandal and action together with sharply-pointed dialogue'.[90]

Although popular with Irish library borrowers, the rural/historical setting in American writing was giving way to the urban. Nonetheless, wholesome romantic and adventure tales about the antebellum South, the declining wilderness and new territories such as California by Elizabeth Garver Jordan, Mary Johnson, Elizabeth Madox, May Stanley, Steward Edward White and Ruth Comfort Mitchell, were popular with library borrowers.

87 *Irish Independent*, 29 May 1922; *Irish Times*, 14 June 2011.
88 *Irish Times*, 19 April 1950.
89 *Irish Times*, 22 October 1955.
90 *Model Housekeeping*, 28 (March 1956), p. 263; 28 (December 1956), p. 551; 32 (May 1960), p. 447.

Mitchell was politically conservative but regarded herself as a feminist and was heavily involved with professional women's organisations. Margaret Mitchell's story of Civil War America, *Gone With the Wind*, was in demand in libraries throughout the country from when it was published in 1936 right through to the end of World War Two. The historical novel *All This and Heaven Too* by Rachel Field was also popular.[91] Booth Tarkington reflected on the American class system in a mid-west setting.[92] John P. Marquand's *Sincerely Willis Wayde* provided a 'gallery of American types' set in an urban Massachusetts setting.[93]

All readers could read the pre-eminent literary expositions on race, class, family, the Depression, materialism and modernism as well as romance, crime, detective and western stories, despite censorship and librarians' and some book reviewers' disapproval. Each reader, therefore, developed a certain view of American life. The American setting of some novels either in urban, city contexts or in rural and expansive territories might not have been quality literature but like US films, they provided an image of America where women and men worked, birth control and divorce were available, life could be dangerous and personal ambitions fulfilled or failed. All was possible in the increasingly consumer-driven society.

The struggle for meaning also applies to newspapers. Mass circulation newspapers such as the *News of the World*, located within the American 'muck-racking' journalist tradition, were aimed at the urban working classes. In the 1920s, the Catholic *New Statesman* maintained that the paper contained about fifteen columns devoted to news, fifteen to serials, ten to sport and forty to crime or divorce. It relied mainly on court cases for reports on crimes, prostitution and divorce proceedings, along with sports news to fill its columns and manipulate popular sentiment.[94] Catholic crusaders in Ireland such as the National Vigilance Association, the Catholic Truth Society and particularly Reverend Richard Devane, SJ, wished to extirpate any type of publication that promoted divorce as well as birth control.[95]

---

91 *Irish Times*, 20 July 1940; 'Librarian's Symposium', *Irish Library Bulletin*, 2, 10 (October 1941), pp. 141, 143–44, 146; 'Librarian's Symposium', *Irish Library Bulletin*, 3, 1 (January–February 1942), pp. 13–14.
92 'American Short Stories', *Irish Library Bulletin*, 8, 6 (June 1947), p. 119. American fiction for juvenile girls developed a following.
93 *Model Housekeeping*, 22 (September 1950), p. 645; 27 (December 1955), p. 118; 28 (January 1956), p. 165.
94 Quoted in Cullen, *Eason and Son: A History*, p. 261; Kevin Williams, *Read All About It: A History of British Newspapers* (London: Routledge, 2011), pp. 3, 21.
95 Cullen, *Eason and Son: A History*, pp. 165, 248, 249, 246–82; Kieran Woodman, *Media Control in Ireland, 1923–1983* (Galway: Galway University Press, 1985), pp. 120, 45; Richard J. Devane, 'Suggested Tariff on Imported Newspapers and Magazines', *Studies: An Irish Quarterly Review*, 16, 64 (December 1927), p. 545.

Most of this hostility was directed at 'English dirt' although both British and American stories filled the newspaper columns. In the inter-war years one view suggested that British mass-produced newspapers portrayed the American people as a 'nation of gun-toting boot-leggers, jazz-mad idlers, immoral divorcées and blood-thirsty lynchers'.[96] Readers encountered a sensationalist view of America where women were characterised by their appearance and dissipated behaviour, although this could also imply evidence of female agency and independence. Such newspapers retained a mainly working-class market in Ireland into the 1960s.[97]

In the eighteenth and nineteenth centuries, mainstream Irish newspapers copied a large amount of information from English newspapers and by the early twentieth century relied on agency reports, such as Reuters and the Associated Press service, for foreign news.[98] By the 1930s, approximately four per cent of total news coverage in the three Irish daily papers was American.[99] News about events in American political, economic and financial life was augmented by articles about American and Irish-American opinion of and support for Irish political, diplomatic and economic affairs.[100] Particular attention was devoted in national, regional and local papers to prominent Irish-Americans and evidence of their success and benevolence to Ireland. Unsurprisingly, any story to do with the premier US company in Ireland, Henry Ford's factory in Cork, was widely reported along with news of returning Irish-American visitors and potential investors.[101] The spectacular and dramatic aspects of life were covered including the kidnapping of the Lindbergh baby, the divorces of Irish-American boxer Jack Doyle and, of course, the marriage of the American divorcée, Wallis Simpson, to Edward, Duke of Windsor. The arrival in Ireland of American aviators such as Amelia Earhart in 1932 and Douglas Corrigan in 1938 created many headlines and

96 *Irish Times*, 15 June 1922.
97 Matthew Engel, *Tickle the Public: One Hundred Years of the Popular Press* (London: Gollancz, 1996); Williams, *Read All About It*, p. xi; Cullen, *Eason and Son: A History*, p. 375; see also PRONI, ESP, D398/19/1, 'Eason and Son, Ltd Order Sheet, Week Ending 26 February 1955'.
98 *Irish Times*, 15 June 1922.
99 NARA, S/D, RG 59, roll 1231.8, James Orr Denby, 12 August 1936.
100 For examples see coverage of events in 1922 in the *Irish Independent* and *Irish Times*.
101 *Irish Times*, 9 November 1922; *Irish Independent*, 25 February 1922; 24 May 1922; *Irish Times*, 2 June 1922; 29 January 1923; *Irish Independent*, 25 March 1922; *Irish Times*, 3 March 1922; *Irish Independent*, 28 September 1926; *Connacht Tribune*, 17 December 1927; *Irish Times*, 19 August 1922; 2 March 1923; *Irish Independent*, 31 January 1931; 28 March 1922; *Irish Times*, 26 May 1922; *Munster Express*, 28 June 1935; 26 June 1936; 28 June 1935; 8 November 1935; 30 May 1947; *Connacht Tribune*, 7 November 1936; *Irish Independent*, 8 August 1936; 2 September 1936; *Connacht Tribune*, 13 November 1943; *Irish Press*, 18 February 1961.

much interest. Earhart personified the 'modern woman' in her appearance and achievement as the first female pilot to fly the Atlantic.[102]

During the 'Emergency', when the censor monitored output, perceptions of America focused on military and security issues with some believing that America 'saved us from Hitler'.[103] Afterwards America's global dominance as a great power combating the evil of communism revived a 1922 view that the 'American way' equated with opposition to communists.[104] A more widespread view of the American 'way of life' after 1945 was as a place where 'every citizen should have a fair chance to attain a decent standard of living and that that standard because of the country's wealth and fertility is and should be higher than standards obtaining anywhere else in the world'.[105] Such opinions confirmed for some readers who had generations of relations and friends in the USA that it was a place of opportunity and prosperity. Local papers emphasised Irish successes in the USA, characterised by the 'Hollywood invasion of Maam Valley' in 1951 for the filming of *The Quiet Man*.[106] This reinforcement of Irish-American success simultaneously reinforced the differences in living standards between the two countries, as noted in chapter three. Against this context, women readers read little about American women in politics but learnt about others in the public eye such as Wallis Simpson who 'Americanised' the future King Edward VIII, film stars and those involved in charitable, humanitarian or social activism such as Eleanor Roosevelt. This Irish media representation of America as a gender-segregated society, where men mostly occupied the political world and women's public roles were an extension of their domestic roles, largely ignored the reality that American women were more prominent in the paid workplace, in political life and in the literary world than ever before, but supported the national agenda for a particular social order which persisted into the 1960s.[107]

---

102 NARA, S/D, RG 59, roll 1231.8, James Orr Denby, 12 August 1936. See *Munster Express*, 28 June 1935; 26 June 1936; 28 June 1935; 8 November 1935; 30 May 1947; *Connacht Tribune*, 7 November 1936; *Irish Independent*, 8 August 1936; 2 September 1936. Doyle's relationship with Movita was covered in the *Connacht Tribune*, 13 November 1943.
103 Donal O'Drisceóil, *Censorship in Ireland, 1939–45: Neutrality, Politics and Society* (Cork: Cork University Press, 1996); ULOHP, Tapes 5, 9, 8.
104 *Irish Times*, 25 August 1922.
105 *Irish Independent*, 24, 26, 27, 31 August; 7, 14 September 1946.
106 *Connacht Tribune*, 21 June 1947; 18 December 1954; 16 July 1949; 2 December 1950; 6 September 1958; 28 April 1951.
107 *Irish Independent*, 14 October 1924; 16 December 1924; 9 December 1924; 24 November 1925; 20 November 1925; 27 April 1926; 28 September 1926; 7 June 1927; 10 October 1922.

Cultural Encounters:
The Consumer

American consumer ways

Chapter two revealed that the Irish female consumer was an important figure in the late eighteenth century. By the twentieth century, she encountered different representations of American womanhood in her every day life. At the turn of the century, as American mass production gathered pace, requiring mass sales, American advertising agencies concentrated in Madison Avenue, New York, spearheaded the professionalisation of the industry which in turn influenced their counterparts in Britain and then Ireland.[108] In the first decades of the twentieth century, the Irish public were already consumers of American bacon and Heinz sauces. The General Motors-produced Buick, Chevrolet, 'Oldsmobile' and the Ford Touring Car were also advertised.[109] The US advertising industry in the twentieth century adopted the public/private or work/home separation of the nineteenth century. American advertisers developed four themes: appearance rather than character was the key to success; consumption was democratising; products could realise nature's intentions; and products could strengthen parental bonds with children. In other words, the home was presented as a sanctuary. The housewife preserved the softer, more cultured qualities of sentiment, beauty and repose, housework was a dignified activity, and labour-saving products and services promised leisure time, though this did not mean decadence. Instead women were to become gardeners or golfers, to read more and become better mothers and wives. On the other side, progress continued in the real world outside the home; thus men could dress conservatively and epitomise control. Grandparents and children featured as supporting actors – healthy, groomed, attired, impeccable in behaviour. Advertisements dealt with class by showing differences between rich and fashionable, while manual classes appeared in supporting roles as servants, although they could occasionally break into the higher echelons of society.[110]

In the twentieth century, the American single female as a consumer with her own income and her married counterpart as a consumer with control, if

---

108 Oram, *The Advertising Book: The History of Advertising in Ireland*, pp. 24, 21; Douglas West, 'Multinational Competition in the British Advertising Agency Business, 1936–1987', *Business History Review*, 62, 3 (Autumn 1988), p. 470.

109 Oram, *The Advertising Book: The History of Advertising in Ireland*, pp. 21–29; *Irish Times*, 5, 8, 21 March 1923.

110 See Roland Marchand, *Advertising the American Dream: Making Way for Modernity, 1920–1940* (London: University of Berkeley Press, 1986); Kate Forde, 'Celluloid Dreams: The Marketing of Cutex in America, 1916–1935', *Journal of Design History*, 15, 3 (2002), p. 187.

not over the family budget, then over household expenditure, were placed at the heart of this multifaceted strategy which was copied in Ireland. One Dublin businessman, like his American counterpart, was convinced that 'It is the woman in the home, the shop, the factory and office who really matters, because the spending of two-thirds of the nation's income is left to her.'[111] By the late 1920s American women were already 'envied' because of the labour-saving equipment in their homes. American 'houses and flats' were 'thoroughly equipped with electrical appliances' which 'reduced 'work to a minimum' while the 'highest standard of efficiency and comfort' was reached. Although *Model Housekeeping* embodied the principle of homemaking as full-time work involving its own standard of professionalism, the adoption of labour-saving equipment was uneven.[112] Income, location and supplies of electricity and indoor water no less than personal interest and ambition dictated acquisition of such goods. Additionally the 1932 Housing Act instigated the building of approximately 70,000 new houses to replace city slums and tenements. Regarded as the 'latest in modernity', these schemes offered extensive opportunities to editors, manufacturers and advertisers to promote their respective agendas.[113] The Electricity Supply Board (ESB) adapted American approaches to selling electrical goods and directed their sales pitches at 'Mrs Consumer' who was categorised as the 'wise' woman, the new bride, the overworked mother, the woman with servants or the working woman living in rented accommodation.[114]

During the war years, fewer imported and native-manufactured labour-saving products were available due to restrictions on currency and transportation, which posed a 'challenge to the housewifely instincts of our nation'.[115] After World War Two, the link between domestic roles and consumption was even stronger with advertisers informing the housewife that her home would be cleaner and run more effectively if she purchased new domestic appliances and household goods. The focus on the home-building agenda in publications was given a fillip by the resumption of private and public house-building with 57,232 houses built in the late 1940s and 101,688

111 Oram, *The Advertising Book: The History of Advertising in Ireland*, p. 585.
112 *Model Housekeeping*, 1 (October 1929), pp. 407–8; Ballaster et al., *Women's Worlds*, p. 121.
113 Conway, 'Recipe for Success', p. 3; http://www.dublincivictrust.ie/buildings.php; Department of Local Government, *Annual Report, 1964* (Dublin: Government Publication Office, 1964).
114 Mary McCarthy, 'Advertising in Ireland, 1922–60' (unpublished MA thesis, University of Limerick, 2004), pp. 18–20, 25; Maria McHale, 'Who Turned on the Lights?' An Exploration of Rural Electrification on Women's Lives in Ireland' (unpublished MA thesis, University of Limerick, 2005), pp. 41, 35; Oram, *The Advertising Book: The History of Advertising in Ireland*, pp. 71, 86.
115 *Model Housekeeping*, 13 (December 1941), p. 3.

in the 1950s.[116] Thirty-eight per cent of advertisements in *Woman's Life* on 14 July 1951 related to household and food items.[117] Unsurprisingly, the ESB launched its Rural Electrification Scheme in 1946 and deployed an extensive advertising campaign in newspaper, magazines and on radio and film. It firmly linked the acquisition of electricity to modern lifestyles and improved quality of life.[118] Some journalists believed that Ireland had 'succumbed' to American influences, particularly labour-saving technologies.[119] Other commentators praised American technological advancements such as the delivery of piped hot water to US public housing because it improved the everyday life of American women.[120]

By the late 1920s Irish readers of *Model Housekeeping* were informed about new dining habits of America working women. There was the 'sandwich lunch' for the 'girl who wants to do a little shopping in her luncheon hour'; the availability of sandwiches and hot coffee in 'drug stores'; the 'automatic restaurant'; the 'cafeteria system' and finally the 'masculine' luncheon clubs which had rooms for women members. In general, New York was seen to 'cater well for its business women at lunch time', unlike the situation in Britain and Ireland.[121] One American purchasing-practice that did take hold was that of self-service shopping. The act of self-selection, as an alternative to counter service, was pioneered by Frank Woolworth in the USA from 1879 onwards as a cost-cutting device. Self-service represented progress and modernity with the 'housewife' at the heart of the process. It was slow to develop in Europe. It was more complex than seemed at first. Women had to change their shopping habits and relinquish the availability of credit, deliveries and sustained contact with the shop owner for speed, cleanliness and convenience and lower prices. On 8 April 1961, Jack Ormston opened the first self-service shop in Limerick, Ireland's third city, and offered a free hair-do to female customers.[122] Ormston had linked the female consumer with consumption while emphasising female beauty and femininity.

---

116 See Clear, *Woman of the House*, pp. 82–85 for a review of content in women's pages and magazines in the period; see also *Model Housekeeping*, 11 (1938–39); 13 (1940–41); 18 (1945–46); 22 (1949–50); 32 (1959–60).
117 Clear, *Woman of the House*, p. 86.
118 McCarthy, 'Advertising in Ireland', pp. 18–20, 25, McHale, 'Who Turned on the Lights?', p. 35; Oram, *The Advertising Book: The History of Advertising in Ireland*, pp. 71, 86, 49.
119 *Woman's News*, April 1957; July 1957; August 1957; September 1957.
120 *The Irish Housewife*, 1 (1946), pp. 9–10; *The Irish Housewife*, 2 (1948–49), p. 15.
121 *Model Housekeeping*, 3 (February 1929), pp. 118, 128.
122 Barbara Usherwood, 'Mrs Housewife and Her Grocer': The Advent of Self-Service Food Shopping in Britain', in Maggie Andrews and Mary M. Talbot (eds), *All the World and Her Husband: Women in Twentieth-Century Consumer Culture* (London and New York: Cassell, 2000), pp. 113–14, 128; *Limerick Leader*, 8 April 1961.

The Hollywood star

For some Irish women, American womanhood came to define standards in personal appearance, glamour and beauty. By the early 1920s, American women were identified by their 'silk stockings, thin shoes, showy blouses and thin shawls'.[123] Another noticeable pattern was that ideas about 'beauty', 'glamour' and 'luxury' were derived from the booming American film industry. It created a new persona, the glamorous Hollywood star. Dyhouse has traced how Hollywood's use of 'light, glitter, sheen ... furs and feathers ... slinky shapes and figures ... cosmetics ... flowers and perfume ... [and] attitude' influenced standards in beauty and behaviour. Hollywood designers dressed the glamorous heroine or anti-heroine 'in a fashion heavy with sexual imagery ... glitter, thick, lustrous furs, slinky dresses over curvaceous but slim figures, exotic flowers and stark red lips'.[124] Moreover, cinemas offered a major advertising platform not least because these products fed into advertisers' marketing ideas about 'self-transformation ... ideas of personal liberty and autonomy' and notions of modernity.[125] People could now see images of flawless female complexions and attendant sexual attractiveness. Dyhouse has gone further to suggest that associating 'glamour' with Hollywood stars allowed women to indulge 'in dreams of escape' from everyday life and to express interest in 'sexual power, the exotic, presence and influence'. One of the earliest marketing strategies revived by the pioneering J. Walter Thompson (JWT) advertising agency in New York brought the use of endorsements by famous people including Hollywood stars to a more profitable level. In 1927 a new JWT advertisement announced that 'Nine out of ten screen stars care for their skin with Lux toilet soap.'[126] The most glamorous film stars advertised Lux and while they might never have stated the words or even used the product, the strategy was set and continued into the 1950s. Woolworths' stores in Ireland, with specialist cosmetic counters, sold a huge range of profitable and popular, 'Hollywood-style' lipstick, mascara and face powder.[127] The 'Hollywood' strategy had become particularly noticeable in the marketing of 'Max Factor', 'Miners', 'Dawn', 'Outdoor Girl' and 'Tangee' and 'Stardust' brands in Irish newspapers and

---

123 *Leitrim Observer*, 10 January 1925; *Irish Independent*, 23 September 1950; 1 May 1953.
124 Carol Dyhouse, *Glamour: Women, History, Feminism* (Zed Books: London, 2010), pp. 36–59.
125 Stephanie Rains, *Commodity Culture and Social Class in Dublin 1850–1916* (Dublin: Irish Academic Press, 2010), p. 125; Charles McGovern, *Sold American: Consumption and Citizenship 1890–1945* (Chapel Hill: University of North Carolina Press, 2006), p. 77.
126 Stephen Fox, *A History of American Advertising and Its Creator* (New York: Vintage, 1985), p. 89.
127 Walsh, *When the Shopping Was Good*, pp. 145–46.

magazines.[128] One example of the Irish slant on the endorsement strategy showed Mrs Desmond Leslie, daughter-in-law of Sir Shane Leslie and the Honourable Judith Browne, daughter of Lord Oranmore and Browne as users of Pond's face cream.[129] Such campaigns easily transferred to the regional newspapers.[130]

Not only did the Hollywood star epitomise the perfect appearance, but from the late 1920s onwards photographs of Hollywood film stars were also used to illustrate the latest clothes in all sorts of public and private luxurious settings. Much of the advice on fashion accepted that Paris and London set the standards in fashion and taste. But the high status gained by American designers during World War One was not relinquished when the war ended.[131] 'Ideas from Hollywood' in *Model Housekeeping* in November 1932 detailed the colour, cut and appearance of clothes worn by Gloria Stuart, Hedy Lamarr and Una Merkel among others.[132] The linking of sex appeal, appearance and emancipation seemed to have worked with journalist Eric Boden, who wrote for *Woman's Life* in the 1930s and wanted to see Irish 'sports girls copy their American sisters' and wear 'shorts for tennis ... one of the most striking signs of their emancipation'.[133] Whether Irish women readers made the same connections is unclear, but they were discerning. Edward H. Symonds, chairman and managing director of the fashion company, House of Reville in London, confirmed to Irish readers in 1933 that his company now designed clothes 'as worn by film stars'. But he believed that women were not only 'intensely interested' in film stars' clothes they were 'critical' of them, and their attitude towards a picture or a star was definitely influenced by 'dress'.[134] Four years later, readers learnt from the young actor, Maureen O'Sullivan who was in the most desirable profession, that she was 'horrified' by what she saw of the girls and women on America's streets because they wore too much cosmetics, 'shockingly' short skirts, bare legs, mascaraed eyes and bleached hair. But, she admitted she would have to 'get accustomed to many things'.[135]

Nevertheless, the Hollywood star remained the source of advice. Film fashion was a recurrent theme in columns in *Model Housekeeping* during

128 *Irish Times*, 27 September 1950, 5 September 1951; 19 September 1951; 8 May 1951; Oram, *The Advertising Book: The History of Advertising in Ireland*, p. 129.
129 *Kerryman*, 14 October 1950; 4 February 1956; *Woman's Mirror*, January 1946; *Irish Times*, 8 November 1948; 10 July 1950.
130 Oram, *The Advertising Book: The History of Advertising in Ireland*, p. 156.
131 Tebbel and Zuckerman, *The Magazine in America, 1741–1990*, p. 106.
132 *Model Housekeeping*, 5 (November 1932), p. 65.
133 *Woman's Life*, 16 April 1938; 7 May 1938.
134 *Model Housekeeping*, 5 (October 1933), pp. 682–83.
135 *Woman's Life*, 2 January 1937.

the 1930s.[136] In 1945, Trudy Marshall, a 'newcomer' to the Fox Studios believed 'in having just the right clothes to suit the occasion'.[137] Joan Fontaine offered 'Dress Chat' and other articles advised that summer holidays required a 'holiday kit' which had to include 'Lesley Brooke's low cut summer floral, Dusty Anderson's three-piece playsuit, Lana Turner's smart serge slacks'. In addition the wedding dresses worn by Anne Millar and Frances Langford should offer ideas to prospective brides.[138] In May 1947, Alexis Smith suggested to readers that 'the stars inspire your kit for sports' and Dianna Lynn heard that 'over in America two types of bathing suits are going out and the new sarong is becoming very fashionable.'[139] In the late 1950s, Delia Dixon in an article in *Woman's Life* entitled 'Fashions from the Films' advised readers to look closely at Vera Miles' dresses from her Paramount Studio-made films.[140] By 1955, 'Hollywood' and 'Florida' dress styles were 'fashion-fresh'.[141] At the end of the 1950s, Nuala Costello acknowledged that the 1950s 'styles came from the [film] stars'. Moreover, there was also a sense of freedom of choice and independence associated with fashions; 'she can have a straight bob by day and transform herself into Nefertiti in the evening ... she can be a clear-eyed business woman for twelve hours and flutter enormous (false) eyelashes from six p.m. ... the style will be within the reach of every woman who wishes to avail of it.'[142] The association of glamour with American film stars was a prominent feature in advertisements in magazines and newspapers available to Irish women from the 1920s onwards even though it belies the exploitative Hollywood star system and the fact that the rich lifestyle was illusory for most people.[143] But simplifying complex messages was part of the craft of advertising.

Over time the terms 'Hollywood' and 'American' were utilised to sell other consumer goods: mattresses, men's footwear, shirts, ties, motoring gloves, women's dresses, sugar, glasses and generally to promote retail business.[144]

136 *Model Housekeeping*, 5 (October 1933), pp. 682–83; 9 (January 1937), p. 229; 9 (April 1937), p. 377; 9 (May 1937), p. 402; 9 (June 1937), p. 44; 9 (September 1937), p. 713; 11 (November 1938), p. 14; 11 (February 1939), p. 243; 11 (May 1939), p. 460; 11 (October 1939), p. 810.
137 *Woman's Mirror*, January 1945.
138 *Woman's Mirror*, November 1945; March 1945; July 1945; June 1946; June 1945.
139 *Woman's Mirror*, April 1945; May 1945; February 1945; January 1947; May 1947.
140 *Woman's Life*, 9 November 1957.
141 *Irish Independent*, 31 May 1955.
142 *Irish Independent*, 12 January 1960. See also a newcomer to the market, *Irish Farmers Journal*, 31 August 1957; 7 March 1959.
143 Dyhouse, *Glamour*, pp. 58–59.
144 *Irish Independent*, 21 February 1922; 1, 3 November 1922; 11 May 1922; 30 June 1939; 4 May 1948; 6 April 1951; 31 May 1955, *Irish Press*, 28 January 1950, *Irish Times*, 28 July 1951, *Cork Examiner*, 13 June 1950.

Daune's Pharmacy in Ballinasloe, County Galway, used the Max Factor image to advertise its existence, as did T. R. Lester in Cork.[145] Mrs James Duignan, formerly Nancy Armstrong, who had worked at Best and Company's Beauty Salon, 5th Avenue, New York announced the opening of the 'Hollywood Beauty Salon' at Menlough, County Galway, on 8 November 1957.[146] Even the traditional knitting pattern from the American firms McCall and Simplicity, which were constantly featured in Irish newspapers and magazines, used accompanying images of smiling, smart-looking women, men and children which conveyed the message that knitting was not just useful and money-saving for a family but resulted in happiness and prosperity.[147] The link between advertisements, consumption and lifestyle refined by American advertising companies gradually proliferated in Irish advertisements. The American 'way' in advertisements found its place alongside existing associations such as the 'Italian look' and 'Paris style' and exemplified the modern and the modish.[148] By 1960, American fashions in clothes, cosmetics, food, health and diet products, domestic furniture and appliances had been added to the list of products available to the Irish public.[149] This evidence offers some sign of the public's interest in US-made products but does not confirm whether or not Irish women believed they were buying the perfect appearance for themselves, their families and home. Other commentators believed they could see a direct link.

Campaigns against foreign consumerism

Previous chapters illustrated that women consumers were urged to protect Ireland's commercial interests and to demonstrate their virtue as well as their patriotism by buying Irish-made goods. In the twentieth century there were various campaigns against foreign influences on Ireland. Although not specifically directed at America, much of it centred on women as buyers and consumers.[150] Self-sufficiency and protectionism were central tenets of

---

145 *Connacht Tribune*, 30 September 1950; *Cork Examiner*, 8 November 1950.
146 *Connacht Tribune*, 9 November 1957.
147 For examples see *Irish Independent*, 14 November 1949; 29 January 1951; 16 April 1951; 5 November 1951; 17 March 1952; 7 April 1952; 17 November 1952; 25 October 1954; 13 June 1955; 26 July 1955; 13 October 1959; 27 October 1959; 5 January 1960; 26 January 1960.
148 *Irish Independent*, 16 April 1958. The description 'American wonder drug' was another feature in Irish advertising to sell all sorts of products. *Cork Examiner*, 28 June 1951.
149 Oram, *The Advertising Book: The History of Advertising in Ireland*, pp. 143, 177, 350; *Cork Examiner*, April 1957.
150 In the 1880s, women often led the campaigns for 'native manufactures'. The Irish Industrial Development Association, established in 1903, campaigned in favour of Irish-produced goods over imports. American-owned Woolworths was never targeted by campaigners. See also Rains, *Commodity Culture and Social Class in Dublin 1850–1916*, p. 95; Walsh, *When the Shopping Was Good*, pp. 20–22, 40–41.

Sinn Féin and later Fianna Fáil economic policy. Beginning in 1908, Sinn Féin organised Aonach na Nodlag, an annual Christmas fair held at the Mansion House in Dublin to establish and promote Irish industries.[151] In the 1920s newspaper advertisements appealed to the 'Women of Ireland' to buy Irish-made commodities. The *Irish Independent* reminded the married woman to buy Irish products and not to spend on 'such scanty drapery as could only be exceeded in the slave markets of pagan countries'. After coming to power in 1932, Taoiseach Éamon de Valera echoed eighteenth-century rhetoric by suggesting that an Irish woman should be dressed 'from head to foot' in Irish manufactured goods and that she should boast about it. Against the background of the Anglo-Irish Economic War (1932–38), and then the 1939–45 'Emergency', 'Buy Irish Goods' headlines featured classified advertisements for Irish-made goods and 'women shoppers' were the principal targets. The Women's Industrial Development Association (WIDA) took over organising the Aonach and in 1940 Linda Kearns MacWhinney, parliamentary senator and WIDA president, criticised the amount of money spent by women on imports as a 'sad commentary on their patriotism'.[152] In 1943, the Gaelic Athletic Association, the governing body for native Irish sports, described Irish fashion as a 'second-rate imitation of Hollywood'.[153]

During the short boom from 1946 to 1950, another 'buy Irish campaign' in March 1950 urged consumers to buy Irish goods and shopkeepers to display them in their windows, and there was an 'all Irish fashion parade' in the Gresham Hotel in Dublin.[154] Despite these campaigns, American imports increased and in the immediate post-war years precious dollars were used to import electrical equipment for the home and workplace. However, Department of Finance officials disputed the use of dollars to import 'non-essential' or 'luxury' items and one official queried whether 'nylons are still obnoxious ... what about ... artificial jewellery, ladies' apparel, furs? And cigars and US cigarettes?' The demand for cigarettes, a hallmark of sophistication in Hollywood films, was insatiable and almost twenty-five per cent of all Irish Marshall Aid funded tobacco imports. Seán MacEntee, the Fianna Fáil Minister for Finance (1951–54), described the demand for consumer goods as an 'orgy of spending' and taunted his predecessors in the 1948–51 inter-party government with accusations about their sanctioning

151 http://www.nli.ie/1916/pdf/3.3.1.pdf.
152 *Leitrim Observer*, 11 October 1930; *Irish Independent*, 14 January 1931; 9 December 1935; http://www.corkarchives.ie/media.pdf; *Irish Independent*, 4 April 1940; 10 December 1940.
153 Quoted in Joseph Anelius, *National Action: A Plan for the National Recovery of Ireland* (2nd edition; Dublin: Gaelic Athletic Association, 1942), p. 100.
154 *Irish Times*, 22 March 1950; *Irish Press*, 4 May 1950.

of dollars for the 'purchase of things like 'permanent-waving pads, combs, imitation jewellery'.[155] Profits in Woolworth stores in post-war Ireland still came from sales of cheap jewellery, 'Hollywood-style' cosmetics along with 'American-style' soft ice cream and fancy goods.[156] Accepting that Britain still provided most Irish imports, 78 per cent in 1929 and 53 per cent in 1950, direct American imports increased from 8 per cent in 1929 to 13 per cent in 1950.[157] Many women now considered American goods, particularly relating to appearance, as part of their everyday lives. American women had presented a physical image which had found a currency with Irish women.

Other representations of American consumerist society provoked similar complex reactions. In the 1920s and 1930s, Catholic commentators believed that American women's clothes offended against 'common decency', America was a place where girls with 'abbreviated costumes ... ostentatiously puffed at their cigarettes' and partook of other 'unhealthy amusement[s]' such as 'jazz' and cinema-going.[158] Yet alongside this, the reader of the *Messenger* learnt from numerous letters of thanksgiving and published petitions that single and married women in America attended high school and college, passed examinations, obtained employment, got increases in salary and were promoted. Letters printed indicated that Irish women continued to send money home, particularly in time of great need.[159] Despite the Roman Catholic church's criticism of emigration and the modern woman, Irish-American 'working girls' in America were applauded because their 'hard earned dollars' paid for the building of churches in the USA and both lay and religious women spearheaded the campaigns to increase the Catholic population and to restrict indecent films, non-Catholic wireless stations

---

155 Bernadette Whelan, *Ireland and the Marshall Plan 1947–1957* (Dublin: Four Courts Press, 2000), pp. 204–5, 228. NAI, D/T, S14106E, Finance memorandum, 21 February 1949; NAI, D/T, S14106E, Hogan to Cremin, 9 February 1949; University College Dublin Archives, Seán MacEntee papers, P67/590(1), Speech, Minister for Finance, at Dungarvan, County Waterford, 22 June 1952.

156 Walsh, *When the Shopping Was Good*, pp. 77, 145, 111.

157 Whelan, *Ireland and the Marshall Plan 1947–1957*, p. 38.

158 Mary Butler, *Modern Fashions in Ladies' Dress*, p. 4; J. L. O'Toole, 'The Value of Comparison, A Story of Irish Life', *Irish Messenger of the Sacred Heart*, 41 (April 1928), pp. 7–8; 'Great National Novena', ibid., 43 (February 1930), p. 97; W. J. Blake, 'Think It Over: Bad Literature', ibid., 59 (July 1946), p. 134; 'From Girl in New York "Child of Mary"', ibid., 42 (May 1929), p. 232; 'An Emigrant's Warning', ibid., 40 (August 1927), p. 376; 'An Exile's Petition for Work', ibid., 41 (June 1928), p. 281; 'Letters of Thanksgiving', ibid., 42 (April 1929), p. 183; 'An Emigrant's Warning', ibid., 43 (December 1930), p. 568.

159 For example see 'Letters of Thanksgivings', *Irish Messenger of the Sacred Heart*, 40 (August 1927), p. 376; 40 (November 1927), p. 523; 42 (April 1929), p. 183; 43 (May 1930), p. 235; 64 (October 1951), pp. 211–12; 72 (February 1959), p. 54.

and reading matter.[160] This apparent contradiction emerges in popular magazines also. Others cautioned that the American working woman made 'sacrifices', which was interpreted by one young Waterford woman in 1939 as the 'American girl' while 'always pert, pretty and smartly dressed' was 'hard as nails'.[161] In 1945 the 'young [Irish] woman of business' was warned to 'Be yourself. Remember there is only one Hedy Lamarr.'[162] But the 'American girl' was defended by Eric Boden in *Woman's Life*; she was 'delightful ... frank ... friendly and amazingly cheerful even in the most trying circumstances ... she wears better stockings and shoes which are ornamental as well as useful ... the American girl knows all there is to know about cosmetics ... she is essentially a great pal.' The example of this fashionable, clever, independent American woman recurs in Boden's columns for his Irish readers.[163]

Similarly, newspapers and magazines defined the 'modern woman' by her bobbed hair, slender figure, short skirts, up-to-date clothes, the use of make-up, cigarette-smoking, dancing certain dances, going to the cinema, drinking cocktails, working in a career and being independent.[164] Yet, side by

160 Mrs. Concannon, 'The Missionary Race: No. 1 Ireland's Destiny', *Irish Messenger of the Sacred Heart*, 42 (January 1929), pp. 24–25; Denis Gwynn, 'Catholic Emancipation and How it was Secured', ibid., 42 (December 1929), p. 536; 'Dangers of the Non-Catholic Wireless', ibid., 43 (July 1930), pp. 335–36; Blake, 'Think It Over: Bad Literature', p. 134.
161 *Woman's Life*, 4 July 1936.
162 *Woman's Mirror*, January 1945.
163 *Woman's Life*, 18 March 1939; 1, 29 April 1939; 24 June 1939.
164 In the late nineteenth century, women cyclists represented the 'New Woman movement' as they were either 'modern and progressive or monstrously unfeminine'. See Tony Farmar, *Privileged Lives: A Social History of Middle-Class Ireland 1882–1989* (Dublin: A. & A. Farmar, 2010), pp. 43–64; Rains, *Commodity Culture and Social Class in Dublin 1850–1916*, p. 131; Louise Ryan, 'Negotiating Modernity and Tradition: Newspaper Debates on the "Modern Girl" in the Irish Free State', *Journal of Gender Studies*, 7, 2 (July 1998), pp. 9–14; Louise Ryan, 'Constructing "Irishwoman": Modern Girls and Comely Maidens', *Irish Studies Review*, 6, 3 (1998), pp. 263–70; Louise Ryan, 'Locating the Flapper in Rural Irish Society: The Irish Provincial Press and the Modern Woman in the 1920s', in Ann Heilmann and Margaret Beetham (eds), *New Woman Hybridities: Feminity, Feminism and International Consumer Culture, 1880–1930* (London: Routledge, 2004), pp. 90–101. Ryan's work is based on an examination of the editorials, articles, letters page and women's pages in the *Irish Times*, *Irish Independent* and *Cork Examiner*. See also Ferriter, *The Transformation of Irish Society, 1900–2000*, p. 74; *Irish Independent*, 25 November 1929; *Leitrim Observer*, 23 June 1923; 18 August 1923; 2 August 1924; 31 January 1925; *Irish Times*, 21 May 1923; 26 May 1930; 30 August 1930; 31 January 1931; 27 October 1933; 22 April 1932; 25 January 1937; 26 June 1937; *Leitrim Observer*, 10 January 1925; *Irish Independent*, 14 October 1924; 16 December 1924; 9 December 1924; 24 November 1925; 20 November 1925; 27 April 1926; 28 September 1926; 7 June 1927; 10 October 1922; 22 October 1929; 15 April 1930; 22 April 1930; 29 April 1930; 30 May 1930; 4 July 1930; 2 August 1932; 17 April 1934; 4 February 1935;

side with this image were advertisements for dances, cinema and cigarettes. Indeed women had smoked as long as men had, but they gained visibility from the 1920s onwards through advertising and film.[165] Moreover, Catholic, political and newspaper figures failed to campaign in a sustained way for social and cultural amenities in Ireland, which contributed to Irish women and men turning to the newest incarnations of the American way: the cinema and jazz.[166] In 1920s rural Ireland there were few halls or clubs. In the 1940s Muintir na Tire commented on the need for local community activities and in the 1950s the 'loneliness, dullness and [the] generally unattractive nature of life in many parts of rural Ireland' was one reason for migration.[167] Those who lived furthest from cities, towns, villages and the main road fared worst of all and, of course, the availability of time, money and transportation dictated the extent of access to organised public entertainment, as did gender. The Irish Countrywomen's Association reported in 1932 that for 'all young girls in the country', the absence of 'recreational and cultural facilities' created a 'leaning towards town life ... such facilities as exist are poorly organised, haphazard and without co-ordination.'[168] Much of the entertainment available to married women in rural areas centred around either their own or a neighbouring home with dancing and music a feature of church-related activities such as stations, rosaries, wakes and weddings. Emigrant departures, markets and fairs also brought people together and concerts, plays and card-playing were popular with married women. In urban areas, the entertainment available to working-class married women also centred on church activities and the home with regular 'hooleys' held in Dublin tenements. Single women in urban areas, depending on income and class, could engage in sporting activities including cycling and tennis and attend plays, theatre and dances.[169] American popular culture promoted more representations of American womanhood.

---

12 March 1935; 2 April 1935; 28 May 1935; 2 July 1935; 1 December 1931; *Irish Times*, 21 May 1923; 26 May 1930; 30 August 1930; 31 January 1931; 27 October 1933; 22 April 1932; 25 January 1937; 26 June 1937.

165 Penny Tinkler, *Smoke Signals. Women, Smoking and Visual Culture* (Berg: Oxford, 2006), p. 59; *Woman's Life*, 12 September 1936.

166 Maria Luddy, 'Sex and the Single Girl in 1920s and 1930s Ireland', *The Irish Review*, 35 (Summer 2007), p. 80.

167 *Irish Statesman*, 4 September 1926; *Intoxicating Liquor Commission Report, 1925* (Dublin: Government Publications Office, 1925), p. 3; NLI, MS 39,871/4, Muintir na Tire, Memorandum for the Commission on Vocational Organisation; *Report of the Commission on Emigration and Other Population Problems 1948–1954* (Dublin: Stationery Office, 1955), p. 175.

168 NLI, MS 39,872/4, Irish Countrywomen's Association, Report to the Commission on Youth Unemployment, 1927–31.

169 Clear, *Woman of the House*, pp. 207–9; Myrtle Hill, *Women in Ireland: A Century*

New Forms of Cultural Encounter

Cinema-going and Hollywood films

In 1939 weekly film attendance in the USA averaged 80 million, in Britain 23 million and in Ireland 21 million.[170] By 1950, one in every three people in Ireland went to the cinema at least once a week and viewed mainly American and specifically Hollywood-produced films.[171] Cinema became the main form of mass public entertainment. In addition to the new or renovated cinemas in the cities, a hall or wall in a village or town was adapted with little financial outlay and capital and admission prices were kept low to attract a wider selection of people than previously attended theatre or concerts.[172] From 1922 onwards, Hollywood on the American west coast became the primary location for film production and the studio system dominated the industry. In the mid-1930s, James Montgomery, the Irish film censor, commented that America 'called the tune in the film industry'.[173] In 1939, Irish film-goers veiwed 1,232 American films and 269 British films, representing 60 more US films than in 1937 and 18 fewer British films.[174] By 1953, 1,965 films were viewed by the public and five times as many American films as British were shown in Ireland.[175]

In 1930s Britain a number of studies examined the impact of cinema-going on women. Except for the Irish censor's records and certain individuals' interest in the cinema phenomenon, no large-scale studies of regular cinema-goers' motivations exist for Ireland, as they do for Britain, and thus oral history, advertisements, articles and public discourse become useful. Rockett's contention, that memories of childhood are often clouded

---

of Change (Belfast: The Blackstaff Press, 2003), pp. 39–40, 110; Kevin C. Kearns, *Dublin Tenement Life: An Oral History* (Dublin: Gill and Macmillan, 1996), pp. 42, 44; McHale, 'Who Turned on the Lights?', appendix 1, interviews, pp. 77–78, 84–85, 95–96, 103–4. See also the evidence in Manuscripts and Archive Research Library, Trinity College Dublin (hereafter MARLTCD), The Arnold Marsh Papers (hereafter AMP), MS 8301, S.S. 1 (a), M. 36, Co. Leitrim VEC, M. 74, Michael O Ciosoig, Connemara; T. 18 Gaeltacht Services.

170 Robert Cole, *Propaganda, Censorship and Irish Neutrality in the Second World War* (Edinburgh: Edinburgh University Press, 2006), pp. 14, 117–18.

171 Terence Brown, *Ireland: A Social and Cultural History 1922–79* (London: Fontana Press, 1985), p. 153.

172 Roy Johnston, 'Music in Northern Ireland since 1921', in J. R. Hill (ed.), *A New History of Ireland, Volume VII: Ireland, 1921–84* (Oxford: Oxford University Press, 2003), p. 653.

173 See 'Discussion' part of T. J. Beere, 'Cinema Statistics in Saorstat Eireann', *Journal of the Statistical and Social Enquiry Society of Ireland*, 15, 6 (89th session, 1935–36), p. 108.

174 *Irish Independent*, 14 January 1939.

175 *Irish Independent*, 24 February 1954.

by nostalgia which undermines evidence on cinema-going, can be countered by the oral historian's view that personal testimony offers a valid source of evidence with the same caveats employed as for all historical sources.[176] Thus, recollections offer some insight. Part of the experience started with the building: many cinemas were converted halls, theatres, shops but there was a wave of purpose-built cinemas. The latter were designed according to new art deco and modernist architectural styles. Among the many examples in Dublin were the Savoy (1929), the Theatre Royal (1935), the Green (1935), the Carlton (1937), and Adelphi (1938); and in other towns there was the Curzon in Belfast (1936), the Tonic in Bangor (1934), the Ritz in Athlone (1939), the Savoy in Limerick (1935), the Savoy in Waterford (1937) and the Ritz in Cork (1939).[177] As in Britain and the USA, most cinemas were warm, comfortable and luxurious and the new buildings were exotic like 'oriental pleasure domes or Moorish palaces'.[178]

Once inside, the film critic C. A. Lejeune, of *The Observer*, commented in 1926 that 'the kinema must please the woman or die'; women and cinema had become more culturally connected than was the case with men.[179] Following from this, one of the few contemporary Irish studies was by Brigid G. McCarthy, a lecturer in University College Cork. In 1944 she identified the appeal of cinema-going: it offered not only 'warmth and comfort' but older people could relax; it was a diversion for children of all classes; and it was 'a meeting place for lovers'.[180] During childhood it was a form of entertainment but also an escape from daily hardship. In 1920s and 1930s Dublin, Alice Caulfield from tenements in Newfoundland Street recalled she went to the 'picture house. Oh, we'd get excited.'[181] Maura grew up in 1950s Ennis and recalled having to 'beg, borrow or steal to get to the cinema'.[182]

---

176 See for example C. Madge and T. H. Harrisson, *Mass Observation* (London: Frederick Muller Ltd, 1937). Kevin Rockett, *Irish Film Censorship: A Cultural Journey from Silent Cinema to Internet Pornography* (Dublin: Four Courts Press, 2004), p. 89; see for example Clear, *Woman of the House*, pp. 216–18.
177 Eve McAulay, 'Cinema Architecture, Art Deco and Modernist Period', in Brian Lalor (ed.), *The Encyclopedia of Ireland* (Dublin: Gill and Macmillan, 2003), pp. 198–99; *Limerick Chronicle*, 14 December 1935.
178 Dyhouse, *Glamour*, pp. 63–64.
179 Melanie Bell, '"Quality", Cinema and the "Superior Woman's" Persona: Understanding Women's Film Criticism in Post-War Britain (1945–59), *Women's History Review*, 19, 5 (November 2010), p. 706.
180 B. G. McCarthy, 'The Cinema as a Social Factor', *Studies: An Irish Quarterly Review*, 33, 129 (March 1944), pp. 45–52. The same edition also contains responses to Dr MacCarthy's paper.
181 See for example Stephanie McBride and Roddy Flynn (eds), *Here's Looking at You, Kid! Ireland Goes to the Pictures* (Dublin: Wolfhound Press, 1996). Also present in Kearns, *Dublin Tenement Life: An Oral History*, p. 72.
182 ULOHP, Tape 8; AOHP, Tape 8.

June Considine who attended cinema avidly as a young girl in 1950s Dublin, came out of the cinema a 'different' person because she had discovered the 'power of imagination', and 'another world' was opened to her which never closed.[183] Other young girls' cinema experience led them to think about potential careers in Hollywood, which surprised the editor of *Our Girls* in the 1930s who received many letters asking for information to be printed. Among the careers promoted by *Woman's Life* in 1936 was that of cinema usherette.[184]

As girls grew older, cinema-going was more than just a leisure activity and other cinematic pleasures emerged.[185] Single young woman attended with female friends. Dublin tenement women were 'very fond' of the pictures because they would 'go in together'.[186] Alice Kelly, aged twenty-five years, worked in the silk department of a Dublin shop and went to the cinema on 'wet evenings'.[187] Most young Irish people grew up ignorant of sex which was rarely, if ever discussed.[188] Cinema, therefore, in addition to the dance hall and the motor car, provided the courting couple with a private, dark space, despite the vigilance of lay and religious organisations and perhaps parents.[189] During her courting days in inter-war Dublin, May Hanaphy recalled that 'maybe the third night you might make a date for the pictures and your fellow would naturally hold your hand. And if you didn't like him you'd just be squirming.'[190] June Considine felt that what she saw both on screen and on the 'back seat' in the Casino cinema 'slowly' eroded her 'innocence'. Similarly, Doireann Ní Bhriain felt the 'sexual excitement' from the screen and surroundings in Sutton Cross cinema in 1950s Dublin.[191] In other words, the whole experience contributed to the woman's sexual awakening.

---

183 McBride and Flynn (eds), *Here's Looking at You, Kid! Ireland Goes to the Pictures*, pp. 14–16.
184 *Our Girls*, 1 (April 1931); *Woman's Life*, 19 September 1936.
185 McBride and Flynn (eds), *Here's Looking at You, Kid! Ireland Goes to the Pictures*, p. 10.
186 Mary E. Daly, *The Slow Failure: Population Decline and Independent Ireland, 1920–1973* (Madison: University of Wisconsin Press, 2006), p. 57; AOHP, Tape 8; Hill, *Women in Ireland*, p. 122; McBride and Flynn (eds), *Here's Looking at You, Kid! Ireland Goes to the Pictures*, p. 10; McHale, 'Who Turned on the Lights?', appendix 1, interviews, pp. 77–78, 84–85, 95–96, 103–4; Ita Meehan, 'The Problem of the Single Girl in Ireland', *The Furrow*, 9 (July–December 1958), pp. 440–41; Edward Murphy, 'The Teaching Sister and the Modern Girl', *The Furrow*, 9 (July–December 1958), pp. 570–72; Kearns, *Dublin Tenement Life: An Oral History*, pp. 80, 167.
187 *Woman's Life*, 29 August 1936.
188 Ferriter, *The Transformation of Ireland 1900–2000*, p. 519; Daly, *The Slow Failure*, p. 80; Kearns, *Dublin Tenement Life: An Oral History*, pp. 44–47.
189 Luddy, 'Sex and the Single Girl', pp. 79–81.
190 Kearns, *Dublin Tenement Life: An Oral History*, p. 218.
191 McBride and Flynn (eds), *Here's Looking at You, Kid! Ireland Goes to the Pictures*, pp. 15–16, 59.

Catholic Church-led vigilance campaigns did not feature in the testimony examined here, suggesting again a gap between Catholic preaching, Catholic beliefs and the personal behaviour of many young women. However, sixteen-year-old Mary Norris, who was working as a domestic servant for a family in Tralee, County Kerry in the 1940s and was allowed out once a week, went out without permission to the cinema on a second night. Following this she was 'taken down to a doctor', and he, 'gave me an internal examination' to see if she was 'intact'. Her punishment for an innocent transgression was to be incarcerated in a Good Shepherd-run Magdalen laundry in Cork.[192] Cinema-going for her was not liberating; instead its association with illicit sexual activity, had dreadful consequences for her life. The censor, James Montgomery, acknowledged cinema's role in the 'the sexual dynamics' of courtship.[193] Cinema-going also contributed to an awareness of changing social behaviour elsewhere.

Dyhouse suggests that the glamour of stars and settings in the films had a significant effect on popular fashion. Stars became fashion and style leaders with their hairstyles, make-up and clothes copied by many and filling pages of magazines. Ginger Rogers, Kay Francis and Lana Turner were favourite role models for hair and make-up.[194] In the 1930s Annie McGlynn, aged twenty years, who worked in Brown and Poulson in Dublin as a packer, loved 'the pictures ... my favourite star is Ginger Rogers'.[195] Into the 1940s, Deirdre was impressed by Shirley Temple whose 'pretty and lovely clothes ... fur collars' were so different from her own 'sparse' clothes.[196] In the 1950s, Maura in Ennis liked Audrey Hepburn and with friends she went 'not for the actual story' but 'to see what they were wearing ... gorgeous, style, the evening dresses and the jewellery'.[197] In addition to newspaper columns and women's magazines offering further insights into stars' lives, fashions and advice girl's magazines such as the weekly *Girls' Cinema* provided more film information. Between 1920 and 1932, this publication tended towards 'sentimentalism rather than sensationalism' and some of its advertisements adopted a 'terrifyingly hectoring tone'. Nonetheless, priced at two pence, it appealed to many working-class women. The longer-running weekly *Picturegoer*, priced at three pence in 1942, featured advertisements and articles on clothes, cosmetics and beauty products as worn by film stars.

---

192 Quoted in Ferriter, *The Transformation of Ireland 1900–2000*, p. 393.
193 Kearns, *Dublin Tenement Life: An Oral History*, p. 46; Kevin Rockett, 'Protecting the Family and the Nation: The Official Censorship of American Cinema in Ireland, 1923–54', *Historical Journal of Film, Radio and Television*, 20, 3 (2000), p. 288.
194 Dyhouse, *Glamour*, pp. 64, 71.
195 *Woman's Life*, 5 September 1936.
196 AOHP, Tape 5.
197 AOHP, Tape 8.

Patterns were provided to allow women make the stars' clothes at home.[198] Hollywood also offered different kinds of femininity which were seen to be dangerously influential in Ireland. Politicians, censor, educationalists, social reformers, crusaders and the film business all took a keen interest in film content.[199]

During the 'silent era', D. W. Griffith's films were preoccupied with 'female honour and chastity'. Others presented images that ranged from the 'exotic, sexually aggressive vamp to the athletic, energetic "serial queen"; the street smart urban working gal, who repels the sexual advances of her lascivious boss; and cigarette-smoking, alcohol drinking chorus girls or burlesque queens.' There was the heroine or 'good woman' and anti-heroine or 'bad woman' and the latter was usually a 'loose or fallen' woman.[200] As early as 1918, John Ryan wrote in the Jesuit *Studies* journal that a 'cosmopolitan gaiety of sin' prevailed in US films, where bedroom scenes and quick marriages 'take place anywhere and everywhere, in spite of *Ne Temere* [decree, 1908] or other impediments'.[201] Later, into the 1920s, films moved from 'Victorian moralism, sentimentality, and reformism' and focused on 'glamour, sophistication, exoticism, urbanity, and sex appeal'. Among the new stars were Greta Garbo, who represented 'the mysterious sex goddess', Rudolph Valentino, the 'passionate, hot-blooded Latin lover' and Colleen Moore, the first on-screen 'flapper' with 'bobbed hair, skimpy skirts, and incandescent vivacity'.[202] Immoral sexual behaviour and divorce became the hallmarks of the criticism levelled at Hollywood films in Ireland, although one motion-picture exhibitor in Dublin believed in 1922 that the majority of 'light or "slap stick" American comedies' did not meet with general approval because of their 'extravagance and their reliance, for full effect, upon slangy sub-titles'.[203]

---

198 Dyhouse, *Glamour*, p. 66; PRONI, Eason and Son Ltd Papers, D398/1/2/1, Order Sheet, Mr O'Dempseys, 25 October 1924; PRONI, Eason and Son Ltd Papers, D398/1/2/1, Order Sheet, Stormont C. S. Club, 5 September 1931; PRONI, Eason and Son Ltd Papers, D398/1/2/1, Order Sheet, W. H. Smith and Son Ltd, 16 March 1942; PRONI, Eason and Son Ltd Papers, D398/1/2/1, Order Sheet, Mr Patterson, Randalstown, 21 August 1948; *Model Housekeeping*, 18 (July 1946).
199 *The Furrow*, 6 (1955), pp. 1–12, 304. Brian McIlroy, *Irish Cinema: An Illustrated History* (Dun Laoighaire: Anna Livia Press, 1988), p. 39; Kevin Rockett, 'The Silent Period', in Kevin Rockett, Luke Gibbons and John Hill, *Cinema and Ireland* (London: Routledge, 1988), p. 39.
200 Dyhouse, *Glamour*, pp. 61–98; Jessica Hope Jordan, *The Sex Goddess in American Film, 1930–65* (Amherst, NY: Cambria Press, 2009), pp. 5, 37.
201 John Ryan, 'The Cinema Peril', *Studies: An Irish Quarterly Review*, 7, 25 (March 1918), pp. 112–26.
202 Jordan, *The Sex Goddess in American Film, 1930–65*, pp. 5, 37.
203 NARA, S/D, RG 59, roll 580.241, Harold Collins, 20 November 1922.

Besides an anxiety about morals, there was concern about the effect of American consumerism on society. The Catholic *Irish Monthly* in early 1925 identified that young women in particular became 'sick with discontent' at the contrast between the glamorous lifestyles on screen and their own dull lives.[204] One campaigner regarded this development as part of 'Americanisation via the films' and it was unwelcome.[205] These campaigns were monitored by US diplomats in Dublin. Four years after the introduction of the Censorship of Films Act 1923, US Consul Harold Collins accepted that some groups, 'super-sensitive Hibernians' and the 'more conservative and anti-American element in the pro-British Unionist class', were hostile to American motion-picture films but he did not see it as 'effective'. He reckoned that American films were 'well-liked' by cinema patrons because most of them had relatives or friends in the USA and were 'especially interested in portrayals of American life'.[206] Deirdre who went to the cinema in Hospital, County Limerick in the 1930s and 1940s felt that 'people were a lot better off in America ... [in] the movies ... there were the cars every place ... every body was living in big mansions.' Later on Peggy who regularly went to the pictures in County Kilkenny felt that 'America was everything' from the films she saw and 'everything they touched turned to gold'. But neither Deirdre nor Peggy emigrated to the USA.[207]

Other new genres to emerge in the 1930s were the 'swashbuckling adventures; sophisticated sex comedies revolving around the issue of marital fidelity; romantic dramas examining the manners and morals of the well-bred and well-to-do; and tales of "flaming youth" and the new sexual freedom'.[208] Threatened by boycotts in the USA because of the prominent sexual themes in comedies and wild gangster films which corrupted the young, Hollywood producers accepted a code introduced by the censor Will H. Hays in 1930 and a Roman Catholic censor, Joseph Breen, in 1934. It was voluntary and resulted in a toning down of the sexual imagery, although more sophisticated techniques were used to present sexual messages. The 'sex goddess'

204 See for example John P. Reardon, 'The Cinema and the Child', *Studies: An Irish Quarterly Review*, 18, 71 (September 1929), pp. 431–42; B. G. McCarthy, 'The Cinema as a Social Factor', pp. 45–67; Dr Alison O' Donovan, 'Children and Cinema', *The Irish Housewife*, 4 (1950), pp. 113–14; Maurice Curtis, *A Challenge to Democracy: Militant Catholicism in Modern Ireland* (Dublin: The History Press Ireland, 2010), p. 62.
205 C. C. Martindale, 'The Cinema and the Adult', *Studies: An Irish Quarterly Review*, 18, 71 (September 1929), p. 448.
206 NARA, S/D, RG 59, roll 580.241, Harold Collins, 3 March 1926.
207 AOHP, Tape 5; ULOHP, Tape 8.
208 Dyhouse, *Glamour*, pp. 61–98; 'Hollywood as History', consulted at http://www.digitalhistory.uh.edu/historyonline/hollywood_history.cfm; Jordan, *The Sex Goddess in American Film, 1930–65*, pp. 5, 37.

stereotype still persisted. There was Jean Harlow in the late 1920s, Mae West in the 1930s and Lana Turner in the 1940s and 1950s. Clarke Gable's 'gaze' at Dorothy Mackail in *No Man of Her Own* in 1933 was excised by Montgomery but the film was passed for viewing in Ireland.[209]

As noted above, these stars attracted both the female as well as the male 'gaze'.[210] They were also backed up by magazines. *Broadway and Hollywood Movies* was regarded by the Catholic Truth Society as part of this 'general pornographic trend' and was so popular that when the Censorship Board requested issues from Eason and Sons in January 1933, there were no copies in stock.[211] Another genre in the inter-war period was the melodrama, particularly maternal melodrama. Such films have also been described as 'women's films' which offered a 'window onto the world of female identity, desire and sexuality'. Usually they starred a well-known female actress with whose 'passions, conflicts and repressed desires the audience could identify and empathise'. The theme of the wealthy, educated, single heroine was often presented either as 'oppositional or parallel' to the married woman and marriage. For example, there was the educated, wealthy, single Bette Davis, 'Judith Traherne' in *Dark Victory* in 1939 who found love too late, and the working woman, 'Kitty Foyle', played by Ginger Rogers in the 1940 film of the same name, who was torn between being single and married. But no matter how poor any marriage might be, it could not be 'destroyed' by the strong, independent heroine. Perhaps an Irish version of this theme was *Song O' My Heart*, the Fox film released in 1930 in which marrying for love and not money was a central theme. The self-sacrificing, good mother was, of course, another theme which was particularly prevalent in films for Irish-American audiences. *Mother Machree* directed by John Ford for Fox and released in 1928 exemplified the genre as did the figure of 'Melanie' in the 1939-released *Gone With the Wind*. Romantic love dominated American melodramas in this period.[212]

Campaigns against American films
The predominance of American films in the Irish censor's work did not unduly concern American officials in Dublin in the 1930s. Consul General Frederick Sterling reported that 'intense or titillating emotional scenes between the sexes' were excised from American films.[213] Another US official

209 www.tcd.if/irishfilm/censor/search.php/q=No+man+of+her+own (accessed 12 November 2012).
210 Dyhouse, *Glamour*, pp. 61–98; Jordan, *The Sex Goddess in American Film*, p. 37.
211 NAI, D/J, H/315/116, O'Reilly to Minister for Justice, 2 April 1932; NAI, D/J, H/315/116, Stationery Office to D/J, 17 January 1933.
212 Fink and Holden, 'Pictures from the Margins of Marriage', pp. 239–45.
213 NARA, S/D, RG 59, 1231, roll 1, Sterling to State Department, 20 May 1932.

Henry Balch focused on the vigilant work of Reverend Richard Devane, SJ, who criticised the 'basic vulgarity of ninety-nine per cent of America productions', their 'materialism' and 'monopoly' of the Irish market.[214] This attention mirrored the campaign of the US Roman Catholic hierarchy, who issued a 'black list' with the names of all films which parishioners should not view. Among its leaders were Dr Cantwell, Bishop of Los Angeles and native of Tipperary, who objected to 'too many bathroom and bedroom scenes' and Dr Curley, Archbishop of Baltimore and native of Athlone, County Westmeath, who started the American Catholic League of Decency against 'filthy films'.[215] Other clergymen such as Bishop McNamee of Ardagh and Clonmacnoise in 1937 took this further and saw a direct link between cinema and female emigration to the USA; 'they are lured by the fascinations of the garish distractions of ... glamorous unrealities of the films.'[216] Once again, following earlier fears about female emigrants in the USA at the turn of the twentieth century, it was young women who were seen to be more susceptible to cinema's messages.[217] As chapter three indicated, the decision to emigrate was more complex than this, but film offered insights into other worlds both real and fictional which made impressions on the young in particular. On the other hand, the film industry promoted a positive view of itself also. In 1933, the results of a survey for the *Kinematography Weekly*, a British film trade journal, revealed that going to the cinema taught some Irish girls 'good bravery, manners, love of country [and] generosity'. In other words, it was suggested that girls imbibed positive values from attending films.[218]

By the eve of World War Two, opponents of American film drew on the experience of other countries to support their arguments about the effect of film on women specifically. Dr J. McAlister Brew, Education Secretary of the National Association of Girls' Clubs in England, believed that the Hollywood film took the place of the 'mother, the home and the lover' in the working-class girl's life. The UCC lecturer, Brigid McCarthy, also referred to in chapter five, described such views as 'unusual' but this did not prevent her from expounding on them in an article and extending the same argument

---

214 NARA, S/D, RG 1231, roll 3, Henry Balch, 2 March 1932.
215 *Irish Independent*, 19 June 1934; 6 July 1934; 16 July 1934.
216 Quoted in Curtis, *A Challenge to Democracy*, p. 100; see also Martindale, 'The Cinema and the Adult', pp. 443–48.
217 Micháel Ó Ciosóig told the emigration commission in 1948 that 'films make the young emigrant more at home ... abroad' because they 'already know Bing Crosby and Mickey Mouse. Dublin is less known than Boston. *Dáil Éireann* is only something in the papers.' MARLTCD, AMP, MS 8301, S.S. 1 (a), M. 74, Micháel Ó Ciosóig, Connemara, p. 6.
218 Finlay, Gavin, '"Celluloid Menace", Art or the "Essential Habit of the Age"', *History Ireland*, 15, 5 (September–October 2007), p. 36.

to working-class Irish people.[219] Meanwhile, Devane and groups such as the Gaelic League, Gaelic Athletic Association and the Irish Tourist Association of Ireland called for the establishment of an indigenous film industry, on the basis that 'we cannot be sons of the Gael and citizens of Hollywood at the same time.'[220] Father Felim O'Brien, professor of Philosophy in University College Galway, believed the Irish 'are fast losing our national consciousness, and are being absorbed into a dangerous, characterless, Hollywood cosmopolitanism that is neutral to our traditional, moral, religious and national values'.[221] Not all Catholic clergy held the same clear-cut position. Bishop Michael Browne in Galway was not opposed to the American motion picture but to the 'gangster' and other types which had a bad influence on children. Neither did he believe that American films harmed the revival of the Irish language, which was part of the Gaelic League-led opposition to film. Monsignor Hynes, president of University College Galway, agreed with the latter point and personally liked 'low-brow' action-type films. Indeed he worked with the management of Cullerton's theatre to punish any students who disturbed film showings. Two priests ran cinemas showing the full range of American films as fund-raising activities for their respective parishes; Fr Connolly in Bundoran, County Donegal, showed the 'sophisticated' films to townspeople and country people saw 'gangster and western films'. Father J. F. Stokes in Dundalk, who operated The Magnet, offered the same selection of films.[222] Nonetheless by 1942 after seventeen years as censor, Montgomery believed that the 'menace of Los Angelesization' had 'lowered all decent conceptions of manly honour and womanly virtue'. Throughout his tenure, his work focused on weeding out sex, divorce, birth control and dancing. But it was the importance given in American films to 'sex appeal' and when the Irish female figure was not dressed modestly and portrayed in a self-effacing, pure manner, which particularly bothered him.[223]

During World War Two, American films no less than German and British films were the subject of the Irish 'censor's blade' due to the

---

219 McCarthy, 'The Cinema as a Social Factor', pp. 45–52.
220 Rev. Richard Devane, SJ, 'The Film in National Life', in *Irish Cinema Handbook* (Dublin: Parkside Press, 1943), pp. 13–28.
221 Quoted in Anelius, *National Action*, p. x.
222 Martin S. Quigley, *A US Spy in Ireland* (Dublin: Marino Books, 1999), pp. 129–34. In the 1930s, the campaigners lobbied for a government levy on cinema revenues to reduce the widespread influence of American film, encourage an Irish industry and provide employment. See also Rex Cathcart and Michael Muldoon, 'The Mass Media in Twentieth-Century Ireland', in Hill (ed.), *A New History of Ireland, Volume VII: Ireland 1921–84*, p. 686.
223 James Montgomery 'The Menace of Hollywood', *Studies: An Irish Quarterly Review*, 31, 124 (December 1942), pp. 420–28; For example see Censors' Records, 'Beauty Contest', 'Callahan's and Murphys – The', http://www.tcd.ie/irishfilm. See chapter five.

promotion of the Allied cause, its challenge to Irish neutrality and the preservation of the state.[224] The arrival of American troops into Northern Ireland not only caused difficulties for the Éamon de Valera-led government from a political perspective but also brought the influence of Hollywood even closer to home. Lake argues that American soldiers personified the Hollywood stereotype which 'coded American men as lovers, as sexual, as men to be looked at'. Concerns about their effects on women's moral and social behaviour were present in the south as well as the north.[225] As the war proceeded, however, film attendance declined, though it was due to import restrictions, film censorship and reduced electricity supplies rather than a response to censorship and vigilance. Among the American films which dominated Irish cinemas were westerns (*Northwest Mountain Police*), literary dramas (*Jane Eyre*), historical dramas (*Cardinal Richelieu*), mysteries and thrillers (*Double Indemnity*, *The Mad Miss Manton*), comedies (*Allergies to Love*, *Hail the Conquering Hero*), musicals (*Can't Help Singing*, *Irish Eyes are Smiling*, *Meet Me in St Louis*) and religious films (*The Keys of the Kingdom*). In 1943, Martin Quigley, the American intelligence officer who worked under the cover of the American film industry, toured the country, meeting cinema owners, clergy, newspaper editors and the public. He confirmed that the Irish motion-picture-goer liked the same types of film which were most popular in America, particularly musicals, comedies, detective, 'Wild West' and newsreel which provided information about relatives and friends in the USA and Britain. Star-studded musical films and particularly those featuring Nelson Eddy and Jeanette MacDonald were 'very well liked' while the *Song of Bernadette* with Jennifer Jones in the lead role was a box office hit in 1943.[226]

Foreign films equated to American-produced and still circulated after the war even though the vigilance campaigns resumed.[227] The portrayal of single women as working, with an income and choices became more normal in American films in the post-war period, yet the traditional concepts of marriage, albeit a companionate one, and the nuclear family remained prominent. The focus on the American family in films presented the audience with the problems and difficulties of marital life but all

---

224 Cole, *Propaganda, Censorship and Irish Neutrality in the Second World War*, p. 117; Cathcart and Muldoon, 'The Mass Media in Twentieth-Century Ireland', p. 688.
225 Quoted in Leanne McCormick, *Regulating Sexuality: Women in Twentieth-Century Northern Ireland* (Manchester: Manchester University Press, 2009), pp. 152, 154.
226 Cole, *Propaganda, Censorship and Irish Neutrality in the Second World War*, p. 172; Quigley, *A US Spy in Ireland*, pp. 135, 175–76; Kevin Rockett, *Irish Film Censorship*, plate 35.
227 *Irish Independent*, 28 April 1937; 14 August 1937; Curtis, *A Challenge to Democracy*, p. 102.

was solved by love and patience. The *Andy Hardy* films made between 1937 and 1958, in which Mickey Rooney played the fictional character, were sentimental, moralistic comedies representing the ordinary American family's life. Family and domesticity remained a constant theme with Doris Day personifying the modern woman. As noted above, the 'sex goddess' persisted and Lana Turner maintained her popularity. The 1954 release, *There's No Business Like Show Business*, starred Marilyn Monroe as the beautiful hat-check girl who becomes the target of Donald O'Connor's attention. The appeal of Rita Hayworth made her another star attraction. Nonetheless, *Gilda* was rejected by the censor, Richard Hayes, although passed by the appeal board in 1946.[228]

Social change and the Cold War also produced more hard-edged films. The dark side of American life, as portrayed in the 'hard-boiled' depression literature of Raymond Chandler and James M. Cain, arrived on screen in the *film noir* genre with male heroes displaying 'masochistic' tendencies and with 'domineering women'. Rockett suggests that many were passed by the censor because the theme echoed official ideology. *The Maltese Falcon* (1941) and *The Asphalt Jungle* (1950) were released as well as *Double Indemnity* (1944) following a successful appeal to the censor. *The Postman Always Rings Twice* starring Lana Turner was not shown until 1962. In *noir* films both men and women led desperate lives trapped in poor circumstances, having failed to achieve the 'American dream'. They evolved from the gangster film of the 1930s and led to the 'youth culture' films which on the one hand, dealt with youth rebellion characterised by James Dean and on the other hand, presented Elvis Presley in 'rock and roll' films. By the early 1960s, young American women and men were portrayed as challenging conventional social norms and adult authority.[229]

Depending on the group, some commentators recognised the power of Hollywood film for good and for ill; it offered cheap, accessible entertainment for all classes and was educational but it also presented poor values, false emotions and illusory glamour which some believed affected women more than men.[230] From the mid-1950s onwards, cinema audience

---

228 Rockett, *Irish Film Censorship*, p. 128.
229 Rockett, *Irish Film Censorship*, pp. 124–25, 142–49; Michael Doorley, *Stella Days, 1957–1967: The Life and Times of a Rural Irish Cinema* (Nenagh: Dubhairle Publications, undated), pp. 92–93; Henry Benshoff and Sean Griffin, *America on Film: Representing Race, Class, Gender and Sexuality at the Movies* (Oxford: Blackwell Publishing, 2004), pp. 238, 235; 'Irish Film and TV Research', http://www.tcd.ie/irishfilm; Quigley, *A US Spy*, p. 200.
230 See *Irish Cinema Handbook* for a discussion on film and society. Post-war discussion on censorship of Hollywood movies became rare. Bryan Fanning, *The Quest for Modern Ireland: The Battle of Ideas 1912–1986* (Dublin: Irish Academic Press, 2008), pp. 167–68.

began to decline due to the continuing growth of suburbs, emigration and increasingly television. From 1953, the British Broadcasting Company (BBC) television signal was received in counties along the east coast and along the border counties from 1955, and Raidio Telefís Éireann was established in 1961. Nonetheless, cinema remained in Beere's words 'one of the greatest social institutions of the world', and Cathcart comments that television replaced cinema in promoting 'the Los Angelisation of Ireland' through American films, situation comedies, crime or cowboy series.[231] In the early 1960s, cinema-going was still synonymous for some in the Catholic Church with 'the luxurious shallow life of Hollywood'.[232] This was an outdated view of Hollywood films which were now an accepted form of entertainment and escapism for many, including many Catholic clergy.

American music and dance

Other American cultural imports that gained widespread following among young women and men were American music and dance, despite the efforts of Irish conservative forces to restrict them. The popularity of dancing in urban and rural areas has been established by Brennan as it moved from house dances, to local halls and later ball rooms.[233] Facilitated by technological developments in recording, the American commercial music industry evolved during the late nineteenth century and popular music became a thriving business in the early twentieth century. John Healy's mother brought a gramophone and records home to Mayo from New York in the 1920s. The records were mainly jigs, reels and hornpipes but she could dance the Charleston also. It was the latter along with ragtime and later jazz, emanating from the black community, that influenced popular music and dance in the USA, Ireland and elsewhere. In 1923, US Consul Henry P. Starrett, reported from his largely urban Belfast district that it was 'probably safe to say' that American popular music 'predominates at all dances'.[234] Writing from Cork in 1929, US Consul John A. Gamon commented that 'American "jazz" music is heard everywhere – on the streets, in the theatres, in the homes, and at the dances.'[235]

---

231 Beere, 'Cinema Statistics in Saorstat Eireann', p. 84; Cathcart and Muldoon, 'The Mass Media in Twentieth-Century Ireland', pp. 693–94. Television was shown at the Royal Dublin Society in 1951.
232 'Religiosus', 'The Promises of the Sacred Heart', *Irish Messenger of the Sacred Heart*, 73, 4 (January 1960), pp. 7–8.
233 Hill, *Women in Ireland*, pp. 106–7, 40; Helen Brennan, 'Reinventing Tradition: The Boundaries of Irish Dance', *History Ireland*, 2, 2 (Summer 1994), pp. 22–24.
234 NARA, S/D, RG 59, roll 580.241, Starrett, 24 October 1923.
235 NARA, S/D, RG 59, roll 580.241, Gamon, 21 November 1923.

Listening and dancing to jazz music offered young women and men another leisure time activity that was mixed-sex, but its effects on young women's behaviour worried some. Conservative forces in the US already viewed jazz as a danger to traditional values because the music was improvised, and as the Catholic magazine *America* noted in 1922, 'moral disaster is coming to hundreds of young American girls through the pathological, nerve-irritating sex-exciting music of jazz orchestras.'[236] It attracted attention in Ireland for exactly the same reasons: popularity with young people, particularly young women and threats to national stability and moral behaviour along with fears of 'denationalising the people'. The Catholic Church hierarchy drove the campaign against jazz dancing in Ireland. Unlike Irish dancing, few jazz dances were 'free from sin' and most were 'the occasion for sin'. Young women's appearance and behaviour were again a focus. Dancing and immodest attire went hand in hand and parents, especially mothers, were publicly criticised for allowing their daughters (not their sons) to go dancing 'immodestly dressed, unchaperoned and unprotected'.[237] Reverend Devane linked young women's exposure to American jazz dancing with emigration.[238] Some priests successfully campaigned to have dances halls closed and Rev. L. P. Muireadhaigh from Dundalk told a meeting of the Maynooth Union in 1928 that there were 'very few people now' who did not admit that there was some 'evil in connection with foreign dances', and of course 'those who practice them, especially girls, after a time cease to have any nobility of mind or sense of shame or desire for anything connected with Faith or Nationality.'[239]

Opposition had come also from the Gaelic Athletic Association (GAA), which introduced a ban on 'foreign dances' in March 1932 with the penalty of expulsion from the association. Some members felt that 'jazz was dead in Gaelic-speaking circles and the GAA had done much to kill it' while others felt 'jazz was not dying.' Although the discussion revolved around jazz, the GAA was unable to define 'foreign dances'. The same question went unanswered at the Camogie Association national convention held in Cavan in January 1935, but the ban was adopted. The Gaelic League favoured the same action against any 'Gaelic Leaguer who took part in Jazz'. It frequently criticised the sponsored radio programmes because of the inclusion of jazz

---

236 Ronald L. Davis, 'Music: Popular Music', in Boyer (ed.), *The Oxford Companion to United States History*, pp. 528–31; John Healy, *Nineteen Acres* (Achill: The House of Healy, 1987), pp. 17, 74.
237 Curtis, *A Challenge to Democracy*, p. 62; Jim Smyth, 'Dancing, Depravity and All That Jazz: The Public Dance Halls Act of 1935', *History Ireland*, 1, 2 (Summer 1993), pp. 51–54.
238 *Irish Times*, 5 January 1938.
239 Smyth, 'Dancing, Depravity and All That Jazz', pp. 51–54.

music.[240] On one occasion, Seán MacEntee, the Fianna Fáil Minister for Finance, was blamed because he 'has a soul buried in jazz and is selling the musical soul of the nation for the dividends of sponsored jazz programmes. He is jazzing every night of the week.' Although Taoiseach Éamon de Valera lent his support to the campaign and the restoration of 'national forms of dancing', in January 1934 neither he nor his ministers attended the opening of a Conradh na Gaeilge 'anti-jazz campaign' in Mohill, County Leitrim.[241] Neither did the de Valera-led government follow up on a suggestion by J. Henecy of Henecy's Gramaphone and Records, 18 Crow Street, Dublin that 'there ought to be a censorship of records.'[242] The visit of the 'Last of the Red Hot Mammas', Sophie Tucker, to Dublin where she performed her jazz routine at the Capitol and then signed autographs on her records in Clery's Gramophone Department in May 1931 provoked no opposition.[243] Neither did any of the nine Woolworth stores receive protests; instead the sales of 'modern' music boomed in the inter-war period.[244] In 1935, the Public Dance Halls Act was passed, which gave district judges the power to grant licences and aimed, in Flann O'Brien's words, 'to wipe out abuses bearing on everything from sanitation to immorality', but it was not fully implemented and dancing continued. O'Brien estimated in 1941 that there were approximately 1,200 licensed halls in the country holding around 5,000 dances annually and 5,000 unlicensed ones, and entry prices suited all pockets. He calculated that one Irish dance was played to every twenty modern dances.[245]

During World War Two, the GAA was clearer in its criticism: 'Jazz is a negro production, while Irish dancing is traditionally Gaelic'. The former had 'undesirable associations' while the latter was 'modest, graceful, stylish and distinct' and the 'nearest approach to contiguity is the joining of partly out-stretched hands.'[246] The stationing of 300,000 American soldiers in Northern Ireland seemed to reaffirm for some the links between jazz, dancing and loose morality. Wills notes that the soldiers transformed the 'social and sexual landscape, for a time at least', but once again Catholic and indeed Protestant clergy seemed to blame the young,

---

240 Oram, *The Advertising Book: The History of Advertising in Ireland*, pp. 512, 522–23; *Irish Independent*, 21 June 1928; 28 March 1932; 11 November 1929; 8 January 1935.
241 *Leitrim Observer*, 6 January 1934.
242 NAI, D/J, H315/61, J. Henecy to P. S. Ua Dubhghaill TD.
243 *Irish Independent*, 7 May 1931.
244 Walsh, *When the Shopping Was Good*, p. 78.
245 Flann O'Brien, 'The Dance Halls', in Sean McMahon (ed.), *The Best from The Bell: Great Irish Writing* (Dublin: The O'Brien Press, 1978), p. 36.
246 Anelius, *National Action*, pp. 109, 111.

Irish female for the spread of licentiousness rather than the American soldier.[247]

The popularity of jazz music was also assisted by the development of Irish radio broadcasting which began slowly with a station in Dublin in 1926 and Cork in 1927. Soon it became a popular medium with the number of licences reaching 100,000 in 1933.[248] Both the Irish radio station, 2RN, and the BBC offered popular music or 'jazz' to their listeners, much to the annoyance of opposition groups. Attempts to ban jazz from the airwaves came from within the station also. T. J. Kiernan, Director of Broadcasting in Radio Éireann, tried to persuade advertisers to use 'quality' music rather than jazz musicians and singers.[249] In 1943, Radio Éireann stopped playing jazz music due to pressure from politicians and did not resume until January 1948.[250] This did not affect its popularity as young people were also loyal listeners to the popular music coming from other sources. The commercial radio station Radio Luxembourg, in existence since 1932, was directed at listeners in Ireland and Britain. The BBC's North American Services radio carried American music as did the many American short-wave transmitters in Europe from 1942 onwards. Beginning in 1943, the American Forces Network located transmitters near major American bases which included those in Northern Ireland, and the American Broadcasting Station in Europe operated from 1944.[251] By the end of World War Two, when the band vocalist had risen to prominence, the music of Bing Crosby, Frank Sinatra, Bob Hope, Doris Day, Peggy Lee, The Andrews Sisters, Lena Horne and Ella Fitzgerald was well known in Ireland.[252]

There was a revival of the vigilance campaigns led by the Legion of Mary and Knights of St Columbus in the post-World War Two period. However,

---

247 See the soldiers' testimony in Mary Pat Kelly, *Home Away from Home: The Yanks in Ireland* (Belfast: Appletree Press, 1994); Clair Wills, *That Neutral Island: A Cultural History of Ireland during the Second World War* (London: Faber and Faber, 2007), pp. 322–23, 345; McCormick, *Regulating Sexuality: Women in Twentieth Century Northern Ireland*, pp. 148–80.
248 Farmar, *Privileged Lives: A Social History of Middle-Class Ireland 1882–1989*, p. 137.
249 Oram, *The Advertising Book: The History of Advertising in Ireland*, pp. 512, 522–23; *Irish Independent*, 21 June 1928; 28 March 1932; 11 November 1929; 8 January 1935; Smyth, 'Dancing, Depravity and All That Jazz', p. 54.
250 See http://www.rte.ie/laweb.
251 See Christopher Morash, *A History of the Media in Ireland* (Cambridge: Cambridge University Press, 2010); Michael Foley, 'Role of Media in Ireland's History Analysed', *Irish Times*, 8 February 2010; Burton Paulu, *British Broadcasting: Radio and Television in the United Kingdom* (Minneapolis: University of Minnesota Press, 1956), pp. 361, 391–95.
252 Tony Gray, *The Lost Years: The Emergency in Ireland, 1939–45* (London: Warner, 1998), p. 145; See http://rte.ie/laweb for public reaction to the visits of Bing Crosby, Ella Fitzgerald in the 1960s.

the Catholic Church's anti-dancing views became 'rather ambiguous' in the 1950s because dances were a source of income for parishes. Arlene Mulkerins recalled that 'dixieland jazz and swing were all the rage' after the 1940s and that rock and roll was the 'next big thing'. 'Rhythm and blues' and 'rock and roll' emerged with singers, such as Ray Charles, Chuck Berry, 'Little Richard', Bill Haley and Elvis Presley, attracted young followers and extensively influenced the Irish music scene.[253] Radio Luxembourg audience report surveys for 1955 noted that 3.9 per cent of its average adult audience was in Britain and Ireland, north and south. Most of its listeners were in the young (16–29 years) category and were in lower income groups.[254] In 1955, when radio presenters Niall and Eric Boden presented a programme with rock and roll music, hundreds of young people flocked into the Henry Street radio centre in Dublin city. The 'ChaChaCha' dance was publicised in Ireland by American disc jockey Ronald Murray Shanik during a round-the-world tour.[255] The style of American performers' music and dance would heavily influence the Irish dancing and indeed show-band scene beginning in the late 1950s.[256] By February 1956, one of the distinguishing features of teenage culture was that a young woman had a 'room of her own' where she could entertain her friends, where she could have a 'jazz session when she feels like it'.[257]

Conclusion

Vance Packard, the American social critic, wrote in 1957,

> For better or worse, most American habits and tastes and institutions are eventually imported in Britain: American tobacco and films, American car-designs and hair styles, even American accents – and American advertising techniques, some of them what many people would term sinister.[258]

Britain was a different place to Ireland. During the forty-year period under

---

253 Arlene Mulkerins, 'The Vocabulary of Silence', in Caledonia Kearns (ed.), *Motherland: Writings by Irish American Women about Mothers and Daughters* (New York: William Murrow, 1999), pp. 211–15.
254 Burton Paulu, *British Broadcasting: Radio and Television in the United Kingdom*, p. 361.
255 *Kerryman*, 21 June 1958; *Irish Independent*, 25 June 1958.
256 Tom Garvin, *News from a New Republic: Ireland in the 1950s* (Dublin: Gill and Macmillan, 2010), p. 19.
257 *Model Housekeeping*, 28 (February 1956), p. 205.
258 Quoted in Jen Browne, 'Decisions in DIY: Women, Home Improvements and Advertising in Post-War Britain', in Andrews and Talbot (eds), *All the World and Her Husband*, p. 135.

review, Ireland was characterised by censorship, clerical dominance, legislation governing sexual behaviour and an under-developed economy. Social divisions and contradictions abounded. There was regular high attendance at mass, novenas, sodalities where 'alien influences' were constantly criticised and, in the public space, vigilance groups were active and politicians upheld Catholic social thinking.[259] Yet as noted in this chapter and in chapter three, American ideas, practices and products slowly permeated Irish society, and Irish women were at the centre of this process. Catholic authorities saw links between Ireland's problems, external influences and women's changing roles.[260] In other words, they saw unwelcome changes in women's behaviour and blamed American influences. Yet the primary reference points for women in their own lives related to domestic contexts centring on economic and social conditions, geographic location and religious and political forces. Just as chapters one and two revealed that the Enlightenment shaped the woman patriot and the educated woman this chapter suggests that American culture influenced Irish women, and Irish society in general.

Different images and models of American womanhood and definitions of femininity were read about, seen in the cinema and imagined. 'America' came to mean certain things for Irish women. The 'American way' incorporated materialism, godlessness, divorce and danger but also progress, modernity, higher standards of living, independence for women, birth control and companionate, loving marriages.[261] 'Americanisation' had entered everyday lives through the dominance of labour-saving equipment, entertainment, fashion and standards of style.[262] For others, American standards were aspirational; American women were 'outgoing', could talk 'freely', 'could work, could have more money ... a woman in business could be doing very well ... driving cars'.[263] This persistent and expanding exposure to different representations of the American woman and her life, combined with the emigrant experience, expanded some women's horizons and contributed to a raising of expectations for a better quality of life for themselves and their families which would not be fulfilled until well into the 1960s.

259 Ferriter, *The Transformation of Irish Society, 1900–2000*, pp. 344, 336–37.
260 Daly, *The Slow Failure*, pp. 36, 44–45.
261 See Daly, *The Slow Failure*, p. 135 for more on women's changing expectations of marriage. Patrick Kavanagh described 'the claim to portray American life' in 'Cat on a Hot Tin Roof' by Tennessee Williams as 'painful to any sensitive person'. *Irish Farmers Journal*, 2 May 1959.
262 *Coimisiún na Gaeltachta, Reports and Minutes of Evidence* (Dublin: Stationery Office, 1926), Minutes of evidence, Rev. James Walsh, CC, Lismore, County Waterford, 9 October 1925, p. 2; J. J. Lee, *Ireland, 1912–1985: Politics and Society* (Cambridge: Cambridge University Press, 1989), p. 265; *Irish Housewife*, 4 (1950), p. 29; AOHP, Tape 8; AOHP, Tape 5.
263 AOHP, Tape 5.

This chapter has provided an historical perspective on the phenomenon of the Americanisation of Irish society. The dissemination of American literature and cinema was an important part of this cultural encounter. The next section will offer a cultural and literary critique of another cultural trend present in early twentieth-century Ireland. It will explore how avant garde modernism became part of Irish women's cultural production.

Modernism

5

Producers and Consumers of Popular Culture, 1900–60

Introduction

The last two sections have been informed by the empiricist approach of the historian and they focused on the process of cultural transfer during two defining historical junctures. By contrast, this section uses the methodology of the literary and cultural scholar to engage in analysis of women's engagement with the cultural movement referred to as 'modernism' and with the popular cultural forms produced and read by women. Combining cultural history and textual analysis, it examines the role of women as cultural producers and consumers and the popularity and marketing of Irish women's writing in the USA.

Traditional literary histories identify two main trends in Irish culture in this period. Avant garde modernism, often but not always conducted in exile, dominates the literary landscape in retrospect in the figures of James Joyce, W. B. Yeats and, eventually, Samuel Beckett. This manifestation of the avant garde which has become a touchstone of Irish cultural achievement in the twenty-first century was very much at odds with the mainstream of Irish culture during the first half of the twentieth century. Where the mainstream was aware of it, it tended to dislike and frequently censor it. In contrast to this experimental and internationalist modernism, critical histories and anthologies have identified a muted, saddened realism as the predominant tone of this period, particularly in the Irish Free State and later the Republic. This construction of cultural and literary history has been challenged in the early twenty-first century from across the spectrum of critical practices.[1]

---

1 Terence Brown, *Ireland: A Social and Cultural History 1922–79* (London: Fontana Press, 1981); Seamus Deane (ed.), *The Field Day Anthology of Irish Writing*, vols 1–3

As chapter four demonstrated, the influence of consumer culture was often denounced as an attack on national and religious identity, and the attractions of consumerism and modernity were rightly, if imperfectly, understood as powerful factors in female emigration. Despite this, as the analysis of the advertising campaigns for rural electrification has shown, the state itself participated in and promulgated the discourses of consumerism and modern advertising to achieve certain goals. In short, there were considerable inconsistencies and tensions in the hegemony of Catholic nationalism. This period was characterised by a conservative backlash against the forces of social change which had been gaining force since the 1890s. Sexual conservatism, religious orthodoxy, censorship and very high levels of institutionalisation and abuse of those who deviated from rigidly enforced social norms are rightly identified as mainstream in Irish state and society during this period. However, it is important to recognise the persistence of spaces of cultural and sexual dissidence and of occasional political resistance to this resurgent conservatism. The characterisation of these spaces as the preserve of a social elite dramatically simplifies the class politics of culture in the period. Bourgeois women did have privileged access to education, especially second- and increasingly third-level education, greater leisure and mobility, all of them factors in their ability to become cultural producers as writers, dramatists, theatre directors and artists. Women without such resources had, as the previous two sections have demonstrated, social and cultural ambitions and challenges of their own. The relationship between working-class women who challenged social and sexual norms and middle-class women who challenged cultural hegemonies was often characterised by misunderstanding and patronising attitudes.

Brigid McCarthy, author of the groundbreaking *The Female Pen*, expressed concern in an article in 1946 about the impact of Hollywood cinema on 'Dublin shop-girls' who assumed that the world on screen, where New York typists wore Schiaperelli evening gowns and lived in glamorous Manhattan apartments, was the world to which they were emigrating.[2] McCarthy was not simply being patronising. Her concern at the way in which Hollywood shaped feminine desire and aspiration and seamlessly fed social dissatisfaction into consumerist aspiration in many ways prefigures the first wave of feminist criticism of popular culture in the 1970s and 1980s. In the context of the 1940s, it also aligned McCarthy with the

---

(Derry: Field Day, 1991); Declan Kiberd, *Inventing Ireland: The Literature of the Modern Nation* (London: Vintage, 1996).

2 Brigid McCarthy, *The Female Pen: Women Writers – Their Contribution to the English Novel, 1621–1744* (Cork: Cork University Press, 1946); B. G. McCarthy et al., 'The Cinema as a Social Factor [with Comments]', *Studies: An Irish Quarterly Review*, 33, 129 (March 1944), pp. 45–67.

prestigious project of cultural nationalism. Such alignment continued to offer women a route to literary esteem and public participation, as it had done since the eighteenth century (see chapter one), almost always with the proviso that issues of gender were subordinated to those of national importance.

In recent years, a more complex understanding of the processes of cultural negotiation and exchange has replaced the implicit middle-class feminist viewpoint in McCarthy's concern about the Dublin shop-girls, that working-class girls were simply dupes who ideally could be educated out of their misdirected desires and ideals.[3] The dreams of shop-girls in the cinematic darkness were surprisingly resistant to the regulatory forces which sought to reform them on religious or national principles. Female emigration continued and female migration from rural to urban life escalated, even as the ideal of the contented rural maiden or mother was ever more stridently articulated by church and state in the period from the early 1920s to the late 1950s. Dissent was not a preserve of those classes or persons with access to highly esteemed cultural forms such as the theatre and literary fiction. Traces of the process of cultural excorporation, where those without such access make do and re-make meaning from the forms of mass entertainment available to them, is evident in the cultural lives of ordinary Irish women throughout this period, in the endless condemnation of their adoption of the signifiers of modern womanhood, such as make-up and fashionable dress and the assumptions of advertisers regarding their appetite for such modernity (see chapter four). Miriam Hansen has argued that

> We must not forget that these films, along with other mass-cultural exports, were consumed in locally quite specific, and unequally developed, contexts and conditions or that they not only had a levelling impact on indigenous cultures but also challenged prevailing social and sexual arrangements and advanced new possibilities of social identity and cultural styles; and that the films were also changed in that process.[4]

Since Miriam Hansen's article in 1999, the term 'vernacular modernism' has been adapted and reconfigured in film studies, architectural history, folklore, jazz studies and more recently literary studies.[5] Common to all

---

3 B. G. McCarthy, 'The Cinema as a Social Factor', *Studies: An Irish Quarterly Review*, 33, 129 (March 1944), pp. 45–52.
4 Miriam Hansen, 'The Mass Production of the Senses: Classical Cinema as Vernacular Modernism', *Modernism/Modernity*, 6, 2 (April 1999), p. 68.
5 Ibid., pp. 59–77.

these disciplines has been a questioning of the old polarity of modernism and mass culture to suggest a much more fluid relationship between the two. This opens up a productive framework for understanding Irish cultural practices in the period, particularly as it undermines any opposition between the local and global, authentic and alienated, identity and universality.[6] Vernacular modernism offers a way of understanding the quotidian cultural life of Dublin in the first half of the twentieth century, which is true to the sources and makes sense of the distance between everyday culture, in the Raymond Williams sense, and both official culture in the form of Catholic nationalism and the received understanding of literary history.[7]

In the US context, Brooks E. Hefner has built on previous work on jazz as a mode of vernacular modernism to argue for the term's application to popular genre fiction and 'ethnic' literatures.[8] This willingness to read popular texts as part of an aesthetic, political and historical continuum with the modernist experiment is particularly useful when applied in the Irish context, where popular and high culture was subject to equal vigilance from the regulatory forces of church, state and communities united in defense of respectability and 'purity'. Perhaps more significant than all the regulation and disapproval is the fact that Hollywood films were imported, occasionally hacked to bits by censors, but avidly watched, as described in chapter four. Popular fiction was the subject of similar constraints and popularity and it was avidly written as well as read. The lens of gender puts the role of cinema spectatorship and reading as sites of negotiation of gender roles into focus as an important counterweight to the dominant ideology of church and state. The latter were increasingly uneasy with the patterns of cultural consumption of the masses in this period.

The appeal of American culture: Melodrama and censorship
The persistent attraction of emigration for young women and the role of American popular culture and consumer goods in this process has been demonstrated in chapters three and four. The appetite for American popular culture in Ireland was a complex process of cultural exchange, which benefits enormously from Hansen's understanding of it in terms of 'modernity's liberatory impulses', but also gives specific insight into the more conservative impulses which America also exported, sometimes in

---

6 See Maken Umbach and Bernd Huppauf (eds), *Vernacular Modernism: Heimat, Globalisation and the Built Environment* (Stanford: Stanford University Press, 2005) for an exposition of these themes from the point of view of architectural history.
7 Raymond Williams, *Culture and Society*, 1780–1950 (London: Penguin, 1958).
8 Brooks E. Heffner, '"Slipping Back into the Vernacular": Anzia Yezierska's Vernacular Modernism', *Melus*, 36, 3 (Fall 2011), pp. 187–211.

the same films, plays and novels.⁹ While official Ireland, in the form of the Catholic Church hierarchy, state commentators and censors, may have deplored it as a craving for foreign, lower-class culture, American fiction and film were immensely popular with Irish readers and film-goers. In the case of fiction, this was not necessarily motivated by deviation from church-prescribed norms. The popularity of American pastoral romance and idealised tales of the antebellum South in Irish libraries may have been influenced by conservative, Catholic Irish-America as well as the success of *Gone With the Wind*. The conflict which this film precipitated between the Irish film censor and the unpopular US Minister, David Gray, is as indicative of US attitudes to the film and its promulgation of a particular construction of American identity and history as of Irish ones to women and the body. Presented with the film for classification in May 1940, James Montgomery, film censor, got busy with his scissors and a prolonged negotiation began with film studios Metro-Goldwyn-Mayer (MGM) through the film's distributor in Ireland. This culminated in a rare official intervention on 22 August:

> I had a visit to-day from His Excellency the USA Minister. He showed me a memo commenting on my cuts, and making various concessions and requests. Most of the concessions have already been agreed upon between Mr Neville [MGM] and myself. There are others where I cannot give way. It should be remembered that only one certificate is issued here – and without reducing a film to a nursery standard – family entertainment is the objective of the censorship. An 'A' certificate has never been granted.[10]

At the end of this process, Irish audiences were still debarred from seeing the full scene where Rhett carries Scarlett off to bed until 1968. However, the censor appears to have been at the least as preoccupied with the representation of childbirth and the avoidance of pregnancy as with sexuality. He was particularly outraged by Scarlett's explicit avoidance of a second pregnancy in the film, but also with the representation of her delivery of Melanie's baby. Montgomery's notes from May 1940 specify cuts to almost all references to childbirth, even to what he refers to as 'midwifery requisites', presumably the hot water, twine, scissors and towels Scarlett requests when she has to deliver Melanie's baby. Montgomery specified cuts reel by reel, with a record of the distributor's response in parenthesis:

---

9 Hansen, 'The Mass Production of the Senses', p. 69.
10 Irish Film Censors' Records, http://www.tcd.ie/irishfilm/censor/show.php?fid=3230 (accessed 10 June 2012).

Reel 4B: midwifery requisites (they offer to give way). Reel 5A: Birth (must come out). Reel 8B: (1) Offers herself (must come out). (2) Speaks of her debasing offer (?). (3) Yankee insults (They agree to this). Reel 9B: Deal with this attempted rape, particularly the C[lose] U[p] of the rough's face (They agree). Reel 10B: Three passionate and prolonged kisses (They agree). Can-can (out agreed). Reel 11A: About babies and figure (?). Reel 12A: Carries her to bed (modified). Reel 12B: (1) Children (modified). (2) Children (modified).

After the US Minister's intervention there are some concessions, but Montgomery records his response as 'I cannot allow Scarlett's declaration of birth control.' Montgomery's continued objection to the scene for which the film is now best remembered continued this preoccupation with Scarlett's body in terms of its maternal (or non-maternal) function:

> This may be of great importance, but it is a scene of strong sexual passion. The tyranny of continuity would almost demand the act of conception to be screened. Why not allow imagination a chance? M.G.M. suggest cutting the kiss and have him simply go over to her and pick her up, and carry her upstairs. The script reads 'They disappear in darkness at the top of the stairs'. I am prepared to reconsider this cut, and to see it as suggested, but they must 'disappear in darkness' and Rhett's remark must come out.

Following his intervention, the US Minister returned to the censor's office on 15 September for a reshow.[11] Despite concessions, Montgomery still insisted on substantial cuts and Irish cinema goers remained protected from references to hot water and towels. The incident indicates the function of censorship in maintaining the monopoly of Catholic concepts in relation to contraception and the maternal.

In this context it is unsurprising that film melodrama, with its emphasis on sexual and familial narratives, should have caused particular unease. The genre was accurately enough described as 'women's films' and classic Hollywood melodrama had a very strong preoccupation with maternal narrative.[12] This, and the influence of MGM, may explain the American Minister's investment in it as an aspect of American identity. *Gone With the Wind* flatters Irish sensibilities in making Irish-American characters

---

11 Ibid.
12 See, for example, Christine Gledhill (ed.), *Home Is Where the Heart Is: Studies in Melodrama and the Women's Film* (London: British Film Institute, 1987) and E. Anne Kaplan, *Motherhood and Representation: The Mother in Popular Culture and Melodrama* (London and New York: Routledge, 1992).

central in a myth of American origins which rewrites history, obscuring the guilt of slavery and the legacy of racism by displacing racial relations into the domestic scenes. The Irish, unlike the slaves, are part of the American family in the film. For the Irish film censor, however, the relationship between the maternal and the sexual at the heart of the melodrama seems to have been so powerfully repugnant that it obscured all else. The extraordinary impact of *Gone With the Wind* derived from combining the feminine form of melodrama with an American national epic. The negation and invisibility of the female body, the power literally to cut it out of the picture, was a matter of national sovereignty in the Irish contexr. Despite this, the appetite of Irish women for such 'women's pictures', romantic novels and domestic sagas had always been high and demand for popular fiction in Irish libraries indicates a strong level of interest in British and American titles throughout the period.[13]

Cultural Exchange:
Irish Women Writing for Export

Nineteenth-century precedents: L. T. Meade and Charlotte Riddell
While the importation of English and American popular culture orientated towards women as readers and viewers caused such unease in Ireland, Irish cultural production also found an audience in the USA, particularly in the area of women's fiction. Irish women writers had been extremely successful internationally in the nineteenth century in popular genres such as mystery, ghost stories and children's fiction, as well as in domestic and romantic narratives. L. T. Meade, who published almost 300 novels between 1866 and 1914, established the girl's school story. 'In 1898 *Girl's Realm* readers nominated her as their favourite author.'[14] As Susan Cahill has analysed, Meade frequently put stories of 'wild', out of place, Irish girls at the heart of this very English genre and the prevalence of her books in advertising, publishers' lists and as school prizes indicated there was very strong demand for this narrative formula. Having moved from Cork to London in 1874, Meade became an influential figure in children's literature, editing *Atalanta*, a magazine aimed at girls and young women from 1887 to 1898. She tended to take a progressive view on gender issues and was a member of the feminist Pioneer Club.[15]

---

13 See chapter four above.
14 Susan Cahill, 'Irish Women Writers of Children's Literature, 1870–1940' (UCD Irish Virtual Research Library and Archive Research Report Series 3, 2010), http://hdl.handle.net/10197/2486.
15 Ibid.

Antrim woman and influential periodical editor, Charlotte Riddell, who wrote a mere fifty books, is not as widely recognised as establishing the literary genre of the mystery and ghost story as are her male contemporaries Sheridan Le Fanu and M. R. James. However, at least one of her stories is always in print, usually 'Hertford O'Donnell's Warning' (also known as 'The Banshee's Warning'), a tale of an Irish doctor who has emigrated to London and who hears the family banshee cry for the young patient whom he does not realise is his own abandoned illegitimate son.[16] Riddell was also an influential editor of women's serial fiction, taking over the editorship of *St James Magazine* in London from another Irish woman, Mrs S. C. Hall, in 1868. Riddell is now widely credited with making the world of business a respectable topic for fiction and making business people, like George Geith in *George Geith of Geith's Court*, acceptable as main protagonists in fiction.[17] This middle-class preoccupation with the professional class, whether haunted Irish doctors or secretly married businessmen, is rather at odds with the general characterisation of Irish fiction in this period as preoccupied with the worlds of landlords and peasantry. Riddell's stories of characters who were geographically, economically and socially mobile, but ultimately tied to the past they sought to escape, resonated in an age of mass urbanisation. In effect, her Irish characters in London merely endured an intensification of a more general condition of nineteenth-century, middle-class life.

The association of Irishness with access to a world of storytelling, natural and supernatural, is one which was consolidated in this period and remains an important part of the marketing of Irish fiction internationally in the twenty-first century. The 'wild Irish girl' was a recurrent character in popular fiction from inside and outside Ireland. This representation of the Irish woman as close to nature, wilful, but attractive, even glamorous, was often completely at odds with the political project of Sydney Owenson's original 1806 novel of that name. However, Owenson's shrewd manipulation of media stereotypes and her self-publicising capacity to play the part of the wild Irish girl beyond the pages of her book was one which was successfully repeated (see chapter one). The image of the charming Irish lady of letters was promoted in conjunction with the ladies' fiction, offering a paradoxical blend of the exotic and the natural in the mix of English domestic fictions.

In the eighteenth century, the emergence of the novel, and even the dismissal of it as a non-learned form of writing aimed at silly women, facilitated the emergence of writing as the first middle-class professional career available

---

16 E-text and bibliographical note available through The Literary Gothic, http://www.litgothic.com/Authors/riddell.html.
17 Ibid.

to women, and which offered financial and social independence.[18] By the late nineteenth century, writing popular fiction had long been both respectable and lucrative though women writers of it remained the target of satire. For example in Anthony Trollope's *The Way We Live Now*, the success of Lady Carbury over more worthy (presumably male) writers is attributed to her deployment of her sexuality and feminine social skills as well as her prolific output. Women writers continued to walk a fine line between fame and notoriety, with some able to exploit public prurience about their private lives to promote sensational fiction.

The modern lady of letters: Katherine Cecil Thurston
In the opening decade of the twentieth century, Katherine Cecil Thurston, daughter of the mayor of Cork, was one of the most popular authors in the USA and England. *The Masquerader* (published in the UK as *John Chilcote, M.P.*) was one of the top-selling titles in the USA in both 1904 and 1905, third in 1904 and seventh in 1905, directly behind her novel *The Gambler*, which was the sixth bestselling title in the USA that year and just ahead of Edith Wharton's *The House of Mirth*.[19] *Max*, which seems very daring even today in its story of a woman cross-dressing in order to study and work as an artist unfettered by society's expectations of her as a woman, was fourth in the bestseller lists in 1910. No Irish writing approached this level of success again in the USA until Frank McCourt's 1996 memoir *Angela's Ashes* and Sarah Ban Breathnach's 1995 lifestyle book, *Simple Abundance*, which were numbers one and two respectively in the non-fiction lists in 1997. Both *The Gambler* and *Max* feature Irish characters prominently, with a substantial section of the former set in Ireland.

The international distribution, consumption and adaptation of Thurston's literary output and persona, combining fiction, dramatisations and film

18 See Betty A. Schellenberg, *The Professionalization of Women Writers in Eighteenth-Century Britain* (Cambridge: Cambridge University Press, 2005) and Cheryl Turner, *Living by the Pen: Women Writers in the Eighteenth Century* (London: Routledge, 1994) for an account of this process.
19 Thurston's bestseller status appears slightly differently depending on sources. The figures are derived from John Unsworth's online database at the University of Illinois, which is an evolving resource for the study of popular fiction, derived from *Bowker's Annual* and *Publisher's Weekly* and the amalgamated listings used by Project Gutenberg 9 (http://www.gutenberg.org/wiki/Bestsellers%2C_American%2C_1900–1922_%28Bookshelf%29) which are derived from Michael Korda, *Making the List: A Cultural History of the American Bestseller, 1900–1999 : As Seen Through the Annual Bestseller Lists of Publishers Weekly* (New York: Barnes and Noble, 2001). The *New York Times* lists, used by Bowling Green University centenary project, for example, vary slightly, but both sources indicate that Thurston's work was consistently in the top ten, very popular and high profile.

adaptation, almost as soon as it became available, with avid reporting of her personal life indicates a form of media convergence and celebrity which is normally considered to be a late twentieth-century development. Her Irishness was very much part of the public persona she cultivated. Thurston promoted an image of herself as the lady of letters, dividing her time between the metropolitan world of London society and her Irish country house in the seaside town of Ardmore, County Waterford. The more negative connotations of Irish 'wildness' became to some extent attached to her image after her divorce and in the lurid reporting of her mysterious death. Despite her marriage to an 'English writer',[20] she was repeatedly referred to in both the London *Times* and *New York Times* as an Irish lady of letters. Indeed she was pre-eminent among a gathering described by the *Irish Times* of 4 May 1910 as 'Irish women of letters: Corinthian Club Banquet brilliant gathering', which boasted the presence of the Lord Lieutenant and Lord Chief Justice, and numerous Irish women writers. Thurston was toasted a month later in the same club at a dinner she attended in honour of John McCormack. Thurston's career indicates not only that Irish women were participants and producers as well as consumers of mass media at the beginning of the twentieth century, but that they were capable of deploying their nationality as an exotic or attractive feature to distinguish them in the international marketplace.

The nation and the marketplace: Dorothy Macardle and Máirín Cregan

A fascinating insight into this is provided by the publication and adaptation of the work of two women, Dorothy Macardle and Máirín Cregan, who were close to the heart of official Ireland and yet active participants in the international Anglophone popular culture that Ireland distrusted. The cover illustrations of the American editions of Macardle's *Uneasy Freehold* indicate how these novels, now readable as expressing in a surreptitious way Macardle's disquiet at the restrictions placed on women in the new Irish state, were marketed as 'female gothic' to an international audience.[21] Macardle's plays were first performed in the 1930s and she combined, not always successfully, these two impulses in her work. Perhaps because the theatre in Ireland was already understood as a political space given the specific 'national' project of the Abbey, issues of nationality and gender were much harder to separate. Hence plays tended to have quite different meanings when staged in Ireland and when staged abroad. Macardle's

---

20 Ernest Temple Thurston, though born in England, in fact spent much of his early life in Cork.
21 Ellen Moers introduced this as a critical term in *Literary Women: The Great Writers* (New York: Doubleday, 1976).

fascinating short play, *Ann Kavanagh*, which was first produced in the Abbey Theatre on 6 April 1922, was by 1937 being published in a collection obviously aimed at amateur dramatic societies by Samuel French, which listed offices in New York, Los Angeles, Toronto and London. Perhaps because so many of the American plays included were comedies, there is a warning on page one of *Ann Kavanagh* that the ending is tragic. That this Irish tragedy is also a commercial proposition is indicated by the stern warnings on the cover against staging without a license from the publisher. A five dollar royalty for each amateur performance is listed, 'professional royalties quoted on application'.[22]

Plays which opened on the Dublin stage, then as now, made most of their money when they transferred to London or New York, but *Ann Kavanagh* indicates that even the unglamorous arena of US amateur dramatic societies offered modest but long-term rewards to Irish writers whose work appealed to US audiences. The appeal of this particular play was undoubtedly partly rooted in the strength of its structure and the element of suspense (if you had not read the warning that this would turn out to be a tragedy). The stage directions indicate interesting attitudes to class and gender in the export of Irish culture, commanding that 'The stage "Paddy" or "Colleen" costume would be wholly inappropriate' and directing 'that Ann has less of a country accent than the men'. While the latter is entirely consistent with the linguistic evidence that Irish rural women spoke with a less pronounced rural accent than the men during the twentieth century, the play is set in 1798 and the function of the stage direction is to direct the emotional identification of a transatlantic audience rather than verisimilitude.[23] The peculiar anxiety about an American audience's willingness to identify with a protagonist whose only fault is compassion is linked to the plot's oblique treatment of intra-national struggle. Ann assumes a young man who asks her to hide him is, like her husband, one of the United Irishmen. When she finds out that he is instead the traitor that her husband, Miles, and the other rebels have been hunting, she cannot bring herself to hand him over: 'he came to me hunted – frightened – like a little child ... I couldn't give him to be killed.' The consequence of insisting the rebels do not search her home is the death of Miles, whom his comrades assume has himself misled them and is a traitor. His brother, Stephen, who knows the truth and tries to convince the others, as he is convinced himself, that Ann is the traitor, nonetheless obeys orders and takes command of the firing squad which

---

22 Dorothy Macardle, *Ann Kavanagh, A Drama in One Act* (New York: Samuel French, 1937).
23 K. P. Corrigan, *Irish English: Northern Ireland* (Edinburgh: Edinburgh University Press, 2010).

will kill his innocent brother, all the while blaming Ann. The destruction of filial attachments by conflicted loyalties here – Stephen's to the 'cause', Miles to his wife – inevitably brings to mind the outbreak of Civil War in Ireland. In this context, Ann's attempt to avoid violence makes more violence inevitable. While the metaphor might have been obvious to Irish and some Irish-American audiences aware of Macardle's politics, the appeal of the play in amateur theatrical circles must surely have been based on its tragic irony, a quality which became associated with Irish themes and characters in Hollywood films in the same period.

The extent to which nationalist women writers like Macardle and Cregan could be successfully marketed to an international Anglophone audience in the 1940s indicates continuity with the publishing strategies of predecessors from Owenson to Thurston, who were adept in making their Irishness a positive attribute in promoting their aptitude as storytellers. The Irish market, especially in the 1930s and 1940s, was not going to provide a living for any of these writers. It is noteworthy, for example, that Cregan could earn more from one children's story broadcast on BBC radio than from the inclusion of *Old John* on the Irish national (primary) school curriculum, with all the sales that implied.[24] If 1930s international audiences sought out Irish material for its pathos, Ireland also fed the American fashion for pastoralism and rural idylls in the 1940s and 1950s. The popularity of Máirín Cregan's children's stories was enhanced, as Susan Cahill has pointed out, by the association of Ireland with simple rural pleasures and fairy tales, but also by the image of Cregan herself, promoted as a warm-hearted Irish mother.[25] Cregan lost out financially when she insisted on undoing a number of changes that her New York publishers, Macmillan, made to the books for their American readers. Her children's books were nonetheless carefully marketed, as her correspondence with the Macmillan children's editor in New York, Doris Patee, makes clear.[26] The association of Irishness and Catholicism was crucial in the commercial success of the fiction, with *Rathina* winning an award from an American National Book Club for Catholic children in 1943, although Cregan worried that children might be put off if this made them think the book was religious in theme.[27]

Cregan was very much an establishment figure in Ireland, married to the prominent Fianna Fáil politician, James Ryan. Ryan in turn was an important link figure between the old Fianna Fáil ethos of economic

---

24 Cregan Papers, National Library of Ireland, MS 46,791/3.
25 Cahill, 'Irish Women Writers of Children's Literature, 1870–1940'.
26 Cregan Papers, National Library of Ireland, MS 46,791/1.
27 Cregan Papers, National Library of Ireland, MS 46,792.

austerity and insularism and the economic policy changes which began in the 1950s, associated with Department of Finance official T. K. Whitaker and Taoiseach Seán Lemass. The promotion of Irish writing for children by a major US publishing firm in terms of shared values of family, idealised rural life and spirituality meshed seamlessly with the way in which Bord Fáilte (Irish Tourist Board) promoted Ireland as a tourist destination, a far away magical place that was also home. It is important not to overlook this conservative cultural convergence as an aspect of women's participation in the production and consumption of culture in this period.

The relationship between external and internal forces in cultural production also needs to be understood in terms of the ongoing necessity to go abroad for artistic training as well as audiences and marketplaces. Modernism exceeded national boundaries even when practised by artists who were very much engaged with ideas of national culture, such as the influential artist, Mainie Jellett. Elizabeth Bowen in her obituary for her friend, Jellett, recalled visiting her in a nursing home in Leeson Street in her last illness: 'Among other things, we talked about the book she had been reading, which had been in her hands when I came in, and about its author, Dorothy Richardson, a woman unknown personally to both of us, whose strain of genius has not yet been enough recognised by the world.'[28]

This meeting of minds of Irish art and Richardson's feminist autobiographical novels were embedded in more practical realities. Bowen's account of Jellett's training as an artist gives an indication of the international foundation of Irish modernism. Jellett, Bowen tells us, studied with two Dublin women, Celia Harrison and then Miss Manning, and

> then, about 1915, went to the Orpen Class in the Metropolitan school of Art in Kildare Street, to study from the life ... in 1917, she went to London, to work under Walter Sickert at the Westminster School ... In 1919 she left London, to go, in 1920, with her friend Miss Hone to Paris, where they both worked in André Lhote's studio. It was in 1923 that both Irishwomen became pupils of Albert Gleizes; and after Mainie returned to live, to paint and to teach in Dublin, yearly visits to France for study with Gleizes, in Paris or at his house in the Rhone Valley, continued up to 1933. During those years, she exhibited paintings in Dublin, London and Paris ... In 1922, on a visit to Spain with Miss Hone, she was profoundly impressed by El Greco's work, as seen in its natural ground of the Spanish landscape. Months in

[28] Dorothy Richardson, British writer, 1873–1957. She was an important feminist writer whose autobiographical stream of consciousness novels were hugely influential; Elizabeth Bowen, 'Obituary of Mainie Jellett', *The Bell*, 9, 3 (1944), p. 251.

Lithuania, in 1931, gave a fresh wave of impetus ... Her last visit to France was in 1939. War clanged a gate shut between her and the Continent.[29]

This was obviously a very privileged life, but it was also workaday artistic training. It was not too far removed from the less privileged world of literary aspiration. Just before war 'clanged its gate shut', on 6 December 1939 Bowen gave a talk to the Irish Women Writer's Club on characterisation in fiction. (This was the same Club which would go on to protest against the banning of Maura Laverty's work.) It is unclear who attended Bowen's talk. The only published account of the club's history appears to be that contained in the *Dublin Evening Mail* on the occasion of the club's silver jubilee in 1958.[30] This account mentions that the club was founded by the poet Blanaid Salkeld and lists Patricia Lynch, Kate O'Brien, Winifred Letts, Teresa Deevy, Constantia Maxwell and Maura Laverty among its well-known members. Rosamund Jacob, a member in 1939, commented of Bowen, 'She has a great stammer but doesn't seem to mind it.' These casual references to Richardson and to Bowen's lectures indicate a relationship between English and Irish modernism, literary and artistic innovation, high modernist aesthetics and modest writing groups. They also indicate a residual but remarkably resilient cultural feminism.

Conclusion

Women's participation in cultural production, consumption and exchange in the first half of the twentieth century indicates that they were neither silent victims of official ideology nor unequivocal upholders of the status quo, but engaged in complex processes of cultural and social negotiation of gender and national identities. It is obvious that all forms of literary criticism necessarily focus on work by those with the educational and economic resources to engage in literary pursuits. This is not an elitist bias, unless it excludes attention to the cultural practice of those without such resources. It is important in analysing women's writing and reading to resist the false dichotomy inherited from the nineteenth century of literary high culture and popular cultural consumption. A quarter of a century ago, Matthew Arnold was a favourite target of deconstruction in Irish literary studies for his views on Celticism, but the Arnoldian disparagement of the culture of the newly literate masses has not attracted sufficient critique

---

29 Bowen, 'Obituary of Mainie Jellett', p. 253.
30 *Dublin Evening Mail*, 26 November 1958, p. 3.

in the Irish context.[31] Irish literary history has produced and contested canons, shadowed by what Franco Moretti, in a global context, has called 'the great unread', that great mass of cultural material which is part of the everyday lives of ordinary people but is invisible in the literary histories and anthologies.[32] The assumption has been that this material is not significant or that it signifies the cultural limitations of the masses. This is a particularly acute issue in relation to women's reading, where disparagement of silly women reading silly novels is almost as old as the novel form itself.

In part, the attachment of literary scholarship to canonical models has been pragmatic. It is not possible to read everything published in any given era and pre-existing and relatively stable canons are knowable and susceptible to traditional modes of literary analysis, such as postcolonial and historicist criticism. Cultural criticism has become increasingly aware, however, of the extent to which 'ostensible indicators of permanence – the canon, heritage, homelands – are … constructed by specific constituencies in order to stabilize the unstable, to hold off inevitable flux, and to create ordered, and politically 'usable', pasts'.[33] Over several decades, these literary and historical canons have been challenged by analysis from the perspective of gender and especially by attention to the history and writing of Irish women. The resources outlined in the introduction to this volume enable a much more detailed, diverse and enlarged view of the cultural lives of Irish women, from subscribers to eighteenth-century journals to soap opera. Identifying and quantifying this material is insufficient for an understanding of the complex processes of cultural and social change, however. This work has drawn on these resources to facilitate interpretation and analysis, combining literary and historical research techniques in the multidisciplinary, collaborative mode demanded by the new range of primary material. It has sought to map the complexity and range of the much disparaged cultural lives of these literate women, readers and writers of novels, playwrights and theatregoers, emigrants writing home and their correspondents, shop-girls at the movies and advertising copywriters. Close attention to the cultural practices of Irish women's writing in the 1930s indicates a dissident milieu which was certainly not brimming with feminist possibility, but which consistently questioned the orthodoxies of church and state and left a record of women making lives and making art in economically and politically difficult circumstances. It also indicates the existence of vernacular dissidence and a degree of continuity between the intellectual and social ferment of the 1890–1922

---

31 See, for example, Brown, *Ireland: A Social and Cultural History*.
32 Franco Moretti, 'The Slaughterhouse of Literature', *Modern Language Quarterly*, 61, 1 (March 2000), pp. 207–27.
33 Astrid Erll, 'Travelling Memory', *Parallax* 17, 4 (2011), p.12.

period and the next wave of social and cultural change in the 1960s, between the first and second waves of feminism. It is not productive, however, to read the period in terms of clearly distinct internal forces of conservatism and external forces of modernisation or a linear and continuous line of feminist history. It is important not to project backward the polarisation of nationalism and feminism that crystallised in the struggles over issues of sexuality, reproduction and religion in the 1960s and 1970s. The concept of vernacular modernism offers a way of thinking about the processes of cultural exchange and excorporation which do not align feminism with a universalising modernity.

Methodologies developed in queer studies and queer theory offer new approaches to the temporality of critical reading practice and to the politics of cultural criticism. Valerie Traub's work on early modern literature advocates 'strategic anachronism' and 'strategic historicism' to 'keep open the question of the relationship of present identities to past cultural formations'.[34] Analysis of the representation, writing, watching and reading practices of Irish women in the literary Dublin of the 1930s reveals the fragmentary traces of dissident aesthetics, different sexualities and lives at odds with the dominant ideology of their day, often invisible to the dominant histories since. The larger context of this book indicates that this was only one end of a broad spectrum of cultural activity in which Irish women negotiated the complexity of their everyday identities. While strategic anachronism and strategic historicism are enabling strategies for literary and cultural analysis, they raise particular problems in an interdisciplinary study of this nature. Historiography is predicated on empirical and archival methodologies which do not aim to fold the present back upon the past, but maintain as objective a standpoint as possible on the historical evidence. Moreover, this case study depends upon the process of uncovering neglected texts and practices and the evidence of their circulation and change. To argue that attention to the cultural production and consumption of women can change our perspective on this era is to assume responsibility for accurately documenting that production and consumption. In challenging the assumptions and limitations of accounts which do not pay such attention, the criterion of accuracy to the sources is of paramount importance. This is not at all incompatible with the acknowledgement that each historical moment reflects differently on the past. At a very basic level, new media, databases and resources have rendered visible hidden cultural practices and abandoned texts. The vernacular modernism of Dublin in the first half of the twentieth century, combining reconfigured relations of

---

34 Valerie Traub, *The Renaissance of Lesbianism in Early Modern England* (Cambridge: Cambridge University Press, 2002), p. 32.

domesticity and intimacy, cultural experiment with traditional forms and imported mass media, is an object of study which yields different insights to literary and historical critique and challenges both. Paying due attention to what shop-girls dreaming in the cinematic darkness actually watched, to what users of public libraries requested and borrowed and to the relationship between Irish writing and global publishing dramatically complicates the cultural history of Ireland and the concept of Irishness.

6

Sexual and Aesthetic Dissidences: Women and the Gate Theatre, 1929–60

Introduction

The previous chapter argued that the concept of vernacular modernism provided a useful framework within which to examine Irish women's cultural practices in the first half of the twentieth century. This chapter elaborates on this suggestion through a focus on theatre and particularly the Gate Theatre in Dublin. The modernist agenda of the Gate Theatre provided women playwrights with considerable opportunity for experiment. More generally the Gate Theatre was a forum where new and often radical ideas about modern women were presented to a public audience untroubled for the most part by the vigilance of the censor's supervision. The aim of this chapter is to examine women's engagement as producers of plays performed by the Gate Theatre and the representation of women in non-Irish authored productions. While film and fiction were censored and policed to an extraordinary degree in the Irish state between the 1930s and 1950s, no official censorship of plays staged in Dublin was established after 1922. Nevertheless, Joan Fitzpatrick Dean's *Riot and Great Anger: Stage Censorship in Twentieth-Century Ireland* has identified a high level of unofficial censorship in operation in the period. Vigilance was exercised by theatre audiences and moral panics were occasionally stirred up by the newspapers or religious groups, but theatrical programming was nonetheless capable of circumventing some of the restrictions operating in other media.[1]

The Gate Theatre, established in 1929 by Hilton Edwards and Micheál MacLiammóir in Dublin, showcased international, experimental theatre

---

1 Joan Fitzpatrick Dean, *Riot and Great Anger: Stage Censorship in Twentieth-Century Ireland* (Madison: University of Wisconsin Press, 2010).

and staged new Irish plays, but it remained financially viable by combining this with reviving classics and staging popular genre theatre. The viability of the theatre was not initially assured and in 1931, after two years in operation, a financial rescue by Lord Longford created a relationship which lasted five years until disagreements resulted in a complex arrangement by which Longford Productions and the MacLiammóir-Edwards Gate Theatre company each occupied the Gate Theatre stage for six months and toured for six months.[2] This compulsory touring meant that the programmes of the two companies had an impact beyond the metropolitan theatre audience. Moreover, it shows both a consistent audience for drama written by women and, by implication from the programming, the importance of women theatre-goers to the theatre's survival. Work aimed at women theatre-goers was extremely important to the viability and programming of the Dublin theatres. Of the fifty-three new Irish plays produced by Edwards-MacLiammóir Gate Theatre Productions between 1936 and 1982, eleven (twenty-one per cent) were by women. They also brought work by European and US women playwrights to the Dublin stage, notably Christa Winsloe and Lillian Hellman. In contrast just eighty-five (twelve per cent) of the Abbey's 685 original Irish plays were by women, which may indicate a correlation between the staging of plays from outside of Ireland by women and openness to new work by Irish women or that the Gate's more eclectic programming was more conducive to women's participation or, more probably, a combination of both factors.

The Gate Theatre, Representations of Women and Women Playwrights

Theatre programmes from the tours of both Longford Productions and Edwards' and MacLiammóir's company indicate a fascinating mix of popular plays, adaptations and challenging modern work, which were promoted in provincial towns through a combination of diverse programming and the trappings of fashion and glamour. Longford Productions' second Irish tour in 1938 presented Christine Longford's adaptation of *The Absentee* from Maria Edgeworth's novel. The production was directed by Peter Powell, who added an odd programme note which referred to the enduring 'wit, humour and characterisation' of *The Absentee* and the extent to which reactions and

---

2 See Christopher Fitz-Simon, *The Boys: A Double Biography* (London: Nick Hearne Books, 1994); and Richard Pine, *The Dublin Gate Theatre, 1928–78: Theatre in Focus* (Cambridge and New Jersey: Chadwyck Healey, 1984). Both give an account of the origins and effect of this arrangement.

motives in the novel can 'appear as laughable to our modern, fashionably disillusioned senses ... I have endeavoured to preserve this charm and sincerity by presenting the play in a slightly mannered style of acting which, while it would not presume to laugh at the novel's sentiments, will allow the audience an enlightened smile at their expression.' Having thus promised its audience delight and flattered them with the implication of modern sophistication, the production offers further glamour, with 'costumes designed by Christine Longford and executed by Eileen Long and P. J. Bourke, hats by Nancy Beckh'.[3] This emphasis on the details of costume indicates that women were a significant part of the provincial theatre audience and the touring companies were keen to attract their interest. The diverse touring programme also included Dorothy L. Sayers' *Busman's Honeymoon*.

The programme offered in the Gate Theatre by Edwards and MacLiammóir from February 1936 to July 1939 shows that the US playwright Gertrude Tonkonogy's *Three-Cornered Moon* was staged in February 1936 in a production directed by Sheelagh Richards. (It also featured in a Longford Production touring programme, reportedly very well received in Sligo.[4]) *Three-Cornered Moon* is a fast-paced romantic comedy which deals with the dramatic economic downfall of a New York family in the aftermath of the Wall Street Crash in 1929. The film adaptation, starring Claudette Colbert, is widely credited as originating the screwball romantic comedy as a film genre. *Three-Cornered Moon* was first performed in the Cort Theatre in New York in 1933. It is concerned with the female-centred family of a wealthy widow, Mrs Rimplegear, who has spoiled her three sons and her daughter while she speculated on the stock market. The adult children are primarily characterised by boredom. The eldest son, Kenneth, cannot see the point of his job as a law clerk and the daughter Elizabeth feels she reached her zenith aged eighteen years. Elizabeth's narrative is initially very dark and expresses a great deal of dissatisfaction with the life available to a well-educated young woman without meaningful employment. She tells her boyfriend, an aspiring novelist called Donald: 'Life's turned sour on me. Ever since I got out of college. I never told you ... But for six or seven months now I've been in despair.' Elizabeth generalises her depression, seeing it as typical of her generation: 'I suppose a lot of young people get this way. It's a sort of *weltschmertz*. I've read about it – but I never knew how real a thing it was till it hit me. I hate everything that goes with life – all its people – all the things it's

---

3 Peter Powell, *The Absentee Programme Notes* (March 1938). See also http://www.Irishplayography.com and the Inventing and Reinventing the Irishwoman website, http://www2.ul.ie/web/WWW/Faculties/Arts%2C_Humanities_%26_Social_Sciences/Inventing/.
4 Longford Production Touring Programme, National Library of Ireland; Pine, *The Dublin Gate Theatre, 1928–78*.

got to offer.' The play makes it clear that her mental state is linked to her lack of intellectual stimulation and motivation: 'I was always so happy in college. There were so many intelligent things to find out – so many people to talk to – people with grand ideas – grand ideals.' It is equally apparent that romance is no compensation for the loss of ideas and ideals. When Donald asks her, 'What about me?', she replies 'I have this dreadful feeling that from now on a person just makes the best of things and grows old. Nothing will ever be the way it was when I was eighteen.' In answer to his contention that she is 'not exactly a person of wide experience', she points out that she is instead a person of wide reading, 'But I've read a lot. I know what I can expect. Only more music – more poetry – more sex. Nothing new. I think as I grow older I can only be content. But I don't want to live if I'm not actively happy. I don't want to compromise.' The play in one of its characteristic reversals of expectation presents the male character as fulfilled by romance, the female one as needing a more purposeful existence. Donald 'sorrowfully' rebukes her: 'You know if you really loved me, you wouldn't feel that life is empty.' Elizabeth, insisting 'Of course I love you,' explains, 'but I'm not so lopsided as you. No man could so completely fill my life that I could forget everything else.' This dialogue takes an even darker turn when the dependent Donald answers, 'If you're unhappy. I am too.' Misquoting philosopher Arthur Schopenhauer (1788–1860), Elizabeth contends 'the best thing about life is that one has the prerogative of leaving it whenever one wishes' and initially terrifies Donald by asking him to join her in 'one grand beautiful exit'. He is nonetheless seduced into contemplating a double suicide by the idea that he could not live with her unhappiness or indeed without her.[5]

Their lurid discussion of means and methods of suicide descends into farce as the three Rimplegear brothers come on and off stage in sequence looking for their mother, expressing increasing agitation about the series of telegrams arriving at the house for her. The telegrams make clear Mrs Rimplegear has taken very bad financial advice and lost the entire $100,000 fortune which she was left outright by her husband on the stock market. At this point, the sons turn on their mother and Elizabeth emerges as the only one willing to take on adult responsibility: 'Now, wait a minute – all of you. [Turning to the Boys] It isn't all mother's fault. She's right. After all, there's a house full of adults here. The least we could have done was to have realised how incompetent she was and taken things out of her hands'. It seems very unfair that the play blames the family's downfall on their mother's ignorance rather than the share speculation of the 1920s and the Wall Street Crash. The scatty indulgent mother becomes a representative of

5 Gertrude Tonkonogy, *Three-Cornered Moon* (New York: Samuel French, 1935), pp. 23–28.

the mindless hedonism of the 1920s, as her newly sensible daughter becomes representative of the seriousness and self-sacrifice of the 1930s. This shift of authority from mother to daughter is at the heart of the play. Mrs Rimplegar insists 'I'm the head of the house and I must sign the checks.' Dr Stevens, the 'practical' family friend, in love with Elizabeth, is the one who suggests she should not, but it is Elizabeth who persuades her, giving her the job of signing off on the weekly household accounts, and it is Elizabeth who takes on the job of signing cheques. While this is part of the traditional feminine task of managing the household, taking on the role her mother has failed to fulfil transforms not only Elizabeth, but the play. At this stage the suicide plot descends into complete farce, as if philosophy and modernism have been made ludicrous by recession. The suggestible Donald rushes down triumphantly having worked out a perfect suicide method but Elizabeth retorts, 'Who the hell is looking for a suicide? I'm looking for a job. Where's the "Help Wanted" section of that paper?'[6] The play is highly ambivalent about traditional gender roles, playing elaborate games with them. The narrative ultimately moves towards a nice normal marriage, however, setting the pattern for the screwball comedy where hapless sensible men and scatty but extraordinarily effective women do always end up together.

The critique of the constraints of proper femininity also recur. Despite her college education, Elizabeth begins her working life as a Macy's shop assistant. She progresses to become a stenographer on better pay, but loses her job for making a slightly racy, witty remark and ends up back at Macy's at half the salary. Finally realising her love for Dr Stevens, she does not lose the sharp edge to her wit, parodying his clinical manner and diagnosing him as the 'strong capable type that breaks down easily and asks very obvious questions'. Continuing the play's series of gender reversals, Elizabeth proposes to Stevens, who responds, 'Now wait a minute, don't rush me.'[7] Even as she reassures him that being her sane and good husband will be enough for her, 'You can leave out the poetry' she reasserts herself, 'and I'll say enough for both of us.'[8] She quells Stevens' misgivings, 'Did you quarrel with Donald? And now you're taking me on to fill the vacancy,'[9] but her mother, who gets the last word, indicates there is something in this when she discovers them kissing:

Mrs R: Why, look, it's Doctor Stevens. I thought it was Donald.
Elizabeth: Yesterday it was Donald, Mother.

6 Ibid., pp. 51–52.
7 Ibid., p. 121.
8 Ibid., p. 123.
9 Ibid., p. 122.

Mrs R: Oh, and today it's Doctor Stevens. [*Pause.*] Well, that's nice.

This scatty mother persona is also the maternal function without any prohibition or blame and Elizabeth's mastery over men and money as well as her frustration with propriety and lack of opportunity indicate the play's happy ending is not an unqualified endorsement of conventional gender roles.[10]

The Gate in the 1930s seems to have been particularly attracted to Broadway and West End plays which express frustration with the limitations of middle-class life and convention. The thriller *Third Party Risk* by Gilbert Lennox and Gisela Ashley[11] opened in Dublin in 1939 and appears to have had a successful run despite an *Irish Times* review praising the acting but dismissing the play as 'feeble'.[12] The play's first London performance was on 2 May 1939 at the St Martin's Theatre, so it was picked up very quickly by the Gate. A well-constructed thriller, the plot is set in motion when an over-worked nerve specialist, Sir David Lavering, has a row with his socialite wife, who is unreasonably jealous of his relationship with one of his patients. The patient, Ann Mordaunt, impulsively invites him to her cottage for the night. On the way they run over a tramp and the ensuing plot turns on their attempts to dispose of the body in order to avoid suspicion of the adultery they never get to enjoy. The incident cures them both of the inclination, though they enjoy one passionate kiss before she goes off to join her husband in Egypt.

This is tame enough fare, but the suggestion of adultery and especially the kiss would have been most unlikely to get past the film censor. The drama depends on our sympathy with the aspirant adulterers. The wife's jealousy is instigated by her mother, Margaret, a silly woman obsessed with one fad after another, fed gossip by her embittered bachelor brother. The plot is very explicit that David's career and his marriage are hugely valued by him. Ann tells him that if they are forced to 'to begin again', it cannot be together as he will hate her for making him lose his career and marriage. His answer, according to the stage directions, comes 'gently, after a brief pause, "Will you hate me?"', and is answered by her parting kiss. The play is both relieved that the potential lovers have got away with their crime and exhibits a definite sense of regret as David returns to his daily routine, ringing 'Next patient, please' to his receptionist.

---

10 Ibid., pp. 95–123.
11 Gilbert Lennox and Gisela Ashley, *Third Party Risk: A Play in Three Acts* (London: The Fortune Press, 1939).
12 *Irish Times*, 1 November 1939.

Bourgeois family values are upheld, but the price that is paid in terms of passion is also acknowledged. It is not *Brief Encounter* by any means, but its emotional economy is similar. Moreover, it is very explicit in linking illicit sexuality and criminality. David and Ann step out of the framework of the sexual morality of the day at the end of Act One and are to be found carrying a body and concealing a hit-and-run by the beginning of Act Two. The figures of the two hikers, Syd and Lil, who intrude upon the scene of the crime and are obviously sexually active outside the social mores themselves indicates that the lower classes have more positive libidinal choices available to them. Once again, however, criminality and sexuality are aligned as Syd turns out to be the escaped burglar they thought was the man they ran over. As everything is neatly wrapped up in Act Three, Syd turns himself in and is returned to prison having married Lil and made an honest woman of her.[13] The neat tying up of all alternatives to sexual and criminal law is authorised by two policemen, who arrive to question Ann and agree to cover up the possible impropriety of her liaison with David at eleven o'clock at night in her isolated cottage. In this respect the play is as morally and sexually orderly as it is formally satisfying, a nice, neat, three-act morality play. There is some desire for another life expressed, but straying exacts a high price and no definitive break is allowed. In this respect the play can hardly be seen as an expression of sexual dissent, but in even broaching the attractions of adultery and presenting a potential adulteress as the play's moral centre, it contravened the social mores of the time, thus indicating a much more tolerant regime in relation to theatre than either film or fiction in Ireland at the time. Novels were frequently banned for dealing with this theme.[14]

It is difficult to avoid the conclusion that the theatre, as an increasingly middle-class past-time, was subject to less routine scrutiny than more populist past-times, such as reading domestic sagas or going to the cinema. As the prosecution of the owners of the Focus Theatre in Dublin in 1957 for staging Tennessee Williams' *The Rose Tattoo* indicates, however, there were definite boundaries which could not be transgressed, though the prosecution was in some ways the beginning of the end of the age of rigorous official and unofficial censorship of sexual and social content in literature in Ireland.

---

13 Lennox and Ashley, *Third Party Risk*, pp. 100–12.
14 See Kevin Rockett, *Irish Film Censorship: A Cultural Journey from Silent Cinema to Internet Pornography* (Dublin: Four Courts Press, 2004).

A Golden Age for Women's Theatre?

The Dublin stage provided a much more hospitable forum for new work by women between the 1930s and 1960s than at any time since. In 1937, the year after the production of *Three-Cornered Moon* by the Gate, three very varied plays by women were staged by Longford Productions: Christine Longford's comedy *Anything But the Truth*, an adaptation of Dorothy L. Sayers detective mystery *Busman's Honeymoon*, adapted by Muriel St Clair Byrne and a revival of Mary Manning's savage depiction of bohemian Dublin, *Youth's the Season–?*

The way in which theatre-going was embedded in the everyday lives of middle-class women is illuminated in the diaries of avid theatre-goer, enthusiastic céili dancer and feminist republican activist Rosamund Jacob. Jacob was a highly unusual woman for her era, given her combination of literary career, political affiliations and social background.[15] Nonetheless her diary entries give a glimpse of the quotidian life of the city in which writing, reading, theatre and cinema-going were embedded and experienced. Culture had to compete with domestic life, friendship, family, politics and other distractions for attention, and cinema- and theatre-going were heavily embedded in social interactions and avidly discussed. Jacob recounts taking a visitor from Waterford 'to *Sweeney Todd* at the Gate' in February 1931 and her recorded impressions indicate the way in which content, costume and the sense of occasion were very much part of the cultural experience: 'It was delicious – H.E. [Hilton Edwards] was grand as Todd, and C.C. [Cyril Cusack] quite good as his accomplice whose throat he cuts in the end. The curate good too, and the chair going over every time was great, but strange that no one really got killed. Micheál [MacLiammóir] looked charming in the eighteenth century costume, and was quite good ... It is a grand style of play.'[16] The following month, after a hard day working on an advertisment for the Friends of Soviet Russia, Jacob went with a friend[17] to the Olympia to see *Goodnight Mr O'Donnell*: 'The play was good, Jimmy O'Dea was a dream, with his intermittent Kerry accent and his "Oh you're awful!" and the crooks and detective and housemaid were all very good – and the Kerlin girl. "These Dublin people has no reticence."' This time the theatre did not end her day for she went home to make more Easter lilies, for the republican commemoration of 1916.

15 See Leeann Lane, *Rosamund Jacob: Third Person Singular* (Dublin: University College Dublin Press, 2010) for a fascinating account of Jacob's many political and literary pursuits.
16 Rosamund Jacob Diary, 24 February 1931 (National Library of Ireland, MS 32,582/1–171).
17 Robert Brennan, father of Maeve Brennan, novelist and short story writer.

Jacob's theatrical taste remained eclectic. Five years later, on Friday 9 October 1936, she set off 'to Clery's and Roche's [department stores in the city centre] to look for lino and rugs'. She was happy to report she 'got some for kitchen and parlour and other room – also winter coats at Roche's, brown'. This was followed by tea with Hanna Sheehy Skeffington, former suffrage leader. This tête-à-tête is followed at the end of Jacob's busy Friday by the trip to the Gate Theatre to see

> Portrait in Marble by Hazel Ellis. Good enough – MacLíammor an admirable Byron, but I think she had him a little idealized in his feelings to his wife, who was certainly horrid in it. He is sent off to die in Greece in 1815. Moore was very nice in it.

The following Thursday 15 October, another fine day, Jacob went visiting herself, first to her friends the Kings in the afternoon

> and then Edmondsons – much as usual, and worried over finance. Went to 'The Jailbird' [by George Shiels] with Helen – at the Abbey. It was very good, a nice comfortable cheerful play with some decent people in it, especially the dressmaker, Eileen Crowe. Martha the Anglicized daughter was overdone by Sheila Richards, her affair with the American was revolting. McCormack was good as Dan, the jailbird, but the Gárda was unnaturally benevolent.

Jacob's dim view of the police force, anglicisation and Americans are as evident as the fact that none of this keeps her from enjoying Shiels' broad farce. As well as illuminating the relationship between the political and cultural avant-garde, Jacob's diaries suggests that high culture and popular entertainment were inextricable experiences for the city's theatre-goers in this period.

Style, Gender and Cultural Exchange: Chekhov, Manning and Tragi-Comic Sensibility

While Irish mass culture was obviously highly influenced by the USA and English cultural imports remained very much in demand and circulation despite religious and political disapproval, it has been customary to see the influence of modernist theatrical experiment and Russian and Soviet culture as exclusive to the avant garde and a minority left wing. The programme for the Gate Theatre shows a more complex picture. Adaptations of Dorothy L. Sayers's detective fiction sat easily alongside work which showed the influence of both Anton Chekhov and German expressionism. The relationship between modernist, nationalist and feminist discourses in the Ireland of the 1930s was complex. It was configured by the exigencies of artistic and dramatic training, the emerging dominance of a radically insular Catholic nationalism in Dublin and the developing international context of the rise of fascism and the inevitability of war. These complexities and the persistence of cultural dissidence come sharply into focus when analysing the staging, reception and influence of Russian playwright Anton Chekhov on the development of Irish theatre. The first production of Chekhov in Ireland was in 1915.[18] Chekhov appears to have been much better received in Ireland than England initially and it was the Irish playwright George Bernard Shaw who championed Chekhov in England. MacLiammóir and Edwards began their collaboration with an Irish-language version of Chekhov's *The Proposal* in 1929 in An Taibhdhearc in Galway.[19] The play's satire on the economic basis of marriage and the lack of romance or even compatibility between the couple who so desire the marriage at the centre of the play may have had a particular resonance in the context of Irish arranged marriages.

After the split between Edwards and MacLiammóir and the Longfords, Chekhov became a mainstay of the repertoire of Longford productions at the Gate rather than those of Edwards and MacLiammóir.[20] Recent work by Elaine Sisson has documented the extent to which Russian theatrical production values continued to influence Irish theatre.[21] While comparisons are often made between the social and psychological stagnation of Chekhov's characters and those of James Joyce's *Dubliners* and the formal influence of Chekhov on Frank O'Connor, the popularity of Chekhov with Dublin audiences in the 1930s is indicative of the public mood in more ways than one. It can be read, as with O'Connor, as an indication of political despair,

18 Robert Tracy, 'Chekhov in Ireland', http://dspace.dial.pipex.com/town/parade/abj76/PG/pieces/chekhov_in_ireland.shtml.
19 Ibid.
20 Robert Treacy has noted that 'Longford's commitment to Chekhov in Ireland is matched only by Mary O'Malley of the Belfast Lyric Players Theatre, who presented "Uncle Vanya" once (1963), and each of the other major plays twice between 1957 and 1978', ibid.
21 Elaine Sisson, '"A Note on What Happened": Experimental Influences on the Irish Stage 1919–1929', *Kritika Kultura*, 15 (2010), pp. 132–48, http://kritikakultura.ateneo.net/images/pdf/kk15/anote.pdf. See also 'Expressionism and Irish Stage Design: 1922–1932', unpublished paper presented to the conference on Irish Modernism, Trinity College, Dublin, October 2007; 'Theatre, Design and the Avant Garde in Ireland: Seeing Things – Irish Visual Culture', unpublished paper presented at the University of Limerick, June 2007. See also Joan Fitzpatrick Dean, 'Rewriting the Past: Historical Pageantry in the Dublin Civic Weeks of 1927 and 1929', *New Hibernia Review*, 13, 1 (Spring 2009), pp. 20–41.

but the characteristic Gate and Longford mode of staging Chekhov is intriguing. Robert Tracy offers other reasons for the appeal of Chekhov:

> These productions, and particularly the performance of the popular Sara Allgood, made Chekhov popular in Dublin, and Edwards' direction eliminated that aura of gloom that had been associated with the playwright since the early days of the Moscow Art Theatre. The Gate was also home to Lord Longford's series of Chekhov plays, done with an admirable lightness of touch. This lightness of touch in the Gate's productions of plays dealing with, amongst other things, historical paralysis, the frustration of sexual desire and personal ambition and the futility of relations between men and women is indicative of a cultural mood that makes the boundaries between comedy and tragedy in the Irish drama of the 1930s sometimes very hard to discern.[22]

This tragi-comic sensibility may explain some of the choices of popular material imported from the West End and Broadway stages to the Gate discussed above. *Three-Cornered Moon*, *Third Party Risk* and even Sayers' *Busman's Honeymoon* veer between comedy and tragedy, or at least melodrama. (Arguably, the comic dimension is precisely what rescues all three from bathos.) This tragi-comic mode also appears to have been hospitable to plays by women, perhaps because it evaded the polarity of modernist poetry and popular verse which proved so difficult for women poets to negotiate, for example.[23] Mary Manning's *Youth's the Season–?*, first produced in the Gate on 8 December 1931 and revived in December 1933, directed by Denis Johnston, was on one level heavily influenced by Chekhov. But the central device of a silent alter ego identifies the play with the influence of expressionism. The fusion of the psychosexual and national in evidence in Manning's play is indicative of the extent to which questions of sexual and national identity were implicated in each other even in the questioning, dissenting social and cultural space inhabited by the Gate's dramatists. The play is also indicative of the social and personal constraints experienced by middle-class women in the 1930s. On the one hand, this is part of a more general, international contraction in opportunity as the roaring, experimental 1920s gave way to the Great Depression and the rise of fascism. On the other, it offers an example of the deployment of theatrical

---

22 Tracy, 'Chekhov in Ireland'.
23 Anna McMullan and Caroline Williams (eds), 'Contemporary Women Playwrights', Angela Bourke et al. (eds), *Field Day Anthology of Irish Writing, Volume 5: Irish Women's Writing and Traditions* (Cork: Cork University Press, 2002), pp. 1234–46.

techniques and forms developed by international modernism to explore the particular instance of political impotence, sexual confusion and social excess characteristic of bohemian Dublin.

Harry Middleton, whom Connie, the younger Millington sister, agrees to marry in the course of the play, is going out to Kenya. Terence Killigrew, with whom she is in love, goads Harry that he is going out to 'beat the niggers', but paradoxically Harry is one of the few characters with any love for the Ireland he is forced by financial circumstances to leave. These self-conscious bohemians are the antithesis of the twin ideologies of imperial restraint and national purity, yet the options facing Connie and her 'effeminate' brother Desmond are no more extensive than those facing, for example, the working-class Annie Kinsella in Teresa Deevy's *The King of Spain's Daughter*. We will inevitably have more sympathy for Annie's horror at a five-year factory contract than Desmond's for donning a bowler hat and following his father into the business, but the basic concept of constraint to repetitive patterns of subordination is the same. The lack of opportunities for marriage among Manning's bohemians is similar to that facing the peasant women in Máirín Cregan's play about women's emigration, *Curlew's Cry*, for example. While the dowry and arranged-marriage system made marriage an unobtainable aspiration for many poor, rural women, the decimation of a generation of men in World War One made it as unlikely a prospect for a generation of middle-class women. The problem of 'superfluous women' was never really addressed in independent Ireland, as noted in chapter three, though it may have played a role in women's attention to and choice of cultural and social pursuits. The men on offer in *Youth's the Season–?* are fairly poor marriage prospects in any case. The cycles of alcohol addiction in which the various unsuitable men to whom Toots, the Millington's friend, finds herself attracted are much more scrupulously delineated than the 'realist' Abbey's oeuvre at the time could have incorporated. The depiction of the remnants of the gentry or indeed the Protestant bourgeoisie as drunkards would not have incited any riots in Dublin in 1931; the depiction of peasants as similarly inclined could have been interpreted as a slur on the national character.

In a sense, *Youth's the Season–?* derives both its comedy and tragedy from the self-indulgent playing out of the vices it excoriates in its characters. It is a comedy of manners that tries by one decisive act to expose the tragedy of a generation. This manoeuvre is focused on the character of Terence Killigrew, 'a young man of twenty-seven' who the stage directions tell us, 'has cultivated his personality at the expense of his intelligence. He started off as a "blood" and has gradually become a shambling literary loafer – untidy, dissipated and frowsy – but with a certain physical attraction.'[24] His

---

24 Fitz-Simon, *The Boys*, pp. 329–30.

alter-ego, Horace Egosmith, who shadows Terence and never says anything, challenges the realist conventions of the play, effectively functioning as an expressionistic device. In order to kill himself in the last act, Terence needs to escape Horace. While Terence derides the Millingtons as 'Circus animals ... born in captivity', he himself is equally futile: 'people have ceased to interest me. Dancing, playing bridge, making love, and writing novels are all equally fatuous occupations, and all have very much the same effect – intoxication. Sobriety is death to me.' How we read *Youth's the Season–?* is very much dependent on how it is staged. Like the Irish Chekhov adaptations and screwball comedy, Manning treads a fine line between tragedy and comedy until the end. An advertisement for the play in the *Irish Independent* on 7 December 1932 describes it as 'A Tragi-Comedy of Dublin Life.'

When Mary Manning went to see her old friend Micheál MacLiammóir on his death bed in the Meath Hospital in 1978, he asked her, 'Mary, would you put a question-mark after *Youth's the Season–?*'[25] In effect Manning's career, which had debuted with *Youth's the Season–?* in 1931, bookended a period of four decades in which the official and remembered version of Irish womanhood was defined by hearth and home, nation and Catholicism, but in which women were highly proactive producers and consumers of international and local theatre which ranged from the experimental to the domestic.

Eugene O'Neill's Irish-American Families

The Edwards-MacLiammóir repertoire at the Gate showed an increasing interest in American drama and in one American dramatist in particular. Of the eight-nine plays produced by them between October 1928 and June 1934, eight were American and, of these, five productions were by Eugene O'Neill. The difficult, expressionist *The Hairy Ape* and *Anna Christie* both featured in their first season in 1928. *Anna Christie* was revived in the third season (1929–30). It is very difficult to imagine the novelistic or cinematic equivalents of this play, with its story of a prostitute seeking a better life through marriage and the back story of Anna's rape as a young girl which precipitated her into prostitution, getting past the Irish censors by the beginning of the 1930s, despite its Pulitzer prize. However, the reviewer in the *Irish Independent* praised the Gate's first season: 'artistically it has been the best venture of its kind that has been attempted in Dublin, and if few of the plays produced suggest the new generation is turning out dramatic masterpieces, all of them were extraordinarily interesting.' The reviewer, 'J.W.C.', astutely identifies *Anna Christie*'s debt to Victorian melodrama

---

25 Fitz-Simon, *The Boys*, p. 300.

and Dickens, objecting to O'Neill's subordination of character to thematic concerns: 'it does not require too much perception to discover that which are ostensibly raw slices of life have been very artfully cooked in both senses of the word.' When the play was revived again by the Gate in 1943, the *Irish Independent* referred to it as 'Eugene O'Neill's great play'.[26]

Mourning Becomes Electra was a terrific success for the Gate in 1938. *Desire Under the Elms*, however, attracted considerable criticism in 1944. While the elements of Greek tragedy in these plays might have precluded automatic censorship in other media, there is no question that O'Neill's themes were very much at odds with the prevailing orthodoxies of Irish society in the 1930s and 1940s. This is particularly relevant in *Desire Under the Elms*, where a family's obsession with landholding and inheritance distorts sexuality and entrenches brutal and perverse patriarchal power. The play's critique of sexual repression and the nuclear, landholding family would have had considerable local resonance in Ireland, where the family farm combined economic and social centrality with iconic national significance. The relevance of the play's critique to Ireland would have been underscored by the prevalence of the theme of conflict between fathers and sons in some of the most influential Irish plays of the preceding decades, for example, W. B. Yeats' *On Baile's Strand* and J. M. Synge's *The Playboy of the Western World*.[27] The play and its productions were not without detractors. An unsigned review in the *Irish Independent* on 16 February 1944 condescends that O'Neill was a young man when he wrote it and that 'it is a common mistake for young men to mistake crudity for power.'[28] The international status of O'Neill's work does not fully account for the licence which the theatre enjoyed to explore material which would simply have been banned in any other medium. The Gate itself had a cachet and status which seemed to protect it even from the disgust occasionally expressed at the plays it staged.

Class privileges partly explain this dichotomy. Material censored in other media, particularly literary fiction and magazines, were available to middle-class and metropolitan readers, especially to those with connections abroad, as indicated in chapter four. The attitude to O'Neill's work in the national newspapers in the 1930s and 1940s was much more receptive than that afforded to the equally renowned American playwrights, Arthur Miller and especially Tennessee Williams, in the post-war period, and there may be a very prosaic reason for this. When O'Neill was awarded the Nobel Prize for

26 *Irish Independent*, 12 October 1943.
27 Elizabeth Cullingford, *Ireland's Others: Gender and Ethnicity in Irish Literature and Popular Culture* (Cork: Cork University Press, 2001); Gerardine Meaney, *Gender, Ireland and Cultural Change* (New York: Routledge, 2011).
28 *Irish Independent*, 16 February 1944.

Literature in 1936, the *Irish Press* ran a front page headline 'Irish-American Author Gets Biggest Prize.' O'Neill famously refused to get off the boat on which he was travelling from England to the USA when it stopped over in Dublin, but Ireland, even Catholic nationalist Ireland in the 1930s, was keen to claim him, with the *Irish Press* prominently reporting that his father was born in Ireland and his parents were Catholic, claiming O'Neill himself for the faith. *Days Without End*, produced at the Abbey, strongly supported a true Catholic attitude in regard to the family, it claimed. Paradoxically, the attraction of O'Neill's work for Edwards and MacLiammóir's Gate Theatre and its audience may have been in its devastating critique of familial and sexual roles and repressions which were recognisable as both Irish and American. It is noticeable that *Days Without End*, where the hero returns to the Catholic faith at the end, was staged by the Abbey, not the Gate. The negative press reaction to *Desire Under the Elms* in 1944 may indicate the limits of tolerance of sexual content or more particularly content relating to pregnancy, childbirth and, specifically in this case, infanticide. It also suggests that while the 1930s saw the rise of censorship and extreme social conservatism, the 1940s and 1950s saw battle lines more finely drawn and an intensification of scrutiny of previous exceptions to the general rule of censorship.

Populist Conservatism and the Laverty Years

The war years made censorship even more mundane, pervasive and paranoid, and the emergence of the Cold War, McCarthyism and new forms of populist Catholic cultural campaigns influenced Irish right-wing opinion to mobilise again against cultural dissidence. By the end of the 1950s the diplomatic niceties had been abandoned. Threatened with prosecution, Longford Productions withdrew its permission to the Pike Theatre group to stage Tennessee Williams's *The Rose Tattoo* as part of the first Dublin Theatre Festival. The carping reviews of 'crude' plays were replaced by four detectives who, according to the *Irish Times* on 24 May 1957, 'arrived in a squad car at the Pike Theatre Club in Herbert Lane, Dublin, last night and took Mr. Alan Simpson, co-director of the theatre, to the Bridewell'. This mobilisation of the forces of the law into the area of theatre censorship just at the point when literary censorship was beginning to recede can be seen as the dying gesture of the efforts to maintain cultural boundaries which had never really managed to impose consistent limits to the imagining and re-imagining of identity and particularly gender identity. Given the context of the material on film censorship discussed in chapters four and five, it was not at all coincidental that this case, which became definitive of Irish censorship, concerned a play which was described by its author as 'Dionysian' and celebrated fertility and the maternal body.

One of the most intriguing conflagrations of theatre, cosmopolitanism and conservatism occurred in the decade most often characterised as the calm before the storm of change in Irish culture and society. Christopher Fitz-Simon, in his joint biography of Hilton Edwards and Micheál MacLiammóir, calls the 1950s at the Gate the 'Laverty' years, where the commercial and critical success of the Gate Theatre depended on the output of Maura Laverty.[29] Laverty's popularity as a playwright came in the wake of stormy encounters with literary censorship. A report of an Irish Women's Writer's Club event on 4 May 1944 at which she was guest of honour noted that her novel *Touched by the Thorn* had won the club's book-of-the-year award despite being banned:

> Senator Donal O'Sullivan [attending the event] said he understood the book had been banned because it was deemed to be 'indecent in general tendency'. 'I am astonished', he said, 'that any group of men could find this book comes under that definition.' Dr Robert Collis, in a highly emotional speech, said Mrs Laverty has been insulted, and there should be a legal right to take the censors to law to prove it.[30]

Ten years later her work remained contentious: Christopher J. Reilly's notebooks indicate he thought *No More Than Human* should be banned, but he was in a minority on the board by this time.[31] Despite this history of the banning of her novels, Fitz-Simon notes that Laverty's *Liffey Lane* was the most successful play of the Gate's spring season at the Gaiety in 1951.[32] Fitz-Simon accounts for the ambivalence with which the Gate was treated:

> It was rather difficult for people of various shades of philistinism to attack the Gate with confidence. It could not be described as 'anti-national' – a favourite label of discredit – for Michael MacLiammóir was, after all, a Gaelic speaker, and he had translated poems by Padraic Pearse ... Hilton Edwards, though English, was a Roman Catholic – as he had told several journalists...[33]

In 1951, Orson Welles, long associated with MacLiammóir and Edwards

---

29 Fitz-Simon, *The Boys*, p. 169.
30 *Irish Times*, 4 May 1944.
31 James Kelly (ed.), 'The Operation of the Censorship of Publications Board: The Notebooks of C. J. Reilly, 1951–55', *Analecta Hibernia*, 38 (2004), pp. 223–369.
32 Fitz-Simon, *The Boys*, p. 169.
33 Ibid., p. 69.

and who had cast them in his Shakesperean adaptations to great acclaim, came to Ireland to see the play as Laverty's work was attracting rave reviews. The Catholic Cinema and Theatre Patrons Association staged a protest against the visit, on the grounds that Welles was a communist sympathiser. Newspaper and contemporary accounts of the disturbances that followed vary. According to the *Irish Independent* there were twenty protestors, according to the *Irish Times* there were twelve, though 1,000 fans thronged around O'Connell Sreet in hopes of getting a glimpse of the star of *The Third Man*. Maura Laverty, according to Fitz-Simon' interviewees, 'was exasperated that a very famous actor that had travelled from the continent to see her play should be treated with discourtesy by a section of the Dublin public' and appeared from the window of the street view of the office in which they were enjoying interval drinks: 'glass in hand, she sang a few lines of "The Red Flag" through the window.'[34] Despite this indiscretion, Laverty's plays became the financial mainstay of the company in the 1950s (though she herself did not benefit as much financially as she should have). In the decade that followed, Laverty's work would find a new medium. *Tolka Row*, her play set in a Dublin Corporation housing estate which dealt amongst other things with the tensions in a family when an emigrant daughter returns with a husband in tow, was originally staged at the Gate in October 1951, directed by Hilton Edwards. In 1964 a serialised adaptation became the first television soap opera of Raidió Teilifís Éireann (the national television station), running for four years through a period of accelerating social change.[35] Laverty's progression from banned novelist through acclaimed playwright to household name indicates a complex and reciprocal relationship between popular and high cultural production in the period.

Sexual Dissidence and Literary History: 'Children in Uniform' in Dublin

Hazel Ellis, who appeared as an actress in Manning's *Youth's the Season–?* and *Storm Over Wicklow*, as well as Denis Johnston's *The Old Lady Says No!*, had two plays staged in 1936 and 1938 respectively. *Portrait in Marble* was an historical drama concerning Byron's relations with the women in his life and *Women Without Men* was set in the claustrophobic environment of a girl's school. Ellis's work was distinguished by atmospheric use of music

---

34 Ibid., p. 173.
35 See Anna McMullan and Caroline Williams, 'Contemporary Women Playwrights', pp. 1247–49.

and credits for both plays include several musicians. *Women Without Men* may have been influenced by German playwright Christa Winsloe's *Children in Uniform*, staged at the Gate in 1934, also set in a girls' school and now usually remembered for its daring treatment of lesbian themes. The staging of Winsloe's play in Dublin just four years after the Berlin premiere raises interesting questions about the extent to which the 'bohemian' Dublin centred around the theatre can be read as a radical, subversive or dissenting space in the conservative 1930s.

Differing interpretations of the significance of the staging of the play and its critical acclaim on the London West End stage were at the centre of key debates in theatre studies during the first decade of the twenty-first century, particularly in defining the practice of theatrical history. The debate was complicated by the increased emphasis on the lesbian aspect of the central character's relationship in the film adaptation. Alan Sinfield, proposing a materialist elucidation of dissident sexualities, draws on Teresa de Lauretis's influential feminist psychoanalytic exploration, pointing out that her

> founding of lesbianism in the loss of the mother seems likely to produce relationships characterized by age difference. Such relationships figure prominently in mid-twentieth-century representations of lesbians, perhaps because they facilitate two hostile manoeuvres. One is to regard lesbianism as a schoolgirl crush, the other is to derive it from a predatory disposition in the older woman.[36]

The most thought-provoking analysis of the numerous variants of the play and film for understanding the Irish staging of the play is probably B. Ruby Rich's argument in 1981 that Leontine Sagan's film adaptation, *Maedchen in Uniform*, was indicative of a much broader milieu which had been concealed from history.[37] In this context, the fact that *Children in Uniform* was staged by a company run by two gay men, Edwards and MacLiammóir,

---

36 Alan Sinfield, *Faultlines: Cultural Materialism and the Politics of Dissident Reading* (Oxford: Clarendon Press, 1992), p. 18. Sinfield also notes that the terms 'erotic dissidence', 'dissident sexuality', and 'sexual dissidence' are used for forbidden and/or stigmatised sex in Gayle S. Rubin, 'Thinking Sex: Notes for a Radical Theory of the Politics of Sexuality', in Henry Abelove et al. (eds), *The Lesbian and Gay Studies Reader* (New York: Routledge, 1993), pp. 22, 23. *Sexual Dissidence* is, of course, the title of Jonathan Dollimore's book, *Sexual Dissidence: Augustine to Wilde, Freud to Foucault* (Oxford: Clarendon Press, 1991). See also Richard Dyer, 'Less and More than Women and Men: Lesbian and Gay Cinema in Weimar Germany', *New German Critique*, 51, Special Issue on Weimar Mass Culture (Autumn 1990), pp. 5–60.

37 B. Ruby Rich, '*Maedchen in Uniform*: From Repressive Tolerance to Erotic Liberation', *Jump Cut*, 24–25 (March 1981), pp. 44–50, http://www.ejumpcut.org/archive/onlinessays/JC24-25folder/MaedchenUniform.html.

whose relationship was semi-public, and that the play was a considerable popular success seems to support Rich's hypothesis. The run of *Children in Uniform* had to be extended due to popular demand and the newspaper advertisements offered refunds or substitutions for theatre-goers who had booked for the scheduled play which had been postponed. The newspaper reviews, on the other hand, offer support for the views that either the play's sexual content was invisible or pathologised. The *Irish Independent* review on 4 April 1934 is curiously constrained and non-committal, merely praising the acting.[38] The absence of an *Irish Press* review is all the more surprising when their theatre critic, Dorothy Macardle, was so obviously impressed by the film version, citing it as an exemplar of film art in her 1940 article on the relative merits of film and theatre in Bulmer Hobson's 1934 collection of programmes and photographs and portraits.[39] This lack of comment may be contextualised by the combination of praise and unease in the *Irish Times* review, which also praised the acting and particularly the striking set design and its evocation of the deprivation of natural joy and affection and regimentation of the girls. Like the London reviewers, the *Irish Times* reviewer read the play as an indictment of 'Prussianism', though it is hard to imagine that the representation of the suppression of children's natural affections and rigid regimentation did not resonate with audience members familiar with the Irish school system in the period.

The photographs of the production of *Children in Uniform* in the Hobson collection show an expressionist set, with a lot of use of shadows and chiaroscuro in the lighting design. Betty Chancellor played the schoolgirl, Manuela, to Coralie Carmichael's Fraulein von Bernberg, the object of her devotion, so though there was an age difference, Manuela was being played by a female romantic lead. Chancellor played Ophelia, for example, in the Gate's preceding production of *Hamlet* and Tatiana in *A Midsummer Night's Dream*. The *Irish Times* reviewer identified Manuela's excess of attachment to her teacher as a neurosis deriving from the absence of 'natural' affections. This reference to neurotic and unnatural attachments in the reviews would indicate that while many of the large audience for the play must have been attracted by the play's reputation for its critique of harsh educational regimes and some by morbid curiosity, they must also have been aware that it dealt with lesbian desire.

The staging of the play in Dublin, where the new state did not have a mechanism for state censorship of new plays comparable to that of books and films but where public opinion was assumed to keep close scrutiny over

---

38 *Irish Independent*, 4 April 1934, p. 2.
39 Dorothy Macardle, 'Experiment in Ireland', *Theatre Monthly Arts*, 8 (1934), pp. 124–33.

theatrical production,[40] raises seductive possibilities. Should we read the popularity of this production as the cultural trace of lesbian and other forms of sexual dissidence? Following Rich's argument, we could argue that the staging of Winsloe's work indicates a lesbianism hiding in plain sight:

> Today, we must take issue with the heretofore unexamined critical assumption that the relations between women in the film are essentially a metaphor for the real power relations of which it treats, i.e. the struggle against fascism. I would suggest that 'Maedchen In Uniform' is not only anti-fascist, but also anti-patriarchal, in its politics. Such a reading need not depend upon metaphor, but can be more forcefully demonstrated by a close attention to the film's literal text.[41]

Conclusion: Interpretation and Re-Interpretation

It is often assumed that the women on the Irish stage are essentially a metaphor for the real power relations, i.e. the national struggle. The alternative is not to find a consistent metaphor for anti-patriarchal struggle, however. It is productive to consider the impact of this German import in the context of an influential discussion of an Irish cultural export. In 1999, Patricia White proposed a radical reading of the film, *The Uninvited*, an adaptation of Dorothy Macardle's novel *Uneasy Freehold*. White argued that 'Because Hollywood films are part of public culture that addresses women, and because they do so through representations of Woman invested with desire, they work with the material – cultural and psychic – that engages lesbian fantasy.'[42] This was one among a number of challenges in the 1990s to the reading of Hollywood film in terms of a polarised active-masculine spectator and passive-feminine object of the gaze.

White's work epitomises a feminist film criticism which can use psychoanalytic theory and address the fact of the audience of women's films.[43] It foregrounds the eerie attraction of the ghosts of her adoptive and natural mothers for the film's heroine, Stella: 'She has been waiting for me,' Stella says, 'in some queer sort of way I always knew it.'[44] Suggesting a parallel between the erotic intensity between Rebecca and Mrs Danvers in Daphne du Maurier's novel and that between the evil, dead, legal mother, Mary,

---

40 Joan Dean Fitzpatrick, *Riot and Great Anger*.
41 Rich, B Ruby, *Maedchen in Uniform*.
42 Patricia White, *Uninvited: Classical Hollywood Cinema and Lesbian Representability* (Bloomington and Indianapolis: Indiana University Press, 1999), p. xv.
43 Ibid., pp. xi–xii.
44 Ibid., p. 68.

and her housekeeper Miss Holloway, White notes that *The Uninvited* was promoted in terms of its similarity to *Rebecca*. Advertisements in the Irish papers repeated the US marketing description of *The Uninvited* as 'the most fascinating mystery romance since Rebecca'.[45] Others chose to emphasis the discovery of a new star in Gail Russell, who played Stella, but were very specific about the local provenance of its source material, billing the film as 'Dorothy Macardle's Ghost Story'. The question that immediately arises from this is the extent to which White's reading of the film can be applied to the novel, but this is less interesting than the extent to which the standpoint of the contemporary critic produces very different texts in retrospect. From the perspective of contemporary Ireland, *The Uninvited* is clearly haunted by the practice of separation of 'illegitimate' children from their natural mothers in the Ireland of its composition.[46] Read from a US perspective in conjunction with *Rebecca*, in the context of the legibility of that film's lesbian narrative to contemporary audiences, a very different suppressed narrative emerges. In effect *The Uninvited* has two unconciousnesses.

From White's point of view, 'The division between good mother and bad is the classic stuff of psychoanalysis and the film follows the script of the family romance', and the ending is disappointing: 'The true mother's ghost seems to be satisfied at delivering her daughter to the arms of the hero and Rick takes it upon himself to vanquish Mary's ghost: "It's time someone faced that icy rage of yours!" he shouts, brandishing a candelabra at the retreating apparition.'[47] In the Irish context, this assertion of sexuality and the defeat of the icy apparition of an idealised and powerful image of Mary who denies both sexual and maternal physical warmth are both more attractive and more subversive. White finds a different agenda:

> The efforts to oppose the two women and to attribute to them opposite qualities ... are confounded and ultimately redouble the discourse of the *sexual* mother ... While the overdetermination of the maternal scenario would seem to lay to rest the lesbian phantom that haunted *Rebecca* ... the fact that motherhood itself is occasion for epistemological doubt threatens to reinscribe the lesbian thematic.[48]

This reading of *The Uninvited* raises key questions for feminist criticism and its relationship with women's history. There is no basis for an opposition between a local and historical knowledge, producing an historically 'accurate'

---

45 Ibid.
46 See Meaney, *Gender, Ireland and Cultural Change*.
47 White, *Uninvited*, p. 70
48 Ibid.

reading, and an intertextual, psychoanalytic perspective, producing a theoretically sophisticated one. Instead White's very different perspective produces a new point of engagement, which is strengthened when one finds Macardle in a 1940 disquisition on the relationship between film and theatre describing the film *Maedchen in Uniform* as a fulfilment of the ultimate poetic potential of film art.[49] The history of Winsloe's play on the Dublin stage raises fascinating questions about Dublin's hidden cultural and sexual histories. The history of the adaptation and interpretation of *The Uninvited* suggests that accessing these histories requires further historical and archival research and the application of a range of different critical and theoretical perspectives. It is a task which challenges the contemporary reader to respect the ambiguities of the past, the complexity of women's lives and work and the ability of popular or neglected texts to produce multiple interpretations and meaning that challenge what we think we know about the women who wrote and read them.

49 Dorothy Macardle, 'Experiment in Ireland'.

Conclusion

This study has explored the complexity of cultural encounters in which Irish womanhood has evolved. In the 'constantly shifting kaleidoscope of give and take' between cultures, women's identities were negotiated and re-negotiated in each of the periods and contexts analysed in this study.[1] We have traced the circulation of ideas, fantasies and aspirations which have shaped women's lives in actuality and in imagination. There are traces in the cultural material of a desire to explore many different ways of being a woman. Attention to women's cultural consumption and production shows that one individual may in one day identify with representations of heroines of romantic fiction, patriots, philanthropists, literary ladies, film stars, career women, popular singers, advertising models and foreign missionaries. The processes of cultural consumption, production and exchange provide evidence of women's agency, aspirations and activities within and far beyond the domestic sphere.

In this tangled web of motive and purpose, it is impossible neatly to categorise cause and effect. It is possible to trace the circulation and readership of texts promoting women's education, for example, but this does not provide conclusive proof of their impact on educational opportunity. Advertisements sold modern appliances by promoting fantasies of new forms of domestic life and personal freedom. Such appliances did change the lives of women who could afford them, but effectively trapped them in a new form of domesticity. Popular films, plays and novels explored real issues for women, particularly in relation to work and opportunities for marriage. The fantasy solutions they proposed to these problems may often have been implausible, but they offered solace to some and space for dissent and change to others. Fantasy is a powerful motivational force and the idea of America, for example, had a profound impact on the actual lives of many Irish women.

---

1 T. C. McCaskie, 'Cultural Encounters: Britain and Africa in the Nineteenth century', in Andrew Porter (ed.), *The Oxford History of the British Empire, Volume 3: The Nineteenth Century* (Oxford: Oxford University Press, 1999), p. 665.

These case studies have explored that 'evolving cultural hybrid', the Irish woman.[2] Womanhood in Ireland is constructed at the intersection of Irish local concerns and international developments. A complex picture of women's reading, writing and aspirations emerges which challenges the assumption that Catholic cultural hegemony was the prevailing force in determining women's roles. The adaptation of European literary modes and genres by Irish-language authors is evident in texts such as 'Párliament na mBan', which continued to be read in manuscript form throughout the eighteenth century. Simultaneously, there was a flourishing market in the reprinting in Ireland of works by English Protestant ministers, London-based bluestocking women and translations into English of French Catholic texts, which circulated irrespective of denominational differences. When Catholic Church control of social and cultural practice intensified in the post-Famine era, there remained a persistent demand for imported novels, newspapers, plays and eventually films which exposed the readership to different values. Censorship, while vigorous, was not always consistent. Eugene O'Neill's explorations of sexual repression and familial neurosis were performed to great acclaim due to his Irish Catholic background.

Widely disseminated popular texts indicate the influence of international debates about the appropriate behaviour, education and appearance of women and concepts of domestic life on Irish opinion. This is not a relationship that can be characterised as an opposition between Irish conservatism and international progress. External influences often reinforced the domestic roles of women, from French religious texts in the eighteenth and nineteenth century to Hollywood films in the twentieth. While many of the literary texts were aimed at women of the cultural elite, advertisements, emigrant's letters, film and radio ensured that women of all classes were by the twentieth century engaged in complex processes of cultural negotiation and exchange.

References to 'new' ways of being a woman, the undesirable modern tendencies in contemporary young women and the dangers of women's fascination with imported ideas and goods were as prevalent in the eighteenth as the twentieth centuries. There was a constant low-level anxiety about the emergence of new and threatening forms of womanhood. Idealisation of domestic womanhood as an unchanging state has been combined with relentless reinventions of good womanhood. There is nothing new about the new woman and nothing static about the role of the housewife.

The assumption that women consumers of imported popular culture participated in a naïve form of consumption which exposed them to corrupting influences was a major preoccupation of Irish cultural commentary from the eighteenth to the twentieth centuries. This has had an enduring impact on

2 Ibid.

the academic construction of the cultural past which has tended to neglect and under-value what women actually read. It is only very recently that literary and cultural critics have begun to pay attention to what Franco Moretti described as the 'great unread'.[3]

Any analysis of women's reading practices problematises the dichotomy between the private and the public in women's lives. From the eighteenth century onwards, reading was for many women an avenue into new forms of culture and education and different types of public access, including political engagement. Consumerism and women's role as consumers opened up the possibility of women's engagement with public and civic space.

The Irish woman writer is a fascinating invention, part marketing strategy, part political intervention, negotiating between an identification with Ireland and an international readership. From the time of Sydney Owenson, Irish women used and adapted forms of fiction which were centrally concerned with women's subjective experience of a broad range of social and historical issues. They invented a persona of the Irish woman writer which appealed to a broad international audience and forged highly successful literary careers.

The process of defining Irish womanhood has, thus, been a key site of ideological tension, from the early reservations about young women reading novels, while encouraging the formal education of girls. In the early Victorian period, Daniel O'Connell's rhetoric promulgated domestic virtues for women, while the political movement he headed depended on their participation in public protest. The female consumer was a constant focus of official anxiety, but she also performed a key economic function. She was crucial to the modernisation of Irish domesticity paradoxically promoted by the Irish state. On the one hand, women were urged to avoid the dangers of modernisation and preserve what was presented as the indigenous purity of Irish womanhood. At the same time the state-funded electricity company urged women to embrace modern utilities in their homes. Similarly, despite the Catholic Church's opposition to female emigration, they produced handbooks advising prospective emigrants. The 1930s was a period of retrenchment and conservatism, but also one where more plays by women were performed in Dublin than at the end of the twentieth century. These apparent historical paradoxes indicate the complexity of the interplay between public discourse and personal conduct, ideas and actions, fantasy and reality. The cultural encounters explored in this volume indicate that Irish women were not passive recipients of imposed models of behaviour. Instead they negotiated, selected and at times defied the representations of womanhood presented to them in official and commercially sponsored media.

3 Franco Moretti, 'The Slaughterhouse of Literature', *Modern Language Quarterly*, 61, 1 (March 2000), pp. 207–27.

Bibliography

Primary Sources

Delargy Centre for Irish Folklore, University College Dublin
MSS 1407, 1408, 1409, 1410, 1411

Dublin Diocesan Archives
Catholic Association Papers, 55/2, Minutes of the Financial Committee of the Association, 1826–35

Friends Historical Library, Dublin
Journal of Margaret Boyle Harvey, 1786–1832

Presentation Order, George's Hill, Dublin
Presentation Order Archive

National Archives and Records Administration, United States
American Foreign Service Inspection Report, Dublin, Ireland, RG 49, roll 1231.9
Despatches from US consuls in Cork, 1790–1906, vol. 10, roll 10, T196
General Records of the Department of State, RG 59, RG 1231

National Archives of Ireland, Dublin
Department of Foreign Affairs, Letter Books, President, 1932
Department of Justice, H305/18/1483
Department of the Taoiseach, S13087A

National Library of Ireland, Dublin
Caroline Hamilton, 'Anecdotes of our family, written for my children', MS 4810
Caroline Hamilton, 'Reminiscences', MS 4810, MS 4811
Cregan Papers, MS 46,791/3, MS 46,791/1, MS 46,792
Irish Countrywomen's Association, MS 39,872/4

Memorandum for the Commission on Vocational Organisation, MS 39,871/4
Minute Book of the Proceedings of the Catholic Association, September–October 1828, MS 3290
Rosamund Jacob Diaries, MS 32,582/1–171

Public Record Office, Belfast, Northern Ireland
Eason and Son Ltd Papers, D3981/2/1
Granard Papers, T3765
Tennent Papers, D1748

Royal Irish Academy, Dublin
Correspondence between Maria Edgeworth and William Rowan Hamilton, MS F 23 3, 1–4

Tipperary Local Studies
The Library Association of Ireland

Trinity College Dublin, Manuscripts Division
Arnold Marsh Papers, MS 8301, S.S. 1 (a)

University College Dublin, School of Archives
Seán MacEntee Papers, P67/590(1)

Ursuline Archives, Blackrock, Cork
Ursuline Archives, *c.*1770–1845

Websites
Dictionary of Irish Biography (Cambridge University Press, http://dib.cambridge.org)
Eighteenth Century Collections Online (Gale Cengage Learning, http://gale.cengage.co.uk/product-highlights/history/eighteenth-century-collections-online.aspx)
English Short Title Catalogue (http://bl.estc.uk)
Inventing and Reinventing the Irish Woman (http://www2.ul.ie/web/WWW/Faculties/Arts%2C_Humanities_%26_Social_Sciences/Inventing/)
Irish Centre for Migration Studies, Breaking the Silence Project (http://migration.ucc.ie/oralarchive/testing/breaking/narrators/)
Irish Film Censors' Records (http://www.tcd.ie/irishfilm/censor/show.php?fid=3230)
Irish Newspapers Online (http://www.irishnewsarchive.com)
Irish Theatre Institute, Playography Ireland (http://www.Irishplayography.com)
The Literary Gothic (http://www.litgothic.com/Authors/riddell.html)
Magazine of Magazines, Limerick, 11751–69 (http://www3.ul.ie/ecrg/digitisation-magazine-of-magazines)

Nineteenth Century UK Periodicals Online (Gale Cengage Learning, http://mlr.com/DigitalCollections/products/ukperiodicals)
Oxford Dictionary of National Biography (Oxford University Press, http://www.oxforddnb.com/)
Project Gutenberg (http://www.gutenberg.org/wiki/Bestsellers%2C_American%2C_1900–1922_%28Bookshelf%29)
Women in Modern Irish Culture Database (http://www2.warwick.ac.uk/fac/arts/history/irishwomenwriters)

Newspapers
Belfast Newsletter
Connacht Tribune
Cork Examiner
Drogheda Journal
Dublin Evening Mail
Enniscorthy Echo
Freeman's Journal
The Galway Vindicator
Irish Farmers Journal
Irish Independent
Irish Press
Irish Times
Kerryman
Leitrim Observer
Limerick Chronicle
Limerick Leader
Munster Express
The Pilot
The Times
Tipperary Star

Periodicals
The Belfast Monthly Magazine
The Bell
Bowker's Annual and Publisher's Weekly
The Catholic Penny Magazine: Published Weekly, Under the Inspection of Catholic Divines
The Dublin Saturday Magazine. A Journal of Instruction and Amusement Comprising Irish Biography and Antiquities
Duffy's Irish Catholic Magazine: A Monthly Review, Devoted to National Literature, the Fine Arts, Antiquities, Ecclesiastical History, Biography of Illustrious Irishmen, and Military Memoirs. …
Eason's Bulletin
Englishwoman's Domestic Magazine

Female Spectator (composite edition, 4 vols, Dublin: George and Alexander Ewing, 1746; reprint, 1747)
The Furrow
Irish Ecclesiastical Record
The Irish Housewife
Irish Library Bulletin
Irish Messenger of the Sacred Heart
The Irish Monthly
Irish Statesman
The Ladies Journal
The Literary and Mathematical Asylum
Madonna. The Official Organ of the Children of Mary Sodalities in Ireland
The Magazine of Magazines
Model Housekeeping
The Monthly Pantheon or General Repository or Politics, Arts, Science, Literature and Miscellaneous Information
The New Magazine
Our Girls
The Parlour Window
Sentimental and Masonic Magazine
Walker's Hibernian Magazine
Woman's Life
Woman's Mirror
Woman's News

Official Publications

British Parliamentary Papers 1826–7 (237), 1826–7, v 2, Second Report from the Select Committee on Emigration from the United Kingdom (reprint; Shannon: Irish University Press, 1968), p. 74, qs 870, 891.
Census of Population of Ireland, 1926, III (Dublin: Stationery Office, 1965).
Census of Population of Ireland, 1961, III (Dublin: Stationery Office, 1965).
Central Statistics Office, *That Was Then, This Is Now: Changes in Ireland, 1949–99* (Dublin: Government Publications Office, 2000).
Commission on Technical Education (Dublin: Stationery Office, 1927).
Coimisiún na Gaeltachta, Reports and Minutes of Evidence (Dublin: Stationery Office, 1926).
Department of Local Government, *Annual Report*, 1964 (Dublin: Stationery Office, 1964).
Hansard House of Commons Debate, 2 June 1833. Consulted on line, 3 March 2012 http://hansard.millbanksystems.com/commons/1833/jun/03/
Intoxicating Liquor Commission Report, 1925 (Dublin: Government Publications Office, 1925).
Report of the Commission on Emigration and Other Population Problems 1948–54 (Dublin: Government Publication Office, 1955).

Report of the Inter-Departmental Committee on Seasonal Migration to Great Britain, 1937–8 (Dublin: Stationery Office, 1938).
Report on Youth Unemployment, 1951 (Dublin: Stationery Office, 1951).
'The Homestead Act, 1862', http://www.nps.gov/jeff/historyculture/upload/homestead.pdf (accessed 16 July 2010).

Printed Contemporary Literature

Aikin, John, *Evenings at Home; Or, the Juvenile Budget Opened. Consisting of a Variety of Miscellaneous Pieces* (Cork: J. Connor, 1794).
Aikin, John and Anna Letitia, *Miscellaneous Pieces in Prose* (Belfast: James Magee, 1774).
Allestree, Richard, *The Causes of the Decay of Christian Piety and The Gentleman's Calling* (Oxford: Printed at the Theater, [1673]).
Allestree, Richard, *The Ladies Calling In Two Parts. By the Author of The Whole Duty of Man: The Causes of the Decay of Christian Piety, and The Gentleman's Calling* (Oxford: Printed at the Theater, [1673]).
Allestree, Richard, *The New Whole Duty of Man* (Dublin: P. Wilson, 1746, 1752, 1764, 1771, 1774).
Allestree, Richard, *The Whole Duty of Man* (Dublin: John Brocas, 1699, 1714, 1720, 1733, 1737, 1800).
Allestree, Richard, *The Works of the Learned and Pious Author of The Whole Duty of Man* (Dublin: Printed for P. Dugan, 1723).
Astell, Mary, *An Essay in Defence of the Female Sex. In Which are Inserted the Characters of a Pedant, a Squire, a Beau, a Vertuoso, a Poetaster, a City-Critick, &c. In a Letter to a Lady. Written by a Lady* (London: printed for A. Roper and E. Wilkinson at the Black Boy, and R. Clavel at the Peacock, in Fleetstreet, 1686).
Astell, Mary, *A Serious Proposal to the Ladies, for the Advancement of their True and Greatest Interest. By a Lover of her Sex* (London: printed for R. Wilkin at the King's Head in St. Paul's Church-Yard, 1694).
Astell, Mary, *Some Reflections Upon Marriage. With Additions* (5th edition, Dublin: S. Hyde and E. Dobson, 1730).
Barbauld, Mrs, *Lessons for Children of Three Years Old* (Dublin: R. Jackson, 1779; London: J. Johnson, 1795).
Beaufort, L. C., 'An Essay upon the State of Architecture and Antiquities, Previous to the Landing of the Anglo-Normans in Ireland', *Transactions of the Royal Irish Academy*, 15 (1828), pp. 101–241.
Le Prince de Beaumont, Jean Marie, *The young ladies magazine, or dialogues between a discreet governess and several young ladies … By Mrs. Le Prince de Beaumont …* (Dublin: James Hoey, Junior, 1765).
Berkeley, George, *The Ladies Library: Written by a Lady. Published by Sir Richard Steele* (1st edition, 3 vols; London: Printed for J[acob] T[onson], 1714).

Boileau-Despréaux, Nicolas, *The Lutrin: an Heroi-comical Poem. In Six Cantos. By Monsieur Boileau. To Which is Prefix'd, Some Account of the Author's Writings, and this Translation: by N. Rowe, Esq* (Dublin: S. Powell, 1730).

Brooke, Charlotte, *Reliques of Irish Poetry: Consisting of Heroic Poems, Odes, Elegies, and Songs, Translated into English Verse: With Notes Explanatory and Historical; and the Originals in the Irish Character. To Which is Subjoined an Irish Tale ...* (Dublin: George Bonham, 1789).

Campan, Jeanne Louise Henriette, *Conversations d'une mere avec sa fille en français et en anglais: avec une jolie gravure* (London: 1816).

Chapone, Sarah, *The Hardships of the English Laws. In Relation to Wives. With an Explanation of the Original Curse of Subjection Passed Upon the Woman. In an Humble Address to the Legislature* (London: W. Bowyer for J. Roberts, 1735; Dublin: George Faulkner, 1735).

Defoe, Daniel, *Essays Upon Several Projects: Or, Effectual Ways for Advancing the Interest of the Nation* (London: Printed for Thomas Ballard, at the Rising Sun in Little Britain, 1702), pp. 282–304.

Edgeworth, Maria, *Letters for Literary Ladies: To Which is Added, an Essay on the Noble Science of Self-Justification* (London: printed for J. Johnson, 1795)

Edgeworth, Maria, *Letters for Literary Ladies*. Edited by Claire Connolly (London: Dent, 1993).

Edwards, Anthony, *A Catalogue of Books, in Most Branches of Literature and Music ... Now Selling by Anthony Edwards, no 3 Castle-Street, Cork* (Cork: Printed for Anthony Edwards, 1785).

Fénelon, François de, *Telemacus, Son of Ulysses*. Edited and translated by Patrick Riley (Cambridge: Cambridge University Press, 1994).

Fénelon, François de Salignac, *The Education of Young Gentlewomen. Written Originally in the French; and From Thence Made English. And Improved for a Lady of Quality* (London: Printed for Nathaniel Ranew, 1699).

Fielding, Sarah, *The Governess; or, Little Female Academy. Being the History of Mrs. Teachum, and her Nine Girls. With their Nine Days Amusement. Calculated for the Entertainment and Iinstruction of Young Ladies in their Education. By the Author of David Simple* (Dublin: Printed for A. Bradley and R. James, 1749).

Fleetwood, William, *The Relative Duties of Parents and Children, Husbands and Wives, Masters and Servants ...* (Dublin: Samuel Fairbrother, 1726, 1753).

Fontenelle, M. de, *A Discourse of the Plurality of Worlds. Written in French, by the Most Ingenious Author of the Dialogues of the Dead. And Translated into English by Sir W. D. Knight* (Dublin: Andrew Crook and Samuel Helsham, 1687).

Fontenelle, M. de, *Conversations With a Lady, On the Plurality of Worlds. Written in French, by Mons. Fontenelle ... Translated by Mr. Glanvill* (Dublin: William Forrest, 1728).

Genlis, Stéphanie Félicité, *Adelaide and Theodore, or Letters on Education: Containing All the Principles Relative to Three Different Plans of Education; to that of Princes and to those of Young Persons of Both Sexes* (Dublin: printed for Luke White, 1783, 1785 (2 reprints); printed for W. Jones, 1794).

Genlis, Stéphanie Félicité, *Nouvelle Méthode D'enseignement Pour La Première Enfance. A New Method of Instruction for Children from Five to Ten Years Old, Including Moral Dialogues, The Children's Island, A Tale, Thoughts and Maxims, Models of Composition in Writing, For Children Ten or Twelve Years Old, and A New Method of Teaching Children to Draw. Translated from the French of Madame de Genlis* (Dublin: P. Wogan, 1800).

Genlis, Stéphanie Félicité, *Théâtre à L'usage des Jeunes Personnes.Theatre of Education. Translated from the French of the Countess de Genlis* (4 vols; Dublin: D. Graisberry, 1781, 1783, 1784).

Gilbert, J. T., *The Streets of Dublin* (Dublin: James Gilbert, 1851)

Griffith, Elizabeth and Richard Griffith, *A Series of Genuine Letters Between Henry and Frances* (3 vols; London: W. Johnston, 1757; Dublin: S. Powell, 1760).

Griffith, Elizabeth, *Essays, Addressed to Young Married Women* (London: T. Cadell, 1782; Dublin: Sold by George Draper, 1790).

Griffith, Elizabeth, *Theodorick, King of Denmark. A Tragedy. Never Before Published. By a Young Gentlewoman* (Dublin: James Esdall, 1752).

Guinan, Rev. J., *Scenes and Sketches in an Irish Parish Or Priest and People of Doon by a Country Curate* (3rd edition; Dublin: M. H. Gill, 1903).

Haywood, Eliza, *The History of Miss Betsy Thoughtless* (London: T. Gardner, 1751; Dublin: Oliver Nelson, 1751, 1752, 1765).

Hickes, George, *Instructions for the Education of a Daughter, by the Author of Telemachus. To Which is Added, a Small Tract of Instructions For the Conduct of Young Ladies of the Highest Rank. With Suitable Devotions Annexed. Done into English, and Revised by Dr. George Hickes* (London: Printed for Jonah Bowyer, 1707, 1708, 1713, 1721; Edinburgh: Printed for James Reid, 1750; Glasgow, 1750; Dublin, 1753).

Hoey, James, *Books Printed by and for James Hoey, Junior* (Dublin: 1763).

Hutch, William, *Mrs. Ball: A Biography* (Dublin: James Duffy, 1879).

Kelly, Anna, 'I Went to America', *The Bell*, 3, 5 (February 1942), pp. 353–56.

Kiernan, George, 'Description of a New Air Pump', *Transactions of the Royal Irish Academy*, 13 (1818), pp. 109–14.

Kiernan, Harriet, 'Essay on the Influence of Fictitious History on Modern Manners', *Transactions of the Royal Irish Academy*, 12 (1815), pp. 61–97.

Leadbeater, Mary, *Extracts and Original Anecdotes for the Improvement of Youth* (Dublin: R. M. Jackson, 1794).

Leadbeater, Mary, *The Leadbeater Papers. The Annals of Ballitore With a Memoir of the Author* (2 vols; London: Bell and Daldy, 1862).

Lennox, Charlotte, *Henrietta* (Dublin: George Faulkner, Sarah Cotter, Hulton Bradley, 1758, 1786).

Leyal, P., Letters *Lately Printed in the Freeman's and Hibernian Journals, under the Signature of P. Leyal: Addressed to His Grace the Duke of Leinster. And now Republished at the Desire of the Apollo Society, and of Several Respectable Citizens* (Dublin: James Porter, 1780).

Locke, John, *Some Thoughts Concerning Education* (10th edition, Dublin: R. Reilly on Cork Hill, 1737).

Lomber, Pére, *Spiritual Consolation, or A Treatise on Interior Peace. Translated from the French of Père Lomber. Interspersed with Various Instructions Necessary for the Promoting the Practice of Solid Piety. Translated By the Authoress of the "Ursuline Manual"* (Dublin: Richard Coyne, 1835).

McCarthy, Mother Borgia, *A Directory, for Novices of Every Religious Order; Particularly Those Devoted to the Instruction of Youth. Translated from the French* (Cork: W. Ferguson, 1817).

McCarthy, Mother Borgia, *The Ursuline Manual, or, a Collection of Prayers, Spiritual Exercises, etc. Interspersed With the Various Instructions Necessary for Forming Youth to the Practice of Solid Piety Originally Arranged for the Young Ladies Educated at the Ursuline Convent Cork* (Cork: 1825; London: Keating and Brown, 1825, 1827, 1830; Dublin: R. Coyne, 1835).

Maguire, John Francis, *The Irish in America* (New York: D. & J. Sadlier, 1868).

Maintenon, Madame de, *The Ladies Monitor or Instructions for the Fair Sex, Written in French by the Celebrated Madam de Maintenon, for the Use of the Young Ladies of St. Cyr's and Now First Translated into English by Mr. Rollos* (Dublin: Printed for Richard Smith, 1758).

Manson, David, *Directions to Play the Literary Cards Invented for the Improvement of Children in Learning and Morals from Their Beginning to Learn Their Letters, Till They Become Proficients in Spelling, Reading, Parsing and Arithmetick* (Belfast: Printed for the author, 1764).

Manson, David, *A New Pocket Dictionary; Or, English Expositor* (Belfast: Daniel Blow, 1762).

Manson, David, 'The Present State and Practices of the Play-School in Belfast', included as an appendix to *A New Pocket Dictionary; or, English Expositor* (Belfast: Daniel Blow, 1762).

Moore, Hamilton, *The Young Gentleman and Ladies Monitor Being a Collection of Select Pieces from Our Best Modern Writers: Particularly Calculated to Form the Mind and Manner of Both Sexes, and Adapted to the Use of Schools and Academies* (Belfast: James Magee, 1788).

Mulholland, Rosa, *A Fair Emigrant* (London: Keegan, Paul Trench, 1888).

Mulholland, Rosa, 'The Hungry Death', reprinted in *Irish Monthly*, 42 (June–July 1914), pp. 297–310, 366–73.

Mulholland, Rosa, *The Return of Mary O'Murrough* (Edinburgh and London: Sands, 1908).

Nicholson, Asenath, *Ireland's Welcome to the Stranger: On An Excursion Through Ireland in 1884 & 1845, for the Purpose of Personally Investigating the Condition of the Poor* (New York: Bakker and Scrivner, 1847).

Ní Mhunghaile, Lesa (ed.), *Charlotte Brooke's 'Reliques of Irish Poetry'* (Dublin: Irish Manuscripts Commission, 2011).

Pascal, Blaise, *Thoughts on Religion, and Other Curious Subjects. Written Originally in French by Monsieur Pascal. Translated into English by Basil Kennet, D.D.* (Dublin: George Faulkner, 1739).
Peyton, Rev. Alex. J., *The Emigrant's Friend; or Hints on Emigration to the United States of America Addressed to the People of Ireland* (Cork: J. O'Brien, 1853).
Springborg, Patricia (ed.), *A Serious Proposal to the Ladies, Parts I and II*, by Mary Astell (London: Pickering and Chatto, 1997), pp. xvii–xxiii.
Toland, John, *Letters to Serena* (London: Printed for Bernard Lintot, 1704).
Ursuline Nun, *The Catholic Lady's Keepsake or Gleanings Offered to Increase the Store of the Young Ladies Educated at St Mary's. By a Member of the Ursuline Community, St Mary's Waterford* (Dublin: James Duffy, 1850).
Ursuline Nun, *The Catholic Offering: Counsels to the Young on Their Leaving School and Entering into the World. By a Member of the Ursuline Community, Blackrock, Cork* (Dublin: James Duffy, 1859).
Ursuline Nun, *A Compendious and Impartial History of England from the Invasion of the Romans to the Close of the Reign of William the Fourth for the Use of Catholic Youth. By a Member of the Ursuline Community, St Mary's Waterford* (Dublin: James Duffy, 1844).
Ursuline Nun, *The Month of Mary: A Series of Meditations on the Life and Virtues of the Holy Mother of God, Particularly Adapted for the Month of May. By a Member of the Ursuline Community, Blackrock, Cork* (Cork: J. O'Brien, 1853).
Ursuline Nun, *The Spirit of Prayer. A New Manual of Catholic Devotion with the Epistles and Gospels for the Sundays and Principal Festivals Throughout the Year. By a Member of the Ursuline Community, Cork* (Cork: J. O'Brien, 1850).
Voiture, Monsieur, *The Works of the Celebrated Monsieur Voiture* (2 vols; Dublin: Samuel Fairbrother, 1731).
Whyte, Samuel, *Modern Education, Respecting Young Ladies as Well as Gentlemen* (Dublin: R. Marchbank, 1775).
Whyte, Samuel, *The Shamrock: or Hibernian Cresses. A Collection of Poems, Songs, Epigrams, etc. Latin as Well as English, the Original Production of Ireland. To Which are Subjoined, Thoughts on the Prevailing System of School Education, Respecting Young Ladies as Well as Gentlemen: With Practical Proposals for a Reformation* (Dublin: R. Marchbank, 1772).
Wilkes Wetenhall, *An Essay on the Pleasures and Advantages of Female Literature* (London: Printed for the Author, 1741).
Wilkes, Wetenhall, *A Letter of Genteel and Moral Advice to a Young Lady. To Which is Digested into a New and Familiar Method, a System of Rules and Information, to Qualify the Fair Sex to be Useful and Happy in Every Stance* (Dublin: Printed for the Author, 1740).
Wilkes, Wetenhall, *A Letter to a Lady in Praise of Female Learning* (Dublin: J. Jones, 1739).
Wyse, Thomas, *Historical Sketch of the Late Catholic Association of Ireland* (2 vols; London: Henry Colburn, 1829).

Young, Edward, *The Complaint, or, Night-Thoughts on Life, Death, and Immortality* (Dublin: Printed for Peter Wilson, 1742–46).
Young, Ursula, *A History of the United Kingdom of Great Britain and Ireland ... Compiled from Various Authors and Intended Chiefly for the Young Ladies Educated at the Ursuline Convents* (2 vols; Cork: W. Fergusson, 1815).
Young, Ursula, *Questions on the History of the United Kingdom of Great Britain and Ireland. Intended Chiefly for the Young Ladies Educated at the Ursuline Convent, Cork* (Cork: J. Geary, 1815).
Young, Ursula, *A Sketch of Irish History: Compiled by Way of Question and Answer, for the Use of Schools* (Cork: J. Geary, 1815).
Young, Ursula, *A System of Chronology Facilitated by the Mnemonics for the Use of the Young Ladies Educated at the Ursuline Convent* (Cork: 1841).

Plays

Lennox, Gilbert and Gisela Ashley, *Third Party Risk. A Play in Three Acts* (London: The Fortune Press, 1939).
Macardle, Dorothy, *Ann Kavanagh, A Drama in One Act* (New York: Samuel French, 1937).
Mary Manning, '*Youth's the Season-?*', *Plays of Changing Ireland*, edited, with introductions and notes by Curtis Canfield (New York: Macmillan, 1936).
Powell, Peter, *The Absentee Programme Notes* (March 1938).
Tonkonogy, Gertrude, *Three-Cornered Moon* (New York: Samuel French, 1935).

Secondary Sources

Adair, Vivyan C. and Sharon Gormley, 'Women and Work', in Carl E. Van Horn and Herbert A. Schaffner (eds), *Work in America: An Encyclopedia of History, Policy and Society* (Oxford: ABC-Clio, 2003), pp. 600–8.
Adburgham, Alison, *Women in Print: Writing Women and Women's Magazines from the Restoration to the Accession of Victoria* (London: Allen & Unwin, 1972).
Aitken, George A., *The Life of Richard Steele* (2 vols; London: William Isbister, 1889).
Akenson, Donald Harmon, *The Irish Diaspora: A Primer* (Toronto and Belfast: Institute of Irish Studies, 1996).
Akenson, Donald Harmon, *The Irish Education Experiment: The National System of Education in the Nineteenth Century* (London: Routledge and Kegan Paul, 1970).
Almeida, Linda Dowling, 'A Great Time to be in America: The Irish in Post-Second World War New York City', in Dermot Keogh, Finbarr O'Shea and Carmel Quinlan (eds), *Ireland: The Lost Decade in the 1950s* (Cork: Mercier Press, 2004), pp. 206–21.
Almeida, Linda Dowling, 'Irish-America, 1940–2000' in J. J. Lee and Marion R. Casey (eds), *Making the Irish American: History and Heritage of the Irish in the United States* (New York: New York University Press, 2006), pp. 548–74.

'An American Magazine', *Hibernia*, 1, 1 (April 1882), pp. 54–55.
Anelius, Joseph, *National Action: A Plan for the National Recovery of Ireland* (2nd edition; Dublin: Gaelic Athletic Association, 1942).
Archer, R. L., *Rousseau on Education* (London: Edward Arnold, 1912).
Arensberg, Conrad A. and Solon T. Kimball, *Family and Community in Ireland* (3rd edition; Ennis: Clasp, 2001).
Armstrong, Nancy, *Desire and Domestic Fiction: A Political History of the Novel* (Oxford: Oxford University Press, 1987).
Aronson, Amy B., *Taking Liberties: Early American Women's Magazines and their Readers* (Westport: Praeger, 2002).
Axtell, James L., *The Educational Writings of John Locke* (Cambridge: Cambridge University Press, 1968).
Bailey, N. (ed.), *The Colloquies of Erasmus* (3 vols; London: Gibbings & Co., 1900).
Balanzo, Wanda, Anne Mulhall and Moynagh Sullivan (eds), *Irish Postmodernisms and Popular Culture* (Hampshire and New York: Palgrave, 2007).
Ballaster, Ros, Margaret Beetham, Elizabeth Frazer and Sandra Hebron, *Women's Worlds: Ideology, Femininity and the Woman's Magazine* (London: Macmillan, 1991).
Barnard, H. C., *Fénelon on Education* (Cambridge: Cambridge University Press, 1966).
Barry, David, 'What the Public Read', *Irish Library Bulletin*, 6, 6 (November–December 1945), pp. 114–16.
Barry, Senator Anthony, 'Library Achievement', *An Leabharlann*, 17, 3 (September 1959), pp. 89–96.
Bayles, Martha, 'Popular Culture', in Paul S. Boyer (ed.), *The Oxford Companion to United States History* (Oxford and New York: Oxford University Press), pp. 608–10.
Beere, T. J., 'Cinema Statistics in Saorstát Eireann (with Discussion)', *Journal of the Statistical and Social Enquiry Society of Ireland*, 15, 6 (89th session, 1935–36), pp. 83–110.
Beetham, Margaret, *A Magazine of Her Own? Domesticity and Desire in the Woman's Magazine, 1800–1914* (London: Routledge, 1996).
Bell, Melanie, '"Quality", Cinema and the "Superior Woman's" Persona: Understanding Women's Film Criticism in Post-War Britain (1945–59)', *Women's History Review*, 19, 5 (November 2010), pp. 703–19.
Benshoff, Henry and Sean Griffin, *America on Film: Representing Race, Class, Gender and Sexuality at the Movies* (Oxford: Blackwell Publishing, 2004).
Berman, David, 'Enlightenment and Counter-Enlightenment in Irish Philosophy', *Archiv für Geschichte der Philosophie*, 64, 2 (1982), pp. 148–65.
Blake, W. J., 'Think It Over: Bad Literature', *Irish Messenger of the Sacred Heart*, 59 (July 1846), pp. 134–35.
Blessing, Patrick J., 'Irish in America', in Michael Glazier (ed.), *The Encyclopedia of the Irish in America* (Notre Dame, Ind.: University of Notre Dame Press, 1999), pp. 454–62.

Blessing, Patrick, J., 'The Irish', in Stephen Thernstrom (ed.), *The Harvard Encyclopedia of American Ethnic History* (Cambridge, Mass.: Harvard University Press, 1980), pp. 524–45.

Bloch, Jean, 'Discourses of Female Education in the Writings of Eighteenth-Century French Women', in Sarah Knott and Barbara Taylor (eds), *Women, Gender and Enlightenment* (Basingstoke: Palgrave Macmillan, 2005), pp. 243–58.

Bloom, Clive, *Bestsellers: Popular Fiction since 1900* (Basingstoke: Palgrave Macmillan, 2002).

Bohan, Sean, 'The Donegal County Library Service', *An Leabharlann*, 13, 2 (June 1955), pp. 81–85.

Bourke, Angela et al. (eds), *The Field Day Anthology of Irish Writing, Volumes 4–5: Irish Women's Writing and Traditions* (Cork: Cork University Press, 2002).

Bowen, Elizabeth, 'Obituary of Mainie Jellett', *The Bell*, 9, 3 (1944), pp. 250–56.

Boydston, Jeanne, 'Women in the Labor Force' in Paul S. Boyer (ed.), *The Oxford Companion to United States History* (Oxford and New York: Oxford University Press, 2001), pp. 834–35.

Bradley, Anthony and Maryann Gianella Valiulis, *Gender and Sexuality in Modern Ireland* (Amherst: University of Massachusetts Press, 1997).

Brennan, Helen, 'Reinventing Tradition: The Boundaries of Irish Dance', *History Ireland*, 2, 2 (Summer 1994), pp. 22–24.

Brewster, Scott et al. (eds), *Ireland in Proximity: History, Gender, Space* (London: Routledge, 1999).

Bric, Maurice J., 'Daniel O'Connell and the Debate on Anti-Slavery, 1820–50', in Tom Dunne and Laurence J. Geary (eds), *History and the Public Sphere: Essays in Honour of John A. Murphy* (Cork: Cork University Press, 2005), pp. 69–82.

Brown, Michael, *Francis Hutcheson in Dublin, 1719–30: The Crucible of His Thought* (Dublin: Four Courts Press, 2001).

Brown, Terence, *Ireland: A Social and Cultural History 1922–79* (London: Fontana Press, 1985).

Brown, Stephen James Meredith (ed.), *Ireland in Fiction, 1910: A Guide to Irish Novels, Tales, Romances and Folk-Lore* (New York: reprinted Burt Franklin, 1970).

Browne, Jen, 'Decisions in DIY: Women, Home Improvements and Advertising in Post-War Britain', in Maggie Andrews and Mary M. Talbot (eds), *All the World and Her Husband: Women in Twentieth-Century Consumer Culture* (London and New York: Cassell, 2000), pp. 130–45.

Burke Savage, Roland, *A Valiant Dublin Woman: The Story of George's Hill (1766–1940)* (Dublin: M. H. Gill, 1940).

Butler, Mary, 'A Medieval Modern', *The Catholic Bulletin and Book Review*, 4 (November 1914), p. 684.

Butler, Mary, *Modern Fashions in Ladies' Dress* (Dublin: Irish Messenger Office, 1927).

Butterwick, Richard, Simon Davies and Gabriel Espinosa Sánchez (eds), *Peripheries of the Enlightenment* (Studies on Voltaire and the Eighteenth Century, 2008: 01) (Oxford: Voltaire Foundation, 2008).

Byars, Jackie, *All That Hollywood Allows: Rereading Gender in 1950s Melodrama* (London: Routledge, 1991).

Cahill, Susan, *Irish Literature in the Celtic Tiger Years 1990 to 2008: Gender, Bodies, Memory*. (London: Continuum Press, 2011).

Cahill, Susan, 'Irish Women Writers of Children's Literature, 1870–1940' (UCD Irish Virtual Research Library and Archive Research Report Series 3, 2010), http://hdl.handle.net/10197/2486.

Campbell, Mary, *Lady Morgan: The Life and Times of Sydney Owenson* (London: Pandora Press, 1988).

Carroll, Francis, *The American Presence in Ulster: A Diplomatic History, 1796–1996* (Washington: Catholic University of America Press, 2005).

Castelyn, Mary, *A History of Literacy and Libraries in Ireland: The long traced pedigree* (Aldershot Gower: Grafton Book, 1984).

Cathcart, Rex and Michael Muldoon, 'The Mass Media in Twentieth-Century Ireland', in J. R. Hill (ed.), *A New History of Ireland, Volume VII: Ireland 1921–84* (Oxford: Oxford University Press, 2003), pp. 671–711.

Clark, Dennis, 'Irish Women Workers and American Labor Patterns: The Philadelphia Story', in Patrick O'Sullivan (ed.), *The Irish World Wide: History, Heritage, Identity. Volume 4: Irish Women and Irish Migration* (London: Leicester University Press, 1995), pp. 112–30.

Clarke, Desmond J., 'The Appreciation, Care and Use of Books', *An Leabharlann*, 12, 1 (March 1954), pp. 5–13.

Clarke, Desmond J., 'Books and the Countryman', *An Leabharlann*, 10, 2 (September 1950), pp. 49–58.

Clarke, Desmond J., 'Presidential Address, Desmond J. Clarke', *An Leabharlann*, 13, 4 (December 1955), pp. 169–76.

Clarke, Norma, 'Bluestocking Fictions: Devotional Writings, Didactic Literature and the Imperative of Female Improvement', in Sarah Knott and Barbara Taylor (eds), *Women, Gender, and Enlightenment* (New York: Palgrave Macmillan, 2005), pp. 460–73.

Clarke, Sister Ursula, *The Ursulines in Cork since 1771* (Cork: Ursuline Convent, Blackrock, Cork, 2007).

Clear, Caitriona, 'Oral History and Women's Household Work in Ireland, 1922–1961: Some Reflections', *Women's Studies Review, Oral History and Biography*, 7 (2001), pp. 53–63.

Clear, Caitriona, *Social Change and Everyday Life in Ireland, 1850–1922* (Manchester: Manchester University Press, 2007).

Clear, Caitriona, *Woman of the House: Women's Household Work in Ireland 1922–61* (Dublin: Irish Academic Press, 2000).

Clear, Caitriona, '"The Women Can Not Be Blamed": The Commission on Vocational Organisation, Feminism and "Home-Makers" in Independent Ireland in the 1930s and '40s', in Mary O'Dowd and Sabine Wichert (eds), *Chattel, Servant or Citizen: Women's Status in Church, State and Society* (Belfast: Institute of Irish Studies, 1995), pp. 179–86.

Clear, Caitriona, 'Women in de Valera's Ireland, 1932–48: A Reappraisal', in Gabriel Doherty and Dermot Keogh (eds), *De Valera's Ireland* (Cork: Mercier Press, 2003), pp. 104–14.

Cohen, David Steven (ed.), *America: The Dream of My Life* (New Brunswick, NJ: Rutgers University Press, 1990).

Cohen, Marilyn, 'The Migration Experience of Female-Headed Households: Gilford, Co. Down, to Greenwich, New York, 1880–1910', in Patrick O'Sullivan (ed.), *Irish Women and Irish Migration* (London: Leicester University Press, 1995), pp. 130–45.

Cohen, Marilyn and Nancy J. Curtin (eds), *Reclaiming Gender: Transgressive Identities in Modern Ireland* (New York: St Martin's Press, 1999).

Cole, Robert, *Propaganda, Censorship and Irish Neutrality in the Second World War* (Edinburgh: Edinburgh University Press, 2006).

Coleman, Anne, *A Dictionary of Nineteenth Century Irish Women Poets* (Galway: Kenny's Bookshop, 1996)

Comerford, R. V. and Kelly Jennifer, *Associational Culture in Ireland and Abroad* (Dublin: Irish Academic Press, 2011).

Concannon, Mrs., 'The Missionary Race: No. 1 Ireland's Destiny', *Irish Messenger of the Sacred Heart*, 42 (January 1929), pp. 211–12.

Connolly, Nora, 'Children's Reading', *An Leabharlann*, 10, 4 (June 1952), pp. 104–7.

Conway, Catherine, 'Recipe for Success in Women's Word: Irish Women's Magazines in the 1930s', http://www.ucd.ie/pages/97/conway.html (accessed 4 April 2012).

Corrigan, K. P., *Irish English: Northern Ireland* (Edinburgh: Edinburgh University Press, 2010).

Cott, Nancy, 'Passionlessness: An Interpretation of Anglo-American Sexual Ideology, 1790–1840', *Signs*, 4 (1978), pp. 219–36.

Critchlow, Donald T., 'Birth Control and Family Planning', in Boyer (ed.), *The Oxford Companion to United States History* (Oxford and New York: Oxford University Press, 2001), pp. 77–78.

Cronin, Maura, 'Of One Mind? O'Connellite Crowds in the 1820s and 1830s', in P. J. Jupp and Eoin Magennis (eds), *Crowds in Ireland, c.1720–1920* (Basingstoke: Macmillan Press, 2000), pp. 39–72.

Cronin, Mike, Mark Duncan and Paul Rouse, *The GAA: A People's History* (London: HarperCollins, 2009).

Cullen, L. M., *Eason and Son: A History* (Dublin: Eason and Son, 1989).

Cullen Owens, Rosemary, *A Social History of Women in Ireland* (Dublin: Gill and Macmillan, 2005).

Cullingford, Elizabeth, *Ireland's Others: Ethnicity and Gender in Irish Literature and Popular Culture* (Critical Conditions: Field Day Essays and Monographs 10) (Cork: Cork University Press and Notre Dame: University of Notre Dame Press, 2001).

Curtis, Maurice, *A Challenge to Democracy: Militant Catholicism in Modern Ireland* (Dublin: The History Press Ireland, 2010).

Daly, Mary E., *The Slow Failure: Population Decline and Independent Ireland, 1920–1973* (Madison: University of Wisconsin Press, 2006).
Daly, Mary E., '"Turn on the Tap": The State, Irish Women and Running Water', in Maryann Gianella Valiulis and Mary O'Dowd (eds), *Women and Irish History* (Dublin: Wolfhound Press, 1997), pp. 206–19.
Daly, Mary E., *Women and Work in Ireland* (Studies in Irish Economic and Social History 7) (Dundalk: Dundalgan Press, 1997).
Daly, Mary E., 'Women in the Irish Free State, 1922–39: The Interaction between Economics and Ideology', *Journal of Women's History*, 6, 4/5 (Winter–Spring 1995), pp. 99–116.
Dammers, Richard H., 'Richard Steele and "The Ladies Library"', *Philological Quarterly*, 62, 4 (Fall 1983), pp. 530–35.
Dancyger, Irene, *A World of Women: An Illustrated History of Women's Magazines* (Dublin: Gill and Macmillan, 1978).
Davies, Rhys, *Marianne* (London: William Heinemann, 1951).
Davis, Ronald L., 'Music: Popular Music', in Paul S. Boyer (ed.), *The Oxford Companion to United States History* (Oxford: Oxford University Press, 2001), pp. 528–31.
Dean, Joan Fitzpatrick, 'Rewriting the Past: Historical Pageantry in the Dublin Civic Weeks of 1927 and 1929', *New Hibernia Review*, 13, 1 (Spring 2009), pp. 20–41.
Dean, Joan Fitzpatrick, *Riot and Great Anger: Stage Censorship in Twentieth-Century Ireland* (Madison: University of Wisconsin Press, 2004).
Deane, Seamus (ed.), *The Field Day Anthology of Irish Writing*, vols 1–3 (Derry: Field Day, 1991).
Delaney, Enda, 'Gender and Twentieth-Century Irish Migration, 1921–1971', in Pamela Sharpe (ed.), *Women, Gender and Labour Migration: Historical and Global Perspectives* (London: Routledge, 2001), pp. 209–24.
Devane, Rev. Richard S., 'The Film in National Life', in *Irish Cinema Handbook* (Dublin: Parkside Press, 1943), pp. 13–28.
Devane, Richard S., 'Indecent Literature: Some Legal Remedies', *Irish Ecclesiastical Record*, 25 (February 1925), pp. 182–204.
Devane, Richard S., 'The Menace of the British Press Combines', *Studies: An Irish Quarterly Review*, 19, 73 (March 1930), pp. 54–69.
Devane, Richard S., 'Suggested Tariff on Imported Newspapers and Magazines', *Studies: An Irish Quarterly Review*, 16, 64 (December 1927), pp. 544–69.
Dhonnchadha, Máirín Ní (ed.), 'Medieval to Modern, 600–1900', in Angela Bourke et al. (eds), *Field Day Anthology of Irish Writing, Volume 4: Irish Women's Writing and Traditions* (Cork: Cork University Press, 2002), pp. 1–6.
Diner, Hasia, *Erin's Daughters in America: Irish Immigrant Women in the Nineteenth Century* (Baltimore: Johns Hopkins University Press, 1983).
Dingley, F. L., *European Emigration: Studies in Europe of Emigration Moving Out of Europe, Especially that Flowing to the United States* (Washington: Bureau of Statistics, Dept. of State, 1890).

Dirrane, Bridge, *A Woman of Aran* (Dublin: Blackwater Press, 1997).
Doane, Mary Ann, *Femmes Fatales: Feminism, Film Theory and Psychoanalysis* (New York: Routledge, 1991).
Dollimore, Jonathan, *Sexual Dissidence: Augustine to Wilde, Freud to Foucault* (Oxford: Clarendon Press, 1991).
Donnelly James S. and Kerby Miller (eds), *Irish Popular Culture, 1650–1850* (Dublin: Irish Academic Press, 1998).
Donovan, Julie, *Sydney Owenson, Lady Morgan and the Politics of Style* (Bethesda: Maunsel & Co., 2009).
Dooley, Dolores, *Equality in Community. Sexuality Equality in the Writings of William Thompson and Anna Doyle Wheeler* (Cork: Cork University Press, 1996).
Doorley, Michael, *Stella Days, 1957–1967: The Life and Times of a Rural Irish Cinema* (Nenagh: Dubhairle Publications, undated).
Dudden, Faye, *Serving Women: Household Service in Nineteenth-Century America* (Middletown, Conn.: Wesleyan University Press, 1983).
Dunleavy, Mairéad, *Dress in Ireland* (London: B. T. Batsford, 1989)
Dunnigan, Diane, 'Coming Home: Return Migration to Ireland, 1890–1920', unpublished paper presented to the Migrations in Irish History Symposium, National University of Ireland, Maynooth, 8 June 2011.
Dyer, Richard, 'Less and More than Women and Men: Lesbian and Gay Cinema', *New German Critique*, 51 (Autumn 1990), Special Issue on 'Weimar Mass Culture', pp. 5–60.
Dyhouse, Carol, *Glamour: Women, History, Feminism* (Zed Books: London, 2010).
E. J. F. and D. B., 'George Berkeley and *The Ladies Library*', *Berkeley Newsletter*, 4 (December 1980), pp. 5–13.
Eager, A. R., 'Some Thoughts on the Classification of Fiction', *An Leabharlann*, 11, 3 (September 1953), pp. 67–69.
Earner–Byrne, Lindsay, 'Reinforcing the Family: The Role of Gender, Morality and Sexuality in Irish Welfare Policy, 1922–44', *History of the Family*, 13, 4 (2008), pp. 360–69.
'Editorial note', *An Leabharlann*, 13, 2 (June 1955), p. 63.
Eger, Elizabeth, *Bluestockings: Women of Reason from Enlightenment to Romanticism* (Basingstoke: Palgrave Macmillan, 2010).
Elias Jr, A. C. (ed.), *Memoirs of Laetitia Pilkington* (2 vols; Athens, Ga.: Georgia University Press, 1997).
'Elinor Glynn', http://www.online-literature.com/elinor-glyn/ (accessed 25 February 2010).
Ellwood, David and Rob Kroes (eds), *Hollywood in Europe: Experiences of a Cultural Hegemony* (Amsterdam: VU University Press, 1994).
Engel, Matthew, *Tickle the Public: One Hundred Years of the Popular Press* (London: Gollancz, 1996).
Encyclopedia Britannica, 11th Edition (London: 1911).
Erickson, Chantelle, *Leaving England: Essays on British Emigration in the Nineteenth Century* (Ithaca, NY and London: Cornell University Press, 1994).

Erickson-Coble, Alana, *Cleaning Up: The Transformation of Domestic Service in Twentieth Century New York* (London: Routledge, 2006).
Erll, Astrid, 'Travelling Memory', *Parallax*, 17, 4 (2011), p. 12.
Fagan, William, *The Life and Times of Daniel O'Connell* (2 vols; Cork: J. O'Brien, 1847–48).
Fanning, Bryan, *The Quest for Modern Ireland: The Battle of Ideas 1912–1986* (Dublin: Irish Academic Press, 2008).
Farmar, Tony, *Privileged Lives: A Social History of Middle-Class Ireland 1882–1989* (Dublin: A. & A. Farmar, 2010).
Fenning, Hugh, 'The Catholic Press in Munster in the Eighteenth Century', in Gerard Long (ed.), *Books beyond the Pale: Aspects of the Provincial Book Trade in Ireland before 1850* (Dublin: Rare Books Group of the Library Association of Ireland, 1996), pp. 19–31.
Ferriter, Diarmaid, '"Bringing Books to the Remotest Hamlets and Hills": The Post-war Public Library Service', in Norma McDermott (ed.), *The University of the People* (Dublin: Radio Telifis Eireann, 2003), pp. 67–79.
Ferriter, Diarmaid, *The Transformation of Ireland 1900–2000* (London: Profile Books, 2004).
Ferry, Georgina, 'The Exception and the Rule: Women and the Royal Society 1945–2010', http://rsnr.royalsocietypublishing.org/content/early/2010/06/30/rsnr.2010.0043.full (accessed 8 March 2011).
Fink, Janet and Katherine Holden, 'Pictures from the Margins of Marriage: Representation of Spinsters and Single Mothers in the Mid-Victorian Novel, Inter-War Hollywood Melodrama and British Film of the 1950s and 1960s', *Gender and History*, 11, 2 (July 1999), pp. 233–55.
Finlay, Gavin, '"Celluloid Menace", Art or the "Essential Habit of the Age"', *History Ireland*, 15, 5 (September/October 2007), pp. 34–40.
Fischer, Lucy, *Designing Women: Cinema, Art Deco and the Female Form* (New York: Columbia University Press, 2003).
Fitzpatrick, David, *Irish Emigration 1801–1921* (Studies in Irish Economic and Social History 1) (Dundalk: Dundalgan Press, 1990).
Fitzpatrick, David, 'The Modernisation of the Irish Female in Rural Ireland', in P. O'Flanagan (ed.), *Rural Ireland: Modernisation and Change 1600–1900* (Cork: Cork University Press, 1987), pp. 167–80.
Fitzpatrick, David, '"A Share of the Honeycomb": Education, Emigration and Irishwomen', in Mary Daly and David Dickson (eds), *The Origins of Popular Literacy in Ireland: Language Change and Educational Development, 1700–1920* (Dublin: TCD and UCD, 1990), pp. 167–87.
Fitzpatrick, Martin, Peter Jones, Christa Knellwolf and Iain McCalman (eds), *The Enlightenment World* (London: Routledge, 2004).
Fitz-Simon, Christopher, *The Boys: A Double Biography* (London: Nick Hearne Books, 1994).
Foley, Dermot, 'A Minstrel Boy With a Satchel of Books', *Irish University Review*, 4, 2 (Autumn 1974), pp. 204–17.

Foley, Marc C. and Timothy G. Guinnane, 'Did Irish Marriage Patterns Survive the Emigrant Voyage? Irish-American Nuptuality, 1880–1920', *Irish Economic and Social History*, 26 (1991), pp. 15–34.

Foley, Michael, 'Role of Media in Ireland's History Analysed', *Irish Times*, 8 February 2010.

Forde, Kate, 'Celluloid Dreams: The Marketing of Cutex in America, 1916–1935', *Journal of Design History*, 15, 3 (2002), pp. 175–189.

Fox, Stephen, *A History of American Advertising and Its Creator* (New York: Vintage, 1985).

Fyffe, Aileen, 'Reading Children's Books in Eighteenth-Century Dissenting Families', *Historical Journal*, 43 (2000), pp. 453–74.

Gabaccia, Donna, 'Immigrant Women: Nowhere at Home?', *Journal of American Ethnic History*, 10 (Summer 1991), pp. 61–87.

Galantière, Lewis (ed.), *America and the Mind of Europe* (London: Hamilton, 1951).

Gargett, Graham and Geraldine Sheridan (eds), *Ireland and the French Enlightenment, 1700–1800* (Basingstoke and London: Macmillan, 1999).

Garrioch, David, 'Making a Better World. Enlightenment and Philanthropy', in Martin Fitzpatrick, Peter Jones, Christa Knellwolf and Iain McCalman (eds), *The Enlightenment World* (London: Routledge, 2004), pp. 486–501.

Garvin, Tom, *News From a New Republic: Ireland in the 1950s* (Dublin: Gill and Macmillan, 2010).

Geary, R. C., 'The Future Population of Saorstát Éireann and Some Observations on Population Statistics', *Journal of the Statistical and Social Inquiry Society of Ireland*, 15, 6 (89th session, 1935–36), pp. 15–35, http://www.tara.tcd.ie/bitstream/2262/4900/1/jssisiVolXV15_35.pdf (accessed 28 April 2013).

Gelbart, Nina Rattner, 'Introduction' to *Conversations on the Plurality of Worlds*. Translated by H. A. Hargreaves (Berkeley: University of California Press, 1990), pp. vii–xxvi.

Gledhill, Christine (ed.), *Home Is Where the Heart Is: Studies in Melodrama and the Women's Film* (London: British Film Institute, 1987).

Gmelch, Sharon (ed.), *Irish Life and Tradition* (Dublin: O'Brien Press, 1979).

Gray, Tony, *The Lost Years: The Emergency in Ireland, 1939–45* (London: Warner, 1998).

Guinane, Thomas, *The Vanishing Irish: Households, Migration and the Rural Economy in Ireland, 1850–1914* (Princeton: Princeton University Press, 1997).

Gwynn, Denis, 'Catholic Emancipation and How it was Secured', *Irish Messenger of the Sacred Heart*, 42 (December 1929), p. 536.

Haining, Peter, *The Classic Era of American Pulp Magazines* (Chicago: Prion Books/Chicago Review Press, 2000).

Hannerz, Ulf, *Transnational Connections: Culture, People, Places* (London and New York: Routledge, 1996).

Hansen, Miriam, 'The Mass Production of the Senses: Classical Cinema as Vernacular Modernism', *Modernism/Modernity*, 6, 2 (April 1999), pp. 59–77.

Harris, Ruth-Ann, '"Come You All Courageously": Irish Women in America Write Home', *Éire–Ireland*, 36, 1/2 (Spring–Summer 2001), pp. 166–84.

Hatton, Timothy J. and Jeffrey G. Williamson, 'After the Famine: Emigration from Ireland, 1850–1913', *Journal of Economic History*, 53, 3 (September 1993), pp. 575–600.

Healy, John, *Nineteen Acres* (Achill: House of Healy, 1987).

Healy, John, *No One Shouted Stop: Formerly the Death of an Irish Town* (Achill: House of Healy, 1988).

Hearn, Mona, *Below the Stairs: Domestic Service Remembered in Dublin and Beyond, 1880–1922* (Dublin: Lilliput Press, 1993).

Heffner, Brooks E., '"Slipping Back into the Vernacular": Anzia Yezierska's Vernacular Modernism', *Melus*, 36, 3 (Fall 2011), pp. 187–211.

Hempton, David and Myrtle Hill, *Evangelical Protestantism in Ulster Society, 1740–1890* (London: Routledge, 1992).

Higgins, Padraig, *A Nation of Politicians: Gender, Patriotism, and Political Culture in Late Eighteenth-Century Ireland* (Madison: University of Wisconsin Press, 2010).

Hill, Myrtle, *Women in Ireland: A Century of Change* (Belfast: The Blackstaff Press, 2003).

Hilton, Mary, '"Child of Reason": Anna Barbauld and the Origins of Progressive Pedagogy', in Mary Hilton and Pam Hirsch (eds), *Practical Visionaries: Women, Education and Social Progress, 1790–1930* (Harlow: Pearson, 2000), pp. 21–38.

Hobson, Bulmer (ed.), *The Gate Theatre* (Dublin: Gate Theatre, 1934).

Hoerder, Dirk, 'From Dreams to Possibilities: The Secularization of Hope and the Quest for Independence', in Dirk Hoerder and Horst Rössler (eds), *Distant Magnets: Expectations and Realities in the Immigrant Experience, 1840–1930* (New York/London: Holmes and Meier Publishers, 1993), pp. 1–34.

Holingshead, Greg, 'Sources for the *Ladies Library*', *Berkeley Newsletter*, 11 (1989–90), pp. 1–9.

'Hollywood as History', http://www.digitalhistory.uh.edu/.cfm (accessed 5 July 2011).

Holmes, Richard, 'The Royal Society's Lost Women Scientists', *The Observer*, 21 November 2010, http://www.guardian.co.uk/science/2010/nov/21/royal-society-lost-women-scientists (accessed 8 March 2011).

Honey, Maureen (ed.), *Breaking the Ties that Bind: Popular Stories of the New Woman 1915–30* (Norman: University of Oklahoma Press, 1992).

Hotten-Somers, Diane M., 'Relinquishing and Reclaiming Independence: Irish Domestic Servants, American Middle-Class Mistresses, and Assimilation, 1850–1920', in Kevin Kenny (ed.), *New Directions in Irish-American History* (Madison: University of Wisconsin Press, 2003), pp. 227–43.

Houston, Arthur (ed.), *Daniel O'Connell: His Early Life, and Journal, 1795–1802* (London: Pitman Press, 1906).

Hovde, B. J., 'Notes on the Effects of Emigration upon Scandinavia', *The Journal of Modern History*, 6, 3 (September 1934), pp. 253–79.

Howley, John F. W., 'Fiction and Culture', *An Leabharlann*, 1, 4 (May 1931), p. 6.

Hoy, Suellen, *Good Hearts: Catholic Sisters in Chicago's Past* (Urbana and Chicago: University of Illinois Press, 2006).

Hoy, Suellen, 'The Journey Out: The Recruitment and Emigration of Irish Religious Women to the United States, 1912–1914', *Journal of Women's History*, 6/7 (Winter–Spring 1995), pp. 64–98.

Hoy, Suellen and Margaret MacCurtain, *From Dublin to New Orleans: The Journey of Nora and Alice* (Dublin: Attic Press, 1994).

Hufton, Olwen, *The Prospect Before Her: A History of Women in Western Europe, Volume 1: 1500–1800* (London: HarperCollins, 1995).

Israel, Jonathan I., *Enlightenment Contested: Philosophy, Modernity, and the Emancipation of Man 1670–1752* (Oxford: Oxford University Press, 2006).

Israel, Jonathan I., *Radical Enlightenment: Philosophy and the Making of Modernity, 1650–1750* (Oxford: Oxford University Press, 2001).

IVRLA, *Research Report: Irish Women Writers of Children's Literature, 1870–1940* (Dublin: IVRLA, 2009).

Jackson, Alvin, *Ireland 1798–1998: Politics and War* (Oxford: Blackwell, 1999).

Jacoby, Susan, 'World of Our Mothers: Immigrant Women, Immigrant Daughter,' *Present Tense*, 6 (Spring 1979), pp. 48–51.

Johnston, Roy, 'Music in Northern Ireland since 1921', in J. R. Hill (ed.), *A New History of Ireland, Volume VII: Ireland, 1921–84* (Oxford: Oxford University Press, 2003), pp. 650–70.

Jordan, Jessica Hope, *The Sex Goddess in American Film, 1930–65* (Amherst, NY: Cambria Press, 2009).

Kanerick, Caroline, '"A Jazzed and Patchwork Modern": "Future" Girls and Modern Masculinities in the Early Popular Romances of Berta Ruck', *Women's History Review*, 19, 5 (November 2010), pp. 685–702.

Kaplan, E. Anne, *Motherhood and Representation: The Mother in Popular Culture and Melodrama* (London and New York: Routledge, 1992).

Katzman, D. A., *Seven Days a Week: Women and Domestic Service in Industrializing America* (New York: Oxford University Press, 1978).

Kearns, Kevin C., *Dublin Tenement Life: An Oral History* (Dublin: Gill and Macmillan, 1996).

Kelleher, Margaret, *The Feminisation of the Famine: Expressions of the Inexpressible* (Durham, NC: Duke University Press, 1997).

Kelleher, Margaret and James H. Murphy, *Gender Perspective in Nineteenth Century Ireland* (Dublin: Irish Academic Press, 1997).

Kelleher, Patricia, 'Young Irish workers: Class Implications of Men's and Women's Experiences in Gilded Age Chicago', *Eire-Ireland*, 36, 1/2 (Spring–Summer 2001), pp. 141–65.

Kelly, James (ed.), 'The Operation of the Censorship of Publications Board: The Notebooks of C. J. Reilly, 1951–55', *Analecta Hibernia*, 38 (2004), pp. 223–369.

Kelly, Mary Pat, *Home Away from Home: The Yanks in Ireland* (Belfast: Appletree Press, 1994).

Kelly, Patrick, 'Anne Donnellan: Irish Proto-Bluestocking', *Hermathena*, 154 (Summer 1993), pp. 39–68.

Kelly, Patrick, 'Perceptions of Locke in Eighteenth-Century Ireland', *Proceedings of the Royal Irish Academy*, 89C (1989), pp. 20–21.

Kelly, Sister M. St Dominic, *The Sligo Ursulines: The First Fifty Years 1826–1876* (Sligo: privately published, 1987).

Kennedy, Kieran, Thomas Giblin and Deidre McHugh, *Economic Development of Ireland in the Twentieth Century* (London: Routledge, 1988).

Kennedy, Máire, 'The Distribution of a Locally Produced French Periodical in Provincial Ireland: The *Magazin à la Mode*, 1777–1778', *Eighteenth-Century Ireland: Iris an Dá Chultúr*, 9 (1994), pp. 83–98.

Kennedy, Máire, 'Foreign Language Books, 1700–1800', in Raymond Gillespie and Andrew Hadfield (eds), *Oxford History of the Irish Book, Volume 3: The Irish Book in English, 1550–1800* (Oxford: Oxford University Press, 2005), pp. 368–82.

Kennedy, Máire, *French Books in Eighteenth Century Ireland* (Studies on Voltaire and the Eighteenth Century, 2001: 07) (Oxford: Voltaire Foundation, 2001).

Kennedy, Máire, 'Women and Reading in Eighteenth-Century Ireland', in Bernadette Cunningham and Máire Kennedy (eds), *The Experience of Reading: Irish Historical Perspectives* (Dublin: Rare Group Books of the Library Association of Ireland and the Economic and Social History Society of Ireland, 1999), pp. 78–98.

Kennedy, Robert E. Jr., *The Irish: Emigration, Marriage and Fertility* (Berkeley and London: University of California Press, 1973).

Kenny, Kevin, 'Part 3. The World of Work. Editor's Introduction', in Kevin Kenny (ed.), *New Directions in Irish-American History* (Madison: University of Wisconsin Press, 2003), pp. 159–62.

Kerber, Linda K., *Towards an Intellectual History of Women: Essays by Linda K. Kerber* (Chapel Hill: North Carolina University Press, 1997).

Kiberd, Declan, *Inventing Ireland: The Literature of the Modern Nation* (London: Vintage, 1996).

Kiely, Benedict, 'The Core of Colum's Ireland', *The Irish Monthly*, 77, 916 (October 1949), pp. 448–52.

'Kilkenny County Libraries Committee, 7th Annual Report for 12 months to 1937', *An Leabharlann*, 6, 3 (December 1938), p. 88.

King, Linda and Elaine Sisson (eds), *Irish Design and Visual Culture: Negotiating Modernity, 1922–1992* (Cork: Cork University Press, 2011).

Knott, Sarah and Barbara Taylor (eds), *Women, Gender and Enlightenment* (Basingstoke: Palgrave Macmillan, 2005).

Koon, Helen, 'Eliza Haywood and the "'Female Spectator'", *Huntington Library Quarterly*, 42, 1 (Winter 1978), pp. 43–55.

Korda, Michael, *Making the List: A Cultural History of the American Bestseller, 1900–1999: As Seen Through the Annual Bestseller Lists of Publishers Weekly* (New York: Barnes and Noble, 2001).

Lally, Bernadette, *Print Culture in Loughrea, 1850–1900: Reading, Writing and Printing in an Irish Provincial Town* (Dublin: Four Courts Press, 2008).

Lane, Leeann, *Rosamund Jacob: Third Person Singular* (Dublin: University College Dublin Press, 2010).

Laverty, Maura, *Never No More: The Story of a Lost Village* (London: Longmans, 1942).

Laverty, Maura, *No More than Human* (London: Longmans, 1944).

Lee, J. J., 'Emigration, 1922–1998', in Michael Glazier (ed.), *The Encyclopedia of the Irish in America* (Notre Dame, Ind.: University of Notre Dame Press, 1999), pp. 263–66.

Lee, J. J., *Ireland, 1912–1985: Politics and Society* (Cambridge: Cambridge University Press, 1989).

Lee, J. J. and Marion R. Casey (eds), *Making the Irish American: History and Heritage of the Irish in the United States* (New York: New York University Press, 2006).

Leeney, Cathy, *Irish Women Playwrights 1900–1939: Gender and Violence on Stage* (Irish Studies 9) (New York: Peter Lang, 2010).

Linkin, Harriet Kramer (ed.), *The Collected Poems and Journals of Mary Tighe* (Lexington: University Press of Kentucky, 2005).

Llanover, Lady (ed.), *The Autobiography and Correspondence of Mary Granville, Mrs. Delany: with Interesting Reminiscences of King George the Third and Queen Charlotte* (2 series, 6 vols; London: R. Bentley, 1861–62).

Loeber, Rolf and Magda Stouthamer-Loeber, 'Fiction Available to and Written for Cottagers and their Children', in Bernadette Cunningham and Máire Kennedy (eds), *The Experience of Reading: Irish Historical Perspectives* (Dublin: Rare Books Group of the Library Association of Ireland and the Economic and Social History Society of Ireland, 1999), pp. 139–42.

Loeber, Rolf and Magda Stouthamer-Loeber, '18th–19th Century Irish Fiction Newsletter' (1999), no. 9. Unpublished. Copy in QUB Library.

Loeber, Rolf et al., *A Guide to Irish Fiction, 1650–1900* (Dublin: Four Courts Press, 2006).

Long, Gerard (ed.), *Books Beyond the Pale: Aspects of the Provincial Book Trade in Ireland before 1850* (Dublin: Rare Books Group of the Library Association of Ireland, 1996).

Luddy, Maria, *Prostitution in Irish Society* (Cambridge: Cambridge University Press, 2007).

Luddy, Maria, 'Sex and the Single Girl in 1920s and 1930s Ireland', *The Irish Review*, 35 (Summer 2007), pp. 79–91.

Luddy, Maria, *Women and Philanthropy in Nineteenth-Century Ireland* (Cambridge: Cambridge University Press, 1995).

Luddy, Maria and Dymphna McLoughlin, 'Women and Emigration from Ireland from the Seventeenth Century', in Angela Bourke et al. (eds), *The Field Day Anthology of Irish Writing, Volume 4: Irish Women's Writing and Traditions* (Cork: Cork University Press, 2002), pp. 567–88.

Lynch-Brennan, Margaret, *The Irish Bridget: Irish Immigrant Women in Domestic Service in America, 1840–1930* (Syracuse, NY: Syracuse University Press, 2009).

Lynch–Brennan, Margaret, 'Ubiquitous Bridget: Irish Immigrant Women in Domestic Service in America, 1840–1930', in J. J. Lee and Marion R. Casey (eds), *Making the Irish American: History and Heritage of the Irish in the United States* (New York: New York University Press, 2006), pp. 332–54.

McAulay, Eve, 'Cinema Architecture, Art Deco and Modernist Period', in Brian Lalor (ed.), *The Encyclopedia of Ireland* (Dublin: Gill and Macmillan, 2003), pp. 198–99.

McBride, Stephanie and Roddy Flynn (eds), *Here's Looking at You, Kid! Ireland Goes to the Pictures* (Dublin: Wolfhound Press, 1996).

McCarthy, B. G., 'The Cinema as a Social Factor', *Studies: An Irish Quarterly Review*, 33, 129 (March 1944), pp. 45–67.

McCarthy, Brigid, *The Female Pen: Women Writers – Their Contribution to the English Novel, 1621–1744* (Cork: Cork University Press, 1946).

McCaskie, T. C., 'Cultural Encounters: Britain and Africa in the Nineteenth century', in Andrew Porter (ed.), *The Oxford History of the British Empire, Volume 3: The Nineteenth Century* (Oxford: Oxford University Press, 1999), pp. 644–89.

MacCurtain, Margaret and Mary O'Dowd (eds), *Women in Early Modern Ireland* (Edinburgh: Edinburgh University Press, 1997).

McCoole, Sinead, 'Lavery, Lady, Hazel', in Brian Lalor (ed.), *The Encyclopedia of Ireland* (Dublin: Gill and Macmillan, 2003), p. 612.

McCormick, Leanne, *Regulating Sexuality: Women in Twentieth-Century Northern Ireland* (Manchester: Manchester University Press, 2009).

McDevitt, Patrick F., 'Muscular Catholicism: Nationalism, Masculinity and Gaelic Team Sports, 1884–1916', *Gender and History*, 9, 2 (August 1997), pp. 262–84.

MacDonagh, Oliver, *The Hereditary Bondsman: Daniel O'Connell 1775–1829* (London: Weidenfeld and Nicolson, 1988).

McDowell, R. B., 'The Main Narrative', in T. Ó Raifeartaigh (ed.), *The Royal Irish Academy: A Bicentennial History 1785–1985* (Dublin: Royal Irish Academy, 1985), pp. 1–92.

McGovern, Charles, *Sold American: Consumption and Citizenship 1890–1945* (Chapel Hill: University of North Carolina Press, 2006).

McGurl, M. K., 'Stray Thoughts on Library Matters', *Irish Library Bulletin*, October 1947, pp. 180–81.

McHale, J. P., 'Ireland and the US Dollar', *Irish Monthly*, 78, 930 (December 1950), pp. 562–69.

McIlroy, Brian, *Irish Cinema: An Illustrated History* (Dun Laoghaire: Anna Livia Press, 1988).

McInerney, M. H., 'Constructive Work for Catholic Irishwomen', *The Irish Monthly*, 52, 610 (April 1924), p. 193.

McInerney, M. H., 'Constructive Work of Catholic Women (continued)', *The Irish Monthly*, 52, 611 (May 1924), pp. 262–68.

McManus, Antonia, *The Irish Hedge School and Its Books, 1695–1831* (Dublin: Four Courts Press, 2004).

McMillen, Sally G., 'Marriage and Divorce', in Paul S. Boyer (ed.), *The Oxford Companion to United States History* (Oxford and New York: Oxford University Press, 2001), pp. 472–73.

McMullan, Anna and Caroline Williams, 'Contemporary Women Playwrights', in Angela Bourke et al. (eds), *The Field Day Anthology of Irish Writing, Volume 5: Irish Women's Writings and Traditions* (Cork: Cork University Press, 2002), pp. 1234–89.

MacMurchadha, F., 'The Countrywoman: Rural Culture and the County Library', *An Leabharlann*, 10, 5 (September 1952), pp. 144–50.

McNeill, Mary, *The Life and Times of Mary Ann McCracken: A Belfast Panorama* (Dublin: Allen Figgis, 1960).

MacRaild, Donald M., *The Irish Diaspora in Britain, 1750–1939* (Basingstoke: Palgrave, 2011).

Macardle, Dorothy, 'Experiment in Ireland', *Theatre Monthly Arts*, 8 (1934), pp 124–33.

Madge, C. and T. H. Harrisson, *Mass Observation* (London: Frederick Muller Ltd, 1937).

Magray, Mary Peckham, *The Transforming Power of the Nuns: Women, Religion & Cultural Change in Ireland, 1750–1900* (New York: Oxford University Press, 1998).

Maguire, John Francis, *The Irish in America* (New York: D. & J. Sadlier, 1868).

Major, Emma, 'The Politics of Sociability: Public Dimensions of the Bluestocking Millennium', *Huntington Library Quarterly*, 65, 1/2 (2002), pp. 175–92.

Marchand, Roland, *Advertising the American Dream: Making Way for Modernity, 1920–1940* (London: University of Berkley Press, 1986).

Markey, Anne, 'Irish Children's Fiction, 1727–1820', *Irish University Review*, 41, 1 (Spring–Summer 2011), Special Issue on 'Irish Fiction, 1660–1830'.

Martin, Peter, *Censorship in the Two Irelands 1922–1939* (Dublin: Irish Academic Press, 2006).

Martindale, C. C., 'The Cinema and the Adult', *Studies: An Irish Quarterly Review*, 18, 71 (September 1929), pp. 443–48.

Matheson, Steve, *Maurice Walsh: Storyteller* (Dingle: Brandon Press, 1985).

Maurer, Shawn Lisa, 'The Periodical', in Ros Ballaster (ed.), *The History of British Women's Writing, 1690–1750* (London: Palgrave Macmillan, 2010), pp. 163–66.

May, Leila Silvana, 'The Strong-Arming of Desire: A Reconsideration of Nancy Armstrong's "Desire and Domestic Fiction"', *ELH*, 68, 1 (Spring, 2001), pp. 267–285.

Meagher, Timothy J., 'The Fireman on the Stairs: Communal Loyalties in the Making of Irish America', in J. J. Lee and Marion R. Casey (eds), *Making the Irish American: History and Heritage of the Irish in the United States* (New York: New York University Press, 2006), pp. 609–49.

Meaney, Gerardine, *Gender, Ireland and Cultural Change* (New York: Routledge, 2011)
Meaney, Gerardine (ed.), 'Women's Writing, 1700–1960', in Angela Bourke et al. (eds), *The Field Day Anthology of Irish Writing, Volume 5: Irishwomen's Writings and Traditions* (Cork: Cork University Press, 2002), pp. 765–975.
Meehan, Ita, 'The Problem of the Single Girl in Ireland', *The Furrow*, 9 (July–December 1958), pp. 440–41.
Meenan, James, 'Some Causes and Consequences of the Low Irish Marriage Rate', *Statistical and Social Inquiry Society of Ireland*, 15, 3 (1932–33), pp. 19–27, http://www.tara.tcd.ie/bitstream/2262/4681/1/jssisiVolXV19_27.pdf (accessed 28 April 2013).
Midgley, Clare, *Women Against Slavery: The British Campaigns, 1780–1870* (London: Routledge, 1992).
Miller, Kerby, *Emigrants and Exile* (New York: Oxford University Press, 1985).
Miller, Kerby, 'Emigration, Ideology and Identity in Post-Famine Ireland', *Studies: An Irish Quarterly Review*, 75, 300 (Winter 1986), pp. 515–27.
Miller, Kerby, *Ireland and Irish America: Culture, Class and Transatlantic Migration* (Dublin: Field Day, 2008).
Miller, Kerby, "Paddy's Paradox: Emigration to America in Irish Imagination and Rhetoric', in Dirk Hoerder and Horst Rössler (eds), *Distant Magnets: Expectations and Realities in the Immigrant Experience, 1840–1930* (New York and London: Holmes and Meier Publishers, 1993), pp. 264–94.
Miller, Kerby A., '"Revenge for Skibbereen": Irish Emigration and the Meaning of the Great Famine', in Arthur Gribben (ed.), *The Great Famine and the Irish Diaspora in America* (Boston: University of Massachusetts Press, 1999), pp. 180–95.
Miller, Kerby A., 'Review – Sending Out Ireland's Poor: Assisted Emigration to North America in the Nineteenth Century', *Journal of Social History*, 38, 3 (Spring 2005), pp. 784–86.
Miller, Kerby and Bruce D. Bolling, 'Golden Streets, Bitter Tears: The Irish Image of America during the Era of Mass Migration', *Journal of American Ethnic History*, 10, 1/2 (Fall 1990–Winter 1991), pp. 16–35.
Miller, Kirby A. and Bruce D. Bolling, 'The Pauper and the Politician: A Tale of Two Immigrants and the Construction of Irish-American Society', in Arthur Gribben (ed.), *The Great Famine and the Irish Diaspora in America* (Amherst: University of Massachusetts Press, 1999), pp. 196–219.
Miller, Kerby, David N. Doyle and Patricia Kelleher, '"For Love and Liberty": Irish Women, Migration and Domesticity in Ireland and America, 1815–1920', in Patrick O'Sullivan (ed.), *The Irish World Wide: History, Heritage, Identity, Volume 4* (London and Washington: Leicester University Press, 1995), pp. 41–65.
Kerby Miller, Arnold Schrier, Bruce D. Bolling and David Doyle (eds), *Irish Immigrants in the Land of Canaan: Letters and Memoirs from Colonial and Revolutionary America, 1675–1815* (Oxford: Oxford University Press, 2003)
Moers, Ellen, *Literary Women: The Great Writers* (New York: Doubleday, 1976).

Moloney, Deirdre M., 'A Transatlantic Reform: Boston's Port Protection Program and Irish Women Emigrants', *Journal of American Ethnic History*, 19, 1 (Fall 1999), pp. 50–66.

Montagu, Violette M., *The Celebrated Madame Campan* (London: Eveleigh Nash, 1914).

Montgomery, James, 'The Menace of Hollywood', *Studies: An Irish Quarterly Review*, 31, 124 (December 1942), pp. 420–28.

Moran, Gerard, *Sending Out Ireland's Poor: Assisted Emigration to North America in the Nineteenth Century* (Dublin: Four Courts Press, 2004).

Morash, Christopher, *A History of the Media in Ireland* (Cambridge: Cambridge University Press, 2010).

Moretti, Franco, 'The Slaughterhouse of Literature', *Modern Language Quarterly*, 61, 1 (March 2000), pp. 207–27.

Morgan, Simon, 'Domestic Economy and Political Agitation: Women and the Anti-Corn Law League, 1839–46', in Kathryn Gleadle and Sarah Richardson (eds), *Women in British politics, 1760–1860* (Basingstoke: Macmillan Press, 2000), pp. 115–33.

Morgan, Lady Sydney, *Lady Morgan's Memoirs: Autobiography, Diaries, and Correspondence, Vol. I*. Edited by W. H. Dixon (London: W. H. Allen, 1862).

Mott, Frank Luther, *A History of American Magazines: 1741–1850* (Harvard: Harvard University Press, 1938).

Mulkerins, Arlene, 'The Vocabulary of Silence', in Caledonia Kearns (ed.), *Motherland: Writings by Irish American Women about Mothers and Daughters* (New York: William Murrow, 1999), pp. 211–15.

Murphy, Cliona, 'Women's History, Feminist History or Gender History', *Irish Studies Review*, 12 (Spring–Summer 1992), pp. 21–26.

Murphy, Cliona, *Women's Suffrage Movement and Irish Society in the Early Twentieth Century* (Philadelphia: Temple University Press, 1989).

Murphy, Edward, 'The Teaching Sister and the Modern Girl', *The Furrow*, 9 (July–December 1958), pp. 570–72.

Murphy, Jeremiah, *When Youth Was Mine: A Memoir of Kerry* (Dublin: Mentor Press, 1998).

Murphy, Maureen, 'The Fionnuala Factor: Irish Sibling Emigration at the Turn of the Century', in Anthony Bradley and Maryann Gianella Valiulis (eds), *Gender and Sexuality in Modern Ireland* (Amherst: University of Massachusetts Press, 1997), pp. 85–101.

National Econimic and Social Council, *The Economic and Social Implications of Emigration* (Dublin: NESC, 1991).

Negra, Diane (ed.), *The Irish in Us: Irishness, Performativity, and Popular Culture* (Durham, NC: Duke University Press, 2006).

Neville, Grace, 'Dark Lady of the Archives: Towards an Analysis of Women and Emigration to North America in Irish Folklore', in Mary O'Dowd and Sabine Wichert (eds), *Chattel, Servant or Citizen: Women's Status in Church, State and Society* (Belfast: Institute of Irish Studies, 1995), pp. 200–14.

Neville, Grace, 'Land of the Fair, Land of the Free? The Myth of America in Irish Folklore', in Anthony Coulson (ed.), *Exiles and Migrants: Crossing Thresholds in European Culture and Society* (Brighton: Sussex University Press, 1997), pp. 57–71.

Neville, Grace, '"She Never Then after That Forgot Him": Irishwomen and Emigration to the United States in Irish Folklore', *Mid-America: An Historical Review*, 74, 3 (October 1992), pp. 271–89.

Ní Annracháin, Máire, 'Literature in Irish', in J. R. Hill (ed.), *A New History of Ireland, Volume VII: Ireland, 1921–84* (Oxford: Oxford University Press, 2003), pp. 573–86.

Ní Mhunghaile, Lesa, 'Anglo-Irish Antiquarianism in County Longford in the 1780s: The Case of Charlotte Brooke', in Martin Morris and Fergus O'Ferrall (eds), *Longford: History and Society* (Dublin: Geography Publications, 2010), pp. 237–58.

Ní Mhunghaile, Lesa, 'Bilingualism, Print Culture in Irish and the Public Sphere, 1700–c.1830', in James Kelly and Ciarán Mac Murchaidh (eds), *Irish and English Essays in the Irish Linguistic and Cultural Frontier, 1600–1900* (Dublin: Four Courts Press, 2012), pp. 218–42.

Nic Eoin, Máirín, *B'ait Leo Bean: Gnéithe den Idé-Eolaíocht Inscne i dTraidisiún Literatha na Gaelige* (Dublin: An Clóchomhar Tta, 1998).

Nolan, Janet, *Ourselves Alone: Women's Emigration from Ireland 1885–1920* (Lexington: University Press of Kentucky, 1989).

Nolan, John, 'Mission of Our Lady of the Rosary', *Irish Ecclesiastical Record* (September 1891), pp. 776–85.

O'Brien, Flann, 'The Dance Halls', in Sean McMahon (ed.), *The Best from The Bell: Great Irish Writing* (Dublin: The O'Brien Press, 1978), pp. 36–57.

O'Carroll, Ide, *Models for Movers: Irish Women's Emigration to America* (Dublin: Attic Press, 1990).

O'Cathasaigh, L., 'The Gaeltacht and Its Problems', *Irish Monthly*, 60, 704 (February 1932), pp. 100–5.

Ó Ciosáin, Niall, 'Oral Culture, Literacy and Reading, 1800–1850', in James H. Murphy (ed), *The Oxford History of the Irish Book, Volume 4: The Irish Book in English 1800–1891* (Oxford: Oxford University Press, 2011), pp. 173–91.

Ó Ciosáin, Niall, *Print and Popular Culture in Ireland, 1750–1850* (London: Macmillan Press, 1997).

O'Conchubhair, S., 'A Day with Monaghan's Mobile Library', *An Leabharlann*, 15, 2 (December 1957), pp. 68–71.

Ó Cuív, Brian (ed.), *Párliament na mBan* (Dublin: Dublin Institute of Advanced Studies, 1952).

O' Donovan, Alison, 'Children and Cinema', *The Irish Housewife*, 4 (1950), pp. 113–14.

O'Dowd, Mary, *A History of Women in Ireland, 1500–1800* (Harlow: Pearson, 2005).

O'Dowd, Mary, 'O'Connell and the Lady Patriots: Women and O'Connellite Politics, 1824–1845', in Allan Blackstock and Eoin Magennis (eds), *Politics and*

Political Culture in Britain and Ireland, 1750–1850: Essays in Tribute to Peter Jupp (Belfast: Blackstaff Press, 2007), pp. 283–303.

O'Dowd, Mary (ed.), 'The Political Writings and Public Voices of Women, c.1500–1850', in Angela Bourke et al. (eds), *The Field Day Anthology of Irish Writing, Volume 5: Irishwomen's Writings and Traditions* (Cork: Cork University Press, 2002), pp. 6–12.

O'Dowd, Mary, 'Politics, Patriotism, and Women in Ireland, Britain and Colonial America, c.1700–1780', *Journal of Women's History*, 22, 4 (Winter 2010), pp. 15–38.

O'Dowd, Mary, 'Thoughts on Gender History', in Maryann Valiulis (ed.), *Gender and Power in History* (Dublin: Irish Academic Press, 2009), pp. 9–18.

O'Dowd, Mary and Sabine Wichert (eds), *Chattel, Servant or Citizen: Women's Status in Church, State and Society* (Belfast: Institute for Irish Studies, 1995).

O'Drisceóil, Donal, *Censorship in Ireland, 1939–45: Neutrality, Politics and Society* (Cork: Cork University Press, 1996).

Offen, Karen, *European Feminisms 1700–1950: A Political History* (Stanford: Stanford University Press, 2000).

Ó Gallchoir, Clíona, 'Foreign Tyrants and Domestic Tyrants: The Public, the Private, and Eighteenth-Century Irish Women's Writing', in Patricia Coughlan and Tina O'Toole (eds), *Irish Literature: Feminist Perspectives* (Dublin: Carysfort Press, 2008), pp. 17–38.

Ó Gallchoir, Clíona, 'Germaine de Staël and the Response of Sydney Owenson and Maria Edgeworth', in Eamon Maher and Grace Neville (eds), *France–Ireland: Anatomy of a Friendship – Studies in History, Literature and Politics* (Frankfurt am Main: Peter Lang, 2004), pp. 79–89.

Ó Gallchoir, Clíona, *Maria Edgeworth: Women, Enlightenment, Nation* (Dublin: University College Dublin Press, 2005).

Ó Gallchoir, Clíona, 'Orphans, Upstarts and Aristocrats: Ireland and the Idyll of Adoption in the Work of Madame de Genlis', in Oonagh Walsh (ed.), *Ireland Abroad: Politics and Professions in the Nineteenth Century* (Dublin: Four Courts Press, 2003), pp. 36–46.

O'Grada, Cormac and Brendan M. Walsh, 'The Economic Effects of Emigration: Ireland', in Beth J. Asch (ed.), *Emigration and Its Effects on the Sending Country* (Santa Monica, Calif.: Rand, 1994), pp. 97–149, http://www.rand.org/pubs/monograph_reports/MR244.html (accessed 28 April 2013).

O'Halloran, Clare, *Golden Ages and Barbarous Nations: Antiquarian Debate and Cultural Politics in Ireland, c.1750–1800* (Cork: Cork University Press, 2004).

O'Halloran, Clare, '"Better Without the Ladies"': The Royal Irish Academy and the Admission of Women Members', *History Ireland*, 19, 6 (November/December 2011), pp. 42–45.

O'Kelly, Hilary, 'Parcels from America: American Clothes in Ireland, c.1930–1980', in Alexandra Palmer and Hazel Clark (eds), *Old Clothes, New Looks: Second Hand Fashion* (Oxford: Berg, 2005), pp. 83–99.

Ó Néill, Eoghan, *Gleann an Óir. Ar Thóir an Staire agus na Litríochta in Oirthear*

Mumhan agus i nDeisceart Laighean (Dublin: An Clóchomhar Tta, n.d.), pp. 79–85.

O'Rahilly, Alfred, 'An Ursuline Writer on Irish History', *Journal of Cork Historical and Archaeological Society*, 47 (1942), pp. 77–86.

Oram, Hugh, *The Advertising Book: The History of Advertising in Ireland* (Dublin: MO Books, 1986).

Oram, Hugh, 'From Paper to Pixels', http://marketing.ie/index (accessed 15 February 2010).

Orr, Clarissa Campbell, 'Aristocratic Feminism, the Learned Governess, and the Republic of Letters', in Sarah Knott and Barbara Taylor (eds), *Women, Gender and Enlightenment* (Basingstoke: Palgrave Macmillan, 2005), pp. 306–25.

Ó Sùilleabháin, Pádraig, 'Catholic Books Printed in Ireland 1740–1820 Containing Lists of Subscribers', *Collectanea Hibernica*, 6/7 (1963/1964), pp. 231–33.

O'Sullivan, Patrick (ed.), *The Irish World Wide: History, Heritage, Identity, Volume 4: Irish Women and Irish Migration* (London: Leicester University Press, 1995).

O'Toole, J. L., 'The Value of Comparison, A Story of Irish Life', *Irish Messenger of the Sacred Heart*, 41 (April 1928), pp. 7–8.

O Tuathaigh, M. A. G., 'The Historical Pattern of Irish Emigration: Some Labour Aspects', in Mary Clancy, John Cunnigham and Alf MacLochlainn (eds), *The Emigrant Experience: Papers Presented at the Second Annual Mary Murray Weekend Seminar* (Galway: Galway Labour History Group, 1991), pp. 9–29.

Owens, Gary, '"A Moral Insurrection": Faction Fighters, Public Demonstrations and the O'Connellite Campaign, 1828', *Irish Historical Studies*, 30, 120 (November 1997), pp. 513–39.

Owens, Gary, 'Nationalism without Words: Symbolism and Ritual Behaviour in the Repeal "Monster" Meetings of 1843–5', in J. S. Donnelly Jnr and Kerby A. Miller (eds), *Irish Popular Culture, 1650–1850* (Dublin: Irish Academic Press, 1998), pp. 242–61.

Parks, Stephen, 'George Berkeley, Sir Richard Steele and *The Ladies Library*', *The Scriblerian and the Kit-Cats*, 12, 1 (Autumn 1980), pp. 1–2.

Paulu, Burton, *British Broadcasting: Radio and Television in the United Kingdom* (Minneapolis: University of Minnesota Press, 1956).

Pells, Richard, *Not Like US: How Europeans have Loved, Hated and Transformed American Culture since World War II* (New York: Basic Books, 1997).

Perry, Ruth, *The Celebrated Mary Astell: An Early English Feminist* (Chicago: University of Chicago Press, 1986).

Pickering, Paul A. and Alex Tyrrell, *The People's Bread: A History of the Anti-Corn Law League* (London: Leicester University Press, 2000).

Pine, Richard, *The Dublin Gate Theatre, 1928–78: Theatre in Focus* (Cambridge and New Jersey: Chadwyck Healey, 1984).

Powell, Martyn J., *The Politics of Consumption in Eighteenth-Century Ireland* (Basingstoke: Palgrave Macmillan, 2005).

'Public Libraries and the War', *Irish Library Bulletin*, 1, 3 (March 1940), p. 22.

Quigley, Martin S., *A U.S. Spy in Ireland* (Dublin: Marino Books, 1999).

Raftery, Deirdre and Susan Parkes, *Female Education in Ireland 1700–1900: Minerva or Madonna* (Dublin: Irish Academic Press, 2007).

Rains, Stephanie, *Commodity Culture and Social Class in Dublin 1850–1916* (Dublin: Irish Academic Press, 2010).

Raughter, Rosemary, 'A Discreet Benevolence: Female Philanthropy and the Catholic Resurgence in 18th-Century Ireland', *Women's History Review*, 6 (1997), pp. 465–84.

Raughter, Rosemary (ed.), *Religious Women and Their History: Breaking the Silence* (Dublin: Irish Academic Press, 2005).

Reardon, John P., 'The Cinema and the Child', *Studies: An Irish Quarterly Review*, 18, 71 (September 1929), pp. 431–42.

Redmond, Brigid, 'No. 3', *Studies: An Irish Quarterly Review*, 33, 129 (March 1944), pp. 57–59.

Regan, Shaun, 'Locating Richard Griffith: Genre, Nation, Canon', *Irish University Review*, 41, 1 (Spring–Summer 2011), pp. 95–114.

Rendall, Jane, *The Origin of Modern Feminism: Women in Britain, France and the United States, 1780–1960* (Basingstoke: Macmillan, 1985).

Reynolds, James A., *The Catholic Emancipation Crisis in Ireland, 1823–1829* (New Haven, Conn.: Yale University Press, 1954).

Richard, Jessica, '"Games of Chance": Belinda, Education, and Empire', in Heidi Kaufman and Chris Fauske (eds), *An Uncomfortable Authority: Maria Edgeworth and Her Contexts* (Newark, Del.: University of Delaware Press, 2004), pp. 192–211.

Rizzo, Betty, *Companions Without Vows: Relationships among Eighteenth-Century British Women* (Athens, Ga.: University of Georgia Press, 1994).

Roberts, Evans, 'Labour Force Participation by Married Women in the United States: Results from the 1917/19 Cost-of-Living Survey and the 1920 PUMS', http://users.pop.umn.edu/~eroberts/evanrobertssshapaper.pdf (accessed 5 August 2009).

Robinson, William H., *The Library of Mrs. Elizabeth Vesey, 1715–1791* (Newcastle upon Tyne: W. H. Robinson, 1926).

Rockett, Kevin, *Irish Film Censorship: A Cultural Journey from Silent Cinema to Internet Pornography* (Dublin: Four Courts Press, 2004).

Rockett, Kevin, 'Protecting the Family and the Nation: The Official Censorship of American Cinema in Ireland, 1923–54', *Historical Journal of Film, Radio and Television*, 20, 3 (2000), pp. 283–300.

Rockett, Kevin, 'The Silent Period', in Kevin Rockett, Luke Gibbons and John Hill, *Cinema and Ireland* (London: Routledge, 1988), pp. 3–146.

Rockett, Kevin and Eugene Finn, *Still Irish: A Century of the Irish in Film* (Dublin: Red Mountain Press, 1995).

Rockett, Kevin and Emer Rockett, *Magic Lantern, Panorama and Moving Picture Shows in Ireland, 1786–1909* (Dublin: Four Courts Press, 2011).

Rockett, Kevin, Luke Gibbons and John Hill, *Cinema and Ireland* (Beckenham: Croom Helm, 1987).

Roddy, Sarah, '"The Emigrants' Friend"? Guides for Irish Emigrants by Clergymen *c*.1830–1882', in Ciara Breathnach and Catherine Lawless (eds), *Visual, Material and Print Culture in Nineteenth-Century Ireland* (Dublin: Four Courts Press, 2010), pp. 244–57.

Rodgers, Nini, 'Two Quakers and a Utilitarian: The Reaction of Three Irish Women Writers to the Problem of Slavery, 1789–1807', *Proceedings of the Royal Irish Academy*, 100C, 4 (2000), pp. 140–41.

Rose, Richard (ed.), *Lessons from America: An Exploration* (London: Macmillan, 1974).

Rubin, Gayle S., 'Thinking Sex: Notes for a Radical Theory of the Politics of Sexuality', in Henry Abelove, Michaela Aina Barele and David M. Halperin (eds), *The Lesbian and Gay Studies Reader* (New York: Routledge, 1993), pp. 3–44.

Ruby Rich, B., '*Maedchen in Uniform:* From Repressive Tolerance to Erotic Liberation', *Jump Cut*, 24–25 (March 1981), pp. 44–50, http://www.ejumpcut.org/archive/onlinessays/JC24–25folder/MaedchenUniform.html (accessed 12 October 2012).

Russell, Elizabeth, 'Holy Crosses, Guns and Roses: Themes in Popular Reading Material', in Joost Augusteijn (ed.), *Ireland in the 1930s* (Dublin: Four Courts Press, 1999), pp. 11–28.

Ryan, John, 'The Cinema Peril', *Studies: An Irish Quarterly*, 7, 25 (March 1918), pp. 112–26.

Ryan, Louise, 'Constructing "Irishwoman": Modern Girls and Comely Maidens', *Irish Studies Review*, 6, 3 (1998), pp. 263–72.

Ryan, Louise, 'Locating the Flapper in Rural Irish Society: The Irish Provincial Press and the Modern Woman in the 1920s', in Ann Heilmann and Margaret Beetham (eds), *New Woman Hybridities: Feminity, Feminism and International Consumer Culture, 1880–1930* (London: Routledge, 2004), pp. 90–101.

Ryan, Louise, 'Negotiating Modernity and Tradition: Newspaper Debates on the "Modern Girl" in the Irish Free State', *Journal of Gender Studies*, 7, 2 (July 1998), pp. 1–14.

Sayers, Peig, *Peig* (Dublin: Comhleacht Oideachas na hÉireannn, undated).

Schaller, Peggy, 'Jeanne Marie Le Prince de Beaumont (1711–1780): Biographical Essay for Chawton House Library and Women Writers', http://www.chawton.org/files/LeprincedeBeaumont.pdf (accessed 12 October 2012).

Schellenberg, Betty A., *The Professionalization of Women Writers in Eighteenth-Century Britain* (Cambridge: Cambridge University Press, 2005).

Schrier, Arnold, *Ireland and the American Emigration* (Chester Springs, Pa.: Dufours Editions, 1997).

Scott, Franklin D., 'American Influences in Norway and Sweden', *The Journal of Modern History*, 18, 1 (March 1946), pp. 37–47.

Sehra, Melissa, *Women in Irish Drama: A Century of Authorship and Representation* (London: Palgrave, 2009).

Seller, Maxine S., 'Beyond the Stereotype: A New Look at the Immigrant Woman, 1880–1924', *The Journal of Ethnic Studies*, 3 (Spring 1975), pp. 59–70.

Sher, Richard B., *The Enlightenment and the Book: Scottish Authors and Their Publishers in Eighteenth-Century Britain, Ireland, and America* (Chicago: University of Chicago Press, 2006).

Shevelow, Kathryn, *Women and Print Culture: The Construction of Femininity in the Early Periodical* (London: Routledge, 1989).

Sinfield, Alan, *Faultlines: Cultural Materialism and the Politics of Dissident Reading* (Oxford: Clarendon Press, 1992).

Sinke, Suzanne, 'A Historiography of Immigrant Women in the Nineteenth and Early Twentieth Centuries', *Ethnic Forum*, 9 (1989), pp. 122–45.

Sisson, Elaine, 'Expressionism and Irish Stage Design: 1922–1932', unpublished paper presented to the conference on Irish Modernism, Trinity College, Dublin, October 2007.

Sisson, Elaine, '"A Note on What Happened": Experimental Influences on the Irish Stage 1919–1929', *Kritika Kultura*, 15 (2010), pp. 132–48, http://kritikakultura.ateneo.net/images/pdf/kk15/anote.pdf (accessed 29 April 2013).

Sisson, Elaine, 'Theatre, Design and the Avant Garde in Ireland: Seeing Things – Irish Visual Culture', unpublished paper presented at the University of Limerick, June 2007.

Sklar, Kathryn Kish, '"Women Who Speak For an Entire Nation": American and British Women at the World Anti-Slavery Convention, London, 1840', in Jean Fagan Yellin and John C. Van Horne (eds), *The Abolitionist Sisterhood: Women's Political Culture in Antebellum America* (Ithaca, NY and London: Cornell University Press, 1994), pp. 301–33.

Smith, Gary Scott, 'Lloyd Cassel Douglas', in John A. Garraty and Mark C. Carnes (eds), *American National Biography*, vol. 6 (New York and London: Oxford University Press, 1999), pp. 799–800.

Smith, James D., 'The Politics of Sexual Knowledge: The Origins of Ireland's Containment Culture and the Carrigan Report (1931)', *Journal of the History of Sexuality*, 13, 3 (April 2004), pp. 208–33.

Smyth, Jim, 'Dancing, Depravity and All That Jazz: The Public Dance Halls Act of 1935', *History Ireland*, 1, 2 (Summer 1993), pp. 51–54.

Springborg, Patricia, 'Introduction', in Mary Astell, *A Serious Proposal to the Ladies, Parts I and II*, edited by Patricia Springborg (London: Pickering and Chatto, 1997), pp. 23–24.

Staves, Susan, 'Church of England Clergy and Women Writers', in Nicole Pohl and Betty A. Schellenberg (eds), *Reconsidering the Bluestockings* (San Marino, Calif.: The Huntington Library Press, 2003), pp. 81–103.

Stearns, Peter, *Gender in World History* (London and New York: Routledge, 2000).

Stevenson, Lionel, *The Wild Irish Girl: The Life of Sydney Owenson, Lady Morgan (1776–1859)* (New York: Chapman and Hall Ltd, 1936).

Strachan, John and Nally, Claire, *Selling Ireland: Advertising, Literature and Irish Print Culture, 1891–1922* (London: Palgrave, 2013).

Sullivan, J., 'Librarian's Year', *Irish Library Bulletin*, 6, 6 (November–December 1945), pp. 115–16.

Synge, John Millington, 'The Inner Land of Mayo', in Alan Price (ed.), *Collected Works, Volume 2: Prose* (London: Oxford University Press, 1966), pp. 305–6.
Taylor, Alice, *To School through the Fields: An Irish Country Childhood* (Dingle: Brandon, 1988).
Taylor, Barbara, 'Feminists versus Gallants: Manners and Morals in Enlightenment Britain', *Representations*, 87 (Summer 2004), pp. 125–48.
Tebbel, John and Mary Ellen Zuckerman, *The Magazine in America, 1741–1990* (New York and Oxford: Oxford University Press, 1991).
Thomis, Malcolm I. and Grimmett, Jennifer, *Women in Protest, 1800–1850* (London: Croom Helm, 1982).
Thompson, Alistair, '"My Wayward Heart": Homesickness, Longing and the Return of British Post-War Immigrants from Australia', in Marjory Harper (ed.), *Emigrant Homecomings: The Return Movement of Emigrants, 1600–2000* (Manchester: Manchester University Press, 2005), pp. 105–30.
Tinkler, Penny, *Smoke Signals: Women, Smoking and Visual Culture* (Berg: Oxford, 2006)
Toal, Catherine, 'Control Experiment: Edgeworth's Critique of Rousseau's Educational Theory', in Heidi Kaufman and Chris Fauske (eds), *An Uncomfortable Authority: Maria Edgeworth and Her Contexts* (Newark, Del.: University of Delaware Press, 2004), pp. 212–31.
Tolles, F. B. (ed.), *Slavery and 'The Woman Question': Lucretia Mott's Diary of Her Visit to Great Britain to Attend the World's Anti-Slavery Convention of 1840* (*Journal of the Friends' Historical Society*, Supplement 23) (Haverford, Pa. and London: Friends' Historical Association and Friends' Historical Society, 1952).
Tracy, Robert, 'Chekhov in Ireland', http://dspace.dial.pipex.com/town/parade/abj76/PG/pieces/chekhov_in_ireland.shtml (accessed 12 October 2012).
Travers, Pauric, 'Emigration and Gender', in Mary O'Dowd and Sabine Wichert (eds), *Chattel, Servant or Citizen: Women's Status in Church, State and Society* (Belfast: Institute of Irish Studies, 1995), pp. 187–99.
Trench, Charles Chenevix, *The Great Dan: A Biography of Daniel O'Connell* (London: Jonathan Cape, 1984).
Turner, Cheryl, *Living by the Pen: Women Writers in the Eighteenth Century* (London: Routledge, 1994).
Tynan, Katharine, *Twenty-Five Years: Reminiscences (1913)* (London: Smith, Elder and Company, 1913)
Umbach, Maken and Bernd Huppauf (eds), *Vernacular Modernism: Heimat, Globalisation and the Built Environment* (Stanford: Stanford University Press, 2005).
Usherwood, Barbara, '"Mrs Housewife and Her Grocer": The Advent of Self-Service Food Shopping in Britain', in Maggie Andrews and Mary M. Talbot (eds), *All the World and Her Husband: Women in Twentieth-Century Consumer Culture* (London and New York: Cassell, 2000), pp. 113–29.
Valiulis, Maryann Gianella (ed.), *Gender and Power in History* (Dublin: Irish Academic Press, 2009).

Valiulis, Maryann Gianella, 'Power, Gender and Identity in the Irish Free State', *Journal of Women's History*, 7, 1, Special Issue on 'Irish Women's Voices: Past and Present', edited by Joan Hoff and Maureen Coulter (Spring 1995), pp. 117–36.

Van Voris, Jacqueline, 'Daniel O'Connell and Women's Rights, One Letter', *Éire-Ireland*, 17, 3 (1982), pp. 33–39.

Van Vugt, William E., *Britain to America: Mid-Nineteenth Century Immigrants to the United States* (Urbana and Chicago: University of Illinois Press, 1999).

Walsh, Barbara, *When the Shopping Was Good: Woolworths and the Irish Main Street* (Dublin: Irish Academic Press, 2011).

Walsh, T. J., *Nano Nagle and the Presentation Sisters* (Dublin: M. H. Gill, 1959).

'Waterford County Library, Annual Report 1959/60', 'Carlow County Library, Annual Report, 1959/60', *An Leabharlann*, 18, 3 (September 1960), pp. 87–88.

Weatherford, Doris, *Foreign and Female: Immigrant Women in America 1840–1930* (New York: Schocken Books, 1986).

Weinberg, Sydney Stahl, 'The Treatment of Women in Immigration History: A Call for Change,' *Journal of American Ethnic History*, 11, 4 (Summer 1992), pp. 25–67.

West, Douglas, 'Multinational Competition in the British Advertising Agency Business, 1936–1987', *Business History Review*, 62, 3 (Autumn 1988), pp. 467–501.

Whelan, Bernadette, *American Government in Ireland, 1790 to 1913: A History of the US Consular Service* (Manchester: Manchester University Press, 2010).

Whelan, Bernadette, 'The Idea of America in the New Irish State, 1922–60', in David T. Gleeson (ed.), *The Irish in the Atlantic World* (Charleston: University of South Carolina Press, 2010), pp. 76–109.

Whelan, Bernadette, *Ireland and the Marshall Plan 1947–1957* (Dublin: Four Courts Press, 2000).

Whelan, Bernadette, *United States Foreign Policy and Ireland: From Empire to Independence* (Dublin: Four Courts Press, 2006).

White, Patricia, *Uninvited: Classical Cinema and Lesbian Representability* (Bloomington and Indianapolis: Indiana University Press, 1999).

Williams, Kevin, *Read All About It: A History of British Newspapers* (London: Routledge, 2011).

Williams, Raymond, *Culture and Society, 1780–1950* (London: Penguin, 1958).

Wills, Clair, *That Neutral Island: A Cultural History of Ireland During the Second World War* (London: Faber and Faber, 2007).

Woodman, Kieran, *Media Control in Ireland, 1923–1983* (Galway: Galway University Press, 1985).

Wright, Eric Olin and Joel Rogers, 'American Society: how it actualy works', www.ssc.wisc.edu/~wright/ContemporaryAmericanSoicety.htm (accessed 2 January 2012).

Wyman, Mark, *Round-Trip to America. The Immigrants Return to Europe, 1880–1930* (Ithaca, NY and London: Cornell University Press, 1993).

Unpublished Theses

Connolly, Tracey, 'Emigration from Independent Ireland: 1922–1970' (Ph.D. thesis, University College Cork, 1999).

de Valera, Anne, 'Antiquarian and Historical Investigations in Ireland in the Eighteenth Century' (MA thesis, University College, Dublin, 1978).

Delaney, Enda, 'Irish Migration to Britain, 1921–71: Patterns, Trends and Contingent Factors' (Ph.D. thesis, Queen's University Belfast, 1997).

Guinan-Dermody, Mary, 'The Establishment of a "Workers' University": A History of Tipperary Joint Libraries Committee, 1927–66' (MA thesis, University of Limerick, 2004).

Kane, Paul J., 'The Life and Works of David Manson, a Belfast School-Teacher 1726–1792' (MA thesis, Queen's University Belfast, 1984).

McCarthy, Mary, 'Advertising in Ireland, 1922–60' (MA thesis, University of Limerick, 2004).

McHale, Maria, 'Who Turned on the Lights? An Exploration of Rural Electrification on Women's Lives in Ireland' (MA thesis, University of Limerick, 2005).

Muldowney, Mary, 'The Impact of the Second World War on Women in Belfast and Dublin: An Oral History' (Ph.D. thesis, Trinity College Dublin, 2005).

O'Connell, Anne, 'Assisted Female Emigration: Vere Foster's Scheme, 1880–1896' (Ph.D. thesis, University of Limerick, 1998).

Riaich, Douglas, 'Ireland and the Campaign against American Slavery, 1830–1860' (Ph.D. thesis, University of Edinburgh, 1975).

Townsend, Lisa, 'The Intellectual and Cultural Interests of Women in Ireland, $c.$1740–$c.$1840' (Ph.D. thesis, Queen's University Belfast, 2007).

Index

A Midsummer Night's Dream, 214
A Series of Genuine Letters Between Henry and Frances, 20
A Serious Proposal to the Ladies, for the Advancement of their True and Greatest Interest. By a Lover of Her Sex, 15, 16, 19
A Vindication of the Rights of Women, 46, 51, 78
Abelard and Heloise, 20
Absentee (adaptation), 197
Adèle et Théodore, 29–31, 57
Advertisements, 5, 83, 89, 147–53, 156, 157, 158, 180, 216, 218
  see also Consumerism
Aesop's *Fables*, 18
Aikenhead, Mary, 61, 65
Aikin, John, 24, 26
Aikin, Anna Laetitia, 24, 26, 50
Alcott, Louisa Mary, 138, 142
All Is Not Butter, 139
All This and Heaven Too, 139, 144
Allergies in Love, 167
Allestree, Richard, 15, 16, 18–19, 21
Allgood, Sara, 206
America, 170
American Catholic League of Decency, 165
American Forces Network, 172
American Philosophical Society, 68–69
An Appeal of One Half the Human Race, Women, Against Pretensions of the Other Half, Men, to Retain Them in Political, and Thence in Civil and Domestic Slavery, 74
An Essay in Defence of the Female Sex, 16
An Essay on the Writings and Genius of Shakespeare, 24
Anderson, Dusty, 152
Andrews Sisters, 172
Andy Hardy, 168
Angela's Ashes, 187
Anna Christie, 208
Anti-slavery movement, 79, 80–81
Anything But the Truth, 203
Aran Island, Co. Donegal, 116
Aran Islands, Co. Galway, 112, 116
Ardmore, Co. Waterford, 188
Aristotle, 66
Armagh, Co. Armagh, 49
Armstrong, Nancy, 14, 52, 153
Arnold, Mathew, 192–93
Ashley, Gisela, 201
Asphalt Jungle, 168
Associated Press Service, 145
Astell, Mary, 15, 16, 17, 19, 20, 51
Atalanta, 185
Athlone, Co. Westmeath, 104, 165
  Ritz cinema, 159
Atlantic Monthly, 133
Austen, Jane, 66

Báile na Gall, Dingle, Co. Kerry, 121
Balch, Henry H., US Consul General, 107, 114, 115, 164–65
Ball, Mary Teresa, 61, 65

Ballaghadreen, Co. Mayo, 99
Ballaster, Ros, 139–40
Ballinasloe, Co. Galway, 153
Ballyhillion, Co. Donegal, 124
Bangor Erris, Co. Mayo, 124
Bangor, Co. Down
    Tonic cinema, 159
Bann, Mai, 111, 120
Bann, Mary, 111, 120
Banning, Robert, 139
Bar Convent, York, 61
Barbauld, Anna Laetitia, *see* Aikin, Anna Laetitia
Bayliss, Marguerite F., 139
Beaufort, Daniel, 67–68
Beaufort, Harriet, 67
Beaufort, Lucia, 67, 68
Beckett, Samuel, 179
Beckh, Nancy, 198
Beecher Stowe, Harriet, 138, 142
Beere, Thekla, 169
Beeton, Isabella, 55
Beeton, Samuel, 55
Belfast, 49, 51–52, 53, 58
    booksellers, 25–26
    Curzon cinema, 159
    printer, 49
    public lectures, 70
    reprints, 25–26
    schools, 39, 60–61, 65
Belfast Natural History Society, 70
Belfast Newsletter, 60
Belinda, 66
Bell, Melanie, 159
Berkeley, George, 15–17, 18, 19, 27, 28, 51
Berlin, Germany, 213
Bernelle, Agnes (Mrs Desmond Leslie), 151
Berry, Chuck, 173
Better Homes and Garden, 135
Bible, 18, 28
Birth control, 112–13, 131, 138, 144, 166, 174, 184
Blachford, Theodosia, 57
Blarney and Whitechurch parish, Co. Cork, 94

Blasket Islands, Co. Kerry, 117, 123–24
Bluestocking circle, 2, 21–26, 42, 52, 66, 72, 219
Boden, Eric, 151, 156, 173
Boden, Niall, 173
Bodleian Library, Oxford, 47
Bohernabreena, Co. Dublin, 77
Boileau-Despréaux, Nicolas, 37
Bord Fáilte, 191
Borden, Lucille Papin, 138, 142
Boscawen, Frances, 23–24, 25
Boston Pilot, 99
Boston, Massachusetts, 92, 95, 99, 105, 110, 112, 115
    Brookline, 109, 111, 113
    Saint Vincent de Paul Society, 105
Boulter, Hugh, Archbishop of Armagh, 38
Bourke, P. J., 198
Bowen, Elizabeth, 191, 192
Boyle Harvey, Margaret, 90
Boyle, Kay, 139
Breathnach, Sarah Ban, 187
Breen, Joseph, 163
Breezy Stories, 134
Bregy, Katherine, 138, 142
Brennan, Helen, 169
Brickley family, Boston, 109
Brief Encounter, 202
Britain, emigration to, 94–95, 108, 109, 116, 120
British Broadcasting Company, 169, 172, 190
Broadway and Hollywood Movies, 134, 164
Brooke, Charlotte, 66, 67
Brooke, Leslie, 152
Brown and Poulson, Dublin, 161
Browne, Judith, 151
Browne, Michael, Bishop of Cork, 166
Buchanan, Alexander Carlisle, 91
Buffalo, New York, 95
Bundoran, Co. Donegal, 166
Burke, Edmund, 46
Burney, Fanny, 25, 72
Bushe, Letitia, 21
Busman's Honeymoon, 198, 203, 206

Butler, Mary, 104
Byrne, Muriel St. Clair, 203
Byron, Lord, 204, 212

Cahill, Susan, 185, 190
Cahirciveen, Co. Kerry, 93
Cailfornia, 143
Cain, James M., 168
Campbell Orr, Clarissa, 32
Can't Help Singing, 167
Cantwell, John Joseph, Bishop of Los Angeles, 165
Cardinal Richelieu, 167
Carmichael, Coralie, 214
Carrenmullen, Malin Head, Co. Donegal, 111
Carter, Elizabeth, 24, 25, 26
Castle Plunkett, Co. Roscommon, 117
Castle Rackrent, 71
Castlerea, Co. Roscommon, 126
Cathcart, Rex, 169
Catholic Association, 77–83
Catholic Book Society, 78
Catholic Cinema and Theatre Patrons Association, 212
Catholic Emancipation, 45, 77–83
Catholic Truth Society, 104, 144, 164
Caulfield, Alice, 159
Cavan, County, 117, 124
Cavendish, Lady Dorothy, 48
Ceárnaí, Seán Tom, 123–24
Censorship, 138, 139, 140, 144, 146, 158, 161, 163-68, 171, 174, 180, 182, 183, 184, 196, 202, 209, 210, 211, 213–14, 219
Centlivre, Susan, 42
Century Magazine, 133–34
Chancellor, Betty, 214
Chandler, Raymond, 168
Chapone, Hester, 20, 24, 25, 26, 52
Chapone, Sarah, 19, 32, 51
Charles, Ray, 173
Charleston, South Carolina, 34, 169
Chekhov, Anton, 6, 204–8
Chilcote, John, 187
Childbirth, 183–84, 210
Children in Uniform, 212–15

Children, 18, 24, 27–28, 29–30, 33–34, 39–40, 50, 71, 72, 74, 78, 140, 147, 185, 190–91, 198
Christian Brothers, 62
Christie, Agatha, 143
Church of England ministers, 16, 22, 36, 60
Church of Ireland ministers, 16, 17, 19, 22, 38, 44, 48, 60
Cinema, 3, 4, 5, 6, 7, 113, 130, 131–32, 150, 151–52, 155–56, 158–69, 173, 174, 175, 180, 181, 182, 184, 195, 202, 203, 208, 212, 214, 218
Clare, County, 117, 124
Clarecastle, Co. Clare, 117, 119, 122, 123, 128
Claregalway, Co. Galway, 124, 128
Clark, Denis, 114
Clarke, Desmond, 140
Clarke, Isabel C., 138, 142
Clarke, Norma, 25
Class, 2, 3, 6, 14, 23, 27, 30, 31, 33, 40, 45, 47, 48, 52, 55, 57, 58, 60, 61, 62, 65, 77, 79, 83, 88, 87, 90, 96, 97, 98, 106, 108, 126, 127, 131, 132, 133, 135, 140, 143, 144, 145, 147, 157, 159, 161, 165–66, 168, 180, 181, 183, 186, 189, 201, 202, 203, 206, 207
Classical education, 28, 37, 42, 65–66
Clear, Caitriona, 95, 106
Clonmel, Co. Tipperary, 49
Clontarf, Co Dublin, 59–60
Coen, Frances Newall, 109
Cohen, Marilyn, 98
Coimisiún na Gaeltachta, 114–15, 121–22
Colbert, Claudette, 198
Coleraine, Co. Londonderry, 44, 65
Collier's Weekly, 135
Collins, Harold, 163
Collis, Robert, 211
Comerford, Máire, 141
Commission on Emigration and Other Population Problems, 122
Conditions of Employment Act (1936), 106
Connacht, 44
Connecticut, 117, 119, 143

INDEX

Connemara, Co. Galway, 100, 110, 113, 128
Connolly, Father, 166
Conradh na Gaeilge, 171
Considine, June, 160
Consumerism, consumers, consumer culture, 1, 3, 4, 5, 6, 7, 14, 55, 75–76, 109, 142, 144, 147–57, 163, 179, 180, 182, 188, 208, 219, 200, 220
Conversations on the Plurality of Worlds, 37
Corine ou l'Italie, 73
Cork City, 25–26, 33, 49, 90, 92, 140, 153, 169, 172, 185
    booksellers, 25–26
    Castle Street, 26
    Ford's factory, 145
    printers, 34, 49
    Ritz cinema, 149
    school, 33, 49, 52, 62
    see also Female Religious Communities
Cork Examiner, 94, 141
Cork, County, 124
Corrigan, Douglas, 145
Corrigan, Maria, 99
Costello, Nuala, 141, 152
Cottage Dialogues, 73–74
Cotter, James, 35
Coyne, Richard, printer, 62–63
Cregan, Máirín, 188–92, 207
Creggagh, Bridget McLaughlin, 111
Crime Busters, 134
Crosby, Bing, 172
Crowe, Eileen, 204
Crusheen, Co. Clare, 107, 117
Cullen, Paul, Archbishop, 94
Curie, Eve, 139
Curlew's Cry, 207
Curley, Michael Joseph, Archbishop of Baltimore, 165
Curran, John, 126
Cusack, Cyril, 203

Dance, 4, 169–70
Dark Victory, 164
Daskova, Princess Ekaterina, 68–69
Davis, Bette, 164
Day, Doris, 168, 172
Days Without End, 210
De Fountenelle, Bernard Le Bovier, 37
De Genlis, Stéphanie-Félicité, 29–31, 32, 57, 60
De Lauretis, Teresa, 213
De Sevigné, Madame, 61
De Staël, Germaine, 72, 73
De Valera, Éamon, 154, 171
Dean, James, 168
Dean, Joan Fitzpatrick, 196
Deevy, Teresa, 192, 207
Delany, Mary, 19–20, 21, 24–25, 38, 51
Delany, Patrick, Dean of Down, 19, 24–25, 38, 51
Delap, James, 48–51
Delgany, Co. Wicklow, 75
Denny, Lady Arbella, 48
Department Stores, 160
    see also Dublin
Desire Under the Elms, 209, 210
Detroit Free Press, 134
Detroit, Michigan, 95
Devane, Richard, 142, 144, 165, 166, 170
Dickens, Charles, 66, 209
Dickson, Barbara, 141
Dictionary of Irish Biography, 83
Dineen, Margaret, 102
Diner, Hasia, 95
Dingle, Co. Kerry, 100
Dingley, F. L., 89, 103
Directory for Novices, 33
Dirrane, Bridget, 110, 112, 115
Dirrane, Ned, 112
Divorce, 131, 144, 174
Dixon, Delia, 152
Domestic service, 92–93, 94–95, 97–99, 100–2, 103, 107–9, 115, 118, 121, 123, 124
Donohoe, Patrick, 99
Donovan, Julia, 73
Double Indemnity, 167, 168
Douglas, Lloyd, 139, 142
Downpatrick, Co. Down, 44
Doyle, Arthur Conan, 143
Doyle, Jack, 145

Du Maurier, Daphne, 215
Dublin Evening Mail, 192
Dublin Family Magazine or Literary and Religious Miscellany, 55
Dublin Ladies' Journal, 133
Dublin, 6, 19, 20, 21–22, 26, 27, 37, 38, 42, 44, 45, 48, 49, 62, 72, 112, 159, 160, 162, 171, 172, 182, 191
    Abbey Theatre, 188–89, 197, 204, 207, 210
    Adelphi cinema, 159
    Apothecaries Hall, 70
    book shops, 135, 137, 140
    Capitol cinema, 171
    Carlton cinema, 159
    Casino cinema, 160
    Clery's Department Store, 171, 204
    coffee house, 38–39
    Diocesan Library, 77
    Dublin Castle, 75–76
    Focus Theatre, 202
    Gaiety Theatre, 211
    Gate Theatre, 6, 196–217
    Grafton Street, 70
    Green cinema, 159
    Gresham Hotel, 154
    Henry Street, 173
    Kildare Street, 70, 191
    learned societies, 69–70
    Leeson Street, 191
    Liberties, 118, 120
    libraries, 137
    Lower Abbey Street, 70
    Mansion House, 154
    Meath Hospital, 208
    meetings in, 81
    Moira House, 25
    Olympia Theatre, 203
    Pike Theatre Club, 210
    public lectures in, 69–70
    printers and publishers, 42, 63–64
    Roche's Department Store, 204
    Savoy cinema, 159
    schools, 32, 33, 39, 49, 61, 65, 76
    Smock Alley Theatre, 42
    social life in, 70, 158
    Sutton Cross cinema, 160
    tenements, 157, 158
    Theatre Royal cinema, 159
    theatre, 6, 7, 22, 43, 188, 196–217, 218, 220
Dubliners, 205
Duignan, Nancy (née Armstrong), 153
Dun Laoghaire, Co. Dublin, 135
Duncan Park Hotel, Boston, 110
Dundalk, Co. Louth, 166, 170
    Magnet cinema, 166
Dundrum, Co. Dublin, 108
Dyhouse, Carol, 150, 161

Earhart, Amelia, 145
Eason and Son Ltd, 132, 133, 134, 135–36, 164
Eddy, Nelson, 167
Edenderry, Co. Offaly, 125, 126
Edwards, Hilton, 196
Edgeworth family, 25
Edgeworth, Maria, 29, 66, 67, 68, 69–74, 197
Edgeworth, Richard Love, 67, 72
Education des filles, 15, 26–29
Education, 2, 3, 13–53, 55–64, 72, 89, 190
Edwards, Anthony, bookseller, 26
Edwards, Hilton, 196–97, 203, 205, 210, 211, 212, 213
El Greco, 191
Electricity Supply Board, 148–49
Electrification, 4, 148–49, 180
Elizabeth I, 38, 42
Ellis, Hazel, 204, 212
Elwood, John, Vice-Provost of TCD, 38
Emergy, Susan, 138, 142
Emile, 30–31
Emmet, Thomas Addis, 92
English Short Title Catalogue, 17
Englishwoman's Domestic Magazine, 55–56, 133
Ennis, Co. Clare, 118–19, 161
Erasmus, 35
Essays, Addressed to Young Married Women, 22
Eustace, Mrs, 47–48
Ewing, George and Alexander, printers, 42

INDEX

Falkiner, Daniel, Lord Mayor of Dublin, 38
Family, 21, 22, 23, 25, 29, 31, 47, 55, 57, 58, 61, 65, 73, 75, 87, 88, 89, 90, 91, 93, 94, 99, 101, 108, 109, 111, 113, 115, 119, 120, 126, 130, 132, 141, 144, 148, 153, 161, 167, 168, 183, 185, 186, 191, 198, 199, 200, 202, 203, 209, 210, 212, 216
Fashion, 5, 20, 28, 39, 41, 45, 54, 55, 57, 66, 69, 73, 75–76, 118–19, 127–28, 141, 147, 150–57, 161–62, 174, 181, 190, 197, 198
Female religious communities, 61, 96, 113–14
    Daughters of Charity, 61
    Franciscan nuns (Illinois), 114
    Good Shepherd order, 161
    Loreto Order, 61, 64
    Missionary of Our Lady of the Rosary, 105
    Presentation Order, 33
    Sisters of Charity (Irish), 61, 114
    Sisters of Charity (San Antonio, Texas), 114
    Sisters of Mercy (Texas and Georgia), 114
    Sisters of St Joseph (Indiana), 114
    Sisters of the Incarnate Word and Blessed Sacrament of Corpus Christi (Texas), 114
    Ursuline convent, Cork, 33, 52, 61–64, 65
    Ursuline convent, Waterford, 82
Female Spectator, 42–44, 62
Fénelon, François, 15, 26–29, 30, 33, 37
Ferguson, William Blair Morton, 138, 143
Fianna Fáil, 154, 190–91
Fiction, novels, 2, 5, 6, 7, 13, 14, 21, 22, 25n, 43, 45, 47, 49n, 50, 51, 55, 61, 63, 64n, 66, 68, 71–73, 102, 103, 104, 128, 131n, 132, 134, 136, 138, 139, 140n, 142, 144, 165, 168, 180n, 181, 182, 183, 185–88, 190, 192, 196, 202, 204, 209, 218, 220

Field, Rachel, 139, 144
Fielding, Sarah, 26, 32
Fitzgerald, Ella, 172
Fitzgerald, Emily, Duchess of Leinster, 31, 32
Fitzgerald, Pamela, 32
Fitzgibbon, Lady Anne, 75
Fitz-Simon, Christopher, 211, 212
Flanagan, Catherine, 99
Flannery, Harry W., 139
Fleetwood, William, 15, 16
Folklore, 9, 103, 123
    see also National Folklore Commission
Fontaine, Joan, 152
Food parcels, 119–20
Ford, John, 164
Forth sisters, 21
Foster, Vere, 99
Fownes, Lady Elizabeth, 56–58
France, 61–62, 192
    see also French writers; Paris
Francis, Kay, 161
Franken, Rose, 139, 143
Freeman's Journal, 76–7, 97
French writers, 26–34, 37–38, 63–64, 72, 74
French, Samuel, 189
Friends of Soviet Russia, 203
Fyffe, Aileen, 24

Gable, Clarke, 164
Gaelic Athletic Association, 113, 154, 166, 170, 171
Gaelic League, 166, 170
Gallagher, Terry, 126, 127
Galway, Co. Galway, 62, 106, 116, 123, 124, 125, 127, 135
    Cullerton's Theatre, 166
    An Taibhdhearc, 205
Gamon, John A., US Consul General, 169
Garbo, Greta, 162
Gardner, E. S., 139, 143
Garoich, David, 74
Generation Without Farewell, 139
George Geith of Geith's Court, 186
Gilda, 168

Gilford, Co. Down, 98
Girl's Realm, 185
Girls' Cinema, 161
Glasgow, Scotland, 27
Gleizes, Albert, 191
Godwin, William, 46
Golf Illustrated, 135
Gone With the Wind, 138, 144, 164, 183, 184–85
Goodnight Soviet Russia, 203
Goorey, Co. Donegal, 117
Goresbridge, Co., Kilkenny, 105
Gort, Co. Galway, 109
Gough, John, printer, 49, 50
Grafton Street, Dublin, 70
Grattan, Henry, 60
Gray, David, US Minister, 183–84
Greenwich, New York, Irish in, 98
Griffith, D. W., 162
Griffith, Elizabeth, 20–22, 26
Griffith, Richard, 20–22
Guinan, Joseph, Father, 104
Guiney, Louise, 138, 142

Hail the Conquering Hero, 167
Haley, Bill, 173
Hall, S.C., Mrs, 186
Haly, James, printer, 49
Hamilton family, 21
Hamilton, Caroline, 56–58
Hamlet, 214
Hanaphy, May, 160
Handcock, Mrs, 21
Hansen, Miriam, 5, 181, 182
Harlow, Jean, 164
Harper's Bazaar, 135
Harper's Monthly, 133–34
Harris, Ruth Ann, 102
Harrison, Celia, 191
Hart, Bret, 138
Hartnell, Henry Crawford, 133, 134
Hastings, Elizabeth, Countess of Moira, 25, 66–67, 70
Hastings, Selina, Countess of Huntingdon, 75
Hawthorne, Nathaniel, 138, 142
Hayes, Richard, 168

Hayes, Tess, 124
Hays, Will H., 163
Haywood, Eliza, 42–44, 62
Hayworth, Rita, 168
Healy, John, 169
Hefner, Brooks E., 182
Hegarty, Margaret, 103
Helen, 71
Hellman, Lillian, 197
Hempton, David, 75
Henecy, J., 171
Hepburn, Audrey, 161
Herschel, Caroline, 68
Hibernia, 138
Hickes, George, 27–28, 35
Hill, Myrtle, 75
Hillsborough, Co. Down, 49
Hobson, Bulmer, 214
Hodgson Burnett, Frances, 138
Hoerder, Dirk, 93
Hollywood, Los Angeles, 150–53, 154, 155, 158–64, 166, 167, 168, 169, 180, 182, 214
  see also cinema
Home Companion, 135
Homestead Acts, 93
Hone, Evie, 191
Hope, Bob, 172
Horne, Lena, 172
Hospital, Co. Limerick, 163
Howley, John F. W., 136
Huguenot school, 59–60, 61
Hynes, Monsignor, 166

Infanticide, 210
Inis Meán, Co. Galway, 116
Inishowen, Co. Donegal, 121
Intimate Romances, 135
Irish Charitable Society, Boston, 92, 105
Irish Countrywomen's Association, 133, 141–42, 157
Irish Emigrant Society, New York, 92
Irish Eyes are Smiling, 167
Irish Farmers Journal, 126
Irish Housewives' Association, 108, 133
Irish Independent, 141, 154, 208, 209, 212, 208, 209, 212, 214

INDEX

Irish language, 34–36, 67, 219
Irish Library Bulletin, 139
Irish Monthly, 116, 134, 163
Irish Parliamentary Party, 82
Irish Press, 141, 210, 213, 214
Irish Times, 141, 188, 201, 210, 212, 213, 214
Irish Tourist Association, 166
Irish Women's Mirror, 133
Irish Women's Writer's Club, 192, 211
Israel, Jonathan, 16
Ivanhoe, 66

Jacob, Rosmund, 192, 203, 204
James, Henry, 138, 142
James, M. R., 186
Jazz, 145, 155, 169–73, 181, 182
Jane Eyre, 167
Jefferson, Thomas, 90
Jellett, Mainie, 191
Johnson, Mary, 138, 143–44
Johnston, Denis, 206, 212
Johnstown, Co. Kilkenny, 93
Jones, Jennifer, 167
Jordan, Elizabeth Garver, 138, 143–44
Jordan, Michael, 127
Jordan, Nancy, 126, 127
Joy family, 39
Joyce, James, 179, 205
Joyce, Nora, 108, 112

Kavanagh, Ann, 189
Keating, George, 34
Keating, Mrs (née Moore), 124
Kelly, Alice, 160
Kelly, Mary Terry, 108, 112, 116–17
Kennedy, Máire, 28, 31, 44
Kennedy, Thomas, 123
    mother, 123
Kenny, Kevin, 98
Kerr, Sophie, 138, 143
Kerry, County, 100, 103, 115, 123, 124, 126, 128
Kerryman, 110, 141
Keyes, Francis Parkinson, 142
Kiernan, Harriet, 68
Kiernan, T. J., 172

Kilkenny, Co. Kilkenny, 20, 21, 49, 66, 78, 82, 111, 163
    diocesan library, 66
Killala, Co. Mayo, 126
Killarney, Co. Kerry, 49
Killigrew, Terence, 207
Kilmore, Co. Cavan, 36
Kilquane, Co. Kerry, 124
Kilrane, Co. Wexford, 124
Kinematography Weekly, 165
Knights of St Columbus, 172
Knott, Sarah, 14
Kruegers, family of, Boston, 109

La Belle Assemblée, 55
La nouvelle Heloïse, 31, 47
La Touche, Elizabeth, 47–48, 75
La Touche, Peter, 47–48
Ladies Home Journal, 134, 135
Ladies Journal, 46
Lady of the House, 55, 133
Lady's Magazine or Entertaining Companion for the Fair Sex, 46
Lady's Monthly Magazine, 46–47
Lake, Marilyn, 167
Lamarr, Hedy, 151, 156
Langford, Frances, 152
Language, 2, 16, 23, 28, 29, 30, 34–36, 38, 41, 52, 57, 60, 83, 89, 93, 102, 106, 132, 166, 205, 219
Latimer, Jonathan, 139, 143
Lavering, Sir David, 201
Laverty, Maura, 119, 128, 192, 210–12
Le Fanu, Sheridan, 186
Le Prince de Beaumont, Jeanne Marie, 32–33
Leadbeater, Mary, 73–74
Lee, Denis, 105
Lee, Peggy, 172
Leenane, Co. Mayo, 111, 120
Legion of Mary, 172
Leinster, 44, 58, 78
Leitrim Observer, 141
Leitrim, County, 118
Lejeune, C. A., 159
Lemass, Seán, 191
Lennox, Charlotte, 25, 61, 62

Lennox, Gilbert, 201
Les aventures de Télémaque, 28–31
Lesbian culture, 213–17
Lester, T. R., 153
Letters for Literary Ladies, 71
Letters on the Improvement of the Mind. Addressed to a Young Lady, 25
Letters, 9, 60
    emigrant letters, 4, 7, 23, 83, 89, 90–91, 99, 101–2, 117–18, 120–22, 129
Letts, Winifred, 192
Lhote, André, 191
Libraries, 28, 29, 31, 66, 132, 135–40, 142, 143–44, 183, 185, 195
Library Association of Ireland, 140
Life, 135
Lifford, Co. Donegal, 62
Limerick, Co. Limerick, 44, 45, 49, 62, 82, 124, 135, 145, 149
    Savoy cinema, 159
Lindbergh baby, 145
Linenhall Library, Belfast, 66
Lisburn, Co. Down, 49
Literacy, 1, 2, 3, 13, 14, 38, 56, 57–59, 61, 82, 83, 89, 132, 192
Lithuania, 192
Little Richard, 173
Little Women, 138
Lloyd, Bartholomew, 70
Locke, John, 15, 17–19, 22, 30, 39, 59
Loeber, Magda, 71
Loeber, Rolf, 71
London salons, 25
London, 20, 21, 22, 23, 25, 38, 45, 46, 72, 74, 78, 80, 185, 186, 188, 191, 213
    Corinthian Club, 188
    fashion, 45, 55
    publishers, 27, 34
    Royal Society, 68
    social life in, 70
    St Martin's Theatre, 201
    theatre, 189, 213
    Westminster School, 191
Long, Eileen, 198
Longfellow, Henry, 138

Longford,
    Christine, 197, 203
    Earl of Longford (Frank Pakenham), 197, 206
Longford, County, 118
Look, 135
Los Angeles, 189
Loughrea, Co. Galway, 81
Lowell, Massachusetts, 99
Loyal National Repeal Association, 80–83
Lucas, Charles, 22
Lucas, Henry, 22
Lynch, Patricia, 192
Lynch-Brennan, Margaret, 100
Lynn, Dianna, 152
Lynn, Massachusetts, 110

Macardle, Dorothy, 188–92, 214, 215, 216, 217
Macaulay, Catharine, 25, 26
MacDonald, Jeannette, 167
MacÉnrí, Mícheál, 124
MacEntee, Seán, 154, 171
Mackail, Dorothy, 164
MacLiammóir, Mícheál, 196, 197, 203, 204, 205, 208, 210, 211, 213
Macmillan, 190
MacWhinney, Linda Kearns, 154
Madden, Samuel, 22
Madox, Elizabeth, 138, 143–44
Maedchen in Uniform, 213, 215, 217
Magasin des Enfans, 32–33
Magazine of Magazines, 45
Magazines, 3, 4, 5, 14, 41–50, 54–56, 71, 90, 131–42, 143, 156, 161, 170
Magdalen laundry, Cork, 161
Magee, William, printer, 49
Magray, Mary Peckham, 52
Maguire, John Francis, 99
Maintenon, Madame, 27
Maltese Falcon, 168
Manning, Mary, 203, 206, 208, 212
Manning, Miss, 191
Mansfield Park, 66
Manson, David, 39–40, 41, 51
Markey, Anne, 49
Marlay, Richard, 60

INDEX

Marquand, John P., 144
Marriage and marital relations, 4, 14, 15, 17, 19–20, 21–22, 27, 42, 43, 51, 54, 93–96, 103, 106, 110–13, 117, 123, 124–25, 127, 131, 137, 134, 145, 147, 162, 164, 167, 174, 188, 200, 201, 205, 207, 208, 218
    Marriage bar, 106, 127, 137
Marshall Plan (aid), 154
Marshall, Trudy, 152
Massey, Mrs, 126, 127
Max, 187
Maxwell, Constantia, 192
Maynooth Union, 170
Maynooth, College, 64
Mayo, County, 103, 118, 121, 127, 169
McAlister Brew, J., 165
McCann, Mary, 99
McCarthy, Borgia, Mother, 33–34, 52, 62–63
McCarthy, Brigid G., 159, 165, 180–81
McCarthy, Margaret, 99
McCormack, John, 188
McCormack, W. J., 71
McCourt, Frank, 187
McCracken, Isabella, 65–66
McCracken, Margaret, 39, 40
McCracken, Mary Ann, 39, 40, 51–52, 53, 66
McDonnell, Sheila, 126, 127
McGlynn, Annie, 161
McGrath, Mary, 123, 125
McGurl, K., 106
McInerney, Father, 134
McLaughlin, Katherine John, 117
McManus, Antonia, 62
McNamee, James Joseph, Bishop of Ardagh and Clonmacnoise, 165
McNevin, Emily, 81
McTier, Martha, 51–52, 53
Meade, L. T., 185–87
Meet Me in St Louis, 167
Menlough, Co. Galway, 153
Merkel, Una, 151
Messenger, 133, 155
Metro-Goldwyn-Mayer, 183–84
Metropolitan School of Art, Dublin, 191

Middleton, Harry, 207
Miles, Vera, 152
Millar, Anne, 152
Miller, Arthur, 209
Miller, Kerby, 83, 93, 101–2
Miller, Merle, 143
Milton, John, 56
Milwaukee, Wisconsin, 95
Mink Lined Coffin, 139, 143
Mitchell, Margaret, 138, 144
Mitchell, Ruth Comfort, 138, 143–44
Model Housekeeping, 133, 138, 139, 148, 149, 151–52
Modern Girl and Ladies Irish Home Journal, 133
Modern Romances, 135
Modern Woman, 135
Mohill, Co. Leitrim, 171
Monaghan, County, 44
Monck Mason family, 22
Monroe, Marilyn, 168
Montagu, Elizabeth, 23–24, 25
Montgomery, James, 158, 161, 166, 183–84
Montague, Lady Mary Wortley, 61
Moore, Colleen, 162
Moore, Margaret, 42
More, Hannah, 24, 50, 72
More, Thomas, 42
Moretti, Franco, 193, 220
Morgan, Lady *see* Owenson, Sydney
Mother and Maid, 133
Mother Machree, 164
Motherhood, 5, 15, 17, 19, 29, 30, 42, 123, 131, 134, 147, 164, 198–201
Mourning Becomes Electra, 209
Movie Spotlight, 135
Moycullen, Co. Galway, 111, 119, 120, 122
Muilreadhaigh, L. P., 170
Muintir na Tíre, 157
Mulally, Teresa, 32, 33, 52, 76–77
Mulkerins, Arlene, 173
Munster, 35–36, 44, 58
Murphy, Jeremiah, 124
Murphy, Maureen, 100, 102, 123
Murphy, Nora, 125

Murphy, William, 92
Murray Shanik, Ronald, 173
Murray, Annie, 117
Murray, Sean, 117
Music, 4, 45, 131, 133, 157, 169–70

Nagle, Nano, 33, 65
National Geographic, 135
National Association of Girls' Clubs, 165
National Farmers' Association, 127
National Folklore Commission, 103, 116
National Vigilance Association, 144
Nationalism, 180, 181, 182
New Haven Journal, 135
New Statesman, 144
New York City Emigrant Industrial Savings Bank, 92
New York Times, 110, 188
New York, 91, 92, 93, 94, 95, 99, 100–1, 108, 109, 111, 123, 125, 143, 149, 150, 153, 169, 180, 198
    Brooklyn, 100, 101
    Carroll Gardens, 101
    Coney Island, 101
    clergy, in, 105
    Hotel Commodore, 125
    Macy's, 200
    Madison Avenue, 147
    Park Slope, 101
    Prospect Park, 101
    publishers, 190
    theatre, 189
    Wall Street Crash, 199
New Yorker, 135
News of the World, 140, 144
Newspapers, 4, 5, 6, 76–77, 89, 90, 131–32, 140–46, 156, 157, 161, 167, 212
Ní Bhriain, Doireann, 160
Ní Dhonnchadha, Máirín, 35–36
Ní Mhunghaile, Lesa, 67
Nicholson, Asenath, 91, 102
No Man of Her Own, 164
No More than Human, 211
Nobody's Fool, 143
Norris, Kathleen, 139, 143
Norris, Mary, 161

Northwest Mountain Police, 167
Novellettes Selected for the Use of Young Ladies and Gentlemen Written by Dr Goldsmith, 22
Nuns *see* Female religious communities

Ó Ciosáin, Nialll, 58
Ó Colmáin, Domhnall, 35–36, 52
Ó Conaire, Micheál, 116
Ó Direáin, Máirtin, 103
Ó Dúbhda, Seán, 121
Ó Murchadha, Tadhg, 128
O'Beirne, Bartley, 106
O'Brien, Felim, 166
O'Brien, Flann, 171
O'Brien, Kate, 192
O'Connell, Daniel, 61, 77, 78–83, 220
O'Connell, Ellen, 61
O'Connor, Donald, 168
O'Connor, Frank, 205
O'Conor, Charles, 67
O'Dea, Jimmy, 203
O'Donnell, 66
O'Donnell, Bridie, 113
O'Halloran, Clare, 69
O'Halloran, Sylvester, 67
O'Kelly, Hilary, 119
O'Malley, Oonagh, 127
O'Neill, Eugene, 208, 209, 210, 219
O'Rourke, Misses, 61
O'Sullivan, Donal, 211
O'Sullivan, Maureen, 151
Offaly, County, 118, 124
Old John, 190
Oliver Twist, 66
On Baile's Strand, 209
Oral history, 9
Ormston, Jack, 149
Ostrander, Isabel, 138, 143
Our Girls, 160
Owens, Nellie, 125
Owenson, Olivia, 59, 60
Owenson, Sydney, 29, 59–60, 66, 67, 70, 71–74, 173, 186, 187, 190, 220

Packard, Vance, 173
Paine, Thomas, 90

Paris, France, 26, 27, 29, 55, 75–76, 153, 191
Parkinson Keyes, Francis, 139
Párliament na mBan, 219
Parliament, Irish, 75
Pascal, Blaise, 37
Passage West, Co. Cork, 120
Patee, Doris, 190
Patriotism, 76–82, 88, 153–54, 174
Pearse, Padraic, 211
Peg's Paper, 140
Periodicals, *see* Magazines
Peyton, Alexander J., 94, 97, 98
Philadelphia, Pennsylvania, 90
Philanthropy, 74–77
Phillips, Katherine, 42
Picturegoer, 161
Pilkington, Letitia, 25
Pioneer Club, 185
Pittsburg, Kansas, 95
Pius X, Pope, 104
Pope, Alexander, 47
Portrait in Marble, 212
Powell, Peter, 197
Practical Education, 72
Presbyterianism, 61, 90
Presley, Elvis, 168, 173
Pride and Prejudice, 66
Protestantism, 3, 14, 49, 50, 58–59, 74–76, 90, 171–72
    see also Church of England ministers; Church of Ireland ministers
Public Dance Halls Act, (1935), 171
Public Record Office of Northern Ireland, 58

Queenstown, Cork, 89
Queer studies and queer theory, 194, 212–15
Quigley, Martin, 167

Radio Éireann, 172
Radio Luxembourg, 172, 173
Raidió Teilifís Éireann, 169, 212
Radio, 5, 172, 173
Rathfarnham, Co. Dublin, 64, 77

Rathina, 190
Reader's Digest, 135
Rebecca, 216
Redbook, 135
Reilly, Christopher J., 211
Reliques of Irish Poetry, 67
Remittances, 91, 92–93, 99, 100, 101–2, 115–16, 116–17, 118, 120, 129, 154
Repplier, Agnes, 138, 142
Reunion, 143
Reuters, 145
Rice, Dorothy, 138, 143
Rich, B. Ruby, 213, 214, 215
Richards, Sheelagh, 198, 204
Richardson, Dorothy, 191, 192
Richardson, Samuel, 61
Riddell, Charlotte, 185–86
Ring, Co. Waterford, 108
Riot and Great Anger: Stage Censorship in Twentieth-Century Ireland, 196
Rockett, Kevin, 168
Rodgers, Nini, 73
Rogers, Ginger, 161, 164
Roman Catholic church and clergy, 4, 14, 52, 63–64, 96–97, 104, 105, 110, 115, 155–56, 161, 165, 169, 170, 171–72, 174, 183, 219, 220
Rooney, Mickey, 168
Roosevelt, Eleanor, 146
Roscommon, County, 124
Rouen, Reed de, 139
Rousseau, Jean-Jacques, 30–31, 47, 57, 62, 72
Rowan Hamilton, William, 69–71, 72
Royal Irish Academy, 66–71
Royal Society, London, 68, 69
Russell, Gail, 216
Russian Academy, 68
Russian literature, 203, 204–6
Ryan, James, 190–91
Ryan, John, 162

Sagan, Leontine, 213
St Catherine of Alexandra, 63
Saint Cyr school, France, 27, 59
St James Magazine, 186
St Nicholas, 133

St Paul, 17
Salkerd, Blanaid, 192
Salons, literary, 23, 24–25, 72
San Francisco, California, 99
Sanger, Margaret, 113
Sappho, 41
Saturday Evening Post, 135
Sayers, Dorothy L., 143, 198, 203, 204, 206
Sayers, Peig, 100
Schools, 1, 2, 14, 27, 29, 31–33, 39–41, 47, 49, 52, 56, 57, 58–60, 61–62, 63, 64, 65, 66, 75, 76, 78, 83, 89, 111, 112, 121, 130, 136, 155, 185, 190, 191, 212, 214
Schopenhauer, Donald, 199
Scotland, 44
Scott, Walter, 66, 71
Scribner's Magazine (formerly, *The Century*), 133–34
Select British Parliamentary Committee on Emigration, 91
Shackleton, Elizabeth, 74
Shakespeare, William, 47, 136, 137
Shaw, George Bernard, 205
Sheehy Skeffington, Hanna, 204
Sheridan, Thomas, 22
Shevlow, Kathryn, 48
Shields, George, 204
Sickert, Walter, 191
Silke brothers, 127
Simple Abundance, 187
Simpson, Alan, 210
Simpson, Wallace, 145, 146
Sinatra, Frank, 172
Sincerely Willis Wayde, 144
Sinfield, Alan, 213
Sinn Féin, 154
Sisson, Elaine, 205
Sligo, Co. Sligo. 62
Smith, Alexis, 152
Society of Friends, 49, 73, 90
Some Reflections on Marriage, 19
Some Thoughts Concerning Education, 15, 17–18
Song O' My Heart, 164
Song of Bernadette, 167
Songs, 102

Spain, 191
Spencer, Edmund, 47
Spiddal, Co. Galway, 106
Split Image, 139
Standards of living, 100–1, 122–23, 125–26, 127–28, 129, 130–31, 146, 148–49, 174–75
Stanley, Mary, 138, 143–44
Starrett, Henry P., 169
Staves, Susan, 16
Steele, Richard, 16
Sterling, Frederick, 164
Stokes, J. F., 166
Storm Over Wicklow, 212
Strictures on Modern Education, 72
Stuart, Gloria, 151
Studies, 162
Subscription lists and subscribers, 7, 18–19, 20, 21–22, 23–24, 25, 36, 38, 43–44, 48, 49, 51, 67, 76–77, 81
Sweeney Todd, 203
Sweeney, George, Mrs, 121
Swift, Jonathan, 25, 38, 51
Swords, Co. Dublin, 77
Symonds, Edward H., 151
Synge, Edward, Bishop of Elphin, 38
Synge, John Millington, 100, 103, 209

Talbot, Catherine, 24, 25, 26
Tarkington, Booth, 139, 144
Tarzan, 135
Taylor, Barbara, 14
Television, 131, 169, 212
Temple, Shirley, 161
Tennent, Anne, 58
Tennent, William, 58
Terson, Madame, 59–60
The Absentee, 197
The Adventures of Huckleberry Finn, 142
The Asphalt Jungle, 168
The Education of Young Gentlewomen. Written Originally in the French, and From Thence Made English. And Improved for a Lady of Quality, 27
The Female Pen, 180–81
The Gambler, 187

INDEX

The Governess or Little Academy ... For the Entertainment and Instruction of Young Ladies in their Education, 26
The Hairy Ape, 208
The Hardships of the English Laws. In Relation to Wives. With an Explanation of the Original Curse of Subjection Passed upon the Woman. In an Humble Address to the Legislature, 19
The House of Mirth, 187
The Irish Countrywoman, 133
The Irish Housewife, 133
The Jailbird, 204
The Key of the Kingdom, 167
The King of Spain's Daughter, 207
The Ladies Calling, 15, 18–19
The Ladies Journal, 41–42, 43
The Ladies Library, 15–17, 27
The Mad Miss Manton, 167
The Masquerader, 187
The Month of Mary: A Series of Meditations on the Life and Virtues of the Holy Mother of God, Particularly Adapted for the Month of May. By a Member of the Ursuline Community, Blackrock, Cork, 63
The New Magazine: a Moral and Entertaining Miscellany, 48–50
The Observer, 159
The Old Lady Says No, 212
The Parlour Window, 46–48, 49
The Pilot, 77
The Playboy of the Western World, 209
The Postman Always Rings Twice, 168
The Proposal, 205
The Quiet Man, 146
The Relative Duties of Parents and Children, Husbands and Wives, Masters and Servants 15
The River Road, 142
The Robe, 139, 142
The Rose Tatoo, 202, 210
The Shamrock, 46
The Smart Set, 134
The Third Man, 212
The Uninvited, 215, 216, 217
The Ursuline Manual, 34, 63
The Way We Live Now, 187
The Whole Duty of Man, 18
Theano, 42
There's No Business Like Show Business, 168
Third Party Risk, 201, 206
Thompson, J. Walter, 150
Thompson, William, 74
Three-Cornered Moon, 198, 203, 206
Thurles, Co. Tipperary, 62, 128
Thurlow, James, 139
Thurston, Katherine Cecil, 187–88, 190
Tighe, Mary, 57–58
Tighe, Sarah, 57
Time, 135
Times, 188
Tipperary Star, 141–42
Tipperary, County, 74, 122, 137, 139
Tobin, Philip, 127
Toland, John, 13, 17, 19
Tolka Row, 212
Tonkonogy, Gertrude, 198
Toronto theatre, 189
Touched by the Thorn, 211
Tracy, Robert, 206
Tralee, Co. Kerry, 161
Transactions of the Royal Irish Academy, 68, 69
Traub, Valerie, 194
Trimmer, Sarah, 24, 50
Trinity College, Dublin, 22, 38
Trollope, Anthony, 187
Tucker, Sophie, 171
Tullyroan, Co. Leitrim, 117
Turner, Lana, 152, 161, 164, 168
Twain, Mark, 138, 142
Tyrone, County, 90

Ulster, 44, 58, 90
Uncle Tom's Cabin, 138, 142
Uneasy Freehold, 188, 215
Unitarians, 24, 26
United Irishmen, 45, 51, 189
University College Cork, 159, 165
University College, Dublin, 127
University College, Galway, 166

Vale, Charles, 143
Valentino, Rudolph, 162
Vallancey, Charles, 67
Vesey, Aghmondisham, 21, 24
Vesey, Elizabeth, 21, 22–24, 25
Vogue, 135
Voiture, Vincent, 37
Voltaire, 62
Volunteers, the, 45, 51

Waggaman, Mary Theresa, 138, 142
Wakefield, Priscilla, 50
Walker, Joseph Cooper, 66, 67–68
Walker's Hibernian Magazine, 44–46, 50, 51, 55, 75
Walsh, Breda, 125, 127
Walsh, Mary, 109, 113
Walsh, S. J. J., 116
Waterford, Co. 44, 62, 116–17, 135, 138–39, 156, 203
    Ardmore, 188
    printer, 49
    Savoy cinema, 159
    Ursuline Convent, 64, 82
Webb, E, printer, 49
Welles, Orson, 211
West, Mae, 164
Western Movie, 135
Wexford, County, 125, 127
Wharton, Edith, 187
Wheeler, Anna Doyle, 74
Whitaker, T. K., 191
White Steward Edward, 138, 143–44
White, Patricia, 215, 216, 217
Whittier, John, 138
Whyte, Edward, 70
Whyte, Samuel, 39–41, 46, 70

Wicklow, County, 100, 138–39
Widows, 15, 17
Wild Irish Girl, 72
Wilkes, Wetenhall, 36–39, 41
Williams, Raymond, 182
Williams, Tennessee, 202, 209, 210
Williams, Valentine, 138, 143
Willkie, Wendell L., 139
Windsor, Edward, Duke of, 145, 146
Winsloe, Christa, 197, 213, 215
Wollstonecraft, Mary, 14, 46, 51–52, 53, 78–79
Woman and Beauty, 135
Woman and her Master, 73
Woman or Ida of Athens, 73
Woman's Life, 128, 133, 149, 151, 152, 156, 160
Woman's Mirror, 128
Woman's Weekly, 133
Women Without Men, 212–13
Women's Digest, 133
Women's Home Companion, 143
Women's Industrial Development Association, 154
Woolworths, 109, 134, 136, 149, 154–55, 171
Wordsworth, William, 71
Work and employment, 4, 5, 93–94, 97–98, 105–6, 107–10, 121, 125, 127, 130–31, 146, 149
Wright, Margaret, 90

Yeats, William Butler, 179, 209
Youghal, Co. Cork, 49
Young, Edward, 56
Young, Ursula, 62–63
Youth's the Season–?, 203, 206, 207, 208, 212